# THE SHIELD
# OF FAITH

## A CHRONICLE OF STRATEGIC DEFENSE

## FROM ZEPPELINS TO STAR WARS

## B. Bruce-Briggs

**SIMON AND SCHUSTER, INC.**  *New York  London  Toronto*
*Sydney  Tokyo*

SIMON AND SCHUSTER and colophon are registered trademarks
of Simon & Schuster Inc.

Designed by Jeanne Joudry
Manufactured in the United States of America

10 9 8 7 6 5 4 3 2 1

Library of Congress Cataloging in Publication Data
Bruce-Briggs, B.
    The shield of faith : the hidden struggle for strategic defense / B. Bruce-Briggs.
        p.    cm.
    Bibliography: p.
    Includes index.
    1. United States—Defenses—History.    2. Strategic forces—United
States—History.    3. United States—Air defenses—History.
4. Ballistic missile defenses—United States—History.    5. Nuclear
warfare—History.    I. Title.
UA23.B78457 1988
355'.00973—dc 19                                                  88-18394
                                                                          CIP

ISBN 0-671-61086-4

*To the memory of the soldiers, airmen,*
*and civilian technicians of the United States Army,*
*the United States Air Force, the National Guard,*
*the Air National Guard, the Royal Canadian Air Force,*
*and the Canadian Forces who have died*
*in the defense of North America, 1950 to ?*

# Contents

9

## III · THE DEFENSE ASCENDANT     81

The One-Man Committee, 82.   The Shadow of Super, 83.   Dwight
Eisenhower's Strategic Defense Initiative, 85.   The Century Series,
89.   Bomarc, 90.   Nike-Hercules, 92.   Hawk, 94.   Civil Defense
Creeps Forward, 95.   NORAD, 95.   SAC Strikes Back, 96.   How
Much Is Enough? 97.   The Other Side in the 1950s, 99.   The Next
War in 1955, 101.   Hitting a Bullet With a Bullet, 101.   Nike-Zeus,
104.   The War of the Brass, 107.   Defending the Deterrent,
109.   Nonmilitary Defense, 114.   Fallout Shelters, 119.   The Strategy
of Civil Defense, 124.   Defending the Missiles, 126.   Defending the
Defense, 128.   The Gaither Committee, 129.

## IV · THE DEFENSE STRAINED     134

The Missile Wars, 135.   The Defeat of CONAD, 137.   Debacle in the
North, 138.   Minor Disasters, 139.   The Vanquished, 140.   The Block-
ing of Nike-Zeus, 141.   Kwajalein, 142.   Civil Defense Finally Rises,
146.   The Democratic Offensive, 149.   McNamara Shoots Down the
Air Force, 153.   The McNamara Defense, 155.   The Defenders Branch
Out, 157.   Nike-Zeus Fights On, 157.   John Kennedy's Strategic De-
fense Initiative, 161.   The Balloon Goes Up, 165.   The Stalling of Civil
Defense, 169.   The Defenders' Kaffeeklatsch, 171.   The Defenders Dig
In, 174.   The Ann Arbor Speech, 176.   The Last Crisis, 177. ARAD-
COM Opens a Southern Front, 180.   The Canadian Missile Crisis, 180.

## V · THE DEFENSE STALEMATED     182

Arms Control, 183.   The Arms Controllers, 188.   ACDA, 191.   The
Problem in Europe, 192.   Finite Deterrence, 193.   Mutual Deterrence,
195.   The Rise of the Kooks, 196.   The Kooks Take On Civil Defense,
199.   The Test Ban, 206.   Nice Nuclear Weapons, 208.   The Last
Fight of Nike-Zeus, 216.   ABM on the Other Side, 218.   Project Defender, 220.   Nike-X, 226.   CD: RIP, 229.   Assured Destruction,
230.   Damage-Limiting, 232.   The Next War in 1965, 233.   The Army
Gets Reinforcements, 234.   The Thin System, 239.   The Nth Power,
241.   Defending the Deterrent Redux, 244.   Fireworks at Kwaj, 247.
Passive vs. Active Defense, 252.   Defense Is Offensive, 255.
The Budget Bleeding Ground, 259.   Cambridge's Last Defense,
264.   The Bleeding of NORAD, 265.   The Defense That Never Was,
269.   Nike-X Reaches Adolescence, 272.   The Conundrum of Arms
Control, 276.   The Other Side Goes First, 277.   Arms Control
Through Defense, 279.   McNamara's Last Defense, 281.   Robert

*Put on the whole armour of God, that ye may be able to stand against the wiles of the devil.*

*For we wrestle not against flesh and blood, but against principalities, against powers, against the rulers of the darkness of this world, against spiritual wickedness in high places.*

*Wherefore take unto you the whole armour of God, that ye may be able to withstand in the evil day, and having done all, to stand.*

*Stand therefore, having your loins girt about with truth, and having on the breastplate of righteousness;*

*And your feet shod with the preparation of the gospel of peace;*

*Above all, taking the shield of faith, wherewith ye shall be able to quench all the fiery darts of the wicked.*

Saint Paul to the Ephesians

---

*Ephesus was . . . the great port to which flowed the commerce of East and West. Its inhabitants were equally noted for licentious and luxurious life, and for cultivation of magical arts . . .*

Concordance to Protestant Episcopal
Sunday School Teachers' Bible, circa 1900

# IN DEFENSE OF THIS BOOK

"**D**efense is the stronger form of war," wrote Major General Carl von Clausewitz. Yet like most other military theorists and practitioners, he emphasized the offense. Defense is the weaker form of military discourse. When the Commander-in-Chief of the armed forces of the North American republic advised his nation in 1983 that he intended to direct his soldiers and civilian agents to examine the technical possibilities of defending the homeland from thermonuclear attack, his initiative was acclaimed as a revelation, or abhorred as an abominable innovation.

In fact, nothing said in Ronald Reagan's "Star Wars" speech had not been said long before—but strategic defense had been buried from public view in a deep shelter. The dominance of the offense in contemporary thinking is reflected in books about the nuclear age: almost without exception, they denigrate or disregard the defense. Most of the authors accept the premise of what this writer calls "the academic strategy," that—in the language of the incisive history *1066 and All That*—defense is A Bad Thing. This book understands, and seeks to inform the decent reader, that defense is A Good Thing—but, alas, good things are not necessarily good enough and are not always easy to gain.

Most public writers on nuclear matters are indifferent to and/or ignorant of what is and is not easy, and how easy. Almost all writings emphasize political squabbles within and between institutions. These vulgar and nasty quarrels cannot be ignored by any plausible account of the defenders of the nation, but it is shallow and cynical to maintain that grubbing for power and money is all that has driven policy. A few people do have principles, some have ideas, and many have competence. To be sure, much history of the American national-

13

security apparatus—*the* Business to its participants—reads like a tale of dogfights—but dirty dogs cannot contest bones in the absence of bones. At bottom, what is done is driven by what can be done. The wars of offense and defense at home and abroad have been determined not only by politics and propaganda, but also by technology.

And much of this book about the defense is devoted to the offense—inevitably so, because offense and defense entwine like two lovers embraced in death. Although strategically quite opposite, they are tactical and technical twins.

Lastly, much of the book necessarily is about matters that may seem distant from the defense of the American homeland—because so many of the doings and undoings of the great world have affected the fortunes of the defenders of the nation. For example, the successful defense of the cities of South Vietnam from Communist attack in 1968 was perceived as an American defeat, and this was decisive in the blocking of Robert McNamara's strategic defense initiative of 1967. The defense cannot be examined in isolation from what and who are to be defended and what and who are the threat.

A chronicle of the fortunes of the defense of the United States from attack from the sky ought to be informative, should be instructive, and is not without some bleak humor—if only because it reflects the humors of the Republic.

# I

# THE DEFENSE DENIED

*We must foresee that our great cities are liable to be raided
by dirigible balloons of great size, raining down bombs
upon the inhabitants . . . And what have we got to protect
us? Nothing.*

ALEXANDER GRAHAM BELL

Surely the offense began when a near-ape tried to seize berries
from his neighbor, and the defense was born when the neighbor
resisted. The resistance initiated warfare. As Clausewitz noted, the
defender causes wars. If you desire peace, submit. Our language
illustrates the validity of his observation: "war" is from the same
root as "guard" and "ward off." In 1947, the United Nations out-
lawed "war" but permitted "defense," so no one thereafter declared
war; nations merely engaged in "conflicts." The "war" departments
and ministries were replaced by "defense" establishments. So "defense" came to mean all military preparations and activities—offensive or defensive, and also kept its original meaning of warding
off attack. "Strategy," from a Greek term meaning the art of war,
has as many definitions as there are authorities, but it has always
meant how main forces are deployed. But in the 20th century, "strategic" also came to mean warfare involving a homeland; so the
American Strategic Air Command exists to lay waste others' home-
lands, yet the term kept its original meaning. So this book is about
defenders: those who have promoted a defense strategy of strategic
defense.

Ancient man devoted his resources to defense by building walls
and organizing cities ("wards") to man the walls. The invention of
ships required manning battlements along the shores. Early in the

15

history of the United States, fortifications sprang up at the major ports, and a ship could not enter an important harbor without passing beneath the sights of the U.S. Army's coastal artillery. Also, a ship at sea might encounter an American armed vessel—for the Army and the Navy had distinct and uncoordinated means of promoting maritime strategic defense.

## The Balloon Threat

In the 20th century, strategic defense gradually became exclusively concerned with attack by things which fell from the sky. But as with so many other modern concerns, the concept began with the Enlightenment. In 1783, in the last days of the War of the American Revolution, the Montgolfier brothers demonstrated a flying device outside Paris. Among the bemused observers of the balloon was the American diplomat Benjamin Franklin. The word of the Montgolfiers' marvelous achievement quickly spread around Europe, and its military significance was presently noticed. Before the year was up, a Prussian named J. C. G. Hayne wrote up a study of What It All Meant. Lieutenant Hayne was an officer of the engineers, who were the first military intellectuals. Brilliant and prescient was his analysis: Aerial warfare promised new horrors to be vented on humanity. Fleets of balloons could bombard fortifications and cities without impediment. The prospect was so hideous that surely the princes of Europe would unite to ban such terrors, or at least be mutually deterred from their use by their mutual vulnerability.

During the Napoleonic Wars, the British newspapers inflated their circulation by frightening their readership with the specter of revolutionary hordes assaulting the sceptered isle by balloon transport, thus initiating a minor literary genre of catastrophe from the skies that became part of the armament of hacks and rabble-rousers into the late 20th century. Fortunately, Lieutenant Hayne and the fearmongers were, as they have so often been, overly sanguinary about the operational practicality of bombardment. The balloons were expensive and unreliable, had a tiny payload, and could hardly be guided at all. Their military use spread very, very slowly. By the mid–19th century they were good only for limited observation of troops in the field. Nonetheless, armament entrepreneurs were quick to try to exploit the new technology. Thaddeus Sobieski Coulincourt

Low peddled his wares to the federal forces during the War of the Rebellion. On 31 August 1861, he raised one of his balloons in northern Virginia, near the intersection of Glebe Road and what is now Wilson Boulevard, just a mile from the swamp where the Pentagon would be erected eighty years later, and just a mile west by southwest of Rosslyn, Virginia. Although the District of Columbia has a profusion of statues of heroes, civil and military, Rosslyn lacks so much as a brass plaque. How appropriate would be a heroic statue of Dr. Low and his balloon. He was a great pioneer—one of the first to offer the Republic quick and painless security via high technology.

Alas, his advanced device had certain inherent drawbacks. Just on the other side of the lines was a battery of Louisiana artillery. The gunners were unappreciative of the wonders of the balloon, and fired on it. They learned that it is nearly impossible to hit an aerial target, but the balloon was very promptly hauled down. On that summer's day, air defense was born. Although no one recognized it at the time, a vital military principle was demonstrated: the defense need not hit the attacker, it merely has to scare him away. Still, Low and his competitors soldiered on for a time, and the rebels briefly engaged in a balloon race, with the ladies of Richmond contributing their silk unmentionables to raise the Confederate cause higher; yet the military clients tired of the innovation. Yes, the balloons were useful, but the generals learned that hauling them around was more trouble than they were worth. The Rebellion was crushed by artillery and infantry assault—by blood, not brains.

## The Dirigible Threat

Later in the century, advances in metallurgy, machining, and the refining of petroleum provided the material base for the invention of cheap and light engines, which permitted improved flying machines. The Prussian Count Zeppelin made a tour of the great brawl between the American barbarians, and took note of Dr. Low's device. Zeppelin's dirigible, essentially a powered balloon, rekindled fantasies of aerial destruction. In his *The War in the Air*, that great concepts man H. G. Wells painted a vision of fleets of Japanese and German airships flattening New York. Count Zeppelin built for the Imperial German forces a dirigible fleet which attempted to demolish

London. The populace was terrified—all the newspapermen had read H. G. Wells.

But not everyone was as much impressed by the threat of mass destruction from the air. A dissenter was Toby Rawlinson, a gentleman of some independent means. He went to war with his chums from the Royal Auto Club, who amused themselves by dashing about northern France hunting Huns in their motorcars. After the front stabilized into bloody trench warfare, Toby needed other divertissements and found himself in the Royal Naval Auxiliary, rushing about southeast of London with a few commandeered cannon attempting to pot zeppelins. The Royal Navy got into the air defense business because the army disdained any activity not involving horses, and because the navy's civilian chief, the First Lord of the Admiralty, was an erratic but clever young politician named Winston S. Churchill who was open to innovative methods. It had been thought to counter the dirigible threat by sending out aircraft armed with machine guns; but the sky is a big place, and the interceptors could not find the targets. The antiaircraft guns were a superior riposte. Because the chances of one shell hitting one zeppelin were trivial, the defense was bolstered by the crude expedients of increasing the rate of fire of the guns and multiplying the batteries.

The defenders killed very few dirigibles, but promoted such fear among the offense that the Teutonic aeronauts changed their tactics and came against the city by night, when they could see little and hit even less. Thus were born measures and countermeasures of strategic defense and offense. The attacks did not stop, but the defense imposed a cost on the offense, requiring it to degrade the effectiveness of its attack. The fear of attrition resulted in offensive countermeasures which reduced the puissance of the attack—a phenomenon that came to be labeled "virtual attrition."

Another solution to the dirigible threat was at the other end of the operational spectrum. Dirigibles were ultralight craft, easily damaged by winds, so they had to be housed in hangars. The hangars were not only large and visible, but vulnerable ("soft"). So Royal Navy aircraft raided the dirigible bases in Belgium and Germany, initiating what later were branded "counterforce" strikes. The defense and counteroffense decimated the German dirigible fleets, and the zeppelins were abandoned.

## The Aeroplane Threat

Yet superior technique was at hand in the form of the increasingly sophisticated and ever-larger heavier-than-air craft, the bomber. The Gotha bombers raided London, and again the population was terrified and again countermeasures were put into effect. Churchill was canned for a gross strategic blunder at Gallipoli, and the Home antiaircraft defenses were transferred to the army. And Toby Rawlinson and his raffish colleagues were forced into some semblance of military order (not agreeable to Toby, who wandered east to engage in some counterinsurgency sport against those Bolshevik fellows in Russia). German losses mounted.

To avoid the guns, the bombers had to fly very high and sacrifice their limited bombing accuracy, or else come in very low and lose speed, range, and visibility. The counter to low-level attacks was barrage balloons—simple, cheap air bags trailing wires to ensnare propellers. Few planes were caught by the barrage balloons, but by their existence they dissuaded the attackers. The defenses prompted the Germans to come by night, which provoked searchlights.

By any measure, the defense had won the air war. But air defense had been forced upon the military by politicians responding to public outcry, and when the First World War was over, the effort was almost forgotten in Great Britain and elsewhere. The army returned to real soldiering and relegated air defense to a minor concern. Others in uniform dominated public discussions of military aviation and how to deal with it. The pilots continued to be sanguine about the sanguinary potential of their favorite vehicles. Britain was the first to create an independent air force, which rapidly developed a doctrine of the primacy of military aviation. The doctrine was greedily embraced by the aviators of the U.S. Army Air Corps. In the 1920s and 1930s was built a theory—carpers would say an ideology—of Air Power.

Unknown to the Anglo-Saxon countries was the most thoroughly worked-out version of the theory, by the Italian General Giulio Douhet. He was not a pilot, but was heavily influenced by the futurist poets, artists, and polemicists who had a vision of the end of history and the beginning of a new era amalgamating technology and heroism. Douhet developed a fascist theory of air power: Armies and navies were obsolete. Command of the Air was all that would matter in future war. Fleets of battleplanes loaded with high explosives, incendiaries, and poison gas would attack one another's cities. Defense was futile. The winner of the war of the future would employ a fleet of bombers to destroy cities one by one until the enemy government surrendered or was overthrown by its victimized and inflamed subjects.

Oddly, although a Fascist himself and offering a criminal theory that seemed to epitomize the fascist worldview, Douhet had little influence upon his own country* or upon the other great enemy of degenerate liberal democracy, Nazi Germany. Italy and Germany both equipped their air forces essentially as mobile artillery to support land operations. The chief of the German Air Force, Hermann Goering, had been a distinguished World War I air commander, but concentrated—perhaps because he himself was a fighter pilot—on fighters and light bombers, not the big planes necessary to carry annihilation to the enemy's heartland.

It was the Anglo-Saxon powers that swallowed the doctrine of air power whole—because it promised war on the cheap. No longer need hordes of proletarians and peasants bleed in the dirt; war could be fought by a few highly trained professionals in flying machines. The masses would participate only by producing the bombers, and, if the preparations were insufficient, by being victims of the air attacks. This view was ballyhooed by air force officers and publicists throughout the 1920s and the 1930s. Not publicized was the little detail that the equipment was not up to the job. Existing planes could not carry sufficient bomb loads, and existing bombing technique could not hit targets. (Only in movies and war comics is it easy to drop something out of an airplane exactly where you want it to fall. To take a simpler task, try to hit a roadside sign with a Coke bottle from a moving car.)

Nonetheless, the idea of air power was politically invaluable. In

---

*Cynics may note that Douhet was bankrolled by Cabroni, the bomber-maker, while the fighter-making F.I.A.T. had superior political connections. The American inventor Hudson Maxim made early back-of-the-envelope calculations showing that bombing must fail, because the payloads were too small and because almost all bombs dropped on even the most crowded city would hit yards, streets, or parks. Maxim was on the payroll of Du Pont, maker of naval munitions. But, in a saying Herman Kahn attributed to Leo Szilard, "The scientist asks if a statement is true; the politician asks why it was said. The first is the more important question." At the state of the art early in the century, Maxim was right.

the 1930s, as the war preparations of the fascist powers became more evident, the liberal countries, loath to rearm and even more loath to face up to the possibility of another world war, took comfort in the idea of air power. The most famous phrase of the era was by the British Prime Minister Stanley Baldwin, who echoed pacifistic propaganda in saying in 1932, "The bomber will always get through." Of course, the formulation of this slogan should make any reader wary—*the* bomber: that is, an ideal bomber, not a real bomber. In fact, no one believed that every bomber would get through; only that some bombers would. Baldwin's statement usually has been interpreted as one of despair, but it was actually meant to be encouraging—because Britain had *the* bomber, while its enemies had not. A line later in the same speech, he said, "The only defense is in offense, which means that you have to kill more women and children more quickly than the enemy if you want to save yourself." Baldwin was reassuring his public and threatening the enemies of Britain. Whether or not he knew that the bombers couldn't hit anything remains open to question. Certainly many high in the councils of the realm knew. But perhaps the capability was irrelevant. Baldwin was a conservative—not an old-line bloody-minded aristocrat like Churchill, but the new breed of prudent, pinchpenny, and pacific middle-class politician. The-bomber-always-getting-through offered Peace and smaller defense estimates. As we shall see, the Baldwin type will appear again in this chronicle.

### Dishing the Bomber

Why the bomber could always get through was explained by the airmen: it had the whole sky to hide in. So the answer to the bomber was not the antiaircraft gun, the fighter-interceptor, or any other weapons system, but by an independent strain of technological development unanticipated by anyone—least of all by the aviators who lusted for bigger, faster, higher-flying, and more numerous aircraft and from time to time puttered with tiresome details such as improved bombs, bombsights, radios, and tactics. In the early 1930s, the menace of air attack was stated succinctly and comprehensively by a marginal member of Parliament, a long-discredited kook and troublemaker but admitted to be deliciously articulate, so quoting Churchill at length is appropriate:

What measures can we take to provide against these very great perils, or at any rate mitigate and minimize their effects? I do not think . . . that it is much use planning to move our arsenals and factories over to the west side of the island. When one considers the enormous range of foreign aeroplanes and the speeds at which they travel . . . it is evident that every part of this small island is, I will not say equally, but almost equally, within range of attack. If enormous sums of money were spent in displacing our arsenals from their present position, it might well be found that before this cumbrous process was completed, improvements in aeroplanes would have more than discounted any advantage which might have been gained. The flying peril is not a peril from which one can fly. It is necessary to face it where we stand. We cannot possibly retreat. We cannot move London. We cannot move the vast population which is dependent on the estuary of the Thames. We cannot move the naval bases which are established along our southern coasts with great hereditary naval populations living around them. . . . I am afraid we shall have to face this peril, whatever it may be, where we stand.

I think it would be a great mistake to neglect the scientific side of defense against aircraft attack—or purely defensive action against aircraft attack. Certainly nothing is more necessary, not only to this country but to all peace-loving and peace-interested Powers in the world and to world civilization than that the good old earth should acquire some means or methods of destroying sky marauders. It is a matter which is of interest to us all that we should be able to meet this present menace which no generation before our own has faced, which shakes the very fabric and structure of all our civilized arrangements, and by spreading fear and danger far and wide, makes it more and more difficult to preserve security and tranquillity in the minds of the different great States. If anything can be discovered that will put the earth on better terms against this novel form of attack, this lamentable and hateful form of attack—attack by spreading terror throughout civil populations—anything that can give us relief or aid in this matter will be a blessing to all.

I hope that the Government will not neglect that aspect of the question. There is a committee, I have no doubt, studying it. It ought to be the strongest committee possible, it ought to have the greatest latitude possible, and it ought to be fed with the necessary supplies to enable experiments of all kinds to be made against this danger. I have heard many suggestions with which I would not venture to trouble the House now, but they ought to be explored and explored thoroughly and with all the force of the Government behind the examination. It ought to be not merely a question of officers of a department doing their best, but of the force of the Government, and I do hope that . . . steps of this kind will be taken; that there will be no danger of service routine or prejudice or anything like that preventing new ideas from being studied, and that they will not be hampered and subjected to so many long delays as we suffered in the case of the tanks and other ideas during the Great War.

The fact remains that when all is said and done as regards defensive methods—and all that you can say now has been said already—pending some new discovery, the only direct measure of defense upon a great scale is the certainty of being able to inflict simultaneously upon the enemy as great damage as he can inflict upon ourselves. Do not let us undervalue the efficacy of this procedure. It may well prove in practice—I admit you cannot prove it in theory—capable of giving complete immunity. If two Powers show themselves equally capable of inflicting damage upon each other by some particular process of war, so that neither gains an advantage from its adoption and both suffer the most hideous reciprocal injuries, it is not only possible but it seems to be probable that neither will employ that means. What would they gain by it? Certainly a Continental country like the one of which I have been speaking [Germany], with large foreign armies on its frontiers, would be most unwise to run the risk of exposing itself to intensive bombing attacks from this island upon its military centers, its munition establishments and its lines of communication at a time when it was engaged by the armies of another first-class Power.

We all speak under the uncertainty of the future which has so often baffled human foresight, but I believe that if we maintain at all times in the future an air power sufficient to enable us to inflict as much damage upon the most probable assailant, upon the most likely potential aggressor, as he can inflict upon us, we may shield our people effectually in our own time from all those horrors which I have ventured to describe. If that be so, what are £50,000,000 or a £100,000,000 raised by tax or by loan compared with an immunity like that? Never has so fertile and so blessed an insurance been procurable so cheaply.

This is profound, and prefigures most mid-century thinking about these matters—but a key concept is absent, surely by Churchill's intent. Britain was troubled not by immediate German eagerness to conquer Sussex or Suffolk, but by Nazi ambitions on the Continent, which might create a Germany powerful enough to overrun the British homeland. The threat of the-bomber-getting-through should deter German expansion; but what if the German bomber can get through too? What deterrence then? And what if deterrence fails? Those were the real issues. That is the problem which defense addresses.

Note the phrase "scientific investigation" in Churchill's speech. He knew that a panel had been set up by the military to examine new approaches to air defense: The Committee for the Scientific Survey of Air Defense, headed by Henry Tizard (rhymes with "lizard"), the rector of the Imperial College of Science and Technology—very roughly the British counterpart of the president of the Massachusetts Institute of Technology. Tizard was the antithesis of the aircraft-potting sportsman Toby Rawlinson. A German-educated chemist, Tizard in World War I was commissioned in the Royal Garrison Artillery, the British equivalent of the U.S. Coast Artillery, which soon converted to antiaircraft. He found zeppelin-hunting uninteresting and transferred to the infant Royal Flying Corps. He was a third-rate scientist, but a first-rate promoter, and sought the application of scientific method to the resolution of military problems, including air defense. Recognizing the resistance of the professional officers to boffins meddling in their time-sanctioned monopoly on the art of war, Tizard was careful to earn his own pilot's wings. His achievements in the Kaiser War were inconsequential, but he stirred the water that would be the wave of the future.

The initial concept examined by Tizard's group was one of H. G. Wells's conceits, the death ray, but a little work on the slide rule revealed that existing means of projecting directed energy via light, heat, or microwaves were insufficient to damage aircraft. More promising was the prospect of burning out the pilots' eyes—but easily countered by goggles. But improvements in destruction were not the requirement. Bullets and shells could chop down a bomber, and fighter-interceptors and AA guns could deliver the bullets and shells. The weak point was in detecting and locating the targets. How to find the incoming aircraft? How to guide its nemesis?

The answer came not from weaponry, nor from science fiction, but from communications. Theoretical work in electricity had led to the invention of radio. Marconi and other pioneers had suggested that radio waves could be bounced off objects and thereby reveal their location. Experiments were conducted under government auspices during the 1920s in Britain, Germany, and the United States. Initially these were purely scientific, intended to discover more information about the composition of the ionosphere, which had been identified earlier because of the surprisingly long range of radio transmissions that had been reflected from this zone in the upper atmosphere. An important breakthrough was achieved by engineers of the Bell Telephone Laboratories, the research arm of the American Telephone and Telegraph Company. The military implications of this discovery were understood almost immediately, and government-sponsored research was accelerated in several countries. Britain felt the need most of all.

There was some controversy in the Tizard committee. It was recognized that radio detection (later labeled "radar") had inherent disadvantages: like radio, it could be jammed; as with radio, the enemy could home in on the transmitter. If the radar could direct fighters to interception range by day, then the bombers would come by night. One member of the committee, Churchill's scientific adviser Frederick Lindemann, held out for infrared detection, gadgetry that would passively read the heat of the enemy aircraft. The technology of the time, however, was not up to the task. The sensors were not sensitive enough, and the planes were not hot enough to be sensed. Instead, preliminary studies began on fitting radio detection to night fighters. Even before a single radar set had been deployed in defense of Great Britain, work began on countering the enemy's expected countermeasures. This was an early battle of the conjectural conflicts, of the paper wars.

While the leadership of the Royal Air Force was proclaiming the benefits of the bomber, ground-based scientists (with the support of a few sympathetic officers) were frantically developing radar. In 1938 there was a crisis over Czechoslovakia, and the British caved in at Munich because—as even Churchill recognized—the deterrence of the bomber had failed, and the defenses were not yet operational. The first primitive radar net was in place by late 1939, and then the British stood and fought for Poland. It was radar, not the sexy Spitfire and the sturdy Hurricane fighters, that won the Battle of Britain. The radars picked up the assembling fleets of bombers and escort fighters and vectored the defensive fighters toward their quarry. The radars alerted the antiaircraft guns which kept the bombers off the naval bases and airfields. The Battle of Britain was almost lost not when the bombers attacked the cities, as Douhet had theorized, but when the Luftwaffe went for the radars and the communications net. A good lesson there: to beat the defense, attack the defense itself. Another lesson: Hitler had hoped for mutual deterrence—we won't bomb your cities if you don't bomb our cities. Churchill's response to the impending loss of the air battle was not a futile attempt to defend the soft radars, but to hit Berlin, to provoke Hitler into reprisals against British cities, and to leave the radars alone. A tough customer was Churchill: burn German and British babies to preserve the radar net, and win the battle.

## The Defense of America

In 1937, the United States Navy offered the Bell Laboratories a contract to research radar. The major radio companies of the United States—among them RCA, Sylvania, and Westinghouse—had already been at work on this new use of radio transmission. Bell Labs was the nation's and the world's largest, most competent, and most renowned industrial research laboratory. AT&T recognized that radio was a potential supplement to, and might even replace, telephone lines, especially in international communications. In any event, Bell Labs had the resources and talent to keep up on all manner of new technologies, just in case they might be useful someday to AT&T and to the U.S.A.

Defense contracting was of no consequence to Ma Bell. Fat and comfortable, by virtue of the telephone monopoly, even in the Great Depression, AT&T had no need to grovel for business. More vital to the company was the goodwill of the government. In those days the federal government was controlled by the New Dealers, who were hostile to large corporations and were vigorously extending the range and intensity of antitrust legislation. Prudence required that Ma Bell be agreeable to Uncle Sam. So Bell Labs rejected the offer of a military contract, and generously engaged in radar research on its own account. A modest radio research operation had already begun at Whippany, in the New Jersey suburbs west of New York. A small team was assembled and in short order put together a simple but effective radar set. The engineers set up their first station on the Atlantic Highlands just off the mouth of New York Harbor, and proceeded to track ships coming in and out. In its first year of unfunded research, Bell Labs designed a radar superior to anything the Japanese developed throughout World War II. One of these engineers was a promising young man named Cliff Warren.

When the war came, AT&T, like other industrial firms, shifted to military production. The manufacturing arm of the corporation, Western Electric, turned out thousands of radars for fire control of guns, for early warning and detection, and for other Army and Navy purposes. Excellent Bell Labs–designed and Western Electric–manufactured radars went onto ships, planes, submarines, and ground stations.

AT&T was not the only producer. Westinghouse was also a leader. Its radars were experimentally deployed on the island of Oahu on 7 December 1941. Two operators reported an unusual formation of aircraft approaching, but were instructed to disregard it and shut down and return to base—to enjoy an exciting Sunday morning. That same morning, another experimental set was being operated outside New York by a Slovak-American engineer named Ivan Getting, who was associated with a nonacademic affiliate of MIT.

Meanwhile, the Americans had been building up their surreptitious support for the British war effort. There was precious little the British could do in return. They had few resources, and their limited technological capability was greatly strained. But they did have one thing the Americans could use. The Americans had become exceedingly impressed by the puissance of the radar defenses of Britain. When Churchill came to power, his crony Lindemann became the chief science adviser, and Lindemann's adversary Tizard was out. For a golden handshake, he was knighted and given a foreign mission. In late 1940, Sir Henry Tizard checked into Washington's Shoreham Hotel with a precious package—in it a small device, a glass tube: the cavity magnetron, a much more powerful and efficient way to generate an intense radio beam to project out to bounce off an incoming target. This gem was transported to Bell Labs to copy.

The magnetron proved difficult to produce in quantity. This drawback was overcome by a Massachusetts firm. Just after the First World War, a group of local venture capitalists and MIT scientists (among them Vannevar Bush) had founded the American Research and Development Corporation. In the 1920s, radio was *the* high-tech product, and companies with radio in their names better attracted the interest of investors. The company became Raytheon, and concentrated on radio vacuum tubes. Its engineers licked the problem of mass production of the magnetron.

With the British experience before it, the American Army recognized the need to involve scientific talent in the quest for better radars, and engaged the nation's leading technical training institution—the Massachusetts Institute of Technology—to found and administer, with military research funds, the Radiation Laboratory (not the radiation resulting from atomic reactions, the radiation of radio waves). Ivan Getting was one of its first hands. MIT's "Rad Lab" was to be the nurturing ground of America's strategic defense system, and it was to hatch the serpents who would kill it.

When America entered World War II, defense against homeland attack was rapidly organized. Although doubtful, and eventually impractical, German assault on the East Coast was considered a possibility in 1942. On the other side of the Zone of the Interior (ZI—"zee-eye"), there was no question of the capability of the Japanese fleet air arm to raid the ports, factories, and cities of the West Coast. A comprehensive air defense apparatus was set up. The coasts were lined with radars linked together by simple communications nets. Controller stations were set up, and squadrons of interceptors were deployed.

The U.S. Army's Coast Artillery, which had long manned the shore batteries for maritime strategic defense, added antiaircraft guns, which, like the AA guns in the field army, were soon converted to fire control by radar. The effectiveness of the antiaircraft systems was hobbled somewhat by a division of responsibilities between the branches of the Army. Radar was an outgrowth of radio, which was a form of communication and therefore the responsibility of the Signal Corps; but the fire control of guns was assisted by complicated mechanical, and then electromechanical, devices that came to be called computers, which were developed by the Army's gun-supply branch, the Ordnance Corps. The integration was always troublesome.

Radars are inherently limited in their coverage because radio waves travel in a straight line, while the earth is curved. Installing enough radars close enough together to achieve full coverage would have been excessively expensive and complex. To fill the gaps, the British recruited ground observers—citizens with binoculars and instructions on how to identify the sight and sound of incoming planes. They were not terribly effective, but helpful. Hundreds of thousands of ground observers were recruited in the United States as well. They manned the coasts with aircraft-recognition manuals and were tested on their ability to identify such aerial exotica as the Blohm & Voss HA 138 and the Savoia-Marchetti SM-79. (The examples are taken from the chronicler's own "Recognition Pictorial Manual" obtained by gift in 1944; as a toddler squinting out over Long Island Sound, he was troubled by his uncertainty of distinguishing a Convair PB2Y from a Japanese "Mavis" flying boat.)

## Passive Defense

In addition, the Americans set up a "civil defense" apparatus. During the 1920s and the 1930s, the threat of air attack had led to development of the guns, fighters, and radars to provide what is labeled "active defense"—to actively intercept attackers. But "passive defense"—modifying facilities and taking measures to reduce damage from an attack—was not ignored. The British were leaders in air-raid precautions (ARP), which we called civil defense. They dispersed their aircraft-production plants and camouflaged factories to hide them from reconnaissance and attack. Warning sirens were installed, air-raid wardens were recruited, fire departments were trained to fight bomb-caused conflagrations and to dig survivors from ruined buildings, and gas masks were distributed to the populace. When war was declared in September 1939, tens of thousands of children were evacuated from the cities into the English countryside. Subways and other underground facilities were pressed into use as shelters. According to a RAND Corporation estimate, the equivalent of $2 billion was poured into ARP in the late 1930s—but not without controversy: in a chilling augury of things to come, the

British civil defense apparatus was harried by the "Cambridge Scientists Anti-War Group."

Little of this was done by the military. Soldiers wanted no part of it. Soldiers want to fight the enemy. Civilians are undisciplined and troublesome, so defense of the population was assigned to the civil authorities and to separate organizations of enthusiastic volunteers, with a bracing of retired military personnel and police—not the cream of the crop, but sufficient to the task. President Roosevelt put the mayor of New York and a World War I military aviator, Fiorello LaGuardia, in command of the American civil defense apparatus. As one of LaGuardia's deputies he named Eleanor Roosevelt, who attempted to turn morale-building into some sort of Americanized Strength Through Joy propaganda operation, which was so ludicrous and inappropriate that she had to be fired by her husband.

The final aspect of passive defense was that of internal security— defense against spies, saboteurs, and defeatists. The Army had responsibility for the air defense of Hawaii, and when a war warning came from Washington in early December 1941, the commander ordered his planes parked close together under heavy guard to defend against Japanese saboteurs. When war broke out, there was a general roundup of known pro-Nazis, pro-Fascists, and members of Japanese "patriotic" organizations. Trotskyite Communists were jailed, and isolationist elements were cowed by raids on the America First Committee. Although we know now that this was no part of the Japanese war plans, it was within the capabilities of the Imperial fleet to sweep down the Pacific coast to bombard it and even to land raiding parties. On the West Coast, resident Japanese nationals and Japanese-Americans were asked, then ordered, then forced to relocate inland. The operation was organized and led by an Army Intelligence officer named Karl Bendetson.

It did not take long for the course of the war to be clear. The Allies quickly went on the offensive against Germany, and seven months into the Pacific war, the Japanese fleet was so badly crippled in the Midway battle that it would have been militarily idiotic to attempt an attack on the West Coast. Attacks on the continental United States were limited to two landings of saboteurs by U-boat, a single shelling of a West Coast oil refinery by a Japanese submarine, and pathetic strategic bombing by balloon (wiping out a Sunday-school picnic in Oregon).

## Bolstering the German Offense

The Battle of Britain stimulated antiaircraft gunnery. The cities, ports, and airfields were ringed with ack-ack batteries. To conserve shrinking manpower, young women manned the guns (a deployment most convenient when the American garrison arrived). When radar direction was added to the guns and proximity fuses (an American child of radar) fitted to the shells, British skies became too hazardous for the Luftwaffe. The kill rate increased from 1/10,000 shells to 1/1,000. Superior means of penetration were required. While heavy bombers and radar were Anglo-American specialties, Germany took the lead in most other areas of military technology. Not only had Germany the most advanced industrial research capability, but following World War I the German military was faced with a particular difficulty: unilateral arms control—disarmament. The Treaty of Versailles denied Germany all manner of military equipment, including aircraft. The German liberal government and armed forces could and did cheat on the controls—intelligently and effectively—but only so much could be accomplished surreptitiously, so new approaches to the security of the Reich were in order. A consequence of the prohibition on aircraft was intensive antiaircraft development, producing the excellent 88-mm gun. During the Battle of France in 1940, German aircraft ranged behind Allied lines, while British and French aircraft were chopped down by German AA. The "eighty-eight" was also found to be a great antitank weapon, initiating the dual-purpose use of AA weapons.

The army also had learned of experiments in rocketry by a club of enthusiastic scientists and engineers, and shortly took them in hand and installed them on the island of Peenemunde in the Baltic, where, modestly but appropriately funded, the research continued which eventually produced the Aggregat-4 rocket, known to history as the V-2.

## The Cruise Missile Threat

The Luftwaffe got wind of the rocketry experiments, and was not about to permit an army monopoly of high-tech bombardment. Air force scientists rushed an alternative means of penetrating British air defenses—a small, unpiloted aircraft designed to undertake a one-way mission from launching sites to the targets: the V-1, the first effective cruise missile. With a primitive jet engine and simple guidance system, the V-1 was easier and cheaper to produce than its army rival and was launched against England in the spring of 1944. The "buzz bomb" created havoc, not so much because the damage was severe—it wasn't—but because being bombarded with no means of response is debilitating to morale.

Very quickly the British and the Americans now ensconced in England devised countermeasures. At 400 miles per hour, the V-1s were not too fast for radar to detect and track and not much faster than manned aircraft, so diving fighter-interceptors could just barely catch them. The antiaircraft guns at first achieved little success; but a new deployment was devised. The guns were stripped out of their established sites around cities and installed in a belt across the southern coast of England. The interceptors were ordered to stay out of the belt; instead, they were stationed over the Channel to take one pass at the incoming V-1s. Then the defense would hand over to the guns. Then any surviving missiles would be exposed to another attack by the fighters which had regained height for another diving attack.

The fighters were reasonably effective, but most of the V-1 killing was done by the guns, because of the advances in radar-and-computer-directed antiaircraft fire. All the gunners did was load and pull the lanyards—the computers did all the rest. The kill rate on the V-1s exceeded 90 percent. The defense could have been foiled by an easy countermeasure: a simple timer could have been fitted to flip the V-1 rudder to zigzag through the gun belt. After the war, an American AA radar engineer met the chief V-1 designer in the United States and asked why the Germans had failed to employ the countermeasure. The ex-German replied that his engineers had indeed advocated it, but had been vetoed by the Luftwaffe chief, Hermann Goering, who told them to stop fooling around with endless modifications, keep punching out the missiles, and continue to attack.

The Luftwaffe did attempt to outflank the defenses by mounting V-1s on Heinkel bombers and launching them against London from the east. This use of the air-launched cruise missile was a waste of precious aircrews, bombers, and fuel—a classic case of virtual attrition imposed by the defense on the offense.

## The First Ballistic Missile Threat

The V-2 soon followed the V-1 against England, and it was not long before the inhabitants were truly terrified. Not only was there no way to intercept it, but they could not even see it coming at a speed of a mile a second. The British had known the V-2 attack was imminent, because intelligence had received good information in 1942, and an errant test rocket had escaped control over the Baltic and crashed in Sweden. Having determined that the Allies would win the war, the neutral Swedes had switched from being neutral on the German side to being neutral on the Allied side, so they tipped off the RAF, which flew in a plane to pick up the V-2 bits and carry them back to England for analysis. Unfortunately, that particular test V-2 had been fitted with a radio-controlled guidance system to test components for another Peenemunde experiment, so the British concluded that the V-2 was radio-controlled and had ginned up countermeasures to jam it. But the production V-2s launched against England were true ballistic missiles, entirely autonomous after launch; they went up into space as ordered by their prepro-grammed on-board gyroscopes, and fell down to their targets in the ballistic trajectory taught in elementary physics. They could not be jammed, but had to be intercepted. At their speed of thousands of miles an hour, there was no way that any fighter plane could get at them even if they could be detected.

Almost in desperation, the defenders turned to the guns. Over the winter of 1944–45, Antiaircraft Command of the British army worked up the first ballistic missile defense system. The radars were aimed up, and the computers were calibrated to track the ballistic trajectories of the missiles coming down. The experiments were delayed for a time because of an apparent flaw in the equipment. The operators found themselves tracking a mysterious image drifting slowly across the screens. It took some weeks for them to realize that the mystery object was the Moon. Ballistic missile defense (BMD) occasioned humanity's first extraterrestrial contact.

The British gun system was the minimum BMD possible—its designers estimated its effectiveness at 3 to 10 percent. The Amer-icans expected to do rather better with their radars and guns in the defense of Antwerp and the Channel ports against V-2 attacks, but in the end the effort was unnecessary because of counterforce attacks by Allied bombers against the rocket-launching sites and because the ground forces had overrun the German launch positions. Still, it was a start.

## The Defense of the Reich

The air defense of the Reich was more formidable than that of Britain. The Battle of Germany engaged exemplary antiaircraft and fighter-interceptor equipment and tactics, both day and night. Nattering with his adoring secretaries in his invulnerable bunkers, Hitler would spin out the last of his totalitarian fantasies—of the entire Reich an air defense command, of an 88 gun in every village and neighborhood, of every citizen assigned to a battery.

By 1943 the Nazi leadership knew they must lose a war of mass production, and for lack of an alternative, played the wild card of high-tech wonderweapons. Though the Germans never quite matched the Anglo-Americans in radar, they opened a box of wizards' tricks for the defense against the Allied bombardment of Germany's cities. The German's managed to get into production limited numbers of jet-propelled fighter planes, unguided ground-to-air rockets, air-to-air rockets, and even a few rocket-propelled piloted interceptors.

Peenemunde tried to contribute to the air defense of the Reich. When the war broke out, its staff was augmented by a physics student at the Berlin Institute of Technology named Oswald Lange; offered a choice between the army and applied scientific work at Peenemunde, he chose the latter. (Many of the characters in this chronicle found military research preferable to military service.) When he reported for duty, he learned that the chief scientist, Wernher von Braun, not only was his countryman (both were from Silesia), but also was a physicist—a Herr Doktor—not a mere engineer. For a time, Lange continued his graduate studies at the technical institute, commuting from Peenemunde in a Junkers transport. Lange was not a rocket man, but a tube man. In America, he would have gone to the Rad Lab at MIT. The prototype rockets were gyroscopically guided, with no need for tubes, so Lange cast about for a plausible use for his particular specialty and hit upon the ground-to-air rocket. His concept was a beam-rider missile, which would read a radar beam fixed on an aircraft and follow the beam up to the target. This became Wasserfall.

American military research has a venerable tradition called "bootlegging"—research not consistent with the formal objectives of the contract, but thought more desirable by the researchers. The creative consultant knows the client's interests better than the client himself. In the German scheme of allocation of military missions, unlike the American, ground-based air defense was the realm of the Luftwaffe, and the rocket establishment belonged to the army, so the work on Wasserfall had to be done on the q.t. And the research soon indicated that the liquid-fuel technology of the Braun team was not optimal for antiaircraft weaponry, because an offensive weapon afforded the time to fill the tanks with the volatile and dangerous liquid fuels before launch, while an antiaircraft missile had to be ready to fire immediately when the target came within range. So surface-to-air missiles (SAMs—"sams") demanded the chemically stable and long-lasting solid-fuel rockets; but the Luftwaffe controlled that technology, and it wanted fighter-interceptors, not rockets.

So Wasserfall never got off the ground. Some of its components were tested on a V-2—inadvertently befuddling British intelligence about its guidance system. A few experimental units were on hand, and it was suggested that perhaps the rocket team might use them to defend Peenemunde itself. Yet when the RAF learned of the operation and laid on a heavy attack in 1943, Wasserfall sat idle. The rocketeers had decided that fighting wars was not their business; they merely designed equipment. The air attack was annoying, but the rocket work was unimpeded. Only a very few people were killed, most of the casualties were slave laborers.

While Wasserfall and other SAMs never got past early development stages, the other new systems took a terrible toll on the attackers. British Bomber Command alone lost 50,000 killed—as many as the total U.S. loss in Korea or in Vietnam. Maintaining the air offensive required the iron will and brutal discipline of the air marshals and generals such as "Bomber" Harris and Curtis LeMay. In the end, the defenses were overwhelmed not by the air assault but by the internal chaos of German industrial production and by the paucity of petroleum.

Another area in which the Germans took a lead was in infrared sensors—devices that could detect the heat of incoming aircraft. This technology never went very far under the Germans, any more than did similar British experiments, but early on it had been identified as having considerable military potential. The many failures and uncompleted projects of the German engineers must be weighed against their fantastic technological successes. The last throes of the Third Reich demonstrated what marvelous military fruits an open-handed and open-ended research cornucopia can yield.

## The Offense Redeemed

In one key area, the Germans were left at the post by the Anglo-Americans. In December of 1938 the German chemist Otto Hahn first experimentally identified what had been theoretically calculated by physicists: nuclear fission. Within a year, at least six countries had military nuclear-energy programs. Fortunately for the anti-German cause, the racial and political policies of the Third Reich had driven many of its most prominent physicists abroad, particularly to the United States. In 1940, two Hungarian émigrés, Leo Szilard and Edward Teller, drove out to Long Island to persuade the most renowned of the refugee scientists, Albert Einstein, to sign a letter urging the American government to pay strict attention to the military implications of the discovery of nuclear fission. Einstein said he would think about it, and then said yes on a second trip by Szilard and another young Hungarian Jew, Eugene Wigner. The result of the petition is famous, but neglected is that the incident contained two innovations: private scientists taking the initiative in military research, and foreigners meddling in American military matters.

Fortunately for the history of humanity, the Germans had rather too much respect for physicists, understanding that such prima donnas could not be managed by mere mortals. Their physicists bickered, and the German nuclear program got nowhere. The crude philistine Americans had quite another view of the role of scientists. When the notion of making nuclear munitions reached the U.S. Army staff, it was noted that the major expense of man-hours and money was for building the factories to make the nuclear explosive materials—plutonium and uranium-235. Therefore the endeavor was just a large engineering project, so an accomplished Corps of Engineers officer, Leslie R. Groves, fresh from completing a War Department office building* named the Pentagon, was put in command of what was given the cover name of the "Manhattan Engineering District." He turned to America's largest chemical company, E. I. du Pont, to build the plants, and the Manhattan Project worked itself out to its immortal conclusion.

The atomic bomb redeemed the concept of air power. While there is great dispute over the effects of high-explosive and incendiary bombing in World War II, only the most enthusiastic air-power devotee would claim that the results had achieved the high expectations of its promoters. Decisive victory had not been attained through aerial bombing. The active defenses had been found to be stupendously more effective than anyone had anticipated. The passive defenses of the factories and cities greatly limited the damage. The Germans and Japanese had resourcefully adjusted themselves to the threat. Civilian and military morale had not collapsed under bombardment. Quite the opposite: involving the civilians in the war directly, putting them on the front line, had bolstered their identification with the war effort. And the governments had not been awed. Germany fought until its capital was overrun and its field armies destroyed; Japan felt the destruction of its merchant marine, navy, and air forces, the entrapment of its armies in China, the nightly burning of its cities by Curtis LeMay's B-29s, and the pinch of half-rations for the entire population, and continued to fight. It required the atomic bomb to bring Nippon to its knees.

The Bomb made aerial warfare look all new, and the world had to contemplate What It All Meant. One of the first to face up to the military implications of nuclear weaponry was a Yale political science professor just released from his military service. Bernard Brodie had begun as a naval historian; his *Sea Power in the Machine Age* is an admirable account of the dialectic between naval offense and defense, with the offense inexorably winning. His *A Layman's Guide to Naval Strategy* was deemed by the Navy staff to be so excellent and succinct that the word "layman" was stripped from the title, the book became prescribed reading for professional officers, and Brodie was called to duty as a staff officer.

He was rather conservative militarily, arguing that the effects of

---

*Later, "The Building" to people in the Business.

aviation on navies were grossly exaggerated and that a major place for the battleship still remained. But when the Bomb was announced, he went to the other extreme: that this new technology had changed everything. In the fall of 1945 he wrote an essay, subsequently published in the anthology *The Absolute Weapon* in 1946, that included the most famous aphorism to have appeared in nuclear-strategic analysis: "Historically the problem of the military has been how to win wars. Henceforth the problem is how not to fight them."

Although his first essay is oft-quoted, Brodie shortly changed his mind—and changed it again and again, because he too often published an incisive and lucid essay before he had systematically and thoroughly thought out the subject. In 1945 he assumed, not unreasonably at the time, that A-bombs were the equivalent of battleships—expensive and few, and to be husbanded for the most vital missions. How peculiar that the learned advocate of the battleship failed to observe that the formidable and expensive weapons system of the armored battle line was never used to bombard a city.

When you pull hard on a piece of fabric, the weakest threads give first. One of the first to break under the strain was Leo Szilard. Even before the Bomb was tested, he tried to block it. Among his other efforts, he wandered down to South Carolina to exhort James Byrnes, then a politician of some note, to implore the President to halt the impending horror. Byrnes considered, and remarked that the Bomb might be a nice thing with which to threaten the Russians. Szilard professed himself to be flabbergasted.

"Don't you care about Hungary?" asked Byrnes, knowing full well that Szilard's homeland was then being raped and pillaged in the course of liberation by the Red Army. No; compared with the dangers of the impending nuclear age, Szilard did not care about Hungary, nor about Poland, or France, or England, or Canada, or Massachusetts. Szilard cared about "humanity" and "civilization." Many in scientific circles thought Szilard's views to be profound. Outside scientific circles, Szilard's reaction revealed how useful were nuclear weapons—against those who have cracked.

## The Not-So-Absolute Weapon

Not everyone was so awed by the Bomb. Anticipating a squabble over the effects of the strategic bombing effort, the British and American governments commissioned independent studies by civilian analysts of the physical, economic, and moral effects of the bombing. The leadership of the American team fell upon a young gentleman banker who had signed on for the war effort, Paul H. Nitze. The work of the United States Strategic Bombing Survey (USSBS) in Germany was completed just in time for application of the method to just-surrendered Japan. The members of the team arrived when the ruins had hardly cooled. They were impressed, but not excessively so. They coolly analyzed the damage and the sensible Japanese civil defense measures. Two volumes of the USSBS were devoted to the attacks on Hiroshima and Nagasaki, and although originally classified, the reports became the elementary texts for work on nuclear-weapons effects—what exactly did a nuclear bomb of such-and-such size, exploded at such-and-such height, at such-and-such distance actually do to structures of such-and-such construction, and to the people in them, or not in them?

Nitze and his colleagues were neither sanguine nor sanguinary about atomic munitions. They were merely another problem, and to establishment operators like Nitze, the affairs of men are fraught with problems which sensible and prudent men must attempt to deal with as best they can. After all, the USSBS merely noted, without need for elaboration, what was obvious: that on the basis of the Japanese evidence, conventional war could do as much damage as a nuclear war, albeit with more ponderous and delayed means; and that even a totally defeated nation could survive a nuclear war. Hiroshima was taken by surprise; nonetheless, people in shelters a few hundred feet from ground zero had survived.

As the USSBS team completed its work, the surviving residents of Hiroshima and Nagasaki were trickling back to their cities and beginning the work of rebuilding them, an enterprise that was accomplished within a few years. Hiroshima, which was not much of a city to begin with, sort of a Japanese Toledo, made the best of a horrid situation, and generated a respectable tourist trade from being flattened in an innovative manner. Nagasaki, at the wrong end of

Japan and lacking an airport, just went back to work—nobody cares about who is second.

Still, not enough was known about the Bomb. The first test, in New Mexico, had been merely to see if the thing would work, and the attacks on Hiroshima and Nagasaki had been uncontrolled experiments. In 1946, the military organized Operation Crossroads. One of the oddities of the outcome of World War II was that the United States found itself in possession of a vast spread of minuscule worthless islands in the central Pacific. One by one, many of these were added to the atomic archipelago. The first was Tinian, whence General LeMay's bombers launched the raids that leveled Hiroshima and Nagasaki. In 1946, Bikini Atoll was added to the archipelago. The Navy needed to know what effects the Bomb would have on the fleet. Among the task force sweltering on the Equator for Operation Crossroads was a small team from the newly formed Naval Radiological Defense Laboratories, including Jerry Strope.

Strope was from Michigan, half German and half Scotch-Irish, and his peculiar Christian name—Walmer—was a family compromise between Walter and Elmer; but when the infant Strope was presented to his aunt, she saw a resemblance to the German side of the family and remarked that "he looks like a little Jerry to me," and the nickname stuck. He earned entrance to the elite all-scholarship Webb Institute on Long Island, which has produced generations of America's leading naval architects. Upon his graduation, the war was on, and he immediately went into government service in the Navy's Bureau of Ships, analyzing war damage to vessels and making recommendations for improvements in ship design and operations to mitigate future damage, to save ships and to preserve American lives.

Nuclear fission, however, was a new way to damage ships and men, so Strope and his colleagues sweated in the hot Pacific sun for six months. The Crossroads tests did not impress the Navy. They showed merely that dropping a bomb in the midst of a tightly packed and immobile fleet would sink many of the ships if no one was on board to perform the requisite damage control. Several fine ships, obsolete but workable, were sacrificed in this way, and some were towed away to be abandoned later. Still, the atomic bomb was no worse than a squadron of kamikazes.

One thing Strope and his colleagues learned in this and subsequent tests was that radiation was a grave threat to the crew and therefore to the operation of a ship, but was easily dealt with by the simple expedient of washing off the ship. Radiation was not the magic poison pictured in the hysterical public press; it was merely some crud to be hosed away.

## The Next War in 1945

Nevertheless, in 1945 and 1946 the popular view of the next war was a nightmare version of Douhet's vision: each side would launch its bombers against the other, pummeling cities into atomic dust, until one side or the other quit, or both were annihilated. This specter was developed in gruesome detail by many of the "atomic scientists"* who had participated in the Manhattan Project. Because of the ballyhoo surrounding the Bomb, they had gained monstrous prestige and felt themselves—and were taken by the press, the politicians, and the public—to be oracles in matters of nuclear energy, military strategy, international politics, and everything else under the sun. Many of them, it turned out in retrospect, had been opposed to using the nuclear weapons against Japan, or so they said.

A more imaginative vision of the next war, which surfaced in 1945 and was a favorite of uninformed commentators, mated American and German technologies. In theory an atomic bomb could be fitted to a V-2, resulting in a weapons system capable of attacking at speeds many times in excess of sound, outstripping any defense, and destroying a city in a single blow—truly the ultimate weapon. But the fearmongers were ignorant of the technical realities. Nuclear bombs were too heavy to fit on rockets, and the V-2s were too inaccurate to warrant the risk of such expensive warheads. Increasing the range, while possible (the Germans had plans to bombard New York in late 1946), would increase the inaccuracy (the Peenemunde scheme was to use pilots who would bail out of the rockets and be picked up by submarine off Montauk Point). Only bombers could deliver bombs in the 1940s. The chief scientific adviser to the war effort, Vannevar Bush, had to take the trouble to beat off the long-range-

---

*The quotation marks are appropriate because 1) many of them were not scientists and 2) in designing the nuclear bomb they were working not as scientists but as engineers. This semantic difficulty was shortly resolved by the labeling of nuclear-weapons engineers as "designers."

rocket fantasy which threatened to divert funds from buying bombers and bombs, which were sorely needed.

## The (Peaceful) Nuclear Wars of the 1940s

The first of the nuclear wars was between the United States and the Japanese Empire—the Americans had the Bomb, and the Americans won. The second nuclear war was between the American military and the American scientific community—the military had the Bomb, and the scientists won. The War Department and the Army quite reasonably felt that they had done an unimpeachable job of bringing the Manhattan Project to fruition. Because these were weapons of war, atomic munitions were merely another variety of ordnance and should be developed and procured under military control. The scientists thought otherwise—and in the ensuing political battles, the scientists won decisively, and their total victory was achieved in the establishment of the Atomic Energy Commission, charged with command of all forms of nuclear energy, including the production and control of nuclear munitions. In the course of the struggle for control, the political activists formed a lobby, the Federation of Atomic Scientists (later . . . of American Scientists) and a journal of advocacy, the *Bulletin of the Atomic Scientists*.

The third nuclear war was over national control of atomic weapons. The British, who had collaborated in the Manhattan Project, were shortly pushed out. This seemed hard on them, but World War II was over, and while the smart money was already being bet on the Soviet Union, there was the possibility that the next adversary might well be the traditional enemy, the British Empire. The solution to nuclear governance adopted as policy by the United States government was that atomic energy should be internationalized under the control of the new United Nations. This proposal seemed to Americans abundantly generous and proper. The U.S.S.R. was not favorably inclined, perhaps because the Soviets believed that the bourgeois states were not to be entrusted with the security of the emerging and inevitable world socialist commonwealth, and/or Russians were not about to let their future well-being be placed in the hands of foreigners, and/or the U.N. may have seemed very international to the Americans, but to the Russians looked like an instrument under American control. So, international control of nuclear energy was left by the wayside. The sovereign nations would have their own nuclear weapons; but how would they use them?

The fourth nuclear war was between the Army Air Forces and the rest of the military. In retrospect, nuclear weaponry conclusively justified and sanctified Air Power, but at the time the air generals were downright hostile. If a city could be leveled with a single bomb, obviously you had no need for thousands of bombers. So there was an air force tendency to pooh-pooh the Bomb in intragovernmental discussions, which was in sharp contradiction to the national policy of making a great to-do about atomic energy.

It became clear within a few months after the end of World War II that the next enemy of the American Republic would be the Soviet Union. But the American public was sick and tired of war, its costs and regimentation; political pressure increased—intelligently or cynically manipulated both by the then-vigorous Communist Party and its swarm of fellow travelers and by the old isolationist, anti–New Deal, Republican right wing—to collapse the U.S. military forces following World War II. The mammoth armies, navies, and air forces that had swept over Europe and Asia were shortly reduced to a rabble equipped with secondhand weapons. Only by the high-pitched promotion of the overweening puissance of the Bomb did American power seem to have any substance. It was all a bluff; there were but a handful of weapons.

## The Next Bomb

Yet it could be forecast that soon the Soviet Union, and God-knows-who-else, would also have the bomb. There were great arguments over how long it would take. Most of the physicists were skeptical about Russian capability. The military, from their few contacts with Russians and from debriefings of German officers, concluded that the Soviets had no technical competence, but won by mass manpower and crude disregard for human life—charging infantry across minefields, for example.

But two men had a different thought. Writing in 1946, the physicists Frederick Seitz and Hans Bethe estimated that a modern country, merely with publicly available information and knowing that nuclear munitions had been achieved by the Americans, could produce a weapon in about five years. Despite their utter ignorance of the Soviet Union, Seitz and Bethe were right on the money; their technical knowledge was sufficient to make the forecast. The Russians first got wind of the Manhattan Project through espionage in 1944 and exploded their first device in 1949. What later came to be labeled (and disparaged) as "mirror-imaging"—projecting our capabilities onto the other side—worked in this first instance.

Also in 1946 one of the stars of the Rad Lab, Louis Ridenour, looked gloomily at the prospect of other powers having the Bomb. He discussed possible counters. He laid out the limitations on air defense in the nuclear age, noting correctly that traditional air defense depended on attrition—that downing 10 percent of the attackers in each raid would destroy 40 percent of the attacking force in five raids, so 10 percent defense kill capability was sufficient to dissuade attack. But that calculation assumed the attack carried conventional chemical explosives or incendiaries.

The atomic bomb entirely changed the equation. Ten percent attrition per raid was not enough; 50 percent was not enough; 90 percent was insufficient. Now it was at last true that if the bomber got through, even one bomber got through, that meant one city was lost. And conventional means of civil defense were pathetic in the face of such formidable offensive forces. Quite properly, Ridenour gave his essay the title "There Is No Defense."

**The Problem Stated**

In the late 1940s we can already see the origins of the fundamental American strategic issue of the nuclear age. Let us call this "The Problem":

1. Any power dominating the Eurasian land mass is a lethal threat to the existence of the United States of America.
2. The Soviet Union is probably hostile and expansionist. Even if it is lazy and benign, we cannot be sure, and we cannot count on its staying that way.
3. The Soviet Union is centrally located in Eurasia and can strike and exert pressure by threats anywhere around its periphery.
4. The dictatorial system of the Soviet Union can extract hordes of troops and a plentitude of conventional military forces from its population and economy.

5. The democratic countries, the United States in particular, are unwilling or unable to match the Soviet Union man for man, gun for gun, tank for tank, plane for plane.
6. Thus the United States must rely on its technological superiority, in particular its ability to match Soviet conventional power with nuclear attack power. The standard scenario for peace is that the threat of a Soviet conventional attack is countered by the threat of a U.S. nuclear attack against the U.S.S.R. Therefore America's allies are reassured and loyal, and the Soviet Union is deterred, and there is relative peace in the world.
7. *But* . . . what if the Soviet Union can strike back? What does that mean? How can we achieve our world-strategic objectives without enfeebling our capitalist economy and democratic polity?
8. *And* . . . what if deterrence fails?

Wrestling with The Problem has not only engendered enduring turmoil in the United States, and stimulated the devising of nuclear-strategic analysis, but also led to the creation of strategic defense systems and organizations.

# II

# THE DEFENSE REVIVED

*It seems the Moscovite*
*Has quite a healthy, growing appetite.*
*We can't be safe, at least we can be right.*
*Some bombs may help—perhaps a bomb-proof cellar*
*But surely not the Chamberlain umbrellar.*

EDWARD TELLER

Not everyone despaired of the defense. As the American forces battered their way across Europe and the Pacific, and fought off the innovative counterattacks of the failing Axis, deep in the bowels of the military services were men who were devising weaponry for future wars. In the summer of 1944, at the Frankford Arsenal in Philadelphia, a young ordnance officer named Jake Schaefer was discussing the V-1 attacks on London. Although the AA guns had been reasonably effective, it was evident that the speeds and rates of maneuver of jet-propelled aircraft flying at near-sonic or perhaps even supersonic speeds would outstrip the capability of mindless shells fired from the ground.

So Lieutenant Schaefer worked up a concept paper advocating the development of a surface-to-air missile. He rejected the radar-beam rider and other types of homing missiles because of excessive complexity and the problem of maneuvering fast enough when closing on a moving target. Instead, he recommended a "command guidance" system, which would be composed of a radio-guided rocket, two radars, and a computer. One radar would track the target; the other would track the defending missile from its point of launch; the computer would calculate the place of impact and

46

would command the missile by radio to make the intercept. If the target changed course, the tracking radar would inform the computer, which would calculate the new intercept point, and inform the missile's controls to correct its course accordingly. Note that the missile did not track the aircraft—it hit a point in the sky determined by the computer.

The scheme was commendable in terms of operating costs: only the rocket, warhead, and radio-control receiver were expended in action, while the radars and the computer—the expensive parts— remained on the ground for reuse. Schaefer suggested that this antiaircraft concept was technologically feasible, indeed conservative, but was a complex system which could be produced by only two American manufacturers, RCA and Bell Laboratories. As he was then in the uniform of Uncle Sam, it would not have been appropriate for Schaefer to mention that he was on leave of absence from Bell Labs for the duration of the war.

The Army picked up on the idea, initially calling it Anti-Aircraft Guided Missile (AAGM), but shortly thereafter the director of advanced research in such matters, Colonel Gervaise Trichel, who was an amateur classical scholar, named the project Nike ("nigh-key") for the Greek goddess of victory (and incidentally established the precedent of naming American missiles and rockets for mythological figures, prefiguring Jupiter, Atlas, Thor, Apollo, *et al.*).

## The First Air Defense War

A bureaucratic difficulty arose because the Army Air Forces also had a very definite interest in air defense. In fact, during World War II the Air Forces, imitating the Luftwaffe, had taken over the antiaircraft guns in the European Theater of Operations. But the Ordnance Corps argued that Schaefer's speculative rocket was merely an extension of the antiaircraft gun and quite within its legitimate research province. After ferocious negotiation, the War Department determined that anything with a wing, even without a pilot, was still an aircraft and therefore meat for air force research, while a rocket with nothing more than a fin was effectively a new type of cannon shell and was therefore artillery and was appropriate for the Ordnance Corps to develop for the antiaircraft artillery.

This squabble took on greater significance when, after thirty years of agitation, the Americans imitated the British in making the air force a separate service, assigned the primary role in air defense. But what about the antiaircraft guns and the proposed surface-to-air rockets? In the original negotiations, the Air Force could have had the ground-based air defense function, but rejected it for an internal administrative reason: the antiaircraft elements of the Army were mostly retreads of the old Coast Artillery Corps. Had antiaircraft been incorporated into the Air Force, those old gunners would have had seniority and would have held most of the top ranks in the new service. Needless to say, the fly-boys wanted none of that, so the antiaircraft guns were left to the Army. The Air Force shortly initiated a parallel project to Nike, which it called ground-to-air pilotless aircraft (GAPA—"gap-ah"). At the Key West conferences at which the Joint Chiefs of Staff sorted out the functions of their services, the Air Force was given overall command of continental air defense and responsibility for "area" defense weapons, while the Army got "point" defense; but the dividing line could not be defined. This was a bad omen for the future of the air defenses of the United States of America.

Another problem of the infant Air Force was that most of the technological competence of the military was concentrated in the technical branches of the Army—in the Corps of Engineers, Signal Corps, and Ordnance Corps—and was unavailable to the Air Force because those tech officers knew that the new service would be the property of men who wore wings on their left breast; other officers would be treated as second-class citizens, and they wanted none of it. The Air Force had to turn to civilians. It responded to a suggestion by engineers of the Douglas Aircraft Company that its small advanced research and development (R and D) shop be converted to a permanent freewheeling institution examining long-range technical issues affecting aerial warfare. The scientific advisers to the Air Force told the generals that the recruitment of top-notch scientific people required that they be treated like university professors, free to research whatever they wanted. So the responsible staff officer, General Curtis LeMay, ordered that the work statement be a single sentence written so expansively that Project RAND could study nearly anything—and funded and trained his Nemesis.

## The Defense Rests

Between 1945 and 1950 practically nothing was done for the strategic defense of the United States, and for good reason. There was no longer any naval threat, so the coastal fortifications could be dismantled and reliance placed upon a considerable and superfluous fleet which the Navy insisted on maintaining. The presumed adversary, the Soviet Union, had a very disappointing record in long-range aviation during World War II. Although they had sequestered a few crippled B-29s which had sought sanctuary in then-neutral Siberia, it was not perceived that the Soviets had much strategic reach. Furthermore, all the German reports said that Russians were lousy pilots. And the Soviets had no Bomb. So the American civil defense apparatus was shut down along with victory gardens and rationing, and the domestic air defenses were dismantled along with the rest of the armed forces, excepting a corrupt gendarmerie in Europe and the Far East, several carrier task forces, and a few squadrons of B-29s. Some of the radars were left, if only because it was too expensive to tear them down.

In 1949 and 1950 the situation changed radically. Presciently, the Atomic Energy Commission had equipped a few aircraft to sniff for evidence of nuclear explosions outside the United States, and in August of 1949 a B-29 detected the debris of an explosion in Central Asia. President Truman announced this to the world. Initially the United States hardly responded, merely stripping down its conventional forces even further and accelerating nuclear-bomb production and the fitting of more bombers for these "special weapons." But little money was available because both the Democratic administration and the Republican opposition were loath to burden the country with high defense spending.

Then North Korea attacked in June 1950, swiftly defeated the South Korean army, and chewed up its American reinforcements with Soviet tanks and artillery. Intelligence picked up the presence of Soviet advisers, concrete evidence that the other side was capable of direct aggression against the West. To a few people high in the administration, the Congress, and the body politic, this was an eagerly awaited opportunity. Now the game was in earnest. The United States remobilized. The U.S. defense budget was tripled in the fol-

lowing year. Everything was built up. There was money for everybody. The new aircraft carriers that the Navy desired were laid
down; the American forces in Europe were raised from a pathetic
garrison to a serious field army; money was dumped into the air
forces. The Strategic Air Command (SAC—"sack"), previously almost entirely a paper organization, was molded by its forceful commander Curtis LeMay into a formidable and well-armed nuclear
strike force. The Cold War buildup of the strategic offensive forces
and the conventional land, sea, and air forces is well recorded by
all accounts of the Nuclear Age/Cold War. What must be added
here is the substantial efforts put into the strategic defense of the
United States.

## CONAD

It became evident that the Soviet Union would shortly have the
capability to strike devastating blows against the United States. In
1950–51 the specter of Soviet attack was by means of the Tu-4, a
copy of the B-29s that had crash-landed in Siberia. The Soviets
appeared to have several hundred of those and soon might be able
to deliver several hundred bombs on American cities and manufacturing installations. In 1951 the Air Force re-created the Air Defense
Command (ADC—"ay-dee-see") and at the end of the year transferred its headquarters from Mitchel Field on Long Island to the
less vulnerable inland site of Ent Air Force Base in Colorado Springs,
at the edge of the Rockies. Initially, its resources were pathetically
thin. Fleets of old World War II fighters were left over, but these
could not deal with a concerted attack by Tu-4s. World War II–era
radars were still emplaced along the coasts, but they were obsolete
and poorly linked together. The Soviets could easily attack over the
North Pole or over the seas against either coast.

The principal asset of the air defense of the United States was
the radar-directed 90-mm and 120-mm antiaircraft guns emplaced
around cities in World War II and mostly transferred to the National
Guard. The Guard had been federalized for the Korean War, so
the gunners were troops on active duty, delighted to be safe from
frozen Chosen. The Guardsmen dusted off the breeches, tuned the
radars, and adjusted their analog fire-control computers. The guns
were deployed around—and in many cases actually in—the major

cities and ports of the United States. New York and Washington rated four battalions, each of four batteries of four guns; Chicago got three battalions; Philadelphia, Detroit, and San Francisco had two; Boston, Baltimore, Pittsburgh, and Los Angeles had one each. Norfolk, main base of the Atlantic Fleet, rated two battalions. Niagara, site of the largest electrical generating plant in the East, was defended by a battalion. The state of Washington rated two battalions, to guard Seattle and the Bonneville Dam and some other vital installations. Most headquarters of the AA battalions, groups, and brigades were based in old Coast Artillery forts. In a few cases the Army continued to occupy space on airfields that had been handed over to the Air Force. One AA brigade found itself bedded down in St. Timothy's School for Girls in Catonsville, Maryland. Less pleasant duty was next to Rosslyn at Fort Myers, quarters for the high Army brass and under their eye.

While presumably the combat firing would be done under operational control of the local Air Force ADC commanders, in the peacetime military the chain of command for equipment, personnel, and especially paperwork is more pertinent. So an overall Anti-Aircraft Command headquarters was necessary, and obviously most conveniently colocated with Air Force ADC. AA Command briefly set up shop at Mitchel Field and then followed ADC to Colorado Springs, where the small cadre took up quarters in the Antlers Hotel. Later in the decade, when it became evident that the antiaircraft gun was shortly to follow the barrage balloon to oblivion, the Army relabeled its AA forces "air defense artillery" (ADA), and the defenders of the Zone of the Interior became Air Defense Command—but an Air Force air defense command was already in being, so the gunners were named Army Air Defense Command (ARADCOM—"ah-rahd-comm").

Shortly it became apparent that a more formal link between the Air Force and the Army continental defense forces was desirable, so the Pentagon established the Continental Air Defense Command (CONAD—"con-add"), a unified biservice command, under an Air Force commander-in-chief (CINCCONAD—"sink-conad") who also wore his blue hat as ADC commander. Working the Army side of the complex negotiations was its Undersecretary, Karl Bendetson. Thus a defense structure was formed, but with old radars, piecemeal communications, fighter-interceptors that lacked night and bad-weather capability, and guns that lacked range and accuracy, so the chances of getting every bomber, or *any* bomber, were slim indeed. Something better had to be done.

## The Valley Committee

The Air Force was conscious of its lack of technical ability to deal with the problem of air defense and hardly knew where to start. A committee was formed of accomplished engineers headed by the MIT physicist George E. Valley, a Rad Lab alumnus. He had resisted offers to go to Los Alamos, and had been very active in the fight to gain civilian control of nuclear energy, but he was not averse to working for the Air Force. His initial AF work was investigating the possibility that the United States was being subjected to reconnaissance by potential attackers from the Soviet Union—or perhaps from Mars. Beginning in 1947, there had been a spate of sightings of unidentified flying objects, and an Air National Guard pilot had been killed pursuing one. Valley joined the team examining these phenomena, most of which were attributable to natural causes (although a mysterious residue remained to bedevil science and delight cranks). The flying-saucer project was a fine introduction to the state of the continental air defense apparatus. Valley described it as "lame, purblind, and idiot-like."

The Rad Lab at MIT had been shut down after the war. Sort of shadow successors struggling on thin funding were the Air Force Cambridge Research Center, abutting the MIT campus, and Project Meteor, an MIT antikamikaze effort for the Navy. Valley served on the electronics panel of the Air Force's Scientific Advisory Board (SAB—"ess-ay-bee"). Encouraged by a colleague to look into the dismal state of air defense, Valley was quickly convinced of its inadequacy, and proposed to the SAB chief, the esteemed aerodynamicist Theodore von Karman, that an air defense committee be set up to investigate the subject. In the proposal was the suggestion that an experimental system be put up to play with radars, interceptor aircraft, and communications. The initial objective set was to raise the estimated kill rate from 10 percent to 30 percent.

The Air Defense Systems Evaluation Committee came to be named after Valley. It was made up almost entirely of MIT professors. One of its first ideas—in retrospect, the most important and long-lasting—was that military use of field radios in the continental United States was foolishness. Why bother when such a superior system was at hand in the form of the domestic telephone lines? Valley approached an old friend, Donald A. Quarles, vice president of the Bell Telephone Labs, to interest them in the problems of air defense. Ma Bell was eager to oblige.

Although the Valley Committee concentrated on the radars and the integration of the entire system, no aspects of air defense were ignored. The group downplayed the potential of ground-to-air rockets (because it was an Army function?) but kept an open mind about interception. A Cornell engineer, noting that the strongest part of any aircraft was its wing, proposed the charming idea of using interceptors as rammers, chopping off the weak tail of the bomber with the strong wing of the interceptor aircraft. Like many others that followed in the saga of strategic defense, the concept was technologically feasible, but was unacceptable to the operators of aircraft because it seemed rather too much like the kamikaze attacks on B-29s.

A major need was better radars. And the main problem was in sorting out the various inputs from the different radars. This could be accomplished only by an enormous calculating device. Early in 1950, Valley encountered a colleague, the engineer Jerome Wiesner, in the hall at MIT and mentioned the need for a computer to process the data that would come into an air defense system. Wiesner pointed out that one was right there on the MIT campus.

## Whirlwind

The Rad Lab had not been MIT's only contribution to the war effort against the Axis. Valuable work had also been done in the Servomechanisms Laboratory, set up to improve fire-control apparatus. One of its stars, Jay Forrester, emerged from working belowdecks on the U.S.S. *Lexington* to discover that the ship had sortied from Pearl Harbor, and he became an inadvertent observer of the conquest of a miserable atoll named Kwajalein. The Navy had need of an aircraft simulator—that is, a device which could imitate the behavior of an aircraft artificially as an aid to design, in order to bypass the time-consuming, expensive, and dangerous business of actually building and test-flying prototypes. The engineers at the Servomechanisms Lab shortly learned that such a device required a very complicated brain which could process elaborate variations of conjectural aircraft performance, and they labored with the primitive analog computers then available.

In 1945 the team learned of a breakthrough at the University of Pennsylvania: the invention of the digital computer, the first modern computer. The Penn machine was founded on the simple idea that controlling computations was easier if you gave up counting by tens, as had been taken for granted by the designers of analog computers, and adopted a Bell Labs idea of counting only by two—because electrical current could be either on or off. This "digital" processing was simpler and faster, although requiring much more circuitry and difficult design.

So the Servomechanisms Lab labored to build a digital computer. Indeed, the project focused on the computer itself rather than on the simulator of which it was to be but a component. To emphasize the intended rapidity of its calculations, the concept was labeled Whirlwind. As the military budgets were cut following the war, and as the project racked up bills, the Navy's research monitors became increasingly nervous. At Princeton, John von Neumann and other brilliant mathematicians were developing the father of modern computers. How could mere servo engineers be qualified to delve into such arcane matters? Although the Navy was very patient, it finally terminated the program, and Whirlwind was placed on MIT's overhead. But that financial bandage would never hold for long; universities are loath to fund anything if they cannot find a patron, so Whirlwind seemed just the thing for the air defense problem. Forrester was an enthusiastic—even maniacal—promoter of his baby, and he was backed up by Robert Everett, an intelligent and tough engineer. Although Valley was initially skeptical, he eventually was sold on the potential utility of Whirlwind's elephantine ruggedness.

As the work developed and the proposed experimental system began to take shape, the AF Cambridge Research Center moved out of cramped quarters along the Charles onto more expansive grounds at Hanscom Field, a former municipal airfield just beyond the western suburbs of Boston, near Bedford. (Hanscom is certainly the only U.S. Air Force base named for a journalist—a reporter for the *Worcester Dispatch*, an aviation enthusiast killed in a crash in 1941.) The experimental system was put together. A new radar was located at Truro, near the tip of Cape Cod, and integrated with existing radars at Long Island's Montauk Point to the south and at Gloucester to the north, and interceptors based at Hanscom and at Otis Air Force Base on Cape Cod—all tied together, at least in theory, by Whirlwind. The work was difficult—but in a decent time, it was possible to direct an interceptor to its target entirely automatically—"the immaculate interception."

The Valley/Cape Cod work gained an enthusiastic supporter in the Air Force's chief scientist, Louis N. Ridenour, who only four years earlier had written "There Is No Defense." He suggested that the country be littered with unmanned microphones to transmit the sounds of attacking bombers. Bell Labs concluded, however, that the mikes would be perpetually confounded by seabirds and hoaxsters; while filtering out such noise was technologically feasible, human beings with real ears would be better and cheaper.

## Project Lincoln

The air defense research was fascinating and useful, and because it would probably require the efforts of highly competent technical people for many years, it would demand an institution permanently devoted to research in air defense of the nation. A name was needed for the project, and Ridenour's deputy, Ivan Getting, looking at a map of the towns around Hanscom Field, noting that there had already been a Project Bedford and a Project Lexington, glanced at the next town—and named it Project Lincoln.

Before starting up the new institution, it was deemed appropriate to first do yet another study, and form yet another committee, this one labeled for Cambridge's river—Project Charles. It too was dominated by MIT personnel—including Valley, G. B. Hill, Ridenour, Wiesner, Forrester, and Jerrold Zacharias. It endorsed Whirlwind and the use of telephone lines to link the radars, computers, and command to the interceptor airfields and the antiaircraft batteries. It rejected a proposal for an Arctic early-warning line, and dallied with the concept of "Porcupine," a monster rocket shotgun to skewer planes with spikes.

Project Charles also took a *pro forma* look at civil defense. It casually listed the various means available, including shelters, but concentrated on trivial economic studies of the vulnerability of a few key industries. This inconsequential effort could be ignored except for the names of its contributors: James Tobin of Yale, later a member of the Council of Economic Advisers under Kennedy; Paul Samuelson of MIT, later a millionaire from selling baby economics textbooks; and heading it, a young Harvard economist, a sometime OSS officer in World War II, Carl Kaysen.

The principal recommendation of Project Charles was to reaffirm that an air defense laboratory should be set up. It did not say MIT outright. The study was not impressive overall; but a few enlightening sentences may have justified the effort; it is well to remember these points—their relevance is nearly universal:

> The problem of defense of the United States is characterized above all by lack of knowledge of what we have to defend against. The enemy has the initiative. Our intelligence tells us essentially nothing about his plans; informs us only partially about his present capabilities; and as to his future capabilities leaves us essentially dependent on assumptions that he can, if he chooses, do about as well in any aspect as we expect to do ourselves. Moreover, we have to assume that he is informed in detail about our present air defense and its weak points and has considerable information about our plans for the future.

Translation: technological "mirror-imaging." What we can do, he can do.

The Lincoln Laboratory was founded in late '51, and its first priority was a really serious, really high-pressure study. The "Project Lincoln" Summer Study of 1952 was the air defense study to end all. It was headed by Jerrold Zacharias, chief of MIT's nuclear-physics department, and was dominated by Tech people—yet heavy hitters were brought in from elsewhere, from Bell Labs and the Pentagon's Weapons System Evaluation Group, including the distinguished physicists John S. Foster of McGill, Isadore Rabi of Columbia, Charles Laurison of Cal Tech, and J. Robert Oppenheimer.

The tone was great optimism, no longer dallying with marginal ideas. In close collaboration with the air staff, the study endorsed an ambitious program to develop advanced interceptor fighters. And a more elaborate scheme for a highly integrated uniform air-intercept control system was laid out; this was surely the principal interest of the study team. But the most striking innovation of the Summer

Study was its strong endorsement of a concept rejected by Project Charles: a distant early-warning system, a screen of radars as far north as possible, pushed forward to the Arctic Circle. This would be expensive and difficult, but it could be done, and the idea was picked up with enthusiasm by elements of the defense establishment.

Another innovation, generally credited to Zacharias, was to blunt an obvious enemy tactic, avoiding radar by coming in from the sea, by putting the radars out to sea on the shallow continental shelf—on platforms modeled on the oil-drilling rigs of the Gulf of Mexico, and thus named Texas Towers. Very closely held at the time were the proposals for the defense of the continent from nuclear attack by means of nuclear weaponry.

So the air defense work became institutionalized as the Lincoln Laboratories of MIT, and attracted many Rad Lab veterans. The operation was put together promptly. Big chunks were taken out of other MIT operations. The Forrester Whirlwind operation was lifted intact and dropped into Lincoln. The labs shortly moved out to Bedford to snuggle near the Air Force's patronage at Hanscom Field. Contrary to many expectations, George Valley did not get the top job but rather became a division head. The first chief was A. G. Hill, a member of the Summer Study (inevitably inspiring poor jokes about "Hill 'n' Valley").

Whirlwind became Whirlwind II, and the progress on the machine did not fail expectations. As it approached fruition, its genius became restless. In 1956, Jay Forrester abandoned his baby, and quit the Lincoln Labs, and dropped out of the Business altogether, devoting the rest of his life to more and more elaborate and single- and simpleminded attempts to compute the world with his "systems dynamics," and collected a bundle of money in a brutal patent fight with IBM regarding the origin of many of the Whirlwind features that went into what became the air defense computer. Forrester was succeeded by Robert Everett, his chief lieutenant and foreman, who kept the original Whirlwind team together and working.

### The Quick-Fix Interceptors

During this period the Air Force used a concise learning device to display the conceptual elements of air defense: detection, identification, interception, destruction—D-I-I-D. Detection was by sensor: by eye, ear, remote microphone, or radar echo. As far as the Air Force was concerned, detection was a boring business just as well left to civilians. Identification was the sorting of the data from the sensors and selection of the hostile targets from the vast quantity of signals from friendly aircraft, false alarms, "noise," and "clutter." The Air Force was happy to dump this tedious function on the civilian technicians.

Interception was dearer to the blue-suited soul, yet interceptor aircraft had a very low priority. Armed forces usually have a plethora of surplus equipment after a war. But the German invention of the jet engine and swept-back wings had made our vast air armadas obsolete overnight. A completely new complement of aircraft was required. Because the Air Force had been erected on the cult of the offensive, its Strategic Air Command was first in line. The priorities went to the B-50 bombers (upgraded B-29s); the B-36, the first intercontinental bomber; the svelte B-47, the first successful jet bomber; and on the drawing boards, the Air Force's great dream, the intercontinental jet bomber, the B-52.

The second Air Force was Tactical Air Command (TAC—"tack"), the barony of the fighter jocks. Their passion was "air superiority," engaging other fighters, dogfighting. The United States had entered World War II when the Allies were going on the offensive, so the Army Air Forces had practically no experience with interception of bombers. An interceptor is not a dogfighter. It does not require high maneuverability or speed, although it should have a high rate of climb to get up to the target if warning time is short. But better to have long range combined with early warning and effective ground control to make a distant intercept. And an interceptor needs powerful but one-shot armaments, and the ability to fly and fight day or night, in fair weather or foul. The USAF in the late '40s and early '50s had no aircraft meeting these requirements, not even on the drawing boards.

So the Air Force resorted to aircraft that had been designed for other purposes. First were a pair of heavy fighter-bombers designed for ground attack, which could carry quite a load of armaments and could be converted to long-range interceptors by substitution of fuel for bombs. The Curtiss-Wright XP-87 was examined and found wanting (and was the last plane produced for the Air Force by that venerable company). More promising was the Northrop XP-89, which was ordered into service. Alas, there was a design flaw, a tail flutter; during a demonstration, a prototype crashed right in front of the selection team. This difficulty was eventually straightened out, and a thousand F-89s were produced, but that was the last plane that Northrop made for the Air Force for 30 years.

So the air staff turned in desperation to a quick fix. A standard U.S. fighter was the subsonic F-80, already obsolescent for dogfighting against the terrific Soviet MiG-15s. The T-33, the two-seat trainer version of the F-80, had been built on the same airframe. It was patched into an all-weather interceptor by installation of a radar in the nose and conversion of the rear seat into the position for the radar operator—"the scope-dope." The resulting F-94 became the workhorse of U.S. air defenses during the 1950s. It was slow, but that mattered naught if the detection and identification could put it in the proper place at the proper time.

Another expedient interceptor was created by installation of a small radar in the F-86, the first-line jet fighter of the early 1950s. The resulting F-86D "Dog"* was faster than the F-89 and F-94 and was greatly loved by the pilots, but it was a single-seater, requiring that the pilot double as radar operator. The limited capability made him little more than an errand boy going out where ground control told him.

## The Battle of the Birds

The culmination of D-I-I-D—destruction—was not easily achieved. The fighter jocks' concentration on air superiority/dogfighting led to conscious emphasis on rate of fire rather than weight of fire. In the swirl of a dogfight, the pilot can get the enemy in his sights for only a fraction of a second, so he wants rapid-firing guns to increase his chances of getting a few bullets into his quarry. So the U.S. Air Force had stuck to the machine gun, useful for killing an enemy

---

*In the 1920s the Royal Air Force began naming its aircraft types—Spitfire, Lancaster, Wellington—and the U.S. air forces adopted the same convention during World War II and into the Cold War era. But these names were strictly for the newspapers and civilians. No one in the services actually called a plane "Shooting Star" or "Stratofortress" or "Delta Dagger"; the planes were coolly labeled by their identifying letters ("F" for fighter) and numbers in series following. Some planes had nicknames, occasionally affectionate but usually derogatory.

But missiles are always called by names—Titan, Sparrow, "Herc" for Nike-Hercules—and the official type designations are disregarded.

fighter, but less so against a bomber, which was easier to hit but much sturdier. Worse, the principal Soviet bomber of the time, the Tu-4, had a tail turret with automatic cannon, one shell from which could shatter a fighter. An American interceptor closing for a tail attack would have been outranged and outgunned, and it would have been no solace to know that the Soviet designer Tupelov had copied the B-29 tail turret intended to chop up Japanese interceptors.

The transitional solution was yet another German invention, the air-to-air rocket—or rather, rockets. The wing tips of the interceptors were fitted with pods stuffed with clusters of small unguided missiles merely aimed by the pilot and fired in salvos of 12 or 24 rockets. The air-to-air tactics took the tail guns of a Tu-4 into account by planning for beam attacks, which also presented a larger target. The intercepting pilot, having made his radar rendezvous with the incoming, would sweep in from the side, would aim ahead of it like a hunter taking a lead on a flying bird, and presumably would blow the target out of the sky.

The ultimate solution to destruction of the bomber was to be the air-to-air guided missile. The intended system was Falcon, made by the Hughes Company. But Air Force design criteria emphasized the performance of the aircraft, not the missile. The aviators wanted their planes to fly ever faster. A large missile would make the plane too bulky if fitted internally, and its drag would slow the plane's speed if hung externally. So the missile had to be small and placed inboard. Thus Falcon was crippled by short range, a tiny computer, and a piddling little warhead. Falcon was a puny bird from its inception.

Here the U.S. Navy took the point. While the Navy will necessarily play a small role in this chronicle because it has had no major mission in strategic defense, it has been the leader in air defense technology. The sailors are intensely devoted to the defense of their ships, and they were badly frightened by the Japanese air offense beginning in late 1944, employing devastatingly effective cruise missiles. The Japanese missiles consisted of ordinary aircraft stuffed with fuel and bombs and equipped with complex and sophisticated sensor and guidance systems—the eyes and brain of a suicide pilot. The U.S. losses were terrible, and the Navy invested heavily in covering its ships with antiaircraft guns, improved radar fire control, and a crash program of ship-to-air missiles and air-to-air missiles for the combat air patrols giving cover to the fleet.

After the war, the Navy gave MIT a small contract for "Project Meteor," to examine ship-to-air missiles, then air-to-air missiles. Little came of it—excepting the finessing of a wind tunnel for MIT by Tech's political operator, the shrewd James Killian—but the project gave many technicians the opportunity for on-the-job training which paid off later. In the late 1940s, the Navy put out three separate air-to-air-missile contracts, all bearing the name "Sparrow." Sperry's Sparrow I was a radar-beam rider which suffered from the same fault as Oswald Lange's Wasserfall: the radar beam spread out as it approached the target, so the missile had trouble making the interception. Bendix' Sparrow II, based on active guidance by an internal radar set that detected the hostile and calculated its own course, was also unsatisfactory.

Sparrow III was a project of Raytheon. It had Navy experience with the aborted Lark missile, intended to kill kamikazes. After the war, Raytheon attempted to convert to civilian production, including an ingenious adaptation of microwave radar technology: Rada-Range, the first microwave oven. The company's human assets were considerable. Returned from the war was Charlie Adams—a.k.a. Charles Francis Adams, one of *the* Adamses, son of a Secretary of the Navy of the same name, but more important, married to the daughter of a Morgan partner, and assigned by Paine Webber to keep an eye on the infant company. A few years later, a guided-missile destroyer was named for his father; it wasn't every vendor in the Business who had such credentials.

In the early '50s, Raytheon's chief engineer was Ivan Getting, rather less than patrician in manner and tastes, but technically brilliant. The Sparrow project was run by a superbright young engineer named Tom Phillips. Sparrow III was a semiactive system: the main radar set transmitting the radio impulse was in the interceptor, and the missile carried only a receiving set and a small brain to instruct it to home in on the signal reflected off the target. This was much simpler than the "active" seeker which required that the missile carry the transmitter and receiver.

The practicality of the design was given a big boost by revival of an obsolete technology, continuous-wave (CW) radar, that had been abandoned in favor of pulsed radar, which could read range by counting the time it took for the pulse to go out and return to the receiver. With Sparrow's guidance scheme of proportional navigation, whereby the missile merely aimed itself at the target, indifferent to how far away it was, the range benefits of pulsed radar were pointless, and the simpler and less-jammable CW radar was more than satisfactory. As a bonus, if the enemy tried jamming, Sparrow III would home in on the jamming signal. This is a model of the "elegant" solutions that engineers adore. The successors of Sparrow III remain the principal air-to-air missiles of the U.S. services.

A group of engineers at the Navy's China Lake testing station in California worked out another excellent system: Sidewinder, a "passive" infrared missile that homed in on the heat of a jet engine's exhaust. This was excellent for air-to-air dogfighting, but of no utility to continental air defense, because it required that the interceptor get right on the tail pipe of a jet—and the original Soviet bombers lacked jet engines and had that hulking turret with guns aimed at the attacker's face. The Navy's missiles had to be forced down the throat of the Air Force, and eventually, the Air Force grudgingly adopted the naval perspective: the missile does not exist to supplement the aircraft; rather, the aircraft exists to carry the missile. And both exist to protect the assets on the ground/sea, not to run up kill scores in the glorious sport of air-to-air combat.

In the mid-'50s, advances in nuclear weaponry offered a resolution to the destruction problem. The size and cost of nuclear munitions had shrunk to the point where it became practical to employ them for what had originally been thought of as purely tactical uses—as artillery shells, depth charges, mines, antiaircraft-missile warheads, and air-to-air-missile warheads. Quickly the Air Force put together Ding Dong, a stupid unguided rocket. The interceptor pilot would aim it in the general direction of the bomber formation, make a fast turn, close his eyes, and pray that his little aircraft was not blown away by the 2-kiloton blast.

When it was tested in the skies over Nevada, five USAF officers observed from the ground immediately below the intercept, protected only by sunglasses. This was an inelegant solution, but seemed effective—provided, of course, the bomber was not flying too low; in which case, a chunk of the terrain and a part of the population might go with the enemy aircraft. The gadget was renamed Genie and pressed into service.

## The Defense Takes Shape

While the big brains at MIT were working on the brain of the air defense system, the Air Force was plugging in other elements. Air Defense Command was located at Colorado Springs as a defensive measure, to better protect the headquarters from attackers coming in over the coastline. (For the same reason, SAC hq was moved from Washington to a former balloon station at Omaha.) The interceptor airfields were relocated for more coherent coverage of the country. They tended to be concentrated in the Northeast and Northwest, with thinner but substantial deployments along the northern border. More important were the radars. There were no major breakthroughs in radar development, merely incremental improvements in range and sensitivity. Unit by unit, coverage spread along the coasts and across the northern border of the United States.

Because the Soviets could end-run around the land-based radars, the lines were extended seaward by Navy ships—at first destroyers, as had been used as radar pickets against the kamikazes in World War II. But the destroyer crews were not happy with dumbly cruising up and down to watch for aircraft, so the Navy reconsidered and equipped old freighters with radars. They were inherently defenseless, but this was consistent with their warning function. Should the Soviets sink them, the alert would be given.

The Navy also deployed four blimps. These almost-dirigibles were constructed for hunting U-boats, but the latest Soviet subs could evade and outrun the lumbering air bags. So the blimps' radars were pressed into service as forward sensors off the coasts.

Radar coverage was necessarily insufficient, because of the line-of-sight problem. So it became necessary to consider filling in the gaps. The Valley Committee had emphasized the obvious Soviet countermeasure to an elaborate system of radar detection and interception: the response of any sensible attacker, and in war one must assume that the enemy will be at least sensible, is not to fly high, where the radar can spot him, but to come down low—come in, if necessary, at treetop height. So another system of sensors had to cover the coasts and frontiers of the United States.

After considering and rejecting a nationwide network of microphones, the United States reverted to World War II practice. The Air Force organized its Ground Observer Corps, a paramilitary militia of public-spirited citizens who manned observation posts watching and listening for enemy bombers. Volunteers poured in. In the early '50s almost everybody feared that war could break out at any time, and civilian cooperation in a war effort was recent experience for the nation. Nearly 400,000 Americans signed up for that unpaid duty—forest rangers, lumberjacks, Great Lakes boatmen, even convicts on state prison farms. The New York region proudly announced its first blind observer (not as queer as it sounds, because he could hear aircraft engines better than a sighted person— but how he could distinguish the sound of a B-29 from that of a Tu-4 is not recorded).

What was tough was keeping people alert in peacetime. This is a fundamental difficulty of defense. The offense has the initiative; he decides when, where, and how to strike. He can rest until he is ready to attack. The defense should be alert at all times, but enduring vigilance cannot be expected of human beings. In a test in 1955, a B-29 crossed the country and was reported by only half of the ground observation posts it passed over. Still, the Ground Observer Corps was deemed a success. While infinitely less than a perfect detection system, it worked as a temporary measure. A more permanent solution was the "gap filler" radars. Smaller radars of less range than the major sets were stationed between the big units. Needless to say, this increased the data load on the air defense analysis and communications system. The last of the ground observer posts was shut down in 1958.

## Nike

The principal concern of the continental air defense planners had been the identification of incoming aircraft and vectoring out of interceptors to meet them—Air Force functions. Yet the Army had not been inactive. As recommended by Lieutenant Jake Schaefer, Project Nike had been given out to a contractor, Western Electric, which passed the research and the systems-engineering responsibility to Bell Laboratories. Again, Bell Labs took its characteristically haughty attitude toward defense contracting. AT&T had been unable throughout the war to invest in new equipment and was eager to begin upgrading the telephone system; it was very conscious that its real business was communications, and treated defense work as an act of civic virtue. Postwar, AT&T ruled that Bell Labs would devote 10 percent, and no more, of its man-hours to defense research. Much valuable work was there to do, especially for the Navy in applying acoustical research to the problem of listening for submarines. As we shall see, some work was done for the Air Force as well.

Project Nike was Ma Bell's patriotic duty for the Army. Among Bell's missile stalwarts was a promising young engineer who had rejoined his old employer after his military service, Jake Schaefer. Immediately, Bell Labs selected Douglas Aircraft as the subcontractor to build the body of the missile. Douglas had been a pioneer in missilery with its experimental ROC guided bombs early in World War II. Douglas also had a bright young man, Maxwell Hunter, recently graduated from MIT. Overseeing the Douglas missile effort at Santa Monica, California, was its advanced-engineering boss, Frank Collbohm, who also had other interesting research and development projects. The level of funding was low, so research progressed slowly, yet by 1950, Nike looked close to being an operating system. A major breakthrough was the abandonment of the original liquid-fueled rocket in favor of a solid-fuel booster first developed for the Navy's Terrier ship-to-air missile.

All the military services had been investing effort in missiles of various types—surface-to-air, air-to-air, and surface-to-surface—and the intense rivalries had spread beyond the Pentagon, engaging the attention of Congress, the press, and the White House. In an attempt to sort this out, President Truman tried to appoint as missile czar K. T. Keller, the president of the Chrysler Corporation (who had hired as Chrysler rocket boss the Colonel Trichel who had named Nike). Keller had been Walter Chrysler's chief production man and knew little and cared less about potential systems. He was told that the nation needed missiles fast, so he picked those which seemed closest to going into production. For offensive missiles, he made some ghastly mistakes that had to be corrected later—most notably, picking intercontinental cruise missiles over ballistic missiles. His priority assignment was "something to knock enemy weapons from the skies," and for the ground-to-air mission he had little choice. The Air Force had let GAPA lapse and had revived it, under the name Bomarc, only because of pressure from the progress of the Nike project. Keller picked Nike, although its development was not completed, for production.

Nike lacked digital computers, but the older analog type seemed satisfactory. The dual requirements of range and sensitivity were too demanding for the original Ordnance target-tracking radar concept. So a longer-range acquisition radar was added to the system; it would first spot the incoming and then hand over the vector and range to the target-track radar. In 1951 the first tests were executed at the Army's White Sands Proving Ground just south of Alamogordo, New Mexico. As is to be expected with experimental equipment, there were some failures, but a successful intercept of a QB-17 drone was achieved, and succeeding tests showed even better performance. In one shot, a Nike without an explosive warhead entered the nose of a radio-controlled bomber and reamed it right through to the tail. Cliff Warren, just assigned to Nike following the shutdown of AT&T's television operation, showed the films to management back in New York, asking: "Do you think that's close enough?" The system* was deemed a success and was pressed into production, the missile by Douglas Aircraft and the guidance systems by AT&T's manufacturing arm, Western Electric.

Nike was a crash program that went into service on budget and on schedule. It was not completely integrated with the Air Force's proposed elaborate centrally controlled air defense system, but the Army could correctly say that the Nikes were in and ready to fire, whereas the Air Force was still fiddling with a paper concept. In the early 1950s, the Army was ahead of the Air Force in missiles, both offensive and defensive. The Air Force was still clinging to manned aircraft—things it could fly. Flying was why there was an Air Force, not to be sitting in a hole in the ground and shooting

---

*A "system" is all that which serves some function. For example, a face-shaving system consists of hot water, soap, razor, blade, arm, eye (acquisition sensor), skin (operating sensor), and brain (computer). "Systems engineering" is the design of systems, especially the integration of components. "Systems analysis" is the attempt to evaluate the performance of alternative systems on paper to reduce expensive and time-consuming construction and testing of hardware. Nike was not the rocket/missile; Nike was the entire SAM system—including also the launchers, radars, computers, and communications.

missiles at some other country or somebody else's aircraft. How to have an Air Force without aircraft was an issue that would take generations to solve, and that issue compounded the problem of defense.

Nike was deployed, beginning in 1953, in the Zone of the Interior. More than 4,000 missiles were emplaced. Some went into the old antiaircraft-gun sites; but with a 25-mile range, the missiles could far outreach the guns and cover a wider area, so the batteries could be placed farther from the cities, to gain more time to shoot at the incoming bombers. America's suburbs became littered with Nike emplacements. The siting of the Nikes was a minor political problem, entailing a few petty local squabbles. Los Angeles managed to keep the missiles off its airport; the battery was installed at the Douglas airport in Santa Monica. The agency of the Army responsible for construction, the Corps of Engineers (*the* Corps), had had much experience building dams and whatnot throughout the country and had learned considerable political skills. Some savings in land acquisition costs were achieved by the simple expedient of emplacing the missiles underground—not so much to protect them from attack as to decrease the risk should something go wrong in the battery itself. One man involved in this business was a bachelor civil servant named Ed Rosenfeld who worked at the interface between the Corps and the missile command at Huntsville, which was the nominal supervisor of Bell Labs and the Engineers. This was when everybody believed that World War III was imminent, that a Soviet attack might come at any time. Who would dare to deny America its right to try to defend itself? The very idea of opposing defense would have been laughed off the continent, or if taken seriously, interpreted as evidence of sabotage and treachery. In the early and mid-1950s, a mild repression was sufficient defense against subversion.

Nike duty was good duty for the troops. The government rented houses for the members of the batteries, and they served their shifts maintaining the equipment and manning the scopes. The handful of officers and sergeants lived in cheerful informality with the men. In those days, America had conscription, which fell mostly on the upper levels of the working class—competent and reliable young men. Occasionally a senior officer would wander in to inspect something or other, but life was peaceful at the Nike sites. In some cases the scenery was gorgeous: from Orangeburg in the Hudson Palisades the skyline of Manhattan was just visible; the sites in the San Gabriel Mountains overlooking Los Angeles offered a fantastic vista. It wasn't really like serving in the military at all—it was more like having a civilian job, or being in the Air Force.

Indeed, continental air defense was so alien to the outlook of the field army that the high command sought to minimize its manpower draw on troop levels. The Deputy Chief of Staff for Operations, Major General Maxwell Taylor, perhaps fondly remembering the British ack-ack girls, suggested manning the batteries with WACs. But his chief, "Lightning Joe" Collins, adopted another scheme: hand many of the Nike batteries over to the National Guard. That sounded eminently sensible. Was not the Guard a militia, intended originally to defend its home communities from Indians and sea-borne raiders? But the Guard had long since converted itself into an imitation field army, and resisted all attempts to assign it lesser military functions. The self-evident policy of making the Guard responsible for civil defense was nixed on those grounds.

And complicated constitutional issues were raised. National Guard units are state forces, placed under direct federal control only in time of national emergency or war. How could CONAD give Guard batteries orders to fire at enemy bombers? The Army's lawyers came up with a devious scheme, writing what amounted to treaties between the federal government and the 31 states with Guard air defense units. Another constitutional roadblock was the provision forbidding the states to have standing forces in peacetime. Obviously, the batteries had to be manned permanently. The solution was truly ingenious: the states hired and the Army trained "civilian technicians" whose jobs were maintaining and operating the missile sites. Those "technicians" were also members of the National Guard, and whether on duty as "state" employees or as Guardsmen in "training," they wore uniforms and were addressed by rank, and only a constitutional lawyer would know they were not soldiers.

The Guardsmen performed their duties commendably, and the system saved the taxpayers a tidy sum of money by relieving them of having to provide quarters and the ancillary services required for active-duty troops. The Guardsmen/technicians lived at home—and defended their homes.

## Not Quite Civil Defense

The last line of defense in the early '50s was the least satisfactory. The U.S. civil defense apparatus created during World War II was for all practical purposes dissolved after the war. The military recognized that civil defense might be needed in the future, but it always had the lowest priority. Still, civil defense was always in every list of requirements for the emerging nuclear age. For example, the famous NSC-68, drafted by Paul Nitze in early 1950 as a broad guideline for waging the Cold War, read:

> The civil defense program should contribute to a reasonable assurance that, in the event of war, the United States would survive the initial blow and go on to the eventual attainment of its objectives. Civil defense programs are designed to serve to minimize casualties in the event of attack, to provide emergency relief immediately after attack, and to help preserve the productive core of the nation. Civil defense programs are tailored to domestic military defense programs and require close and continuing coordination with them.

That turned out to be an incomplete description of the issues. The last thing the soldiers wanted was close coordination with the military efforts. Dealing with civilians was a migraine headache. The military was quite happy to see civil defense placed elsewhere in the government. Initially, the military took an interest in a single palliative to the Bomb: shelters. The thrust was the passive defense of military installations and defense production, not the civilian population. The Army had been much impressed by the effective German and Japanese countermeasures to aerial bombardment, especially the German underground plants, such as the V-2 production line at Nordhausen. However, the Army did not anticipate having swarms of slave laborers to dig out subterranean sitings, so existing underground facilities were investigated. The Corps dispatched teams to explore existing caves and mines suitable for factories and warehouses for war matériel. The criteria in terms of "floor" area, "ceiling" height, ventilation, and drainage were stiff—but millions of cubic yards of usable space were identified.

Practically nothing was done with the information. In the constrained budget environment of the late 1940s, the Army had higher priorities for its few dollars. And the idea was misconceived on both strategic and tactical grounds. Underground factories were valuable only for production in a long war—a total atomic war probably would be fought to a rapid conclusion with the forces in being at the outset of hostilities. Protected factories were as irrelevant as were the Army's elaborate mobilization plans for building up World War II–model mass armies. And on the tactical level, the Achilles' heel of the subterranean facilities was power—the caves and mines might survive attack, but how could the electric lines, the power plants, and the dams? Auxiliary generators only pushed the difficulty back a step—how could the oil or coal be delivered? Fixes were possible for many of those problems, but the issue became too complex to warrant great investment, and the Army's attention shortly was diverted to the defense of Korea.

The hiding option did have one positive and lasting result. To the north of Washington, near Camp Ritchie on the Maryland–Pennsylvania border, the Army dug a little Pentagon—the Alternate Joint Communications Center, burrowed into the granite of Raven Rock Mountain. Over the years, the facility was expanded to the Alternate Military Command Center, with provision and plans for evacuating key government personnel if the nation came under attack. If Washington went, Fort Ritchie was planned to be the capital of the United States—unless it too was taken out.

Another option was favored by many scientists. After the disappointment on international control of weaponry, some politically active atomic scientists began to agitate for a solution to the impending nuclear threat: civil defense through dispersion—prepare the nation for nuclear attack by speading it out. Those who had built the Bomb believed that nuclear weapons were bound to be few and expensive, so damage could be reduced—on paper—by elimination of prime urban targets. The infant city-planning profession was eager to illustrate its new skills by designing cities to minimize bomb damage—cities of long narrow strips, or complex webs, mixing industry and countryside in the manner prescribed by the "garden city" concept of the intrawar period. These ideas were vigorously endorsed by many of the scientists for more than a decade, and their leading publication, the *Bulletin of the Atomic Scientists*, was crammed with civil defense propaganda. An early advocate of dispersion was Edward Teller, and the notion was most visibly promoted in a popular book, *Must We Hide?*, by a big thinker of the time, Ralph Lapp. Initially, nothing came of dispersion either.

During the 1950–51 defense buildup, the World War II defense apparatus was revived. The programs were entirely prenuclear: sirens, wardens; even the term "air-raid drill" was employed. People were taught to take cover. The chronicler recalls being a pupil shepherded to the central hallway of his schoolhouse and taking the fetal position on the floor with his classmates. The structure was of brick, just three miles from the Pentagon, and would have been blown down on top of the huddled schoolchildren by a mere 20-kiloton blast. Still, no child of the 1950s can forget "duck and cover."

Probably some money was usefully spent on fire engines, ambulance services, and other emergency equipment. Four hundred field hospitals left over from the Korean War were distributed around the country to help provide emergency care for the injured. The CONELRAD (CONtrol of ELectronic RADiation) system was imposed on commercial radio: to prevent enemy bombers from homing in on radio stations, yet to keep stations on the air to broadcast emergency information, a scheme was worked out for all stations to transmit the same information on only two frequencies. (This system still existed in the late 1980s, although all references to enemy attack long ago were excised from the canned message.)

An idiot idea for national identification tags to label our corpses was put forward. Some discussions of building shelters of some sort were held fitfully, but nothing was done. Some educational films were distributed around the country which taught some very simple but practical lessons. For the individual faced with an atomic attack, the action was (and is) the same as when anything unpleasant is occurring: get down, get under cover, get out of the way. As one of the federal civil defense chiefs said casually to the Congress in the early '50s, the basics of civil defense were described simply: "dig, die, or get out."

Digging was very expensive, and digging deep enough to escape the effects of a nuclear blast was believed sufficient to bankrupt the country. Getting out was cheaper, but required some means of exiting. In those days barely half of the urban population had its own automobiles. Evacuation was a program for the upper classes, who were prepared to leave the proles behind to die. The intensive advocacy by atomic scientists of dispersion met with failure—the last major effort, Project East River of the Brookhaven Labs, came to naught. A few government agencies were moved out of Washington in the early 1950s; for example, the Quartermaster Corps research division went up to Natick, Massachusetts, just down the road from the Hanscom complex. But the Republicans and more conservative Democrats fought off dispersion for the same reason that liberals were supporting it. Dispersion meant that the government could tell industry where to locate plants: yes, dispersion meant national economic planning—just what the liberals had wanted all along, and had not been able to get, even at the height of the New Deal. The National Planning Association was a leading supporter of civil defense.

Here and there around the country, individuals promoted CD. In Phoenix, a newly elected reform city councilman named Barry Goldwater pushed civil defense, and elicited only indifference. In New Jersey, the Bell Labs engineer Cliff Warren tried to interest his fellow school-board members in building shelters in new schools, to no avail. Dying was seen by all too many people as a necessary consequence of nuclear war. Because official ballyhoo immediately after World War II had made so much of the "absolute" nature of nuclear weapons, the ignorant and semieducated considered any countermeasures to be inherently futile.

Small wonder that civil defense was mostly a peripheral sectarian program of some liberals, promoted by flat pamphlets of the National Planning Association and shrill cartoons of the arch-liberal Herblock. The civil defense leader in the House, Chet Holifield, was a protégé of the California radicals Upton Sinclair and Jerry Voorhis. Mayor Frank Zeidler of Milwaukee, America's most socialist city, was an outspoken advocate. The liberal reform mayor Joseph Clark of Philadelphia said in 1953 that it was "time to stop playing with tin soldiers and sand forts" and to face up to the "vital function which may well mean life or death for our civilization." Senator Hubert Humphrey of Minnesota wrote vigorously in support of the program and advocated a joint congressional committee on civil defense. But all to no avail. Collectively, the pols wouldn't touch the idea. Each year the civil defense agency would ask for substantial sums to begin executing its mandated duties, and the Congress would slash appropriations to a fraction of the request. For example, for 1951 the civil defense agency asked for $730 million, the Budget Bureau approved $403 million, the House appropriated $187 million and the Senate $84 million, and the compromise appropriation was $32 million. In Eisenhower's first year, the request for $285 million was whittled down to $46 million.

Leadership was needed, but was conspicuously absent. The federal civil defense administration was typically headed by defeated state governors, who exemplified what shall be labeled Yarmolinsky's Rule: "Every administration needs jobs for political hacks; civil defense is a job for a hack." Jerry Strope described one of these worthies as "a functional illiterate with a one-week memory bank and twenty-second attention span." The CD rank-and-file was an embarrassment. In every nation there are little men who lust to push other people around. Such men require uniforms and other emblems of rank and prestige. Serious security forces, the police and the military, impose a rigorous regime of discipline and training to keep this type in line; no such restraint controlled the little men who put on civil defense armbands and swaggered about the country boasting of how they would take over and run things when "the day" came. To be sure, such men were a minority, but there were too many of them and they quickly turned off the public and the pols. All this was a consequence of the refusal of the military and the militia to touch CD and the reluctance of the politicians to give them authority over civilians.

## The Northern Glacis

A glance at the map of North America will reveal that the Canadian–American border dips southward at the Great Lakes, and that substantial and important U.S. cities and military bases are but a few miles south of the line. These geographical facts were not ignored by the air defense planners, and they sought increased cooperation from America's northern neighbor. The first informal combined planning for continental defense began in 1940, and was continued fitfully after the war. Few Americans are sensitive to the raw fact that the traditional enemy of Canada is the United States. The Canadian ruling class, of both British and French origin, had looked to Britain for protection against the coarse, aggressive, and land-hungry Yankees. But the decay of the British Empire had led to a policy of appeasement of the Colossus to the South, and the Canadians eagerly grasped the American hand—as a temporary measure, to be sure, until Canada itself became a great power.

In the immediate post–World War II era, the Canadian Dream was grandiose: England had had its place in the sun, the States were having their turn, and the 21st century would be Canada's. Like the British, eventually Canada would have to have a nuclear arsenal, but this was officially put on the back burner for the time being. A first step toward superpower status was in the military high-tech of the time—first-line combat aircraft. The first effort was the CF-100 all-weather fighter, a commonplace first-generation jet that went into service in the early 1950s. Down the line, and the real symbol of Canada's playing in the big leagues, was the CF-105 fighter, the supersonic "Arrow" which was to come into service in the 1960s.

Nor was Canada remiss in meeting the organizational and technological requirements of air defense. The Royal Canadian Air Force established its own Air Defense Command; ground control stations were established, and the radar net was extended. As in the States, the World War II British-model civil defense organization was resurrected. To be sure, Canada had some special air defense problems. Most obvious, Soviet bombers attacking by the polar route would arrive first over Canada. If their plans were thwarted, they might then resort to secondary targets—say, Toronto or Vancouver or Halifax. And it was not inconceivable that Soviet pilots might mistake Winnipeg for Minneapolis, or simply miss and take out Windsor instead of Detroit, or Niagara Falls, Ontario, instead of Niagara Falls, New York. Were that not enough, the U.S. Air Force suggested that the Soviet bombers were fitted with "deadman's fuses"—gadgets to automatically detonate the bombs if the plane dropped below a prescribed altitude. (The reader who wonders how the Air Force imagined such a vicious tactic for the Soviets is advised that the bulk of American bombers were like the Soviets' in being unable to make a round trip to enemy territory—and the reader is also reminded of the concept of "mirror-imaging.")

And Canada presented a different target pattern from the States. A much greater proportion of the population and economy was located in a few metropolitan cities, and those targets were more difficult to defend because they were spread in a narrow strip along the American border. However, the core of Canada is in the valley of the St. Lawrence, in that part of Ontario and Quebec jutting southward below the 49th parallel. So the American radar net along the 49th parallel was extended eastward through Canada. Both countries contributed to the building of the radars and the communications southward via (need it be said) Bell Canada, to link with the emerging American air defense network. This was the Pinetree Line. Although there were no formal discussions of the issue, because the Canadians were extremely sensitive about their sovereignty, informal arrangements were made between the USAF and the RCAF to allow for U.S. fighters to intercept Soviet bombers in Canadian airspace should the need arise. Canadian acquiescence in this policy—as in subsequent continental defense schemes—was at least partly prompted by full awareness that the Americans were not about to ask permission to engage southbound bombers in Canadian airspace. Nuclear war is not a time to be punctilious about international law.

But the Pinetree Line was inadequate, especially for the defense of the Canadian cities just to the north of it, so Canada began to install a new line roughly along the 50th parallel. The concept was called the McGill Fence, after its designers at the Radiation Laboratory of the university of that name, in imitation of the MIT operation. The sparkplug was the physicist John S. Foster. The untended radars were cleverly primitive—they merely reported the passage of something overhead and its speed. This simplicity was possible because of the absence of commercial air traffic in the North. As Project Mongoose, the undertaking was approved early in the 1950s; it was completed by 1957 and named the Mid-Canada Line. Yes, the communications were provided by Bell Canada, much of the equipment manufactured by Northern Electric, and some particularly ticklish technical problems had advice from some engineers who came up from New Jersey.

## The Strategy of Continental Defense

Everybody took for granted the desirability of a continental air defense. Yet only the professionals gave any thought to what it was all about. To the public at large, the principal problem was exemplified by the metaphor "Pearl Harbor," which had happened only a decade before Project Charles. American propaganda in World War II had made much of the "sneak attack." The public had for-

gotten, if it had ever known, anything about the circumstances leading up to the Pearl Harbor debacle, and had paid scant attention to
the official investigations of the great air defense disaster.

So few outside the Business were more than dimly aware that the
Japanese attack had not been unexpected. To be sure, the exact
timing and place of the raid was a great surprise; the Japanese
accomplished a brilliant tactical coup. But there was no strategic
surprise; indeed, the United States had perhaps deliberately provoked a war by imposing a steel and oil embargo on the Japanese
empire. Some Japanese response was expected; the only question
was what. The American forces in the Pacific had been alerted.
Intelligence had picked up sufficient signals to indicate that something was afoot; but there was, as there often is in intelligence, too
much information to process successfully. In hindsight, one could
point to this or that intercepted signal and ask why on earth the
responsible authorities had not seen the significance and taken appropriate action. But, as brilliantly discussed in the classic RAND
study by Roberta Wohlstetter, the debacle at Pearl Harbor was a
failure to select the few shreds of relevant data from a vast quantity
of intelligence "noise."

In the 1950s, the professionals were not really expecting that
Soviet bombers would appear on the radar scopes with no warning
whatever, that our fighters would have to scramble to meet the
enemy, and that the antiaircraft guns and missiles would hurriedly
be primed to fire at any planes that got through. Quite the contrary.
Some of the war plans, or what purport to be the war plans, of the
early 1950s have been released. Whether these are genuine or not
is a question that must be left to future historians. However, we
can read the defense plan in the deployment of the American forces.

The initial concentration of radars and interceptors was in the
state of Washington, home of Boeing, the bomber maker. Of equal
or perhaps even greater significance was the Hanford nuclear-power
complex, the manufacturer of plutonium. Then there was an air
defense district around Knoxville, Tennessee. Just to the northwest
of the city was Oak Ridge, where the uranium-235 was extracted
and bombs were assembled. Another one of the original air defense
districts was around Albuquerque, home of Kirkland Air Force
Base, the principal base of the military Special Weapons project,
the successor to the Manhattan Engineering District, the soldiers

who handle the nuclear weapons for the U.S. military. Here also was the Sandia Corporation, set up under the management of Western Electric to supervise the production of nuclear weapons. And in the mountains north of Santa Fe was Los Alamos, the original weapons lab, where, until the late '40s at least, weapons production was undertaken.

The next coverage was provided for Washington, the national command center, and adjacent Baltimore and Norfolk. Then, as expected, thick cover was laid on over the industrial heartland of the East and Midwest—Boston, New York, Philadelphia, Pittsburgh, Cleveland, Cincinnati, Detroit, Chicago, Milwaukee, St. Louis, and Minneapolis. Separate air defense systems were built up for the major Western technical centers of San Francisco and Los Angeles.

All that seems obvious. But consider what was not defended. Little or no effort was made to protect the bomber bases of the Strategic Air Command. Now, it shouldn't take a lot of thought to realize that bombing another country's cities and disregarding its attack forces is criminally foolish. The cities are of military value only because they support defense production. Defense production can hurt you in a long war, but the bombers can get you in a few hours.

The United States did not prepare to defend its bomber fields in the early 1950s, and the reason very slowly trickled through the Business. The bomber bases needed no defense because they would be empty when the Russian attack came. The bombers would have long since been over Soviet targets. The bomber bases did not need to be defended against Soviet attack because the United States planned to attack first. The North American air defenses were to take a Soviet second strike.

To be sure, the American first strike would include attacks upon the Soviet bomber bases—what staff planners called the BRAVO "blunting" mission and RAND analysts later labeled "counterforce"—so the air defense of the continent would have to receive only a partial and ragged second strike of some indeterminate surviving fraction of the Soviet bomber force. The warning would be sufficient because the dispatch of the American bombers would be the signal to generate the continental defenders to full alert. And the air defense would probably have to take only one attack, because the American war plans, one must conclude, intended that the war would last only about twenty-four hours, in the expectation that the Soviet Union would last only about twenty-four hours. The counterattack would surely come—how could the Soviets not exact a few crumbs of vengeance after their countrymen have received the full loaf of nuclear bombardment?

Now, these deduced American war plans must not be casually attributed to the Commander-in-Chief, or to the Department of Defense, or even to the Air Force, because the planning then was closely held by the Strategic Air Command and its chief, Curtis E. LeMay, who took his duties with deadly seriousness and was loath to share his intentions with persons not properly responsible for and cognizant of the terrible possibilities of the unconstrained bomber offensive. Everything would be thrown at the Soviet Union all at once, expecting the country to be completely knocked out as a fighting force by the time the surviving bombers returned to their bases.

An operational difficulty was that the bulk of the American bomber force of the mid-'50s was medium bombers lacking the range to get to the Soviet Union and back. Forward bases and aerial refueling, a USAF invention, partially overcame this limitation, but even so, SAC could not count on getting the bombers back again. For the medium bombers, the attack plan was a slightly modified kamikaze mission. They could hit their targets, and try to escape from Soviet airspace before ditching in Afghanistan, Iran, Scandinavia, or the Canadian Arctic. So the crews were given training in how to survive in unfavorable terrain. Carefully selected and highly disciplined crews were required for this duty, and it is to LeMay's everlasting credit that he built a force which, as best we can determine, would have executed the orders faithfully. Certainly by the calculus of total war, throwaway bombers were cheap—one bomb, one crew, one plane for one Soviet air base or one major military installation or one major industrial city.

Still, it was necessary that the SAC bombers exit from American airspace safely and that at least the surviving heavy bombers be recovered for "reconstitution" for possible future strikes and to deter potential scavenger countries from trying to profit from the nuclear war. The bombers were the most important military asset of the United States. It would not do to have them shot down by our own air defense. Yet the strike might not be entirely successful—

some Soviets would get off as our planes entered Soviet airspace and were engaged by Soviet air defense. Even in a twenty-four-hour war, the skies over North America likely would be littered with bombers, both ours and theirs, both healthy and crippled. In air defense parlance, the sorting of ours from theirs is Identification Friend or Foe (IFF—"eye-eff-eff"). So the first criterion of the continental air defense system was to avoid shooting down our planes, both on their exit routes and in their hoped-for return from their Soviet targets; this was a crippling limitation.

In retrospect, Curtis LeMay and the other SAC generals seem monstrous, with their grotesque boasts of "blasting a ditch from the Baltic to the Black Sea" in a one-shot "wargasm." But their doctrine and strategy were exquisitely functional—and technologically determined. Most of the bombers—the B-29s, the B-50s, and the B-47s—could make one strike. Already the Soviet air defenses were building up; the more bombers attacking at once, the more easily were the defenses penetrated. It was the bomber generals' duty to expend their entire force if necessary, but they didn't relish the notion, so they screamed for more of the long-range bombers—the B-36s and B-52s—which could have a decent chance of coming back. SAC saw any diversion of funds from the strategic offense as murdering its own people. So SAC fought the Navy, the Army, and strategic defense.

### The Great Shmooz

Not only Cambridge sought to answer The Problem. New York weighed in. Throughout the 1950s, the great establishment foundations, Ford and Carnegie, were supporting a continuing strategic seminar under different labels. What amounted to a keynote address was offered by J. Robert Oppenheimer at the Council on Foreign Relations in February 1953, when he offered his immortal metaphor of "two scorpions in a bottle." Continental defense was one solution. "There is . . . a highly qualified panel . . . looking at the technical problems of continental defense. There are lots of things that haven't been used and that ought to be used. Natural but healthy developments in the obtaining and analyzing of information; developments in aircraft and missiles, and above all the use of space. There is a lot of space between the Soviet Union and the United States."

He was referring to the Kelly Committee on continental defense set up at the Defense Department level to adjudicate between the rival claims of the Army and Air Force. Merwin Kelly was the director of Bell Labs. He was prodefense, but not fanatic about it. The offense was also necessary—if your optimum kill was 70–75 percent of incomings. The establishment worthies accepted the idea of a powerful continental defense, but without enthusiasm. The "internationalists" looked to Europe for a solution. And the Army looked to *the* Council for reinforcements.

Traditional balance-of-power strategy was bolstered by advanced technology. Nuclear munitions promised to be plentiful and cheap, which permitted a complete rethinking of how they might be used. One of the pioneers in the field was Oppenheimer, who led Project Vista, advocating that nuclear battle be returned to the battlefield. The first of the big guns equipped to propel atomic artillery shells into the massed Red armies arrived in Germany in late 1953. With artillery shells and with tactical air-dropped bombs, it became possible to think of having a nuclear war rather like World War II, and with no attacks on the homeland.

With Eisenhower slashing the Army budget, the high brass was eager to make the new options known to the establishment. For eight years, relationships with establishment liberal Democrats were cultivated by such political generals as Maxwell Taylor, James Gavin, and Earle Wheeler. A minor reflection was the appointment of a protégé of the Army's chief political adviser to be the study director of phase I of the Council's big shmooz. Henry Kissinger elegantly wrote up the Army case. Unfortunately, he failed to take into proper account some details: that the Soviets would themselves obtain nuclear munitions; that if the Soviets thought they were losing at the theater level they would be motivated to strike directly at us; that it was disputed, even within the U.S. Army, that nuclear weapons gave an advantage to the defense in land warfare; and that the Europeans might not appreciate the benefits of being atomized to be saved the horrors of communization. His book was bludgeoned in reviews by Paul Nitze and W. W. Kaufmann of RAND. Although Kissinger earned instant public fame as a "nuclear strategist," the judgment was not shared by the real ones. The Great Shmooz went on, and the establishment turned its ear to new voices out of California.

# III

# THE DEFENSE ASCENDANT

*Invincibility is in the defense; victory is in the offense. The experts in defense conceal themselves as under the ninefold earth; those skilled in attack strike as from above the ninefold heavens. Thus they can both protect themselves and gain total victory.*

SUN TSU

**D**wight D. Eisenhower came to power in 1953 representing a Republican constituency that had been draggings its feet on defense spending for twenty years. In those days, the Republicans didn't like any kind of big government. Quickly, the new administration moved to a new defense posture. Imitating a British concept produced by a team led by RAF Air Marshal John Slessor, the Eisenhower administration announced "A New Look" relying on "massive retaliation" by SAC against any aggression. To be sure, no one actually said just that, nor was that actually the policy, but the implication in the declaration and in the reduction of other forces to bolster SAC was troubling enough. Peace would be kept on the cheap by the Deterrence of the Bomber. It was Stanley Baldwin all over again. And the British government that stimulated the policy was headed by an aging Winston S. Churchill.

But the New Look did not deal with The Problem. What good was our threat, if the other side could hit back? By the time Eisenhower came to power, the Soviets had more than 1,000 Tu-4s, possessed at least dozens of A-bombs, and were assumed to be working on jets. However agreeable was the New Look to Republican businessmen in Peoria, the more thoughtful members of the Eastern internationalist establishment were disturbed.

## The One-Man Committee

As the concepts of continental air defense evolved, and as the equipment was designed, the budgets swelled, and the matter required decisions at the highest levels of government. And Congress took a considerable interest—at least the military affairs and atomic energy committees, which in those happy days were expected to have an exclusive overview of defense spending and operations. An early supporter of air defense was Senator Leverett Saltonstall (Republican, Massachusetts), who was troubled by how slowly the matter was being pursued. In late 1953, he established a one-man investigating committee to look into the issues of continental air defense: Robert Sprague.

As Bob Sprague would be the first to admit, he was the son of an even more distinguished man, Frank Sprague, a Naval Academy graduate who in the late 19th century devised numerous breakthrough inventions that made possible the electric railroad and the trolley car. His imagination transformed America and the world: it was the electric trolley that permitted the first spreading out of cities and suburbanization. Frank Sprague also served on the Navy's scientific advisory board in World War I with Edison, Hudson Maxim, and others; one project was Elmer Sperry's "aerial torpedo," the first cruise missile. He made enough money to give his son a patrician's education. Young Bob attended the Hotchkiss School just before the first World War, but then followed his father's footsteps to the Naval Academy. (He is probably the only Hotchkiss boy to have attended Annapolis.) While in the Navy in the 1920s he went to graduate school at MIT, where his thesis project was the design of a submarine. But a naval career seemed less attractive than one in business, so in 1930 he established the Sprague Electric Company in abandoned textile plants in North Adams, Massachusetts, to make a promising advanced electrical device, the condenser.

Sprague Electric had a good product, necessary for the emerging radio industry, and consequently, of course, radars. The company flourished during the war. One minor transaction was of some interest: Sprague Electric received an order for a small number of condensers of extremely exacting specifications from a peculiar government client identified only as the Manhattan Engineering District. Sprague's condensers worked perfectly in the millisecond before they were atomized in New Mexico and Japan.

It is hard to imagine a more appropriate figure than Bob Sprague to play a leading role in the Business in the 1950s. Not only had he impeccable breeding, education, and social and political contacts, but he was also an engineer, conversant with the technologies involved, and an industrialist, a practical man who had met payrolls and turned out a quality high-tech product. Moreover, he was disinterested; his substantial personal holdings in Sprague Electric precluded a paying government job because of problems of nominal conflict of interest deriving from the company's petty defense business. He had to refuse the Undersecretaryship of the Air Force for that reason. So he served as an unpaid consultant, first with Senator Saltonstall's committee and then in the Executive Branch. His greatest qualification was that, like most of his patrician contemporaries, he was a great patriot.

Saltonstall, however, was not entirely disinterested in promoting air defense. The establishment of Massachusetts as the air defense research and development center was of enormous benefit to the then-decayed economy of that venerable state.* Sprague reported back to Saltonstall and helped to push Project Lincoln. Shortly thereafter, a major pro–air defense piece by James Killian and A. G. Hill was published in *The Atlantic* (and condensed in *The Boston Globe* and *The Christian Science Monitor*) and copies were circulated by the House minority leader John McCormack (Democrat, Massachusetts) to all high government officials. Eisenhower was pushed into signing off on the continental air defense project in early 1954. Sprague, as unpaid consultant, became the continental defense expert of the National Security Council.

## The Shadow of Super

During this period, occurring in parallel with and closely connected to the air defense agitation, was the bitter internal fight over the proposed Super program. The Manhattan Project recognized that

---

*Students of the recent industrial history of the United States will have noticed already that this is also an account of the origins of the Massachusetts high-tech complex. Hanscom Field is just off Route 128.

even more plentiful energy might be popped by use of the intense heat and pressure of a fission reaction to fuse hydrogen. The scheme was put on the back burner; surely fission was sufficient. With the evidence of Soviet possession of atomic weapons, the fusion concept—labeled "Super" by insiders—gained increased attention, and was pressed especially by Edward Teller. Resistance was strong. Many of the scientists quite reasonably thought that they had unleashed adequate horrors on the world. But the counterarguments— that if we can do it, they can do it, and that the prospect of parity in fission weapons with the Soviets meant that the United States could maintain superiority only by jacking up the nuclear-munitions competition another notch—were in the end persuasive. The opponents of Super cast about for other militarily useful alternatives to divert attention and activities from the fusion program. This fight had several effects on the saga of strategic defense. One alternative was tactical nuclear weapons, pressed heavily by J. Robert Oppenheimer and others, and embraced by the Army.

Many of the same people also supported continental air defense. The air defense scientists tended to overlap with those who had not worked on the fission bomb, such as George Valley, and those who had dropped out of the nuclear-weapons business or were at least very skeptical about its desirability, such as Jerrold Zacharias, head of the nuclear department at MIT. He was the "Z" of the supposed "ZORC" cabal of scientists plotting to thwart Super at the 1952 Summer Study on Air Defense, so accused by the chief scientist of the Air Force, David Griggs. "O" was Oppenheimer himself, "R" was the esteemed Rabi, and "C" was Charles Lauritsen of Cal Tech.

Because many scientists refused to work on Super, the working staff at Los Alamos was overstrained and perhaps less than entirely enthusiastic. So the promoters of Super drew upon reinforcements from a cache of talent in physics and mathematics that belonged to the Air Force. The RAND Corporation had early on become involved in the abortive nuclear-aircraft project. A nuclear-energy department, later renamed the physics department, was established under David Griggs, a Rad Lab grad whose personal plane had been used as a target in early radar experiments; among its luminaries were Ernest and Milton Plessett, Albert and Richard Latter, Herman Kahn, and Sam Cohen; and the department was drawn into the Super program. The mathematics was devilishly elaborate. A key part of the fusion puzzle was how to estimate the movement of subatomic particles through the medium of hydrogen to calculate what rates of pressure were necessary to make the hydrogen fuse, or "burn." At times, all of the (few) large computers in the nation were linked up to the Los Alamos–RAND calculating shop.

Also, the perceived foot-dragging by Los Alamos led to the perception, in particular by Edward Teller, that another weapons shop was needed; less influenced by academic values; harder, tougher, more aggressive, more imaginative. Teller went to his patrons in the Atomic Energy Commission and in Congress and achieved his dream of creating the second weapons lab, located over the mountains to the east of Berkeley at Livermore. Alumni of the Livermore labs will play a prominent role in the chronicle of strategic defense.

But for the record, it was Los Alamos that produced Super. The original explosion was announced in November of 1952. The announcement was rather coy, mentioning a thermonuclear "device." Elaborate overdesign ensured that it would work, and the resulting 50-ton machine that blew away Eniwetok Atoll was of no military use whatever. Not until January 1954 did the United States explode a usable weapon, a thermonuclear bomb that could be dropped from an aircraft or delivered by other means. In the meantime, the Soviets had achieved the same or better results. Although the evidence is somewhat clouded, the most reasonable interpretation of the analysis of the Soviet tests in August 1953 is that they did then have an air-droppable bomb. Translation: the Soviets had the hydrogen bomb first. It was a near thing, and the United States lost not through technological ignorance, parsimoniousness, or lack of will, but through internal opposition delaying the program.

The advent of Super, and of the Soviet's Super, had a fundamental and far-reaching effect, which in the end changed the entire nature of strategic defense. But in the short run, the H-bomb broke the back of resistance to continental air defense. How could you not be serious about defending against such a threat?

## Dwight Eisenhower's Strategic Defense Initiative

The fear of the Soviet Super provoked a colossal undertaking to defend the continent. The most ambitious measure was adding a forward screen of distant early warning for North America. The concept had long been discussed of going all the way north, into the Arctic. Some bits of the far north system already existed in the air defenses of Alaska. In 1952, the world was startled to learn that the United States had surreptitiously constructed an enormous military installation at Thule, at the northern tip of Greenland. Although the base was announced, its function was omitted from press accounts: Thule was intended to be a forward SAC base to refuel bombers on their way to Soviet targets. Yet it too had to be defended and equipped with radars. And other radars were in Greenland, along the Newfoundland and Labrador coasts, and farther east in Iceland.

Still, an enormous gap remained in the Far North. Soviet bombers could approach unimpeded directly over the Pole. Radar stations in these forbidding environments had been rejected as too expensive by Project Charles and by RAND. But further consideration led to a change of mind, and the money was found. The resulting Distant Early Warning (DEW—"due") Line was one of the great engineering feats of all time. The job was done by the Corps of Engineers, moving a half-million ton of equipment and building in the most forbidding environment this side of the Moon. The line was begun in the early 1950s, and 78 radars were eventually strung across the edge of the Arctic Ocean. This was outrageously expensive; but how does one measure the value of six hours' more warning?

By 1959, the air approaches to North America were strewn with radars. There were the three main radar lines: from north to south, the DEW line, the Mid-Canada Line, and the Pinetree Line. Covering the flanks were the Alaska and Aleutian island defenses to the west and the Greenland and Iceland defenses to the east. The most ingenious idea for pushing the radars forward to gain more warning time and to improve reception by reducing "ground clutter," or reflections from the land, was a baby of Project Lincoln. Along the coasts of Texas, Louisiana, and California, oilmen had erected large structures from which to drill for oil and gas in shallow waters. Men lived on the rigs. The rigs could support considerable equipment—a big radar set and a crew of operators. A test tower was built off Nantucket and seemed to work, so three more were added on the continental shelf off New England. The Navy said "no way" to the Texas Towers, so they were manned, like almost all the continental defense radars, by the Air Force. So "airmen" huddled against the fierce winds and salt spray of the North Atlantic and experienced flight only in the radar signatures on their scopes and in the swirling patterns of the seabirds. Because they were in the Air Force and were not on ships, their requests for sea pay were rejected.

The grandiose MIT air defense command and control system pushed by Saltonstall, Sprague, Killian, McCormack, *et al.*, also went into the budget. When it came time to give a name to the system, a colleague of George E. Valley's made a combination of acronyms with Valley's initials: SAGE ("sage"), for Semi-Automatic Ground Environment. SAGE was not the whole body of continental air defense. It was its brain and nervous system. It comprised the communications links from the sensors/radars to the interceptors/missile batteries, together with the analytical capability of the computer and the operators on the scopes. Note the term "*semi*-automatic": not all operations were automatic; men were deliberately involved in the system to monitor and check it.

The systems engineers at Lincoln Labs went out to identify prospective subcontractors to build the system. For communications, obviously AT&T had no competition. For overall engineering supervision of the construction of the SAGE centers and their buildings, it was equally obviously AT&T's manufacturing arm, Western Electric. For the computers, three candidates were evaluated, and the decision team came down strongly for the International Business Machines Corporation, which turned Whirlwind into a major endeavor. A former glove factory was converted to produce what the Air Force designated the AN/FSQ-7 computer, which greatly influenced later IBM computers. While this contract was not the only factor, it is doubtful that IBM would have become the world's dominant "mainframe" computer manufacturer without SAGE. It was good business. And IBM's chief, Thomas J. Watson, Jr., became an enthusiast for the defense.

Forty-six SAGE centers were planned. Each was to be housed in a four-story concrete structure resembling a blockhouse. Each computer had 55,000 vacuum tubes and 175,000 diodes, and weighed 175 tons. The computers were so large that men could walk around inside them. If not at the right temperature, the computers would go berserk; an enormous amount of electricity was needed for the air conditioning alone. Of course, the data links in from the radars and out to the interceptors' bases were handled by the telephone company, which for a time, and not unreasonably, charged normal commercial rates. Congress got wind of this, and telephone bills were something the solons could grasp, so AT&T had to oblige by cutting the rates to the Air Force. Congress might be accused of being pinchpenny, since Ma Bell had been investing substantial sums of money to harden its own facilities against attack—or rather, passing on the costs, without complaining, to the ratepayers. But in the end, Ma Bell benefited mightily, because the installation of the data-processing links for SAGE became the basis of AT&T Longlines' vast data-communications business.

As SAGE began to be installed, the Air Force and everyone else involved in the project recognized that this was not the end of the engineering line. The system, particularly the computer, was not a fixed piece of machinery like an aircraft or a gun; it had to be continually modified and reprogrammed. As SAGE went into service, it could be operated only for the very simplest programs, and the problems of air defense were enormous and presumably growing. Somebody needed to be competent to continue to develop the system—employing a term just then coming into use—to provide "the software."

This would have been excellent follow-on work for Lincoln Labs. But MIT had a surfeit of military-research riches; it was supposed to be an institution of higher education, yet the military work was coming to dominate the operation. Research to help the national defense and to develop useful ideas and even equipment was one thing; it was quite another matter to be permanently baby-sitting the Air Force. Another institution was necessary. The Gaither committee, which included many MIT-connected people, recommended, "It is imperative that a competent technical group be given the responsibility for planning a balanced defense system in the light of *continually* changing technology and the *continually* changing threat. By the very nature of the problem we face this group must be heavily technical with military support, as opposed to the present concept of being heavily military with technical advice."

The institutional answer was provided by Major General James McCormack, USAF (retired). This accomplished man had been one of the few Army engineers who transferred their allegiance to the Air Force. A West Point graduate and Rhodes scholar in the 1930s, who bore a striking resemblance to the Duke of Windsor, he had risen rapidly in the Air Force's R&D hierarchy in the 1950s. He retired in 1955, at the age of 45, reportedly for bad health, but retained sufficient vigor to have a second career as a top-level operator in the Business. He helped found the Institute for Defense Analyses and was appointed vice president of MIT for military research.

McCormack's solution to the organizational problem of technical advice to air defense was the formation of an imitation RAND, with the same sort of establishment board and operation by engineers. The founding board included McCormack and J. A. Stratton of MIT, Sprague, Rowan Gaither, William T. Golden, an investment banker active in defense and science circles, and William Webster, president of the New England Telephone Company, AT&T's man in Massachusetts. McCormack also christened the new organization—in imitation of RAND again—The MITRE Corporation. The name was normally translated as MIT Research and Engineering, or something of the sort, but McCormack denied it and MITRE officially maintains to this day that its name is not meant to remind anyone of the Massachusetts Institute of Technology. Some wags, recognizing who was to be the real power in the operation, translated the initials as "Must I Trust Robert Everett." Everett was still too young and not sufficiently established to be the top man, so the experienced research manager C. W. Halligan was brought in from Bell Laboratories. He made a very agreeable front man, if only because he could match the generals drink for drink, while Everett and his colleagues from Lincoln Labs Division VI, most of them going back to the Whirlwind days—including John Jacobs, David Israel, and Charles Zracket—ran the show. Perhaps it is needless to say that MITRE moved out to Bedford, near to Hanscom Field and got to work to get SAGE running.

## The Century Series

SAGE was to have some impressive equipment to command and control. In the early '50s a series of projects had led to production fighters numbered over 100 in the Air Force's sequence, thus the "century-series" fighters began to be deployed to the ADC squadrons.

The McDonnell F-101 was originally intended as a long-range fighter escort for bombers, but its configuration lent itself to the interceptor role. It was bought in some quantity by Air Defense Command, and later, as the CF-101, by the Canadians. The first squadron was activated at Massachusetts' Otis Air Force Base in 1959. Also pressed into service by ADC was the Lockheed F-104, not originally meant to be an interceptor either, but intended as an air-superiority fighter for theater warfare. It was rather a hot rod, lacking range and firepower; but it did have a high rate of climb and was available.

The dart-shaped Convair F-102 was designed to be a continental defense interceptor from its inception, and was approved for mass production by Air Force Undersecretary Roswell Gilpatric in 1952. But its execution was found wanting, and so it was purchased only in small quantities, necessitating its supplementation by the F-101 and F-104. The Air Force finally settled on the F-106, an upgraded F-102, which became the standard air defense fighter, programmed to come into the inventory in large numbers around 1960 and expected to stay in service through the mid-'60s until replaced by even hotter stuff. The F-106 was specially designed to be an interceptor, deployed in North America only; it was delta-winged (the design was assisted by the German inventor of the delta wing, Alexander Lippisch), long-range, fast, and capable of carrying the available weapons. Air Force flackery labeled it "the ultimate interceptor." It was a strong aircraft—that turned out to be its greatest virtue. The F-106 buy was originally intended for more than 1,000 planes.

### Bomarc

Although the Air Force had a definite preference for manned aircraft, it did not entirely ignore the role of missiles in air defense. The GAPA project was revived as Bomarc in 1950 with the same contractor, Boeing—thus "Bo." The "marc" was the Michigan Aeronautical Research Center. After World War II, the University of Michigan attempted to build a large research operation to compete with those of MIT, Cornell, and others. Indeed, when the SAGE system was under consideration, Michigan attempted to counter it. But MIT's president James Killian informed the Air Force that Tech thought it demeaning to engage in vulgar competition, and killed Michigan's chances.

One peculiarity of Bomarc was its power plant, a ramjet (another German invention). Unlike the conventional turbojet engine requiring intricate, expensive fans and bearings, the ramjet is merely a slightly constrained pipe; fuel is injected into it, burned, and expelled from the rear end. This simplicity commended it to engineers who consider clean technical solutions to be "elegant." Early experiments showed that the ramjet could operate effectively only at very high speeds, so the machine was fitted with a rocket engine to propel it up to velocities where the ramjet could burn.

Because the interservice allocation of missile design required the Air Force to concentrate on what were presumably pilotless aircraft, Bomarc had to have wings, unlike Army finned missiles. And as an area defense weapon, it had to have long range. So Bomarc eventually evolved as a huge device, as large as an intercontinental cruise missile. Bomarc was intended to have a 200-mile reach, much farther than the Army's Nike, although its speed—1½ times the speed of sound—was less. It had to be controlled by the SAGE center to the vicinity of the target, where it would switch over to its own active homing radar for the kill.

When the history of failed weapon systems is written, Bomarc will certainly rank high on the list of superturkeys. The ramjet had an incorrigible tendency to flame out and fail. It took Boeing and the Air Force ten years and several redesigns to get it working. The original estimated price was $25,000 per unit; the delivered price was $750,000. A complete redesign produced the Bomarc B with double the range, and the brute force of nuclear warheads helped make up for its inaccuracy. Even in those cheerful days of the 1950s, when the Congress and the public automatically assumed that the military knew what it was doing, the smell of Bomarc began to penetrate to the outside world. Nonetheless, there had been problems with weaponry before, and the Air Force had full confidence that eventually it would sort out Bomarc.

So the final and ultimate plan for the North American air defense system was that the incoming enemy would be faced by layers of sensors and layers of interceptors. If he came across the North Pole, he would have to cross three lines of radars; if he came in over the sea he would have to face at least two lines of radars. First, he would be hit by the fighters operating at longer range; if he got through them, he would be hit by Bomarc; if he got through them, Nike would down him. It was a formidable system—on paper.

## Nike-Hercules

The Army/Bell Labs were not idle while the elaborate Air Force plans were being pressed forward. Hardly was the deployment of Nike begun when the follow-up system began to be developed. While there was no complaint about the performance of Nike in the field, further testing found a fundamental flaw in the design that embarasses Bell Labs engineers to this day. While Nike performed with exemplary precision against a single bomber, two or more bombers in formation would confound the computer. It could not decide which bomber to select as a target and would switch back and forth between them, transmitting conflicting orders to the rising missile, which, likely as not, would pass between the bombers and leave them all unscathed.

Fortunately, a fix was immediately at hand. The 1950s progress in reducing the size, weight, and cost of nuclear munitions permitted the Army to put one into an artillery shell a mere eleven inches in diameter and later into a small rocket fired from the back of a jeep, unfortunately labeled "Davy Crockett." Nuclear weapons became cheap enough that they could be deployed for the defense as well as the offense. With a nuclear warhead, the defender need not hit a bomber, or even near a bomber; a single blast would blow the entire formation from the skies, like dry leaves from a tree in a heavy wind. And little Nike could be fitted with a nuclear warhead of the narrow uranium gun-type design employed over Hiroshima.

The idea had distinct drawbacks. The gun-type warhead was definitely inferior to the fatter plutonium implosion devices used in almost all nuclear weapons. Worse, Nike's short range raised the ugly prospect of the defense frying our own cities along with the Soviet bombers. As originally conceived, Nike would not do at all; so Bell Labs generated the Nike-B, later labeled Nike-Hercules, or "Herc" for short.

Nike-Hercules had the same guidance and controls and could be used interchangeably with its predecessor—relabeled Nike-A, and presently Nike-Ajax; only the missiles themselves were changed.

Following the guidelines from Whippany, Max Hunter and his colleagues at Douglas used a trick of the Germans (and not knowing it, the contemporary Soviets) of producing a more powerful rocket that was merely four of the old Ajax boosters welded together. The resulting unit, rather larger, heavier, and more expensive than the original Nike, had a much longer range, more rapid acceleration, and vastly greater punch—40 kilotons.

Beginning in 1958, the Hercs began deployment throughout the country. In a considerable sense they initially replaced the antiaircraft guns, because those were just being phased out for the Nike-Ajax when the Hercules began to come in. (The last guns defended the canal locks at Sault Ste. Marie.) With the Herc's higher costs and longer range (100 miles), it was no longer efficient or necessary to maintain as many batteries, but the problems of obtaining sites were still considerable, so many of the closer-in Nike-Ajax batteries were relinquished (although many were saved for another purpose), and the Hercs tended to be distributed in the most distant suburban locations. The plan was for 8,300 to be deployed.

The official announcements were deliberately vague about the Nike-Hercules warheads. Congress was told that they could be conventional or atomic, which was true. In practice, of course, the nuclear warheads were why the Hercs were made. The warheads had to be on-site ready to be fired at any time. So beginning in the late 1950s, thousands of nuclear explosives were emplaced in the suburbs of America's great cities, many of them under the control of the National Guard. Of course, elaborate security precautions were established. The introduction of nuclear weapons to America's close-in air defenses obliged the Army to invest considerably in another form of defense—vicious sentry dogs. Yet the job was accomplished without serious incident. The Nike-Ajax was phased out in 1963, and all the air defense batteries from then on were fitted with the Hercs.

The Air Force fighter pilots complained that the Army's firing doctrine was "shoot them all down and sort them out on the ground." Of course, it was a great deal more elaborate than that. A Nike battery was under the direct command of a CONAD regional center, usually in a SAGE unit. The batteries were alerted to hostile targets. Backup plans provided for continuing the defense should the headquarters be destroyed or communications cut. The rules of engagement for the Nike defenses were complicated and worked out in careful detail with the Air Force. Very definite corridors were established for returning SAC bombers and American interceptors. In the remainder of the airspace, an elaborate hierarchy of rules was laid down for the battery commanders. Planes heading north were to be ignored; planes heading south were to be hit. Anticipating that the Soviets would come in low to evade radars and interceptors, a rule was fixed that a target popping over the horizon and appearing on the radar at short range would be fired upon. But the accuracy of the Nikes degenerated rapidly under 500 feet, and below 200 feet of altitude they were worthless.

## Hawk

Moreover, the Nikes suffered from the same drawback as the long-distance radars. Because their guidance information came from radars on the ground, the Nikes could operate only at line-of-sight. Enemy bombers could go down low and penetrate the coverage. Many solutions were suggested to resolve the problem. Bell Labs contrived a variant of the Nike which could dive down on the incoming bomber, but this raised the possibility that the nuclear warhead attacking a low-flying target might well cause what was gingerly called "collateral" damage.

Raytheon had the answer. *Ex post facto*, its missile was named Homing-All-the-Way-Killer, but this label was obviously ginned up. Hawk was a fledgling of an earlier bird, built around a semiactive radar system derived from that of Raytheon's Sparrow III. The missile was not fired vertically, as was Nike, but was mounted on a small launcher that would be swung in the direction of the incoming, and the missiles fired off at an angle immediately ready to lock in on the reflected radar signal. Hawk was an excellent weapon (and at the time of writing, still is). Whippany coolly evaluated the competing systems, and as the Army told Raytheon, "Bell Labs declared your proposal was better and more efficient than its own." Hawk was the answer for low-level interception, and Raytheon got the contract. It was planned that Hawk would be deployed both for low-level air defense of the field army and for continental air defense early in the 1960s. The first was achieved more or less on schedule.

## Civil Defense Creeps Forward

The last line of defense was linked to the first. The DEW Line would alert the civil defense apparatus and provide time to evacuate the cities. The Republicans were more willing than the Democrats to leave the lower classes behind. In the mid-1950s, ambitious paper evacuation exercises were conducted, including the participation of the Commander-in-Chief. The usual complaint that evacuation will merely create a horrendous traffic jam is spurious: in eight hours, "bumper-to-bumper" traffic at 5 miles per hour will go 40 miles, well beyond range of direct nuclear-weapons effects. Still, improvements were needed. A stated objective of the National Defense Highway Act of 1957 was to help defend the country against attack. A glance at the design of interstate highways funded by the Feds reveals their defensive pattern. The loops around the cities were built in anticipation that the cores would be gutted by nuclear explosions. Massachusetts Route 128 is an exemplar. Furthermore, the urban expressways running from downtown to the suburbs and to the countryside beyond were intended for evacuation. But no such exit routes were built for Washington—the Congress was aware that the voters would not permit them to protect themselves first. In the long run, of course, the interstate highway system helped to disperse the nation.*

## NORAD

As the defensive system became more and more elaborate, and as the range of the radars and the interceptors extended, it became increasingly impractical to continue to rely upon casual arrangements between the United States Air Force and the Royal Canadian Air Force. A more formal link was required. That was achieved not by treaty, but by an executive agreement between the two governments. The American and Canadian Air Defense Commands con-

---

*Ironically, the only major institution to disperse from Washington in the Eisenhower days was the civil defense agency itself. In 1954 its headquarters was transferred to a disused veterans' hospital in Battle Creek, Michigan. The selection of this metropolis seems to have had something to do with the fact that Republican Senator Homer Ferguson was up for reelection in 1954 and needed some benefit to call to his Michigan constituents' attention. He was beaten, but Battle Creek became known for Kellogg's Corn Flakes and civil defense.

tinued to exist, and above them was placed a supranational command, the North American Air Defense Command (NORAD—"nooradd"). Henceforth, the institution responsible for the air defense of North America would always be NORAD; but it must be kept in mind that the NORAD commander was principally the commander of CONAD and also the commander of ADC, and that the Canadian deputy commander of NORAD and the other Canadian officers were not answerable to the American chief, but to their own military and civilian superiors in Ottawa.

The Canadians shortly showed up at Colorado Springs, and found it very much to their liking. Indeed, many of them stayed there so long, and enjoyed the climate and the company so well, that the first Canadian deputy NORAD commander, Air Marshal Slemon, and hundreds of his compatriots later retired to Colorado to savor the light mountain air at the edge of the American Rockies.

## SAC Strikes Back

As the continental air defense system built up, the fighter jocks began to get cocky. Some trial raids by SAC against the defenses had results credible to ADC. Needless to say, some care had to be taken not to shoot down our bombers, so ADC officers were placed in the control centers to ensure that no mistakes were made; but SAC began to suspect that the exercises were being rigged to favor the defense. So SAC arranged a little exercise of its own. Unbeknownst to the defenders, SAC posted observers in the civil traffic-control centers. ADC was not notified when SAC flushed its bombers, exited through Mexico, deployed its squadrons into the Atlantic and Pacific, refueled in-flight out to sea, and threw its force against North America. SAC blew away the continent—on paper. SAC even got a bomber over Colorado Springs unscathed. There was joy in Omaha that day.

An ideological attack was also mounted, using a spurious historical analogy: SAC smeared continental air defense with the epithet "electronic Maginot Line." To this day, the metaphor of "the Maginot Line" is commonly employed to illustrate the futility of defense. The metaphor is false. In the 1930s, France erected a barrier of sophisticated fortifications along its German border, named for the minister of war, André Maginot. The line was not continued north along the Belgian border, because Belgium was an ally and could not be written off. Belgium could not afford equivalent fortifications, and in any event counted on the threat of French and British intervention to deter German attack.

Faced with the Nazi military buildup, the Belgian government in 1936 lost its nerve, renounced the alliance with France, declared its neutrality, and refused even joint planning with France. Nevertheless, the French assumed that the Maginot Line would block a direct German invasion of France and would channel the Germans through Belgium, thus forcing them to deal with Belgian and British forces, as well as an advancing French field army generously equipped with tanks and supported by a considerable air army.

In 1940, the Germans attacked Belgium as anticipated and were engaged as expected. Although the French had better, though fewer, planes and better and more tanks, the Germans had superior morale and tactics and decisively defeated the Allies in Belgium. Nonetheless, the Maginot Line held until France surrendered, and thereby achieved all that was intended. Now, it may be that France's taking an overall defensive posture was an error, or that posture may have been a necessary consequence of internal conditions in France—but the Maginot Line itself was a strategic and tactical success. The metaphor is spurious.

## How Much Is Enough?

Eisenhower, desperate to fight off the demands of the Air Force and the other services for more money for the offense and the defense, found a useful agent in Donald Quarles. He came from Arkansas, had been an artillery officer in World War I, and had worked his way up through the Bell Labs research-management hierarchy. He obtained his first prominent defense post when the AEC organized the nonprofit Sandia Corporation to supervise production of nuclear munitions. The management contract was awarded to Western Electric, and Quarles was seconded as its chief.

Quarles was also a Republican politician, several times elected mayor of Englewood, New Jersey. Under Eisenhower, he was made Assistant Secretary of Defense for Research and Development, not then a powerful post because the infant Office of the Secretary of Defense (OSD—"oh-ess-dee") was feeble. The muscle was still in the hands of the services. Still, Quarles did well enough to be promoted to Secretary of the Air Force, already established as a slot for a development and procurement executive.

Donald Quarles should be better remembered. He was one of the first prominent Americans to publicly identify two vital concepts. Here is an extract from 1956 hearings before the House defense-appropriations subcommittee; his interlocutor is George Mahon (Democrat, Texas):

### MUTUAL DETERRENCE

MR. MAHON. We are approaching a period of atomic plenty. What do you visualize will develop as this era of atomic plenty comes upon us?

SECRETARY QUARLES. I believe it will mean that each side will possess an offensive capability that is so great and so devastating that neither side will have a knockout capability, and, therefore, a situation in which neither side could profitably initiate a war of this kind. The point is that if either side did initiate it, before that side could knock out the other one, the other could not [sic— "do"?]so much mortal damage to the aggressor that the aggressor would still come out of the war worse than he went into it, which means he would have no advantage in going to war. This has been frequently referred to as a position of mutual deterrence, and I believe we are moving into that kind of a situation.

I must hasten to say that you only have mutual deterrence as long as both sides retain that kind of capability, and the only way we can retain that kind of capability is to be most determined and most progressive to keep our forces up to that requirement.

MAHON. It certainly is far from a desirable picture to be in a period of mutual deterrence, is it not?

QUARLES. It is far from the millennium, but it is a lot better than war, and it is a tremendously lot better than nuclear war.

I console myself, working in this field, that maybe we are working toward something that will be better through this very difficult travail.

MAHON. Hard on the nerves and on the pocketbook.

QUARLES. Yes, it is. It takes a strong stomach and a strong pocketbook both.

Later in the year, addressing the Air Force Association, he titled his speech with a question: "How Much Is Enough?" He meant to remind his audience that there had to be a limit on peacetime defense spending, but he did not offer an answer to his own question. His successors would try—and for lack of a better answer, would resort to mutual deterrence to try to cap defense spending.

But Quarles himself, and others after, would concentrate less on mutual deterrence and how-much-is-enough than on "working toward something that will be better through this difficult travail." And as we shall see, others demonstrated in a negative way the importance of "a strong stomach and a strong pocketbook."

## The Other Side in the 1950s

In 1956 the other side provoked an air defense flap. At a Moscow flyover, the Soviets displayed a fleet of long-range jet bombers. And there were intelligence indications of substantial Soviet bomber production. Certainly the Soviet Union had the capability to produce the engines, the airframes, the electronics, and the nuclear bombs. American air intelligence, dominated by the air-power cult of the offensive, quite reasonably calculated that the Soviets were building an enormous fleet of jet and turboprop bombers to bombard the United States. The Soviets could not possibly be so stupid as to eschew the advantages of the big bombers.

Much later it became evident that the Soviet bomber menace had been misinterpreted. The mistake was strategic "mirror-imaging"; since *we* thought that long-range strategic bombing was the ultimate, certainly the Soviets would hold the same doctrine. But they in fact were old-fashioned military types, unimpressed by high-flying theories. They saw their weaponry as a means to threaten their immediate enemies, and emphasized forces to project power in the areas around the Soviet periphery—precisely where the United States was using its own strategic air power to deter them from expanding. The estimates on Soviet jet-bomber production were remarkably accurate—but it turned out that the Soviet Union was building considerable fleets of medium bombers, what NATO designated "Badgers," to attack Europe, Japan, and Western shipping.

The analysts of air intelligence had ignored the most striking feature of the Soviet military establishment: it was not dominated by bomber pilots, aircraft-carrier admirals, or paratrooper generals;

rather, the high prestige and the promotions had gone to the artillerymen. To the Soviets, rockets were not "strategic weapons," they were long-range artillery. And the Soviets saw no particular need to emphasize mere airplanes when rockets were such a superlative and more technically advanced means of intercontinental bombardment. In the late 1950s, the U.S.S.R. created an independent military entity that is rendered in English as "strategic rocket forces." And American analysts still argue whether or not the Soviet long-range aviation and submarine-launched missiles are under its command. No matter; the Soviets, then and into the mid-'80s, concentrated on being good artillerymen.

Yes, there was a Soviet reaction to the Strategic Air Command: not building equivalent Soviet bomber fleets, but, quite sensibly, erecting an enormous air defense apparatus. Like the later Rocket Forces, this was created as a separate military service almost from scratch, because Soviet air defenses had been primitive or nonexistent before 1948. The *protivo vozdushnaya oborona strany, PVO Strany*—conventionally translated "Troops of Air Defense," but "Air Defense Forces" would be better—were smeared over the Eurasian land mass. The Soviets laid on fleets of fighters, originally almost entirely day fighters, with practically no night or bad-weather capability. And the Soviets papered their empire with antiaircraft guns. Much is disputed about Soviet military doctrine and practice, but all commentators agree that the Soviet military adores artillery as much as Anglo-Saxons lust for aircraft. The PVO Strany kept their guns in service into the 1960s, as if they couldn't bear to give them up. (The Soviet army kept horse cavalry until 1955.) Looking more to the future, the Soviets began to erect comprehensive radar networks. Soon, the Soviets began, at just about the same time as the Americans, to flood the country with surface-to-air missiles.

The system was organized like a field-army air defense system— no central control; everybody shoots at anything that looks hostile with everything he has. What is facinating in retrospect is how similar the Soviet air defense system was to the early-1950s paper concepts at The RAND Corporation and Stanford Research Institute. The Soviet system is what you do when you are *serious* about continental air defense.

## The Next War in 1955

So the next war in 1955 looked like this: the Soviets would commit some aggression; then the Strategic Air Command would blow away the Soviet Union, and Continental Air Defense Command would try to intercept the ragged counterblow. But none of that would happen—because the Soviets wouldn't dare act in the first place. So that is how the next war looked from Omaha.

Not everyone was so sure. If the Soviets knew they would be blown away by SAC, then the initial step in an aggression was to blow away SAC first; to get at SAC, it had to penetrate CONAD.

How the next war looked to Moscow we cannot know. We can guess from its force deployments that it did not so much intend to nail SAC on the ground as to kill it over Soviet territory. And we also know that the Soviet leadership, then under Nikita Khrushchev, was sufficiently impressed by American power to make some minor conciliatory gestures—withdrawing from its naval bases exacted from Finland; evacuating the Soviet zone of occupation of Austria and handing it over to a bourgeois republic, supposedly neutral but neutral on the American side.

We also know from Soviet research investments that came to fruition later in the decade that the High Command had in mind a whole new way of fighting the next war.

## Hitting a Bullet With a Bullet

Recall that long-range rockets were deemed impractical because they were too inaccurate to justify risking expensive nuclear war-heads? Well, the Super solved that problem. With ten megatons, you could miss by more than the proverbial mile; a five-mile miss would still kill your target. To be sure, when the first analyses of the intercontinental ballistic missile—originally abbreviated "IBM," shortly changed to ICBM ("eye-see-bee-em") for obvious reasons—were made circa 1953, no deliverable thermonuclear bombs existed, and nothing resembling an intercontinental rocket was operational. There was some evidence that the Soviets were working on ballistic rockets—they were known to have captured part of the German rocket organization—but more important was the rule of techno-logical mirror-imaging: what-we-can-do-they-can-do. Although the threat then was still from the bombers, and would be for some time to come, the writing was on the wall. As we shall see, it was expectation of the inaccurate large-warhead ICBM that drove Air Force researchers into the passive defense of SAC. Others took up investigation of active defenses against the impending ballistic-missile threat.

Among the booty of World War II were the German scientists and engineers scooped up by the Soviets, the British, and the Americans. The bulk of the Peenemunde rocket team offered itself to the Americans and was surreptitiously flown into the Army's antiaircraft school, headquarters, and concept center, Fort Bliss, just south of the New Mexico White Sands Proving Ground. In 1946 most officers were idle, taking a well-deserved rest after the world war, and having ample time to contemplate some of the implications of the exotic new technologies put forward by their German guests. To an antiaircraft man, the advent of the ballistic missile immediately provokes the notion of anti–ballistic missile defense. The officers worked through some crude concepts on paper, but nothing of any great import. Nevertheless, in order to show off their forward thinking, the ballistic missile defense material was briefed to the Chief of Staff, General of the Army Dwight D. Eisenhower, during a visit to Bliss. Ike was unimpressed. He characterized the antimissile problem as "hitting a bullet with a bullet." In the rear of the room, listening respectfully, was a young officer named C. J. LeVan.

When the V-2 appeared, the Army had modified an existing advanced air defense research contract with General Electric, Project Thumper, to examine missile defense. It was rejected at the time as being technologically inconceivable. The Air Force had a similar Wizard program (not to be confused with the program of the same name of the late '50s) which was also shut down in the late 1940s.

The offense and the defense work together. The Atlas ICBM program began in earnest in early 1954. Immediately, the analysts had to consider countermeasures. What might the other side do to blunt its effectiveness? And what, therefore, should be the counter-countermeasures to counter the countermeasures? This research program was labeled Project Wizard. Convair, the prime ICBM contractor, and RCA were deeply involved. The RAND Corporation was concerned with the issue. The first cut was that defense was impossibly difficult. An ICBM would fall at 24,000 miles an hour—more than four miles a second. Interception would require an astoundingly rapidly closing missile. If its speed was the same as the ICBM's, then the closing rate was eight miles a second. And the warhead of a missile is tiny compared with an aircraft—it has no wings or tail and presents a much smaller radar signature.

Conversely, plotting the course of a ballistic missile is easier than that of an aircraft. An airplane has a wonderfully flexible computer, the human brain, which can make it perform erratic maneuvers, while the ballistic missile is very stupid; it just falls. After any segment of its fall has been plotted, the rest can be drawn with precision. Furthermore, the missile is falling down from space, where there is no ground clutter or flying objects to confuse the radars. Even if our side's ICBMs are in flight, they are not coming our way, and they do not return from their missions. So intercepting a ballistic missile required "only" figuring out how to get something up to a predetermined spot in the sky.

The AICBM* researchers employed a special terminology to parse the problem. To actively defend against an ICBM, you had to "acquire" it, or notice that it was coming; "discriminate" it from other things which might be in space; and "intercept" and "kill" it. The only available means of acquisition then was radar, and contemporary sets lacked the range. And radar could identify only at line-of-sight, and an ICBM would come low over the curvature of the Earth. (The common image of missiles dropping from space is false. On the optimal trajectory, an ICBM comes in at about 20 degrees above horizontal—not a high fly ball, but a long line drive.) Nevertheless, acquiring was seen as relatively easy—long-range radars were expensive, but raised no impossible technical problems. The range was achieved by the generously-funded work of California's

---

*In the 1950s, "BMD" meant the Air Force's Ballistic Missile Division, the vital agency which supervised development of the ICBM, so the term "Anti-ICBM" (AICBM—"ay-eye-see-bee-em") was used for ballistic missile defense; this was shortly shortened to ABM ("ay-bee-em"). In the early '60s, the Air Force unit became the Ballistic Missile Office, so "BMD" was freed up. During the '60s, "ABM" came to be applied to the Bell Labs–Army developmental system, and BMD came to be the generic term. Because the Bell Labs system had several names in its evolution, the term "ABM" will be used to identify them collectively in this book, while "BMD" will refer to all concepts and means of ballistic missile defense. Offensive countermeasures were first "Anti-AICBM" or "double-auntie," but this cumbersome formulation was presently changed to "penetration aids," "pen-aids" for short.

Varian brothers in developing the monster klystron radar tubes. Interception and kill of an ICBM required "merely" putting something lethal up in its path—but very rapidly.

Discrimination was the weak link in AICBM. The attacker wanted to confuse the defense. The most obvious method was to use the ICBM rocket booster, or "tank," that was separated from the warhead but followed it through space; a simple explosive could split the tank into many fragments, complicating the defender's radar picture. Other "penetration aids" (pen-aids) were immediately devised on paper. As in aerial attack, active jamming by broadcasting false signals on the defenders' radar frequencies was a practical ploy, and strips of metal foil, "chaff," could be cast from the warhead to confuse the radar. It was fairly simple to deploy very light balloons made of aluminum or other material that would reflect the radio waves. Or more elaborate decoys could be employed. None of these was without cost—pen-aids cost money, and more important, they took up payload on the missile, forcing virtual attrition on the attacker.

But the simplest pen-aid was the easiest and the cheapest. The earliest warheads were bulky and generated so much friction that they were slowed enormously on reentry to the atmosphere. Some primitive early missiles were slower than an aircraft at impact. And the heat generated by the friction left a long trail, creating a blatant target for the defense. So the first counter-countermeasure was to design the warhead aerodynamically so it would come in faster and smoother. The more aerodynamic warheads were less affected by the perturbations of the atmosphere, and were more accurate, smoother, and harder to spot and track. This was a prototypical example of what was later labeled "stealth" technology. Project Wizard paid for itself right there.

### Nike-Zeus

It did not take a lot of thought to realize that AICBM required an immensely elaborate system to tie together the radars, the computers, and the interceptors. The Air Force asked for proposals from three teams: Convair-RCA, Lockheed-Raytheon, and Western Electric–Douglas. The last, prepared by Bell Labs, won hands down. At almost exactly the same time, the Army, seeing anti–ballistic missile defense as an extension of its established ground-based air defense role, also approached the institution with the best reputation for systems engineering and for hitting a spot in the sky—Bell Labs. Agreeable to the national interest, Bell studied the problem for both the Army and the Air Force. The Labs were not without some direct experience in the field, having the services of Jake Schaefer, who as an Ordnance Corps officer had written one of the first concept papers on dealing with the V-2 threat. He had assumed that the initial antimissile missiles would be slower than their prey, so the size and shape of the area that could be defended by an AICBM battery ("the footprint") was determined by how early the target was acquired, which is to say, by the range of the defender's radar. Lieutenant Schaefer had calculated the first "measures of merit" of the trade-offs between interceptor speed and radar range.

Bell Labs delivered the same report, written by Schaefer and Cliff Warren, to both the Army and the Air Force. Both were delighted and were eager to brief it to the higher reaches of the Pentagon. There was a little squabble about who would brief first, and the Army pulled seniority on the upstart Air Force. Then the Air Force hesitated. It had too many high-tech irons in the fire at once—advanced bombers, advanced tactical fighters, advanced interceptors, and the emerging ICBM program. The Army had only shorter-range rockets and surface-to-air missiles to justify its role in the atomic age. The Army cared more about AICBM, and the Army went ahead. In 1956, Bell Labs got the green light to begin research on an anti–ballistic missile system. At the Army rocket center at Huntsville, an antimissile systems office was established in late 1957, but it was devoted to minor paper shuffling and casual oversight, with Bell Labs in real control of the research and development. Because it was sold as a follow-on to the Army's Nike missiles, the program was first labeled Nike II; soon it became Nike-Zeus. Its original configuration was intended to also deal with high-flying aircraft and cruise missiles (by carrying active radar) as well as ballistic missiles.

The conservative prudence of the Bell engineers exhibited itself in the project. Nike-Zeus was Nike-Ajax and Nike-Hercules, and then some. The design had computer-commanded guidance, an acquisition radar to pick up the incoming, and a tracking radar to plot its course; a battery of missiles would be launched, tracked, and guided by yet another radar to the spot in the sky where the intercept would take place. The initial scheme required forward acquisition radars located in Canada backed up by a local acquisition radar near the firing batteries. Rapid radar development shortly reduced this to a single U.S.-located Zeus Acquisition Radar (ZAR). As we shall see, the history of the ABM project is a steady progression of combining radar functions and reduction of number of sets. For the missiles themselves, Bell Labs turned to its old collaborator, Douglas Aircraft, and its rocket whiz, Max Hunter. An ABM interceptor required a rocket that could climb at least into the upper reaches of the atmosphere at a rapid rate of speed, to kill the incoming as high as possible to minimize possible damage to the ground, and to permit the timing of more intercepts should the initial ones fail. Rocket technology had progressed since the early days of Nike, but the range required a two-stage, and later a three-stage, rocket to meet the requirements.

Of course, the controls were designed by Ma Bell's manufacturing arm, Western Electric, as were the earlier Nikes. Tying the whole system together required a formidable computer, something much faster than the vacuum-tubed models that had gone into SAGE. Here Bell Labs had presolved the problem. In 1948 a team of engineers, including William Shockley, had invented the transistor, which could do the job of the vacuum tube but much more cheaply, in much less space, with much less electricity, and generating a tiny fraction of the heat. And Bell began developing computers and programs to operate the system that could calculate precisely how to hit a bullet with a bullet.

The kill was a difficulty. For obvious reasons, the higher the better. But the higher the kill, the thinner was the atmosphere. Conventional chemical and nuclear explosives kill with blast caused by the compression of the air by the rapid heating of the initial molecular or atomic reaction. In the thin air of the higher atmosphere, the blast was puny; in the vacuum of space, it was nonexistent. The difficulty was mitigated conceptually by the adaptation of nuclear munitions. What more appropriate use for atomic weapons than to nullify other atomic weapons! Still, nuclear blast also required air to harm a target. Knowledge of the effects of nuclear explosives developed at breakneck speed during the testing programs of the 1950s, incited by the competition between Los Alamos and Livermore. The weapons designers directed their attention to smaller, more efficient, and more highly tuned nuclear explosives. The earliest idea was to equip Nike-Zeus with the largest-yield warhead practicable, and to explode it at the very edge of space, counting on its brute power to produce a big mess of blast, heat, and radiation that it was hoped would foul the incoming. The original range of Zeus had to be limited to a hundred miles, because a sorting out of Air Force and Army functions had defined the Army's "point defense role" as limited to that much.

## The War of the Brass

Now, this seems a digression from a chronicle of the defense, but the defense and the offense work together, technologically and politically as well. Nike-Zeus was drawn into the missile wars, as was Nike-Hercules. President Eisenhower was cutting budgets, which put the squeeze on the services and was increasing the temperature in the Pentagon. The Navy, defeated in the "revolt of the admirals" against air power in the late 1940s, was making an end run with its Polaris submarine-launched-missile program. It was the Army and the Air Force that fought it out in the late '50s. The principal bone of contention was the intermediate-range ballistic missile (IRBM— "eye-are-bee-em"), either the Army's Jupiter, produced by the German team at Huntsville, or the Air Force's Thor, designed by the same team of crack Douglas rocketeers that made the Nike missiles. At the second level was a fight between Nike-Hercules and Bomarc. But every other missile was drawn into the fray. The Army's Nike-Zeus represented money that could not be spent by the Air Force. Furthermore, the success of any AICBM system might cast some doubt on the Air Force's growing emphasis on the ICBM. The Army wanted to go into production with Nike-Zeus; the Air Force said it was a waste of money, and anyway, ballistic missile defense should be an Air Force function. But the Air Force was hoisted with its own petard: it had concentrated on interception in space, and had demonstrated on paper that the offense could lay on penetration aids to fool the defense. The Army used the Air Force's research to support its own late-intercept concept.

At this time, to be sure, there was no Nike-Zeus—no missiles, no radars, no computers. It was just paper. But previous weapons systems in the '40s and '50s had been pushed into production before they were thoroughly developed and tested. If you waited to test thoroughly before you began producing, the weapons could become obsolescent, leaving open a window of risk. The standard '50s military procedure, which did not always work but usually did, was to research until there was a credible theory that the system would work, then begin to prepare for production while continuing the development, and then fix any flaws that showed up in the prototype. This was how the Air Force had developed the interceptor-fighters for continental air defense in the 1950s. It may seem inefficient, but probably was less costly than more careful development, which, as we know from the '70s and '80s, can devour enormous sums of money without compensating savings or effectiveness. The Army wanted the go-ahead to produce and deploy Nike-Zeus before development and testing.

The Air Force won most of the interservice battles in the Pentagon and in the White House, so the Army tried to recruit reinforcements in the Congress and in the public-at-large. The near-mutiny by Army officers over the missile program, with equally belligerent counters from the Air Force, led to a war of leaks. The contemporary specialized and general press are filled with nasty little stories spilled out to confound the opposition.

The contractors were expected to back up their clients. Raytheon, for example, was laying on huge Hawk ads at the time. Boeing was putting on a hard press for Bomarc, and its Senator, Henry "Scoop" Jackson, was a powerful support in the Congress. It occurred to the Army's missile command that the Nike contractor was an American institution with considerable clout. So the chief Huntsville flack flew to New York to pay court to America's premier public relations man at AT&T, to propose that Nike-Zeus be featured on the front cover of all telephone books. In his monster office, the great flack deigned to suffer the pitch of the pathetic civil servant. Then, in reply, he picked up from his desk a small black device made by Western Electric; caressing it and cradling the telephone, he said, "You see, every time someone lifts this handset, we make money. Every time someone puts a nickel in this, we make money. *This* is our business."

If Uncle Sam wanted Ma Bell to make missile systems, the great lady was pleased to oblige. But Ma Bell did not hustle for business, and she was not about to raise the political heat in her kitchen. The Army had to make do with endorsements by Donald Douglas. Nike-Zeus was reasonably funded for further development, but did not get the go-ahead for production and deployment. This was seen as a temporary setback. How could we not defend ourselves from the ICBM threat?

## Defending the Deterrent

To the Air Force, the terrible significance of the ICBM was that SAC's airfields would be vulnerable to near-instant attack. This became the special concern—some might say the fetish—of a now-renowned institution, then but barely perceived even by educated Americans, The RAND Corporation. A mythology has grown up around the RAND of those flush times. Reportedly, RAND's role was as a fount of unrestricted intellectual activity. Many of the projects of the '40s and '50s suggest that the place was thoroughly ripping off its blue-suited patron. But so long as valuable product came out—and it did—and no large waves were raised—and for a decade only ripples appeared—the sweetheart deal continued to the satisfaction of both parties.

Still, the RAND executives knew perfectly well who was their patron and that they had better deliver what the Air Force wanted. Writings about RAND have concentrated on those few men who published extensively in the open literature. And the influence of RAND has been grossly exaggerated because its staff did publish and moved on to more visible academic and political positions, while the Air Force officers and civil servants mostly stayed in their own career channels, were subject to strict censorship, and remained anonymous. In fact, RAND was not a haven of strategic thinkers or political analysts but essentially an engineering consulting firm, organized and run by aircraft engineers, and concentrating on engineering problems. Most of its most valuable men are unknown.

Take Ed Barlow, a World War II radar man who had gone into advanced tube work at Sperry Corporation on Long Island while continuing graduate studies at NYU (and had the extraordinary experience of going down to Princeton to lecture on a subject related to the theory of relativity, and during his discourse looked into his audience and saw there in the front row the frizzled hair and wizened face of Albert Einstein). Rather than finish graduate school he came out to RAND, where he was put to work on air defense.

An assistant was another bright young engineer named Jim Digby, also a radar man, drawn out of the Air Force's Watson Laboratory (where he had participated in early work in tracking V-2s). In 1950, Barlow and Digby led the first RAND air defense study, which was pedestrian and conservative, taking for granted the technology of the day (including even the Army's antiaircraft guns) and simply plastering the country with radars, guns, and interceptors. And the cost was unacceptable—about $10 billion, when the Air Force wanted a system priced at about a billion.

That and subsequent RAND examinations of air defense in the early 1950s were uniformly pessimistic. There was no way to achieve, even on paper, high enough attrition rates to ensure protection of cities against air attacks. One calculation was that an expenditure of a third of the Gross National Product would be required for a high confidence of 95 percent kill rate. And certainly most important of all, though RAND should interest itself in any matter of concern to the Air Force, air defense was clearly not the central air-warfare issue. The Air Force was built around the offensive forces—the bomber squadrons were its heart and soul—so RAND prudently and properly addressed the bulk of its considerable technical and analytical skills to the offense. It was from this concern that RAND made its great contributions to the defense.

It has often been the case that investigation of an apparently mundane problem has given rise to a major advance. The particular case at issue was how to base SAC's bombers. To simplify somewhat, SAC could locate its planes forward on fields close to the Soviet Union, or back in the continental United States,* refueling them on the way out and back. The question was which option offered better operational results and which was cheaper. The Air Force, and RAND, were always very conscious of the budget. This question was addressed by a RAND analyst who came into the Business though the back door. Albert Wohlstetter was the epitome of the late bloomer. His family had suffered financial reverses, but not so severe as to deny him the resources to be an academic/intellectual

---

*Then the Zone of the Interior (ZI—"zee-eye"); after the admission of Alaska and Hawaii to the Union, CONUS ("cone-us").

idler in his youth in the 1930s, dallying in the gentlemanly but commercially feckless pursuits of modern dance and mathematical logic.

During World War II, however, with the threat of the draft, one could not sustain intellectual vagrancy, so he found himself engaged in production control for a small aircraft electric-parts firm controlled by his investor brother on the East Side of Manhattan in a tacky district later occupied by the edifice of the United Nations. After the war, he wandered off to government service and to an abortive venture in mass-produced housing. Then he moved to Los Angeles, where his wife, Roberta, a political scientist, had taken a position with the RAND social science department and suggested to her husband that perhaps something there might amuse him. Wohlstetter seemed an interesting fellow and was hired in the economics department for lack of any other place to put him. For some time his output was not noticeable, and his position was reportedly somewhat shaky. (Unlike civil service and the university, RAND offered no job security or tenure—this was one of its virtues.)

Wohlstetter's solution to the basing problem was worked out in the excruciatingly comprehensive and meticulous detail that became his trademark—to site bombers in the continental United States, and refuel them on the forward bases. A principal reason was that the financial costs, while important, were fairly trivial when compared with the strategic cost of basing the bombers forward, which was their vulnerability to a Soviet surprise attack. In the course of the study, Wohlstetter and his colleagues noticed that the bombers were naked to a Soviet first strike. While SAC intended to strike first against the U.S.S.R. in the event of war, Soviet knowledge of that intention meant that SAC had to expect Soviet preemption and be prepared to strike second. (Indeed, the famous "first strike/second strike" distinction was devised in this analysis.) Insofar as the ability of the United States to execute a devastating nuclear strike constituted the threat to the other side—"the deterrent"—the deterrent itself needed to be defended. In his early forties, Albert Wohlstetter had discovered the cause to which he would devote the rest of his life.

This was to be a predominant requirement for The Problem—necessary, but not necessarily sufficient to its resolution. Maintaining a credible second-strike capability soon became what everybody (except pacifists and enemy propagandists) favored, the minimum requirement for strategic forces. When RAND began serious work on this issue, the deterrent consisted only of the bombers. (RAND was not concerned with the paltry forces on the Navy's carriers; their survival was of no concern to the Air Force.) RAND looked again at air defenses to defend the deterrent, and again found them wanting. A very optimistic appraisal was that at most the planned system might get, say, 30 percent of the incoming. Even with calculations on the basis of 50 percent attrition, SAC's bases would be easily wiped out.

Several solutions were examined, and some adopted. The most obvious was augmentation: to increase the number of SAC bases, to raise the number of targets and to reduce the enemy's certainty of getting almost all of them. From a dozen bases in 1951, SAC expanded in a decade to more than 50. Another solution was surface-to-air missiles: grudgingly, the Air Force accepted close-in airfield defense by the Navy's Talos and the Army's Nike-Hercules; but these did not survive Eisenhower's budget knife. Another solution was the one favored by Wohlstetter—"hardening" the bases; fortifying them against attack, passively defending them. Wohlstetter and colleagues worked on designing underground shelters for the bombers.

For protective construction, the economists and aeronautical engineers needed help from civil engineers, so RAND engaged J. J. O'Sullivan and obtained the consulting services of Paul Weidlinger. The latter was an émigré from Hungary who had wandered through Czechoslovakia, Switzerland, and Bolivia before arriving in the United States during the war and becoming the chief engineer for the Acme Aircraft Company, where Wohlstetter had worked. The two men had also been postwar colleagues at the National Housing Authority after the war and in the abortive industrialized housing venture. When Weidlinger first appeared at RAND, Charles Hitch, the head of the economics department, took note that he was Hungarian—as were, among others in the Business in those days, Theodore von Karman, John von Neumann, Edward Teller, and Eugene Wigner. "It may be," Hitch asserted "that being Hungarian is necessary to being a genius, but it is not sufficient; you must actually do something brilliant." Weidlinger did. He discovered that structures could be hardened to levels far above those then assumed. A normal house can be blown down by five pounds per square inch of blast, or "overpressure," and 10 psi ("pee-ess-eye") will take out just about any normal structure. The Air Force, and the military in general, had estimated that a heavily fortified building might perhaps be able to take twice as much overpressure. Weidlinger escalated hardness. He calculated that certain types of concrete construction toughen under pressure. He started talking about 40 psi, and before he left RAND he was working up around 200 psi.

These numbers are vital because they interplay with accuracy. The blast of a nuclear bomb, like any other explosive, decreases very rapidly with distance from the point of impact. Something hardened to 50 psi will withstand a much closer hit than something of less strength. The relationship between the explosive power, or "yield," of a nuclear weapon, the accuracy of its delivery, expressed in circular error probable (CEP—"see-ee-pea"), and the psi of the target can be crudely approximated in a simple formula that is understandable to anyone who has had high school algebra, including even a pilot. Wohlstetter, Weidlinger, *et al.* had hit upon a wonderfully persuasive form of analysis.

The RAND people exhaustively examined how to put the bombers underground, in shelters tailored to the exact shape of the plane, with provision for the high tail to fold. This was very expensive, requiring that money be diverted from bombers and bombs. The Air Force wouldn't buy the idea. Reportedly, Curtis LeMay got up in the middle of a briefing of this scheme, spat, "You can't drop concrete," and stomped from the room. Unable to sell the client directly, Wohlstetter eventually took his story public in his famous essay "The Delicate Balance of Terror." In retrospect the title was unfortunate, because he was only arguing that the balance was not as robust and automatic as many people believed. So long as the strategic forces were vulnerable, the other side might be tempted to attack them, if only in crisis, so the situation was inherently "unstable." Better to stabilize it by hardening, by the passive defense of the "deterrent."

Another solution to SAC vulnerability was the one that was ultimately adopted, passive defense through mobility: a number of bombers kept on short-term ready alert at the edge of the runways, with fuel tanks filled, batteries charged, bomb bays armed, and the crews alerted to be airborne in a few minutes. A more intensive defense-by-mobility was permanent airborne alert: a few of the bombers in the air at all times. This was a very effective solution, although very expensive in terms of cost of operation, in wear and tear and reduction of the life of the aircraft, and in the potential of planes' having accidents with nuclear weapons on board. (Not that they could explode accidentally, but the debris was radioactive and poisonous, and components might conceivably fall into enemy hands.)

Wohlstetter also needed technical assistance on the other side of the defense calculations, on what nuclear weapons could do to SAC. In those days information on nuclear weapons' effects was very closely held. The RAND Corporation's physics department had labored mightily on the abortive nuclear-powered aircraft, and had done very useful work on the Super project. Because the nuclear work was sponsored by the AEC rather than the Air Force, the physics department was sealed off from the rest of the corporation, and the conflicting security regulations meant that the two factions could hardly speak to each other about professional matters. Fortunately, one member of the physics department was willing and eager to stretch the security mandates to their limit and perhaps a little bit beyond.

### Nonmilitary Defense

Herman Kahn was as different a character from Albert Wohlstetter as one could imagine. Whereas Wohlstetter affected *fin de siècle* urbanity, Herman* was a cheerful slob. Whereas Wohlstetter was lean and austere, Herman was fat and hilarious. Herman's family had been among the last refugees out of Eastern Europe, having fled the ravages of the Bolshevik Revolution. He was eight years younger than Wohlstetter, but his history was almost as vagrant. He had been a prodigy in high school and won a scholarship in chemistry to the University of Southern California, but did not feel at home at that tony school and transferred to the more proletarian UCLA before he was drafted in 1943. At induction, he achieved the highest score anyone had ever made on the Army's intelligence test. His friend and UCLA classmate Sam Cohen had tried to get

---

*A character weighing 300 pounds with the demeanor of a borscht-circuit comic and the joyous enthusiasm of a 4-year-old child could not be "Kahn" to anyone who knew him.

him into Los Alamos, but Herman had become tired of attending special schools for bright recruits and requested shipment overseas; the Signal Corps sent him off to Burma, where he worked behind the lines tending telephone communications equipment.

After the war he finished up at UCLA, attended Cal Tech for a while, and bounced around at several flunky jobs in the L.A. aircraft industry before his friend Sam Cohen suggested he come over to the beach at Santa Monica and join RAND's nuclear physics department. At first he was a human computer, hired to do calculations for brighter minds. He quickly showed his colleagues that he was one of the brighter minds and went on into reactor work for the nuclear-aircraft project and to the Super project.

Just as he was becoming bored with that matter, there was the distraction of a security case involving his new bride, Jane, who had come out to RAND from Sperry with Ed Barlow and had been courted by both Herman and Jim Digby. There was no taint on Jane, but her screwball sister had been an actual card-carrying Communist, and in 1954 these things rubbed off an awfully long way. Herman beat the security rap, but in the meantime he wandered down the hall and came upon the Wohlstetter operation, and was fascinated. While Restricted nuclear-weapons-effects information could not be revealed to Air Force hirelings with mere Top Secret clearances, Herman held that physics was physics, and that usable estimates of blast and radiation could be made from open-source data and could be explained to men with a modest amount of technical training. This was very useful to Wohlstetter. But it was not long before Albert learned that by introducing Herman to nuclear strategy he had played Frankenstein.

Herman needed to make his own mark. Air defense had already been deemed to be a bust; Wohlstetter had SAC defense sewed up; others at RAND were working effectively on ICBMs and countermeasures. What had not been analyzed in the serious, thorough, comprehensive, imaginative, quantitative RAND manner? Herman looked briefly at tactical aviation and found it wanting, and perhaps inevitably he found his way to civil defense—to passive defense of the civil population.

Although some desultory individual papers had been done on civil defense in the early '50s (including ones by the economist Jack

Hirshleifer and by a summer visitor named Carl Kaysen), and although RAND itself had a civil defense plan instituted in 1954, the management had considerable qualms about a group study of what was called "nonmilitary defense." But Herman was an emerging star, and in the loose structure of the RAND of the day he could not be denied his own small project. He gathered a team and became "an instant expert" in civil defense.

The fundamentals of civil defense research had already been laid down at Stanford Research Institute and other contractors to the federal civil defense agency. An already established convention was to design an enemy attack upon your own country, count the damage, then consider how to reduce it. The original work had concentrated upon economic damage, a carryover of the World War II belief that the vital effect of bombing was the crippling of a country's war-making potential. This concept was made irrelevant by the thermonuclear age. As pointed out by Brodie and the earlier commentators on atomic warfare, the ability to conduct a long war with mass production of weaponry was irrelevant in the atomic age. A war would have to be fought with the preparations and the forces in being at its outbreak.

Earlier RAND work had also used a World War II concept: how many people were "dehoused" by bombing. The firebombing of Germany and Japan had burned out large urban areas, but usually without causing high casualties. Atomic warfare was quite another matter, and the measure of success or failure in civil defense that came to be generally accepted was the number of fatalities, counted in the tens of millions. The conventional means of counting was the "cookie-cutter" technique. A bomb of such-and-such yield would create such-and-such overpressure within such-and-such a circle around its "ground zero," blowing down all buildings in that circle, killing all people there. In wider rings would be less damage and lower casualty rates. The cookie-cutters would be laid down over the maps of major U.S. cities. Estimates were made of where the attacker would mark his ground zero in order to maximize casualties. The calculations would assume that the U.S. Census was accurate (although everyone knew that it was not quite so) and that everybody was home when counted by the Census on April 1 (knowing full well that many would be elsewhere). In some sense, the crudeness of the estimates mattered little, because the variations were "only" a few tens of millions. It was easy to design Soviet attacks that would slaughter more than a hundred million Americans. So the immediate analytical problem was how to bring those numbers down.

Initially, Herman and his team paid little attention to possibilities for evacuation in war. They had good information on how short the warning times would be. A few hours was not sufficient to pull the population out of the cities. Remember that the Distant Early Warning Line had been constructed to provide for six hours' warning of air attack. The RAND people were planning defense against missile attack—less than a half-hour. People had to be protected where they were. From the testing in the Pacific and in Nevada in the early 1950s, a considerable body of information had been gathered about the effects of blast upon differing types of construction. For example, 10 psi overpressure would destroy all normal buildings; the optimum way to impose that blast with a megaton bomb on the largest area of a city was an air burst at an altitude of about 7,000 feet. But the maximum overpressure immediately under the blast would then be 40 psi. Therefore, if the enemy was sensible about his targeting, you could save the entire urban population with shelters against 40 psi.

In 1956, RAND had conducted a seminar on protective construction. One topic was the work sponsored by the Army Corps of Engineers in the late 1940s. Among the Engineers' contract researchers had been the civil engineering firm of Guy Panero. His son Robert addressed RAND on the subject and greatly impressed Herman with his quick wit and fantastic imagination. Panero thought very, very big and began to scratch together rough plans for blast shelters under New York City. Manhattan is built over granite bedrock, and Panero was able to design a shelter system that could temporarily hold the entire population, and be filled in 20 minutes. Alas, the geology of Staten Island and Brooklyn was less favorable, although the limestone under Chicago was also promising. A variant was to use existing large underground structures—a huge salt mine under Detroit reaches all the way to Dearborn. While helpful, there were not enough of these natural shelters to hold more than a tiny fraction of the population.

In the course of the nonmilitary defense study, Herman and his colleagues traveled around the country scrounging up all the work that had been done on civil defense. They visited the federal civil defense headquarters at Battle Creek, and found a staff not terribly impressive, with the exception of a clever engineer named John Devaney, a former Navy Seabee who had worked on the DEW Line construction in the employ of the Corps of Engineers. He had already been working on blast-shelter calculations. The RANDites also called on the Naval Radiological Defense Laboratory at Hunter's Point, near San Francisco. Jerry Strope and his associates had long since shifted from alleviating nuclear effects on ships to methods of defending the Navy's shore establishment. Their research led them to shelter design. The NRDL folk were practical people who were not satisfied with paper calculations. They actually built shelters, and they addressed the question of how people would live in shelters until the radiation had worn down. They solicited volunteers from the county prison farm, who were put in the shelters for lengthening periods of time and in decreasing space. The crowding sounds unspeakable to the average middle-class American accustomed to spreading over several hundred square feet of floor space, but remember, the designers were Navy people, whose idea of how people lived and worked for months on end was a ship with bunks stacked one above the other. To naval architects, anything more than a few cubic feet was an unwarranted luxury.

But perhaps prisoners were not a properly representative sample of the population, so the NRDL people jammed ordinary citizens into their prototype shelters. Putting their bodies where their research was, they recruited workers, clerks, and scientists from the lab, with their wives and their children, and had them occupy shelters for longer periods of time, diverting themselves with charades and such. They learned some interesting things that would not have occurred to a theoretician, such as that bunking teenage boys and girls too close together was ill-advised, because they thought it a lark and would giggle and flirt and keep everybody awake all night.

These experiments showed that it was practical to greatly shrink the space needed to shelter large populations, and therefore to reduce the cost. But the costs were still astronomical, even perhaps prohibitively so in peacetime, and in war insufficient time would be available to build the elaborate shelters that NRDL envisioned.

## Fallout Shelters

Sheltering against blast was not the only possible countermeasure to nuclear attack. In the mid-1950s, attention slowly but inexorably turned to the menace of radioactive fallout. If exploded at ground level, a hydrogen bomb would generate huge amounts of poisonous debris which would spread downwind. If you knew which way and how briskly the wind was blowing, the fallout pattern could be roughly calculated. (RAND used an egg-shaped cookie-cutter.) But you could not know that in advance, so potentially the whole country, not just large cities, might be damaged by nuclear war.

Whereas blast shelters were primarily for urban population, fallout shelters defended everybody. Although most of them could withstand low levels of blast, fallout shelters essentially protected from the deadly falling dust. In the mid-'50s, the concept of "protection factor," immediately abbreviated to pf ("pea-eff"), was devised. A pf of 10 would reduce the amount of radiation inside a shelter to a tenth of the outside radiation. Outside radiation of 600 rads is probably lethal, while 60 at worst causes the sniffles. Stanford Research Institute researchers made a major breakthrough by noting that even very modest levels of shelter could reduce fatalities to illness and reduce illness to good health—not for everybody, of course: tens of millions would be lost; but many tens of millions more would be saved.

The great virtue of the fallout shelters, however, was simply that they were cheap. Unlike blast shelters, they did not require expensive materials or elaborate design, just simple timbers and dirt. And fallout shelters could be rigged in almost any basement. Still, this approach meant writing off the cities. What did that mean? That led the researchers inevitably into the question of what is labeled "postattack recovery." Could America survive without the cities? Herman and his colleagues divided the nation analytically into the "A country" and the "B country"—A being the big cities, B being the rest. Examination of the census figures for industrial production and other economic activities revealed that the nation could go on without the A country. The B country was a substantial country in itself; if it survived, it could rebuild the A country. This point had been made in another way by another civil defense enthusiast, Edward Teller, who remarked that the principal asset of a country is its people; if the plants and equipment are destroyed and the people survive, the people will rebuild. Abandoning the people and saving the plants and equipment would merely leave a prize for the victor. Save the people.

The RAND team also looked at least superficially at some other aspects of the recovery phase. There had been economic studies of this question, even by economists at RAND earlier in the '50s, but their quality was minimal. Indeed, many of the economic studies of postattack recovery were undertaken by economists who wanted funding to develop their elaborate input–output models of the economy. Such models were never (and still are not) of any value, because the operations of the economy are too complex and intricate to be captured by any simplified analytical models. And no model of peacetime economy can represent how people will respond after a major attack has knocked huge chunks out of the productive capability. Instead, Herman counted on the workings of market forces to reconstruct the economy.

One obviously severe problem, which bedevils civil defense planners to this day, is food. Where will it be, and how can it be gotten to the survivors? An SRI analysis of this problem was rather dismal, because it failed to consider that food could be moved before or after the attack. Certainly enough food was (and is) in normal storage in America to feed survivors under the most optimistic survival conditions. Some of the food would be contaminated by radioactivity, a problem that Herman cheerfully solved by suggesting that the different levels of contamination be labeled for different consumption groups—the cleanest stuff for nursing mothers, and so on down to the worst to be fed to cattle.

Another problem in the postattack regime is money. How will people pay for things? Where will they get the money? How will we take care of the damage costs? Insurance policies uniformly renege on paying for war damage. Here an easy answer was at hand: a government war-damage-equalization corporation, of the type that had existed in World War II. The government would pay off obvious claims immediately, thus reestablishing credit and putting money back into circulation.

In trying to find the best answers to these frightening problems, the RAND people wandered all over the intellectual map. A particularly useful researcher was Fred C. Ikle, a Swiss who had come to the States immediately after the Second World War and had interested himself in the moral effects of bombing. A Swiss took civil defense for granted. The Swiss defense policy was to dig in the country, both the military and civil assets, and to dissuade attack by threatening the aggressor with the prospect of expending his forces against Swiss stone, steel, concrete, and national will. The Swiss army and air force are dug deep into Alps, and for generations all new Swiss construction, including housing, has been required to include shelters.

Ikle's Ph.D. dissertation at the University of Chicago was later published as *The Social Effects of Bomb Damage,* one of the classics of a 1950s genre called "disaster studies." A large team of sociologists at the Social Science Research Council examined these dismal matters. Everyone granted that a heavy nuclear attack was quite different from other catastrophes; nonetheless, all investigations of major wartime and peacetime disasters showed that people rarely panicked or abandoned hope, and society did not collapse into anarchy. Rather, people clung to life and hope, cooperated, dug themselves out of the ruins, and did the best they could. It is hard to think of a post–nuclear-war experience more terrible than the conditions of the proscribed races of Europe under National Socialism, yet what is striking is how the great majority of the Jews, Gypsies, and Slavic prisoners of war clung to life. A few committed suicide, and doubtless many more gave up and accepted death in preference to the misery of the ghettos and the death camps, but the great bulk struggled as long and as well as they could. Similarly, the German refugees from Eastern Europe fleeing the vengeance of the Red Army, many of them aristocrats, merchants, and intelligentsia, adapted themselves to loss of status, position, and all worldly possessions and a life of hard manual labor—because they had no choice. (Opponents of civil defense would always claim that society would go to pieces—doubtless another example of "mirror-imaging"; imagine the reaction of a university to a major disaster.)

The RAND team examined post-postattack recovery, considering the long-term health and genetic effects of radiation. Here a key man was a restless physician named Hal Mitchell, who had joined the physics department in the early 1950s to concentrate on medical effects of nuclear weaponry. RAND had a great deal of relevant material gathered by the Atomic Energy Commission, reflecting experience with the industrial use of radioactive materials plus the Japanese nuclear bombings plus the very limited experience of the Marshall Islanders and the Japanese fishermen who had been dusted with fallout from a Bikini H-bomb test. Insofar as the data were relevant—and there were legitimate questions about their validity—the health and genetic effects were nasty, but did not seem to be intolerable. There would probably be a few more leukemia cases, a few more misshapen newborns, but nothing that was beyond recent human experience. The environment after a large attack would seem to be perhaps as unhealthful as the living conditions of an industrial worker around the time of the First World War—not a life preferred by a middle-class American, but not an impossible situation. Or so thought Herman and most of his colleagues, not anticipating the hysteria that would be aroused by such a matter-of-fact estimate. The real evidence, such as it was, directly contradicted unsupported claims by leading scientists that nuclear war would surely destroy civilization or humanity.

An alternative view was expressed by Hal Mitchell's father, who remarked that his response to a nuclear attack would be to stand on the roof of his apartment house watching the fireworks and going out in a flash, rather then scratch out a miserable existence after the war. Of course, he was an old man, and the prospect of rooting about in the woods was not attractive to him. Some younger people felt the same way and argued that life would not be worth living after "a nuclear war." One might expect that some cosseted Americans would not want to live in the postwar world. But what was ugly—and is ugly—is the agitation to prevent others from making the other choice, to live and to recover. During the civil defense furor of the early '60s, a neighbor accosted Jane Kahn at a reception at the Chappaqua Jewish Community Center: "Do you *really* want your children to survive a thermonuclear war?"

"They are *very nice* children," said Jane.

The RAND team did not overlook the other side. A White Russian émigré analyst, Leon Goure, investigated the Soviet civil defense capability. He found it to be an impressive effort, far exceeding that of the United States, with substantial resources—and, of course, with advantages inherent in a totalitarian command system. Critics within RAND and elsewhere were more skeptical. American intelligence had not devoted much of its limited capabilities to this peripheral Soviet military activity, so Goure had to rely almost exclusively upon official publications. He described what the Soviets *declared* their civil defense should be; not everyone was persuaded that that was what it actually was. And as Herman noted, even if you took the Goure analysis at face value, the Soviet system was antediluvian. It was a well-designed World War II–type civil defense apparatus, concentrating on air-raid wardens and firefighting, with little to indicate any adaptation to the realities of the atomic age. It was, however, under direct military control.

After he completed the civil defense study, at least insofar as Herman Kahn could finish anything, and prepared to circulate its results, a serious roadblock was encountered in the person of Frank Collbohm, RAND's president, who was extremely dubious about the whole matter. He had been a high manager at Douglas Aircraft during the war, and among his responsibilities was the civil defense of the plant at Santa Monica. The task had been a gigantic bother to Collbohm. The needs of the war effort had brought many women into the plant, hours were long, there was a housing shortage, automobile backseats were unavailable because of gasoline rationing, so the shelters became trysting places for the young Douglas workers.

Collbohm also saw that publishing the RAND results might help ignite a civil defense boom. The money that went into sheltering the population might well come out of the Air Force budget. The Air Force would not like that, and would not look kindly upon RAND for having promoted it. Collbohm put his foot down, and made Herman and the team cut back sharply on their recommendations, reducing their report to little more than proposals for further research. This slowed Herman down some, but not enough. The intensity of feeling on this issue grew so heated that Charlie Hitch, the head of the economics department, had to be brought in as the mediator, and a team negotiated the final RAND report for six months. One required change was that no reference to Air Force sponsorship appear on the report.

## The Strategy of Civil Defense

"The Report on Non-Military Defense," as Collbohm desired, primarily recommended a research program; but nonetheless, it elegantly developed the strategic case for civil defense—indeed, for any type of partial defense. To be sure, much is to be said for the purely humanitarian side of civil defense in saving lives should there be—God forbid—a nuclear attack. This "insurance" function in itself ought to justify civil defense. But the strategic case was a great deal more interesting to the RAND crew. This was a mitigation of The Problem; if the other side can hit you back, but cannot hurt you as much as he might otherwise, your threats are more credible. If the Soviets could retaliate and kill 120 million Americans, that effectively means the end of the country; so our threat to strike first is of trivial credibility to him, to our allies, and to us. However, if he hits back and kills "only" 20 million Americans, then (in those days) 160 million survive, so we still have a viable working country, and therefore the threat to strike first becomes necessarily more credible, and presumably more deterring.

Not in the report was Herman's favorite tactic—strategic evacuation. During a crisis, the government would order the evacuation of cities in order to demonstrate American resolve. The evacuees would join the denizens of the "B country" in fallout shelters. Fallout shelters were the main feature of the RAND report. That emphasis made brilliant operational sense. It was not so expensive as to frighten taxpayers and politicians, or to draw large sums from the military budgets. And unstated in the published RAND report, but noticed by some critics, was that fallout sheltering was necessary only because of RAND's greatest defensive achievement—the theory of defending the deterrent, of passively protecting the offensive forces. An air burst to blow away a city does not produce substantial radioactive fallout. Large amounts of fallout are generated by ground bursts. Ground bursts are necessary to attack heavily protected targets. Ground bursts are the other side's response to hardening of the strategic offensive forces. Defending the deterrent means putting the entire nation at risk. It was wonderfully logical as long as the deterrent deters; but what if deterrence fails? In a sense, Herman Kahn was cleaning up after Albert Wohlstetter.

Herman took his story on the road and gained a national reputation with it. Chet Holifield's Joint Atomic Energy Committee loved it. The civil defense operators, long laboring in the political darkness, were delighted to have such an articulate, intelligent, and well-connected standard-bearer. And the RAND story had marvelous utility to others as well.

In 1958, Albert Wohlstetter was invited to Sweden—presumably neutral in the Cold War, but then neutral-on-our-side. The Swedes were particularly interested in the RAND people because they perceived them to be moral comrades—serious-minded, rigorous, positivist social democrats. And the Swedes were debating whether or not to go nuclear.* For the nonce, they had invested heavily in defense. In fact, Sweden was to devotees of strategic defense as Kenya was to big-game hungers. With the population of New York City, it had the sixth-largest air force in the world, mostly interceptors; was covered with high-quality radars; and had an excellent ground-control apparatus copied from that of Sweden's erstwhile Luftwaffe friends.

The country was also dead serious about passive defense. So Albert brought along John O'Sullivan, Paul Weidlinger, and Herman Kahn. Everything in Sweden was dug in—in deep. The key factories were dug in, the command centers were dug in, the fighter hangars were dug in; even the navy was dug into blast shelters in the islets along the Baltic coast. Huge underground shelters underlay the cities—intelligently employed as parking garages until The Day. Unfortunately, the shelters were pre-atomic or atomic, not thermonuclear. The RAND people gave the Swedes some useful hints about the latest findings in nuclear-weapons effects, and left their grateful hosts some samples of "the Sharkey rule"—the RAND circular slide rule for doing quick-and-dirty calculations of weapons effects.

Albert and company found it a delight to see how serious a liberal society could be about defense. The Swedish policy was (and on paper still is) "Total War—Total Defense." The Swedes were not given to overstatement—they meant *total*. The potential aggressor was warned that Sweden would fight to the last man, the last bullet, the last rock, if need be. Every family had a pamphlet beginning,

---

*The length of the debate approximated the time it would have taken for the country to develop nuclear munitions. In 1968, Sweden declared that it would eschew them.

"Sweden *wants* to defend itself, *can* defend itself, and *will* defend itself . . . We will never give up! Any announcement that resistance will cease is false." The total defense comprised the military defense, the civil defense, the economic defense—and the psychological defense.

The RAND team concentrated on the excellent hardware and concrete of the defense, and perhaps bedazzled by the superficial similarity of Sweden to a liberal nation, did not pay enough attention to the psychological defense. It was contrary to Swedish law to even challenge the defense openly; it was illegal to oppose the draft. No official in America has the command of a high Swedish bureaucrat. The RAND team returned impressed and refreshed, and at least one of them, Herman, may have learned the wrong lesson. They overlooked the psychological defense.

### Defending the Missiles

The offensive missile programs were pushed forward. The Convair Project Atlas was narrowed to a particular liquid-fueled ICBM of that name. Other missiles were added. As a short-term fix, Douglas' intermediate-range Thor was given high priority. Lockheed took on the Titan project, an enormous rocket more advanced than the Atlas, although its original Bell Labs guidance system was a failure. And Boeing got into the act with a yet more forward concept, the solid-fueled Minuteman, much more cheaply stored in ready alert condition and far less vulnerable to attack.

The defense of the offensive missiles was not disregarded. While there was not much to be said for sheltering bombers, because of the vulnerability of airfields to attack, missiles had the sweet advantage of not requiring any runways. Although the first Atlases sat naked and exposed on the ground, Wohlstetter's notion of defending the offense shortly was applied to the missiles. Harry Rowen of RAND was deeply involved in this research. The original concept was to use a similar configuration to that of the Army's Nikes. The ICBMs would be stored underground horizontally and elevated to a vertical position prior to firing. Those missiles were huge and heavy, requiring enormous jacks. Blast doors sized to the entire length and breadth of the missile would have been expensive and made a large target of only 50 psi hardness.

The desire for simplicity and a smaller target led to vertical storage of the missiles. The Titan I was to sit in a hole in the ground and be elevated to the surface to be fired. The RAND people went off the California coast to examine the powerful elevators on the oil platforms. The next logical step was followed for Titan II and the subsequent Minuteman: the missiles would fire directly from their holes in the ground, from permanently emplaced canisters of reinforced concrete—which in plan looked like the grain silos on the plains, and the metaphor stuck.

To the greater enthusiasts for passive defense, these measures seemed wishy-washy. Herman, Panero, and crew wanted to go really deep—to burrow the missiles into hard-rock mountains, with preplaced demolition charges to blow the side off the slope, exposing the ICBMs for launch.

Not only the missiles, but the command centers needed to be defended. The SAC headquarters at Omaha was in a disused aircraft factory, easily blown away by even a badly aimed Soviet bomb. SAC hq was the Vatican of the offense, so it is understandable that the high priests of the first strike were loath to defend it. That would cast doubt upon the efficacy of the offense, both in peace and in war. A properly equipped and planned offensive force should deter attack and should destroy the other side on the ground. Finally SAC put its command center in a bunker two stories underground, which would provide protection from radioactive fallout or from a distant miss, but could be crushed flat by anything resembling a direct hit.

Herman thought he knew better. In a 1956 briefing for the Air Force Science Advisory Board, he exploited a current movie: "There has recently been released a picture called 'SAC.' The ostensible stars are June Allyson and James Stewart, but the real lead of the picture was without question the B-47 bomber. Now I am hoping that ten years from now we will find a new picture being released called 'SUC'—Strategic Underground Command.

"The first scene of this picture might start out as follows: Three fellows are sitting around a table playing pinochle in what is obviously an underground shelter. There is suddenly a terrific shaking.

"One of the fellows gets up to look at a meter.

"The other asks, 'How much was it?'

"The first says, 'About 100 megatons.'

"The second says, 'I can always tell by the shaking.'

"Finally the third one says with a great deal of irritation, 'Write it down on the morning report and sit down and deal.' "


## Defending the Defense

Continental air defense was more sympathetic to passive defense. NORAD thought to build a shallow bunker like SAC's, but the RAND analysts persuaded the CINCNORAD, Earl Partridge, that his headquarters bunker, the Combat Operations Center (COC—"see-oh-see") of NORAD, should be dug in deep. As the analysis continued, and as the size and accuracy of our missiles improved, so did the assumption that the Soviets could do as well, so the original idea of going down 800 feet was changed to 1,800 feet. NORAD headquarters was already at Colorado Springs, so neighboring areas were canvassed for likely sites. On purely engineering criteria, the winner was Cheyenne Mountain, just southwest of Colorado Springs. The site was selected, and the money appropriated.

The next stage in the hardening of the air defenses against attack was the SAGE centers, the brains of the network. If the Soviets took them out, air defense would be headless. So work began on the concept of "SuperSAGE." The centers would be burrowed into the ground—a concept now practical because the Bell Labs transistor shrank computer volume by a factor of a hundred and cooling requirements by factors of thousands. Many sites were examined for SuperSAGE. One was at Kennesaw Mountain, Georgia, appropriately the locale of one of the bloodiest battles of the War between the States. Another was at White Horse Mountain, at Cornwall, New York. The military has exhibited a perversely suicidal streak. Cheyenne Mountain is not deep in the Rockies; it is on the outskirts of Colorado Springs, right across the road from Fort Carson, the base of a full infantry division, and just across town from Petersen Air Force Base. Colorado Springs is the home of some 18,000 retired military personnel and the site of the United States Air Force Academy. Cheyenne Mountain is near the top of the Soviet target list, and the Air Force will lose its old and its young. Likewise, a near miss of Fort Ritchie would take out Carlisle Barracks and the Army War College. And White Horse Mountain is just up the road from West Point. In the 1950s, SAC intended to fly away to Soviet targets, and leave its ground crews and its families to die.

But as if to show its willingness to kill civilians as well, when the Air Force first started deploying ICBMs, instead of putting them out in the middle of nowhere, it located many, for cost and convenience, close to major cities, most notoriously in a noose of death around Tucson. This was rectified in later missile deployments, but one wonders how the original sites were selected.

The planners also began to be concerned about the location of the air defense bases relative to those of SAC. Not only was SAC vulnerable, but the second-highest-priority target set for the other side was the air defenses. Initially, Soviet ICBMs would be few in number—perhaps too few to get SAC. How might they be used? Perhaps a better strategy for the Soviets would be to use their missiles to take out the defenses, giving their bombers a free ride to burn SAC or whatever targets they chose. To be sure, the notion might have been yet another example of mirror-imaging, because that was how SAC planned to use its first few missiles—to blast paths for the bombers through the Soviet Troops of Air Defense.

But RAND established that the other side need not choose between targeting the offense and the defense. So many ADC centers were colocated with SAC bases that the Soviets could take out both with only 15 more bombs than it would take to eradicate SAC alone. Fewer than a hundred bombs not only would kill all of SAC that had not launched, but would decapitate the air defense apparatus as well, leaving only the Army's autonomous Nike batteries to defend the nation.

## The Gaither Committee

While RAND analysts were rummaging through civil defense research, the officials of the civil defense agency had put a hand grenade in President Eisenhower's pocket. Taking advantage of the great publicity given the "bomber gap," public fears of the hydrogen bomb, and insider rumors of intelligence reports about an emerging Soviet ballistic missile program, they tried to prod Eisenhower into action by exercising their legally mandated obligation to recommend measures to protect the country from nuclear attack. Battle Creek sent to the White House a plan drawn up by Jack Devaney for blast shelters in 315 prime target areas, and fallout shelters for the rest of the nation, priced at $32 billion! (Multiply by about four for late-'80s dollars—and note that the gross national product then was only $450 billion.)

Eisenhower was flabbergasted and put the matter off onto yet another committee, headed by Rowan Gaither. A San Francisco lawyer of impeccable breeding and reputation, he was one of the central figures of the Business in the 1950s. Among his myriad accomplishments, Gaither had been a founder of the Rad Lab, had been chairman of RAND, and as chairman of the Ford Foundation had been bankrolling much of the national-security research at American universities. The Gaither Committee was officially a subcommittee of the paper National Security Resources Council, but it quickly took on an independent life. Gaither's deputy was Bob Sprague. On the panel or consulting to it were some familiar names; James Killian, General McCormack, and Jerry Wiesner of MIT, several people from the Bell Telephone Labs, Paul Nitze, the physicists Rabi and Lawrence, Albert Hill (of Hill and Valley), Jerry Strope, and Herman's colleague and friend Andy Marshall of RAND. (Herman and Albert were not listed, but were both in Washington as consultants.) Gaither took sick with the cancer that was soon to kill him, so leadership devolved on Bob Sprague.

The Gaither committee was a classic case of bootlegging. Sprague *et al.* went far beyond their mandate of evaluating the civil defense programs and made an across-the-board investigation of the U.S. strategic posture. A team including Sprague and Wiesner called on Curtis LeMay at his headquarters in Omaha, and Sprague told him something to this effect: "After talking with everybody, including your staff, it seems to me that if the Soviets attacked tomorrow, you could only get about a dozen bombers off the ground to hit back." LeMay replied, "No, Mr. Sprague—nine."

Sprague was appalled by the casual admission of SAC vulnerability. LeMay led him to an adjoining room where wall charts displayed the world situation and informed him, "We're overflying Russia twenty-four hours a day. If those bastards start to mass their planes for surprise attack on the United States, I'll knock the shit out of them before they get off the ground."

"But General, that's not the national policy."

"I don't care. That's what I am going to do."*

This was a terrifying revelation for Sprague—if only because the LeMay plan, if that really was his plan, was wonderfully naive, since no President would give such an order. Or would he? Or would a crisis reveal that SAC's plan was the only plan, and had to be executed as it was written? Or would LeMay perhaps execute it on his own? Shaken, Sprague returned to Washington and asked to brief the Commander-in-Chief himself on his discovery. In the Oval Office in the presence of the Joint Chiefs of Staff and Donald Quarles, Sprague told what he had learned in Omaha. The American high command listened impassively. Upon completion of the briefing, Sprague expected the conventional interrogatory period. He waited for questions. There were no questions. He waited. Finally he rose and excused himself. That terminated Bob Sprague's role as a White House adviser.

The final Gaither report was drafted by Nitze (quietly, because he was *persona non grata* to the Eisenhower administration). Very much under Wohlstetter's influence, it recommended short-term measures such as implementing SAC's alert situation, active missile defense of SAC bases, increasing the numbers of IRBMs and ICBMs, speeding up the Polaris program, and putting in anti-ICBM defenses against the emerging Soviet threat. The report stated elegantly the mainstream solution to The Problem:

> The main protection of our civil population against a Soviet nuclear attack has been and will continue to be the deterrent power of our armed forces, to whose strengthening and securing we have recorded the highest relative value. But this is not sufficient unless it is coupled with measures to reduce the extreme vulnerability of our people and our cities. As long as the U.S. population is wide open to Soviet attack, both the Russians and our allies may believe that we shall feel increasing reluctance to employ SAC in any circumstance other than when the United States is directly attacked. To prevent such an impairment of our deterrent power and to ensure our survival if nuclear war occurs through miscalculation or design, we assign a somewhat lower

---

*Of course, the account is by Sprague. General LeMay contradicts it, saying, "I wouldn't *out loud* advocate a preemptive strike." LeMay also denied remembering who Sprague was, his voice laced with utter disdain. At the mention of the name "Nitze," the cordial general's face screwed into a grimace of pure hatred.

than highest value, in relation to cost, to a mixed program of active and passive defenses to protect our civil population. . . .

A massive development program to eliminate weaknesses in our present active defenses [here they recommend coverage against low-level attacks and counter-countermeasures against enemy electronic jamming] . . .

A nationwide fallout shelter program to protect the civil population. This seems the only feasible protection for millions of people who will be increasingly exposed to the hazards of radiation. The Panel has been unable to identify any other type of defense likely to save more lives for the same money in the event of a nuclear attack.

The construction and use of such shelters must be tied into a broad pattern of organization for the emergency and its aftermath. We are convinced that with proper planning the post-attack environment can permit people to come out of the shelters and survive. It is important to remember that those who survive the effects of the blast will have adequate time (one to five hours) to get into the fallout shelters. This is not true of blast shelters which, to be effective, must be entered prior to the attack.

We do not recommend major construction of blast shelters at this time. If, as it appears quite likely, an effective air defense system can be obtained, this will probably be a better investment than blast shelters. However, because of present uncertainties, on both active and passive fronts, it seems prudent to carry out promptly a research and development program for such blast shelters since we must be in a position to move rapidly into construction should the need for them become evident.

The estimate was that a countrywide system of fallout shelters could save 35–50 million lives at a cost of $25 billion, whereas investing heavily in blast shelters would not be as cost-effective. (The Gaither calculations found that the civil defense agency estimates were about $20 billion low.)

Another recommendation was "A program to develop and install an area defense against ICBMs at the earliest possible date." Jerome Wiesner was especially enthusiastic about BMD. As an immediate step, the creation of an early-warning system against ballistic missile attacks was urged. Although the fallout-shelter program was consciously presented as more acceptable than the inordinately expensive blast shelters, Eisenhower nonetheless tried to put the entire study aside; but the results were leaked, and the outcry in the press and in the Congress (by Senator Joseph Clark of Pennsylvania, among others) was too great. The missile programs were accelerated, the Gaither-recommended ballistic missile early-warning system was set in process, and MITRE was established; the rest of the program, however, was put in the drawer.* In particular, nothing whatever was done about civil defense. And the reprogramming of Air Force appropriations for the offensive missiles and ballistic missile early warning led to a sharp cutback in the planned deployments for continental air defense.

The work of the Gaither Committee was given heightened importance when the Soviet Union announced that it had successfully test-fired an ICBM in August of 1957 and then proved it by placing an artificial satellite in orbit the following month. The Soviets had seized the technological high ground, and the Americans panicked.

---

*A mythology has grown up around the Gaither report. Wiesner has several times reported Eisenhower responding to the civil defense briefing, "Where are the bulldozers we'll need for scraping the bodies off the streets?" Sprague does not recall it, and cannot imagine Eisenhower making such a smart-aleck remark. (In an unrelated context, Ivan Getting attributed such a remark to his brother, a Massachusetts public health official; perhaps Wiesner confused him with Ike.) Wiesner has said that Gaither proposed astronomical defense costs; the Gaither recommendations in fact were a hair less than actual expenditures in the next five years. It is commonly said that none of the proposals were adopted by Eisenhower—and falsely. When the report was published in 1975 by a Senate committee, a preface by Senator Proxmire's staff said that the report was a glaring example of exaggerated forecasts of Soviet capabilities—yet the preface was falser than the projections.

# IV

# THE DEFENSE STRAINED

*Only poets make strategy without budgets.*
GIULIO DOUHET

Sputnik could not have appeared at a more inopportune time. That thing up in space going "beep beep" confirmed Soviet boasts of possessing intercontinental ballistic missiles. The booster that could put a satellite in orbit could deliver a thermonuclear weapon to a North American target. Immediately it was revealed that the Army's Huntsville team had been ready, willing, and able to launch an American satellite, but had been blocked by higher authority. For years earth-orbiting satellites had been considered for reconaissance of the closed world of the Soviet Union. The very first paper of The RAND Corporation, written by David Griggs, Louis Ridenour, and others in 1946, and delivered to the U.S.S.R. by the Rosenberg spy ring, described the utility of reconnaissance satellites. The Eisenhower administration had determined to first fly a civilian satellite in order to establish the principle that orbiting vehicles could legally pass over nations without violating their sovereign territory— to distinguish outer space from airspace. Sputnik achieved that objective for us—to the enormous long-run strategic benefit of the United States, but at staggering short-run political costs to the presidency.

Eisenhower was under heavy pressure to rush the U.S. space program and missile force. Actually, excellent plans for Atlas, Thor, and Jupiter had already been laid down, and some modest acceleration was about all that could be usefully done. The political heat was intense. Eisenhower had a heart attack in the midst of the crisis,

134

as did the Pentagon research chief, Herbert York. And Louis Ridenour and Donald Quarles—who was then Deputy Secretary of Defense and slated for the top job—dropped dead in this period. But Ike held firm. He was not about to spend any more money. In fact, he cut the defense budget in real terms.

## The Missile Wars

The interservice struggles of the 1950s, already exacerbated by Eisenhower's pinchpenny budgets, became vicious. The Army wanted larger conventional forces. The Navy wanted money for Polaris and its aircraft carriers. The Air Force wanted bombers, missiles, and continental air defense—in that order. The Army was especially bitter. A Colonel Nickerson had to be court-martialed for leaking stuff out of Huntsville. A revolt of colonels had to be suppressed by a facile staff general named William Westmoreland. The Army's Chief of Staff, Maxwell Taylor, retired, wrote a blistering book against Eisenhower's defense policies, and attached himself to the Kennedys. The Army's research chief, John Gavin, retired, wrote a blistering book against Eisenhower's defense policies, and went into big business. The Army's rocket chief, John Medaris, retired, wrote a blistering book against Eisenhower's defense policy, and took the cloth as an Episcopal priest.

The Congress, led by a battery of competent Democratic senators such as Stuart Symington and Henry M. Jackson, held widely publicized hearings calling for radical changes in defense policy. Even staunch Republicans like Congressman Gerald Ford complained, "I am sick and tired of this [interservice] bickering, and I think the public is likewise."

A good working rule of government is—if you don't want to spend money, reorganize. So Eisenhower handed the power of arbitrator of the missile wars to the scientific politicians. A minor Executive Office science advisory council was elevated to President's Scientific Advisory Council (PSAC—"pee-sack") under James Killian of MIT, who had already charmed Ike with his bureaucratic skill in prior committees. He was not a scientist, or even an engineer (he had a B.A. from Tech), but an accomplished courtier. At MIT he was essentially a top-drawer fund-raiser, who knew that nothing was for nothing and that MIT ought to earn its way, whether from industry or from government. Earning Tech's keep drew Jim Killian onto scientific panels, where he displayed a genius for committeemanship. He would listen patiently and empathically to all parties, and wait until they were exhausted, then propose a consensus position as reflecting the public interest—it almost always was the public interest, and always was the interest of the Massachusetts Institute of Technology. For PSAC, Killian gathered like-minded folk, many from Cambridge, to sort out the defense budget. Almost all of the "Charles River Gang" were liberal Democrats.

To better coordinate defense research, the assistant secretaryship was upgraded to Director of Defense Research and Engineering (DoDR&E—"dee-oh-dee-are-'n-ee"). The first Director was Herbert York, a Livermore man. Under him was established a new body dedicated to service-independent high-tech research: the Advanced Research Projects Agency (ARPA—"are-pah"). It was given responsibility for far-out BMD research, including the Air Force's Project Wizard, renamed Project Defender. Earlier reforms had created the mostly civilian Weapons Systems Evaluation Group (WSEG—"wess-egg") as an advisory group to the Joint Chiefs of Staff, and the RAND-like Institute for Defense Analyses to provide scientific advice to WSEG. The influence of both was strengthened.

In the battle of the offensive missiles, the Army took a severe drubbing. Its prize, the Jupiter, was handed over to the Air Force, and the Army was nevermore to have a role in long-range rocketry, or so it was thought. Only the short-range Honest John and Pershing missiles were left, and because their development was nearly completed, the Army no longer needed the German-American team at Huntsville or the Army's original rocket research facility at Cal Tech's Jet Propulsion Laboratory. Both these precious institutions were handed over to the newly formed National Aeronautics and Space Administration, commissioned to wage the space race with the Soviets.

The Navy was also driven from space. The Air Force was given the military space mission. And the Air Force continued its Atlas, Titan, and Minuteman ICBM programs under its own research command and systems-engineering contractor. Because too many important people were asking too many pointed questions about the relationship with the profit-making Ramo-Woodridge Company (later TRW) for its missile programs, the Air Force organized a nonprofit corporation on the model of RAND and MITRE—Aerospace Corporation. However, Aerospace did not take over the ICBM work, which remained with what was to become TRW, but concentrated on the Air Force's own emerging space program, especially for reconnaissance satellites. General James McCormack was on the original board of Aerospace. Its first president was Ivan Getting; among his lieutenants was Ed Barlow from RAND.

The Secretary of Defense approved recommendations that the Air Force control the ballistic missile early-warning and command-and-control system, as the Air Force had controlled the radars and SAGE for continental air defense. As a consolation prize, the Army was given ground-based ballistic missile defense development, which meant the Bell Laboratories' Nike-Zeus work, nominally as the agent of ARPA.

## The Defeat of CONAD

The major casualty of the missile wars was continental air defense. If the Soviets could cream us with ICBMs, why bother with improving defenses against mere bombers? In a few months continental air defense went from being the politician's delight to being a boondoggle. Perversely, Fiscal Year 1958 saw the peak in real-dollar spending for strategic defense; in the year of Sputnik, the United States spent more on strategic defense than on strategic offense. Although the Democratic-controlled Congress forced some money on him, the President remained parsimonious, and funds were needed for the Air Force's ICBMs, for the Navy's Polaris program, and for the civil and military space investments necessary to counter Sputnik, so cuts came out of the hide of continental air defense.

- The planned 4,500 interceptors were cut to 1,000. The original buy of 1,000+ F-106s was chopped to 340.
- Even better stuff had been on the drawing boards. In 1955 the Air Force had established a requirement for the LRIX—Long-Range Interceptor Experimental—on paper a marvelous aircraft: a two-seater, with two engines, Mach 3 speed, range from the continental United States to the North Polar regions, there to loiter and kill incoming bombers with long-range missiles. North American Aviation was supposed to produce it as the F-108, but the

Air Force was forced to choose between the LRIX and the proposed XB-70 superbomber. Of course, the Air Force went for the bomber; no new interceptors were added after 1960.

- The Nike-Hercules buy was cut back from 8,300 to 2,400. Only part of the planned close-in defense was installed.
- The Hawk procurement for continental air defense was terminated. Hawk was delivered to the field army only.
- Bomarc deployments were cut from 30 squadrons to 18 squadrons, and then to 8. The supposed supermissile, finally made reasonably operational, was deployed in the northeastern United States and adjoining Canada, but the West Coast bases were scrubbed, so Bomarc did not even defend Boeing's own state of Washington.
- The SAGE centers still in blueprint were scrubbed. Of the 46 planned, only 22 were built.
- The hardened Super-SAGE was cancelled. Only one was dug in, at North Bay in Ontario, because this center was not only a regional SAGE but Canada's own air defense center, its little Cheyenne Mountain.
- While it stayed in the program, a stall was put on the construction of Cheyenne Mountain. And SUC was put on the back burner.
- New radars on the drawing boards were killed.
- The Navy pulled its blimps out of service.

To be sure, most of the extant elements of continental air defense stayed in place. The DEW Line, the Mid-Canada Line, and the Pinetree Line remained. The fighters were on the airfields. The SAGE units under construction were completed. The planned replacement of Ajax by Hercules continued. The Texas Towers stood on the continental shelf. But the heyday of continental air defense was history—in a few months.

### Debacle in the North

Nineteen fifty-eight was a miserable year for air defense north of the border as well. The Avro Arrow fighter was cancelled. Although in the basic design and the airframe there were no insurmountable problems, the radar was supposed to have been provided by RCA, and the U.S. government scrubbed it. Its Sparrow II missiles were supposed to have been provided by Bendix, and the U.S. government scrubbed them. The Canadians would have been left with a plane without brains and claws, with the costs climbing and no national capability to develop the vital subsystems themselves. And Canada had a new prime minister, a pinchpenny conservative who also could read the forecast for air defense as well as any American. John Diefenbaker shot down the Arrow.

In place of Canada's own fighter plane, American Bomarc missiles were offered, and the Canadians, like damn fools, took them. Two squadrons went in at North Bay and at La Macaza, Quebec. In the early '60s another deal was made for the Canadians to operate additional radars and receive 66 McDonnell F-101 fighters in return. As the CF-101, these planes remained in service as Canada's most visible contribution to North American air defense until the early 1980s.

## Minor Disasters

Air defense disasters were not merely political and budgetary— some were petty and local. When the Nikes were installed, some neighbors were concerned about having deadly weapons nearby— and were assured of their safety. They were very safe, but not perfectly safe. On May 22, 1958, maintenance on a Nike-Ajax at Battery B, 526th AA Missile Battalion, at Middletown, New Jersey, seems to have been bungled. A missile got loose on the site and exploded and blew up other missiles—killing six soldiers and four civilians. This was especially embarrassing because it was the nearest Nike site to the Bell Labs. Some modifications were in order—and there was no more difficulty of that sort.

Two years later, a fire in a Bomarc hanger at McGuire Air Force Base, also in New Jersey, reached the missile and its nuclear warhead. While heat and spark cannot ignite a nuclear reaction and all firing mechanisms are fail-safe, melted plutonium can badly contaminate its immediate surroundings. The ex-Bomarc building is still off-limits—and will be for centuries.

And the DEW Line was not working as well as had been hoped. It had been manned through competitive bidding. A division of ITT made the low bid. ITT was able to make the low bid by paying lower wages to radar operators. So ITT recruited low people to watch scopes in the Arctic. Many of them watched the scopes badly— some of them watched the scopes not at all.

Worst of all, in 1961 a heavy storm on the Atlantic Coast swept away Texas Tower No. 4, committing the resident airmen to Davy Jones's locker. They got no sea pay there either.

And over the years, unnoticed and untabulated, and mourned only by their families and friends, pilots and radar operators of USAF and Canadian interceptors were lost in training missions and routine exercises.

## The Vanquished

Now, we ought not to forget that many people were involved in the rise and fall of continental air defense. We should not ignore the devoted effort that went into it, especially by people at MIT. We should not disregard the role played in the decisions to terminate the development of continental air defense by the President's Scientific Advisory Committee and its various subpanels, the newly organized Advanced Projects Research Agency, the office of the Director of Defense Research and Engineering, and the Weapons Systems Evaluation Group and the Institute for Defense Analyses, which were advising it. We should not forget their disappointment at having failed.

We should not underestimate their understandable distaste for the dirty bickering of the uniformed military.

We should not disregard the trauma of discovering that continental air defense was to cover for retaliation after a first strike.

We should never forget their terror of SAC.

We should remind ourselves of some of the men engaged in the debacle: Hans Bethe, Richard Garwin, James Killian, Spurgeon Keeney, George Kistiakowsky, Wolfgang Panofsky, George Rathjens, Jack Ruina, Jerome Wiesner, Herbert York, Jerrold Zacharias. There is a story that at a meeting of the Military Operations Research Society, perhaps in Chicago, around 1960, someone said, "The smartest people in the country tried to make air defense work, and couldn't." According to the story, the speaker was from MIT, perhaps one of those named above.

Herman wrote in 1964 that "One of the startling things about working in the ABM field today is to note how few of the 'defense intellectuals' are willing to take an enthusiastic stand behind ABM. This is not solely a result of the weaknesses of ABM. Many of the same intellectuals gave enthusiastic support to air defense systems which had equally grave or even graver weaknesses. One rather suspects that for various reasons the disillusion created by some of the badly designed air defense systems has had a more or less permanent effect."

## The Blocking of Nike-Zeus

In this atmosphere, it would have been a wonder if Nike-Zeus had been approved for production; and it wasn't. Of course, the Army heralded Zeus as the answer to the Russian missile menace. And the Army had much support in the Congress. The irrepressible Representative Dan Flood of Wilkes-Barre, who affected the demeanor of a riverboat gambler and the rhetoric of a carnival pitchman, hailed Zeus as the answer to "the Red-triggered nuclear hailstorm." But Eisenhower did not want to put up the estimated $13–14 billion for thousands of short-range missiles in 1,200 batteries ringing 35 cities, mostly in old Nike-Ajax sites, warned by 9 forward acquisition radars.

With relief, the Defense Department passed the decision on to the President's Scientific Advisory Council, headed by the Harvard chemist George Kistiakowsky, who put it out to a subcommittee under Jerry Wiesner, with the physicists Hans Bethe, Wolfang Panofsky, and Harold Brown of Livermore. PSAC turned thumbs down. The Air Force had provided the key arguments: the offense could always outstrip the defense; the individual city defenses of Zeus could be saturated by concentrated attack; the radars were soft and vulnerable. Among the advisers to the subcommittee were Richard Latter and William Graham of RAND. In 1959, Zeus again went to PSAC, to the same subcommittee, plus Zacharias, and was again nixed.

Defenders of the Nike-Zeus program maintain that it was defeated only on paper, that had the system been deployed, it would not have faced the visionary decoy threats ginned up by the imaginative analysts of RAND and the Air Force. Soviet reentry vehicles, up to the late '60s, had slovenly aerodynamics. In the atmosphere they decelerated at 100 times the force of gravity, trailing a huge radar signature, and slowing to subsonic speeds at 20,000 feet. The primeval Soviet missiles were far easier targets than aircraft. Had the orders been given in 1958, Nike-Zeus would have been first deployed by 1963, and would have provided effective ballistic-missile defense against the Soviet Union at least until the early '70s, and against everybody else to this day. No one could have anticipated this in 1958—but had Zeus been deployed, it would have been an accepted part of the military and urban landscape of America. ABM would not have become a football for cynical politicians. Zeus in place—like Herc and Hawk, like Sparrow and Sidewinder—could have been upgraded over and over again. Had Nike-Zeus gone forward in 1958, America would not have been naked to attack, and would not have been convulsed by frenzy later.

## Kwajalein

Although a hold was put on Nike-Zeus production and deployment, it was time to consider where to test the system. The established Army test range at White Sands, between Alamogordo and Fort Bliss, was obviously inadequate—indeed, a few of the shorter-range Nike missiles had gotten away and terrorized passing road traffic. The Navy's test station at Point Mugu, on the Pacific Coast, was also considered, but rejected for lack of space. What was needed was a place that could be bombarded at intercontinental range. Because the Army's main long-range test facility was already established at Cape Canaveral, it seemed reasonable to seek a target island downrange in the Atlantic. Caribbean locations were too near. Arrangements were made with the British to establish a station at Ascension Island, in the South Atlantic, but the international dealing threatened to be too complicated. A test site on U.S.-controlled territory was imperative—"Site X" it was designated.

Attention turned to the Pacific. A team of Army officers, Huntsville bureaucrats, and Bell Labs engineers climbed into a Constellation transport for a tour of the Central Pacific. A promising candidate was Christmas Island, but its incomprehensible status of condominium of sovereignty with the Brits made it too politically convoluted. The team then concentrated on the Marshalls and Gilberts, to the east of Eniwetok and Bikini, and were struck by the virtues of Kwajalein. They hit on the atoll principally for its airfield and existing structures already prepared by the Atomic Energy Commission to support earlier nuclear testing. The Navy had nominal suzerainty over Kwaj, but the place was just a burden on the Navy's overhead, so the seamen were glad to have Army occupants to justify its tiny garrison's existence.

The Huntsville landscape architect Ed Rosenthal was commissioned to write up the required specifications for the Army's missile test site; he wrote them so that the competition would be won by Kwajalein. The name is native, supposedly meaning "an abundance of material and spiritual blessing." According to the *Guinness Book of World Records,* Kwajalein is the world's largest atoll, formed by the carcasses of untold billions of dead coral piled on the rim of a long-submerged volcano. The main island, also called Kwajalein, at the south end of the rim was the scene of bitter fighting in World War II. Chastened by the horrible casualties of the Marine landing at Tarawa, 700 miles to the south, a few months earlier, the American task force had thoroughly leveled Kwaj by air and naval bombardment. When the Army stormed shore in Operation Flintlock in January 1944, the Japanese defenders were exterminated in short order (although a straggler hid out until 1948). Several of the troops who invaded or occupied Kwajalein later returned as BMD researchers.

The main island was just over a square mile large, and the remainder of the 90-odd islands ringed the largest lagoon in the world, of nearly a thousand square miles of water. While the airfield was important, and the lagoon made an excellent target, shallow enough for the recovery of missile debris, the great advantage of the atoll was its location: 4,800 miles—ICBM range—from the Air Force's just-completed launch complex at Vandenberg Air Force Base, on the California coast.

Kwajalein was added to the atomic archipelago in 1946 when a B-29 named *Dave's Dream* took off for Bikini and returned 20 kilotons lighter. Among the targets at Bikini had been the *Prinz Eugen,* a fine heavy cruiser which had accompanied the *Bismarck* on its last sortie into the North Atlantic, made the renowned Channel dash from Brest back to home port evading Allied air, and managed to survive the Third Reich. It had also—for a time—survived nuclear attack by the Americans and been towed back to Kwajalein's lagoon; but it was highly radioactive, and no one cared to save the ship when it began to list, so it had capsized and turned belly up. The *Prinz* was the leading tourist attraction at Kwajalein, an ever-present reminder of the power of nuclear munitions.

During the Korean war, the island had been used as a refueling station for the then short-range piston transports crossing the Pacific to support America's growing Far Eastern forces. Increased activity had led to the moving of the natives off the main island to permanent quarters on the nearby islet of Ebeye. There were no complaints—the Marshallese had long acquaintance with the odd ways of the outsiders, and had been pushed around in succession by Spaniards, Germans, and Japanese. The Americans at least paid them a modest wage for their cheerful and lackadaisical labor. At the end of the Korean war, the Eisenhower cutbacks in conventional forces and the shifting of most nuclear testing to Nevada had provoked a serious depression in the local economy. In 1958, the Navy had placed Kwajalein on its list of surplus bases.

In early '59, DoD approved the selection of Kwaj as the cradle of Nike-Zeus. The original Army plans called for also occupying Johnston Island, some 1,300 miles to the northeast, using it as a launch pad to fire the Army's Jupiter rockets on pseudo-ICBM trajectories at the defenders of Kwaj. This was interpreted by the Air Force and by DoD as a transparently desperate attempt to keep the Jupiter program in being. Furthermore, the DoD research chief, Herb York, suspected that if the Army was doing the firing, the validity of the tests results might be doubtful. Why bother, when real ICBMs could be fired by the real operators, the Air Force, from Vandenberg? Johnston Island came to be the site of "high altitude" experiments for the AEC, the Air Force antisatellite program, and some other "black" activities.

Kwaj was so perfectly sited for missile defense research that ARPA picked the second-largest island in the atoll, Roi-Namur, for its separate ballistic missile defense research. To study how ICBM reentry vehicles behaved, it erected elaborate radar facilities for Project PRESS (the Pacific Range Electromagnetic Signature Studies Program). Again, the offense and the defense were working together.

In 1960, the Army and Bell Labs took possession of Kwaj. Among the inspectors were Cliff Warren, the chief project engineer, and Jake Schaefer, chief of the Nike-Zeus systems department. The Bell Labs engineers, snug in the New Jersey suburbs, were offered the opportunity to establish their families in the mid-Pacific. To be sure, Ma Bell provided them with every reasonable incentive and created the equivalent of a military-base facility on the atoll; certainly they enjoyed excellent communications with their families Stateside; but Kwaj was not exactly New Jersey. The heat and rains necessitated informal dress. No white shirts or neckties were required, and men and women wore shorts. But culture is stronger than environment, and Kwajalein became a suburb of Whippany. Recreational facilities were lacking, and one could not go into New York to shop or to the theater, and there were no country clubs on Kwaj, so many of the wives of the AT&T and subcontractors' staffs brushed up their typing skills and took jobs as secretaries and clerks. Life was pleasant, albeit rather dull, brightened by swimming parties in the lagoon, with scuba diving to the carcass of the *Prinz*.

At least, family and friends could not drop in unannounced. Kwajalein was a military base—a closed facility. Passes were required to get onto the atoll, and they were not easily obtained. The authorities had been much embarrassed by the newspaper photographs and the television coverage of failed shots at Cape Canaveral, so journalists did not get passes. There were no nearby motels for snoopy reporters. The only way in was on the weekly charter flight from Honolulu—ten hours of DC-6.

To be sure, there were some uninvited visitors. Apparently ABM systems development and radar research are beneficial to sea life. Very soon after Nike-Zeus operations began, fishing boats appeared on a regular basis—very large, very well-equipped vessels of the Union of Soviet Socialist Republics, especially remarkable for the plethora of radars and communications antennae ornamenting their deckhouses and masts. There is no record of any of the fishermen coming ashore. Soviet submarines also enjoyed the tropical waters.

On the whole, the snoopers were disregarded. The testing of rockets requires the fitting of small radios to transmit information about their performance—"telemetry." The Western Electric–Bell Labs engineers fiddled some signals, just to make the interpretation more interesting to eavesdroppers. On one occasion, a Soviet ship was idling in the planned impact area of a missile about to come downrange from California. It disregarded admonitions to move out. Finally, Kwaj resorted to an "SOS." This prompted a Soviet protest in the United Nations that the United States was misusing the international distress call for its sinister military purposes.

Life on Kwaj was enlivened by regular Fourth of July celebrations. Not only were ABM rocket components being tested at the atoll, but ICBM rockets were being fired at it from across the Pacific. So one place under the American flag had a serious civil defense effort, where people had to take shelter—against American missiles.

## Civil Defense Finally Rises

What the politicians can take away the politicians can give. As air defense collapsed, civil defense was on the rise. The reasons are clear enough. Continental air defense could do absolutely nothing against a ballistic missile threat; civil defense could mitigate both bomber and rocket attacks. It is improper to make too much of the influence of any individual in any of these matters, but key people ofttimes appear in the right place at the right time. Herman Kahn was feeling too much heat at RAND and in early 1959 solicited a six-month sabbatical as a research associate at Princeton's Center for International Studies. Its chief, Klaus Knorr, had been one of the last people to write on dispersion, several years after it was rejected by everybody else.

Herman was supposed to be writing a book on civil defense, but instead spent a great deal of time proselytizing in New York and Washington. Through an old schoolmate of Wohlstetter's, he got to Time Inc. and found a warm reception. About this time the Luce magazines had switched from their early-'50s emphasis on the offense to a promotion of the defense, which continued for a decade. Herman also showed up at the Council on Foreign Relations, the Carnegie Endowment, and numerous other establishment institutions. He was still in contact with the Gaither crowd. A public operation similar to the Gaither Committee had been conducted under the auspices of the Rockefellers, with the usual list of establishment names, and it strongly endorsed civil defense. Probably converted to the faith by Edward Teller, Nelson A. Rockefeller became a true fanatic—on strategic grounds, to limit Soviet blackmail. Yet with all his money and all his power at the height of his popularity, he could not force a major program through the legislature of his own State of New York.

At Princeton, Herman attended another major conference with Nitze and many other American and European worthies on what to do about NATO—how could we credibly threaten to defend Europe with nuclear weapons if the Soviets could respond to our attack by striking back? The generally accepted answer was improving the conventional defense of Europe. This seemed at least to mitigate The Problem, and became standard establishment strategic fare.

Instead of writing his civil defense book at Princeton, Herman fulfilled his publishing obligation with a little sleight-of-hand. Over the years he had been elaborating his briefings on thermonuclear strategy. He had them up to three full days. Herman laboriously hand-typed them, complete with his charts, into a manuscript, "Three Lectures on Thermonuclear War," shortly trimmed to *On Thermonuclear War,* which was published by the Princeton University Press in 1961. This book was to a remarkable degree a summation of the nuclear-strategic thought of the American professionals and of the American establishment in the late 1950s. Without giving excessive credit to the book itself, the ideas in it were those generally held by serious people at the time. Grossly oversimplified but not distorted, Herman argued these points: first, the word "deterrence" meant little in and of itself: what was it you were deterring? He distinguished between three general types:

Type I—Deterrence of attacks against the homeland. This was the most widely thought-about threat, and was the easiest to deter. You needed a force that could survive an attack (in Wohlstetter's sense) and strike back in a terrible reprisal. When hit hard, men and nations hit back. Herman considered this so obvious that he did not spend a lot of time on it (rather to Wohlstetter's annoyance; Herman would cheerfully allow that SAC could park all its bombers in Times Square, disperse the crews to 42nd Street bars, and turn off all the warning radars—and the Soviets would not attack). And he thought the framework of Type I deterrence to be the least likely scenario for nuclear war. Why would nations engage in a suicide pact? In this he shared the near-universal RAND view.

Type II—Deterrence of other major threats to vital American interests—a veiled way of saying defense of Western Europe. To defend Europe the United States had to be able to credibly threaten to hit the Soviet Union with nuclear weapons. In other words, the United States should have a credible first-strike capability. A first strike against what? To strike against Soviet cities (as posited by SAC) would earn a Soviet attack in return—that is, the Soviets had Type I deterrence of our Type II deterrent strike. Instead, following the lead of many of his RAND colleagues, especially his close friend Andy Marshall, Herman advocated counterforce strikes against the other side's weapons, not his cities. This had certain ethical and moral advantages, to say the least, although it would raise the levels of fallout around the world. And Type II deterrence also required heavy defenses of the strategic forces—because the threat of our first strike would incite the other side to knock it out before venturing on a major aggression.

Type III—Deterrence of lesser provocations and acts. We were not about to blow up Kiev and lose Boston because the Soviets had sunk a ship or supported an insurgency movement on our turf. For this, he argued, we needed substantial conventional forces and the ability to launch strictly limited nuclear attacks under careful control.

Now, for all of these forms of deterrence, we must worry about "war-fighting"—about exactly how we will use the weapons and how the other side will respond. We also must be concerned about our defenses and his defenses, because our ability to limit damage from his reprisals affects our war-fighting ability and, more important, our ability to make threats short of war. Herman supported arms control, as long as it did not seriously downgrade any of the above, and even advocated world government, which he thought preferable to all-out thermonuclear war, but he could not see how we could possibly get global governance except after the shock of a brutal nuclear war.

*On Thermonuclear War* created a high furor and gained Herman an international reputation far exceeding his previous identification as a promoter of civil defense. Yet civil defense promised substantial strategic advantages in the scheme. In a crisis situation, one or both sides could improve their bargaining position by ordering a strategic evacuation of the cities, so that the enemy's threat to burn the urban areas would be largely nullified. As a consequence of the popularization of analytical work by Herman and by many other people— most notably Jerry Strope on the inside—the establishment, for the most part, came to accept the principle that civil defense was a partial answer to The Problem, part of the package of bolstering national strength against the constructive Soviet menace.

But not Herman nor anyone else involved at that time who knew the technology believed that defense substituted for offense. The best solution to The Problem was no nuclear war; the best way, short of surrender, to prevent nuclear war was deterrence; defense strengthened the deterrence.

Oh, yes—while deterrence is the name of the game, *what if deterrence fails?*

## The Democratic Offensive

While many of these matters were then classified, they were known at least in their broad outlines to the politicians. In the perceived weakness of Eisenhower's pinchpenny policies, the Democrats smelled red meat. Paul Nitze had been a Republican and had been offered the Defense Department International Security Affairs (ISA—"eye-ess-ay") slot when Eisenhower came in, but the right-wingers knew he had been a principal lieutenant of the hated Dean Acheson, and nixed his appointment. As subsequent Presidents were to learn, Nitze was a bad man not to give a job to. He immediately began a guerrilla war against Eisenhower. An early shot was his criticism of Ike's lackadaisical air defense program; in 1953, he advocated a $3 billion supplement. In the Council's schmooz, he argued that augmenting the offense would return decreasing marginal security utility, while defenses promised higher return on investment.

Early in 1956, long enough before the election not to make his endeavor too obvious, Nitze slashed at the supposed "massive retaliation" policy of John Foster Dulles in a famous essay that introduced a wonderful distinction to the strategic vocabulary: between "declaratory policy" and "action policy"—between what is said to be the policy and what the policy really is. Nitze was too prudent to state nakedly that they could not be identical because the public could not tolerate the truth, but he recognized that it was bad policy to let the declarations get too blatantly out of step with the actions. Of course, "massive retaliation" was mostly hot air—the U.S. would not resort to full atomic attacks against the U.S.S.R. for piddling aggressions; we would employ lesser and more appropriate methods of resisting and retaliating—but the U.S. administration had not provided adequate means to perform such action, and according to Nitze, it had better. In 1959, he became the principal defense-issues adviser to Senator John F. Kennedy of Massachusetts.

Another politician who smelled blood was the junior senator from Washington, Henry Jackson, who had entered the Congress in 1940 and had subsequently made himself probably its most knowledgeable single member on defense issues—despite his epithet "the Senator from Boeing." He was an important member of the Joint Committee on Atomic Energy, played a key role in pushing through the Super program, and even supported Bomarc. In 1959 he announced to the world that "America is losing the cold war." Jackson had hoped to become Kennedy's vice-presidential candidate, but had been shunted aside to the figurehead position of chairman of the Democratic National Committee while Kennedy's own brother ran the campaign. Alas, Jackson was a flaming liberal, and the Kennedys perceived themselves to be vulnerable on the right flank, so the vice-presidency went to Lyndon B. Johnson.

Previously, John Kennedy had exhibited small interest in defense. As congressman, he had made a *pro forma* statement in support of civil defense, and seems to have left continental air defense to Saltonstall and McCormack. In his run for the presidency, Kennedy had leaned hard on the military inadequacies of the great golfer and his minions, thus confuting the soft-on-Communism canards smeared on the Democrats by Joseph McCarthy and his ilk in the late '40s and early '50s. Kennedy had already been in contact with Maxwell Taylor, the Army Chief of Staff who had fought and lost the missile wars with the Air Force. Taylor elegantly reflected Army opposition to reliance upon the striking power of SAC and favored more emphasis on fighting in "the gray areas," less than total war. He was also a star supporter of the Army's Nike-Zeus ABM system.

Almost everyone named in this book was a liberal Democrat who supported Kennedy in the 1960 election. (Bob Sprague, a Republican loyalist, was an exception.) Kennedy had organized a cell in Cambridge. He knew well how to exploit intellectuals—pretend to pay attention to their advice, and they will tout you as a thoughtful person. Daniel Ellsberg, a Harvard graduate student and RAND consultant, made the link to Santa Monica. Harry Rowen advised the campaign, and Wohlstetter crafted an elegant broadside against Ikish prudence and parsimony in *Life*.

The opposition made much of a supposed "missile gap." It was a remarkable replay of the "bomber gap" of the mid-'50s. Yes, the Soviets had ICBM potential—Sputnik proved that. Yes, there were intelligence reports of substantial rocket production. But again, the other side put priority on the shorter-range weapons to threaten its neighbors in Eurasia. At a 1956 Council meeting, William Bundy of the CIA estimated operational Soviet ICBMs in 5–8 years—right on the money.

Yes, the other side would soon have intercontinental capability. But counting their missiles versus our missiles was specious. What mattered was what they could do with them; with fewer than a hundred ICBMs, they could take out SAC and NORAD. Pinch-hitting for Wohlstetter at an off-the-record Council meeting, Herman made the Soviet-first-strike case rather too enthusiastically, presenting some speculative numbers of SU strength. Contrary to Council fiats, Nitze cited them elsewhere, Roger Hilsman used them at a public meeting in Washington, and they appeared in *The Washington Post* as a RAND forecast of Soviet capabilities. In consequence of "the Hilsman Leak" the Council made bad Paul sit in the corner for a year, and the wrath of Ike came down on RAND. The damage was irreparable.

After the usual jockeying for power, the President-elect selected an unobvious national-security apparatus. Nitze wanted to be Deputy Secretary of Defense, the number two slot in the Pentagon, usually the "Mr. Inside" who really administers the place, but was offered the post of National Security Adviser, which he turned down. He settled for ISA, the Pentagon's foreign office, the job Ike had reneged on—sweet revenge. The deputy secretaryship went to Roswell Gilpatric, a Wall Street lawyer of impeccable establishment connections and Air Force Undersecretary under Truman, when he had tried to broker the early air defense squabbles. The National Security Adviser was McGeorge Bundy, an academic politician of considerable skills, but with a thin résumé for the affairs under his charge. Any man of broad education can understand foreign policy, but defense requires considerable detailed knowledge, particularly of technology. His assistant was W. W. Rostow of MIT. One of the staffers was the economist Carl Kaysen, who wrote on passive defense for Project Charles; part of Kaysen's brief was civil defense. The new presidential Science Adviser was Jerry Wiesner, who had been brought into the Kennedy circle by the Harvard law professor Abram Chayes, who himself got a State Department job. Never before in human history had academics occupied high national-security positions.

Other positions in the Building were filled by unobvious men.

The Director of Research and Engineering was unexpected—a young prodigy out of the Livermore Labs named Harold Brown. The top Pentagon job was quite a surprise. Although Robert S. McNamara was an automobile executive and a Republican, he fitted well in the Kennedy circle, who were also mostly nominal Republicans; the Kennedy people constituted a royal court, and McNamara was an accomplished courtier. He had started off as a Harvard professor before joining the Air Force during the war; had sold his services with the famed team of "whiz kids" to the Ford Motor Company, then the absolute monarchy of Henry II; and had elbowed his way to its presidency. Much has been made, for better or worse, of his "scientific management," mostly by people ignorant of the automobile industry. McNamara was purely and simply, from beginning to end, what they call in Detroit a "bean-counter": an accountant, a man who expects the numbers to add up, and who expresses initiative and creativity by making the numbers add up. Such men make fine controllers, but are rarely good salesmen or leaders, although McNamara certainly stood above most. And he was tormented by ambition—from Day One in D.C., he was running for Vice President.

During the transition, he was put in touch with Charlie Hitch, and was greatly impressed by RAND's rigorous analytical approach. So Hitch came in as the Pentagon controller, and good jobs were given to Harry Rowen and Alain Enthoven and to a few other RAND people. Wohlstetter was offered a post, but preferred to be a consultant, as did one of RAND's shrewdest minds, W. W. Kaufmann, who had fled to MIT but among other duties edited McNamara's exquisitely lucid annual Posture Statements. Still, too much has been made of the preeminence of RAND in the Department of Defense in those days. While the RAND style and approach had great influence and while certain RAND hobbyhorses—especially passive defenses—were ridden hard, RAND-type thinking should not be blamed for what finally fermented in McNamara's Pentagon.

One of the odder DoD appointments was an earnest young lawyer named Adam Yarmolinsky, who had no experience whatever in defense matters. He had been slated for a job in HEW, but the Secretary-designate thought it ethnically imprudent that Ribicoff be backed up by Yarmolinsky. He was a Kennedy loyalist right down the line, so perhaps that is why he was placed in the Pentagon as a political troubleshooter, and as a political commissar to keep an eye on the people over there, none of whom totally belonged to the Kennedys. On the transition team, Yarmolinsky's job was filling jobs. One responsibility was finding a civil defense director. Herman Kahn, then knowing that his exit from RAND was inevitable, offered himself for the job by sending a copy of his recently published *On Thermonuclear War*. This unique manner of soliciting a post certainly attracted bemused attention, but Herman did not get the appointment. It might have been amusing to see what would have happened; but as Yarmolinsky pointed out, newly elected administrations have many political debts to pay, mostly to people of mediocre quality, so there need to be jobs in the government suitable to be harmlessly filled by political hacks. The civil defense job was just such a post. Yarmolinsky's Rule required that it go to a man named Frank Ellis, who had done something or other to deliver some key convention delegation to Kennedy—perhaps Louisiana or wherever; it does not matter. He was nobody, because civil defense was nothing and nowhere.

Except for those who lost their jobs in the turnover, the serious people in the Business were delighted. In response to their campaign promises to bolster America's presumably cloudy defense posture, the McNamara crew quickly pushed through an increased budget allocation for strengthening the strategic forces. The Minuteman and Polaris programs were accelerated. A substantial portion of SAC was put on airborne alert.

## McNamara Shoots Down the Air Force

Although a billion and a half was added to the defense budget for Fiscal Year 1962, the reprogramming was mostly financed by cuts elsewhere. Two squadrons of the Air Force's Snark intercontinental cruise missile had just entered the inventory. They were at the same time slow, inaccurate, vulnerable to attack, and expensive to maintain; McNamara hunted the Snark out of existence. A plan to defend the forthcoming Minuteman missile by making it mobile—which actually progressed to shuttling dummies around the West on railroad cars—was scrubbed in favor of silo hardening. And the nuclear-powered airplane, which had been the *raison d'être* of the founding of the RAND physics department and which had burned over a billion in research money, was at long last terminated.

None of these deletions were mourned, but one item was a stake in the heart of the Air Force. McNamara killed the B-70 program. B-70 was to be the superbomber—supersonic, flying at 70,000 feet, capable of intercontinental range. This was where the Air Force saw its future. But the plane had been designed like the contemporary 1950s interceptors, to maximize speed, so nothing could be hung on the outside of it. The B-70 could only drop bombs, not carry the air-to-ground missiles that were already being fitted to the B-52s to stand off beyond range of Soviet antiaircraft defenses.

Belatedly, the Air Force tried to repair this drawback by relabeling the beast the *RS*-70—"reconnaissance-strike"—and gave it the mission of cruising over the Soviet Union following initial U.S. strikes to identify and to hit anything that might be left. This role required radars that could distinguish targets from 70,000 feet at Mach 3 in a nuclear-war environment. Some people were convinced that this capability was within the state of the art, but apparently no one who was not wearing a light blue suit. Except for some further development money, because the prototypes had almost been completed, the B-70 was scrubbed, and McNamara earned thereby the undying, intense, total enmity of the Air Force.

Worse was yet to come. The following year, McNamara shattered the Skybolt, the air-launched ballistic missile that was to extend the life of the manned bomber. Not understanding why the Air Force and the Navy both needed to develop similar tactical aircraft, he ordered a shoot-out between the F-106 and the Navy's latest fighter. Since World War II, McDonnell had been apprenticing with such efforts as the F-101; with the F-4H, the company produced its masterpiece, the greatest fighter that ever was. The Air Force was whipped at the start. And it also was obliged to accept the Navy's Sparrow and Sidewinder air-to-air missiles.

Furthermore, the Air Force had been remiss in ground attack, so McNamara stuffed the Navy's Vought A7U down its throat. And he killed the Dynasoar, which was to fly the Air Force out to space. To be sure, on the debit side was the TFX debacle—but that did not become evident until much later. And the belt-buckle battle provoked by an inane attempt to impose a single buckle on all military uniforms was a harbinger of the malignant effects of number-crunching gone cancerous. But almost everything that Mc-Namara and company did to the Air Force was unexceptionable.

Now, he could not have been able to scourge the Air Force without the scorpions of RAND. They knew where all the sky-blue bodies were buried. Had they been Navy analysts, perhaps McNamara might have sunk as many ships as he shot down airplanes. The Air Force was not appreciative. Its rancor especially turned on Alain Enthoven, soon to be the Assistant Secretary for Systems Analysis, doubtless provoked by his cool, confident—some said arrogant—style, but perhaps exacerbated by his tall, erect, long-striding physique, right out of *Steve Canyon*. Had he not sold his soul to the civilian Satan, what a superb Air Force officer he would have been!

The Air Force was thrown a bone: Curtis LeMay was made Chief of Staff—the better to keep an eye on him.

## The McNamara Defense

On continental air defense, the McNamara crew maintained the general freeze imposed by the late Eisenhower administration. They read the same numbers about the shift of Soviet priorities from bombers to missiles. Enthoven had worked on SAGE at RAND and knew its weaknesses. But the last Eisenhower program was tolerable for the nonce. Even the discredited Bomarc was left in service—on the grounds that it cost only $20 million per year for operations and would draw enemy fire. And the replacement of the Nike-Ajax by the Hercs was completed on schedule.

The principal initial emphasis of the McNamara defense was purely Albertine—defense of the strategic offensive forces; defending the deterrent. The Navy's missile submarines were promoted, as were the hardened ICBMs. Minuteman shortly was successfully tested, and the hardened silos begun. Unhardened missiles, some of them deployed for only a few months, were already obsolete. As the Corps of Engineers dug holes in the ground in North Dakota, South Dakota, Montana, Wyoming, and Missouri; as the silos were poured and wired, the crews trained, and the missiles and their warheads carefully inserted and capped with concrete, the Atlases and the Titan Is were taken out of service (not to be wasted, because they were used to launch satellites and, as we shall see, to make flights to destruction across the Pacific Missile Test Range).

However, the hardening of command and control was treated more gingerly. The McNamara Pentagon looked again at the RAND concept of a deep underground command post for SAC, and concluded that the costs had been underestimated. A better idea was more congenial to SAC and the Air Force: a flying command post—a real airplane, a converted Boeing KC-135 tanker which a SAC general could fly himself to earn his flight pay while deterring the next war. It was named Looking Glass, and it still flies. It isn't cheap, but it seemed to be cheaper and more survivable than SUC. So SUC was sacked.

Another passive defense casualty was the Deep Underground Command Center (DUCC—"duck"). The Fort Ritchie alternative command center was designed for the nuclear-bomber age, not the thermonuclear-missile age. The high command would not be able to relocate fast enough to escape incoming ICBMs. The planned solution was to dig an enormous cavern thousands of feet under the Potomac, with tunnels down from the White House and the Pentagon. The cost would have been considerable; the politicians feared adverse public reaction to such elaborate measures for protecting themselves; and the Air Force was negative on the ground that survival of the government would be an impediment to war-fighting. General LeMay is alleged to have said, "What could those poor dumb bastards do in a nuclear war?"

McNamara did break the freeze on the Cheyenne Mountain project, and the digging began in 1961. Tunnels were driven into the rock from either side, and a great cavern chopped in the heart of the mountain. Because a strong blast would generate powerful shock waves, the entire interior structure had to be cushioned against the resulting vibration. A small city was built inside Cheyenne Mountain cushioned by springs. In the tunnels were blast doors to be closed in the event of emergency. The digging went on until 1966, when the complex was declared ready for operation.

At that time Herman, gone from RAND for several years to form his own Hudson Institute, visited NORAD headquarters. He was shown the result of the concepts of his colleagues. He was suitably impressed. But with one demurrer: "You put it in the mountain; you should of put it *under* the mountain." In the interim between concept and construction, the accuracy of ICBMs had greatly improved. When completed, Cheyenne Mountain was vulnerable to attack. A ground burst could knock it out. NORAD's Combat Operations Center had an Achilles' heel; Herman knew how to fix it, but he and his colleagues had left RAND, so no one was left to lean on the system. To be sure, a backup command position was located elsewhere, but it was no more secure.

## The Defenders Branch Out

Obviously, people in the air defense business had to find other lines of work. As we shall see, the Army's air defense consultants found another cause. Ed Barlow of RAND went over to the Aerospace Corporation and worked the offense. Jim Digby, who was suspected by Wiesner of leaking PSAC findings, took deep cover and headed for Europe, where SAGE was to be imitated by NADGE—NATO Air Defense Ground Environment. A little later in the '60s came BADGE—Base Air Defense Ground Environment, for Japan. MITRE worked on all these projects—littering the Free World with little SAGEs.

But MITRE found a better function. A principal reason for SAGE was sorting out the hostiles, the friendlies, and the normal civil aircraft. The advent of Boeing's jet airliners triggered an explosion of civil air traffic and a need to watch over it. So MITRE found itself serving the Federal Aviation Administration and advising on shifting SAGE over to the FAA's radars, computers, and tracking consoles for air-traffic control.

Better yet was a shift in emphasis at Bedford. What was SAGE generically? Was it not a means of commanding and controlling interceptors and SAMs? Air Power could not send messages by runner or jeep. MITRE was willing and able to advise the Air Force how to command and control* everything everywhere.

## Nike-Zeus Fights On

The Army was delighted with the change of administration. After all, had not the Kennedy people taken up what was essentially the

---

*Was not command and control a form of communication? The terms command, control, and communications were combined into "C³" ("see-cubed") by Richard B. Foster of Stanford Research Institute, an air defense specialist and close collaborator of Bell Labs who was en route to becoming the Army's principal strategic adviser.

Army's line? Was not Max Taylor right there in the White House as the "military representative" of the President? After his resignation as Chief of Staff, General Taylor complained, "I view the coming years, the next two to five years, let us say, with very great concern. I feel that we will have to do better than we have in order to close the missile gap. By the missile gap I don't simply mean the deficiency in numbers of our operational missiles, but our entire missile system, to include protective devices, particularly the anti-missile missile requirement." Had not Kennedy himself, addressing the Senate, quoted General Gavin's complaint that "our defensive missile capabilities will lag behind" the Soviets', and argued that "our continental defense system . . . must be redesigned for the detection and interception of missile attacks as well as planes"?

The Army laid it on for Nike-Zeus. In January of 1961, the Army orchestrated the first successful ballistic missile intercept. The missile-killer was not Nike-Zeus; it was not yet ready to emerge from the labors of Bell Labs and Douglas. As a proxy, as a demonstration, an Honest John short-range ballistic missile was intercepted by, of all things, a Hawk, a low-level air defense missile. This was accomplished at the White Sands Proving Ground. The Army took films of the event and released them to television news. Alas, the Hawk did not make a head-on intercept of the Honest John, but nailed it from the side; the speed was too fast for the eye to follow, so at the point of impact the Army slowed down the film so that the Hawk could be seen drifting across the path of the dropping Honest John. When this was shown on television, David Brinkley casually mentioned that the Army had doctored the film.

Later in the year, the Army used a Nike-Herc to intercept another Nike-Herc dropping down at White Sands. This sounds irrelevant to ballistic missile defense, but remember how slow were the short-range ballistic missiles of the time. Herc, with its command guidance, could be ordered to turn over and dive faster under power than any other missile then available to be used as a target.* Ballistic missile intercepts were demonstrated to be possible. But it must be noted that neither of those missiles was dropping at ICBM speeds. Hitting

---

*Indeed, this feature gave the Nike-Hercules deployed with the field armies in Europe and Korea dual capability as antiaircraft weapons and as surface-to-surface missiles; in the secondary role, the missile is commanded out to the limit of its range, and then it falls in a ballistic trajectory.

a bullet with a bullet is not too difficult if you know where the bullet is dropping and if it is not going frightfully fast.

The Army mobilized its public relations apparatus. A major campaign was organized through the Association of the United States Army, the private lobby organized in the 1950s to counter the long-established Navy League and the enthusiastic and effective Air Force Association. The Army itself was producing Nike-Zeus materials. The push attracted Kennedy's attention, and also his annoyance. Despite Maxwell Taylor's efforts, McNamara and his Pentagon colleagues were no more impressed by the prospects for Nike-Zeus than were their Eisenhower predecessors. They were intimately familiar with RAND's skepticism about BMD. Nonetheless, in the fall of 1961, McNamara formally requested authorization for production and deployment of Nike-Zeus. The draft FY63 budget proposed that the United States begin to build an anti–ballistic missile defense system. The proposal was rather less than enthusiastic. The deployment was to begin in 1967, at the very end of the five-year budget cycle, as late as it could be and still be in the budget. The numbers also were as small as possible—1,200 missiles in 12 batteries defending 6 cities. The request offered no hope of blocking an ICBM barrage, merely offering arguments for secondary benefits of limited deployment.

But even a token deployment of Nike-Zeus was excessive for the White House. The Budget Bureau knew full well that a limited deployment would be the camel's nose in the tent. Six cities were defended—would the hundreds of other cities remain naked? The Army had requested 3,500 missiles defending 27 cities. And when the proposal came over the river from the Building, the administration was embroiled in another defense flap. And Zeus had an inherited enemy in Wiesner, the Science Adviser. To persuade the President, McNamara sent over the Army's civilian research chief together with Harold Brown and ARPA's Jack Ruina—who transmitted a mixed message. In any event, the Kennedy administration was interested initially in quick fixes, and Nike-Zeus, even with the most ambitious crash program, could not be on board for several years.

So Nike-Zeus lost again; but the Army did not lose. "Flexible response" meant more troops, tanks, and guns for the Army. Furthermore, Kennedy—perhaps excessively influenced by the plethora of ex-OSS types around him or by romantic recollections of his own experiences as very-small-unit commander of a patrol torpedo boat— was entranced by the potential for countering Communist insurgency with imaginative and highly trained elite forces. This too was grist for the Army.

The Kennedy-McNamara emphasis on conventional and unconventional warfare took much wind out of the sails of Nike-Zeus. For insofar as Nike-Zeus was part of the Army's response to the strategic-warfare emphasis of the Eisenhower days, a movement toward a more balanced posture, the sort of posture the Army itself had proposed, eroded Army interest in the strategic role. But making too much of this factor would be unwise, at least circa 1961. The issues can never ignore politics, but with Nike-Zeus, and as we shall see, with ABM in general, it was the technology factors that drove the decisions. The most devoted supporters of Nike-Zeus, from Maxwell Taylor on, did not maintain that it was an effective system, much less a cost-effective system, but that it was: 1) something with some promise; and 2) the only system we had—even if its best estimated performance was a 25 percent kill of incomings one at a time, firing two anti-missiles at each ICBM.

For ballistic missile defense, the McNamara team did endorse the BMEWS deployment to the north. The massive 4,800-mile-range RCA radars at Thule in Greenland and Clear in Alaska were completed in 1961, and the third unit, at Fylingdales Moor in Yorkshire, was in service the following year. For the time being *at least,* a few minutes' early warning was to be all the defense against ICBMs.

More important, a system of even earlier warning went operational in 1961. The first reconnaissance satellites disgorged their film to the waiting transports poised to pluck the parachuted canisters from the skies. The photos showed fairly conclusively what most intelligence analysts had expected: not only were there not the large numbers of Soviet bombers, but the supposed ICBMs were sparse. In retrospect, the Soviet IRBM choice seems singularly sensible, because, all things being equal, accuracy in ballistic missilery decreases with range. And it seems as certain as any of these "black" matters can be that the Soviets were at that time far behind the United States in the all-important technology of guidance.

That was extremely good news, but it was also decidedly bad news. The Soviets lacked the strategic superiority that some trembling folk of the late '50s had feared, but they did have enough to do terrible damage to the United States. While the first recon satellites had picked up a corporal's guard of ICBMs sitting exposed and easily killable, no one thought that was all the missiles there ever would be.

## John Kennedy's Strategic Defense Initiative

Worse, in 1961, a crisis broke over Berlin. The Problem reappeared in all its ugly ramifications: anytime they wanted, the Soviets could swallow West Berlin in a gulp, and what was America to do about it? What good was our strategic superiority if they could strike back and there were no defenses? With weak continental air defenses and nonexistent ballistic missile defenses, the Kennedy administration turned toward the only available means of bolstering America's strategic defenses.

The original Kennedy quick-fix strategic program was announced in March 1961. It failed to mention civil defense at all, nor is there any record of the President's having paid careful attention to it. He was shortly made aware of this omission. Frank Ellis may have been a political hack, but he was an energetic one. He began to proselytize with evangelical vigor, even planning a trip to Rome to persuade the Pope to support the installation of fallout shelters in all church basements. And Congressman Chet Holifield leaned on the President. And Stuart Symington proposed that all the reserve forces of the United States, including the National Guard, be combined in a single formation, and that civil defense be made one of its missions.

On the White House staff, Carl Kaysen did a quick and dirty study of civil defense and argued that the current program was entirely out of date and that spending more money as in the past would be a waste, so "the United States should either face up to the problem in a serious way or forget it."

Many people think that a greater influence was Nelson Rockefeller, who visited the Pentagon and the White House in early 1961 to make a pitch for civil defense. Politically astute observers will note that it may not have been that Rockefeller was so persuasive, but that he was the most probable Republican presidential candidate in the next election. Rocky made a pitch for CD at a governors' conference in early May, backed up by Oscar Reubhausen, and supported by the Democratic governor of South Carolina, Fritz Hollings. Whatever the reason, in May the President sent a second appeal to the Congress to reprogram the 1962 budget. The most famous elements were a plan for tax cuts and a commitment to send an American to the Moon. Hardly noticed among those big stories was this section:

> One major element of the national security program which this Nation has never squarely faced up to is civil defense. This problem arises not from present trends but from past inaction. In the past decade we have intermittently considered a variety of programs, but we have never adopted a consistent policy. Public considerations have been largely characterized by apathy, indifference, and skepticism; while, at the same time, many of the civil defense plans proposed have been so far reaching or unrealistic that they have not gained essential support.
>
> This administration has been looking very hard at exactly what civil defense can and cannot do. It cannot be obtained cheaply. It cannot give an insurance of blast protection that will be proof against a surprise attack or guarantee against obsolescence or destruction. And it cannot deter a nuclear attack.
>
> We will deter an enemy from making a nuclear attack only if our retaliatory power is strong and so invulnerable that he knows he would be destroyed by our response. If we have that strength, civil defense is not needed to deter an attack. If we should ever lack it, civil defense would not be an adequate substitute.
>
> But this deterrent concept assumes rational calculations by rational men. And the history of this planet is sufficient to remind us of the possibilities of an irrational attack, a miscalculation, an accidental war which cannot be either foreseen or deterred. The nature of modern warfare heightens these possibilities. It is on this basis that civil defense can readily be justified—as insurance for the civil population in the event of such a miscalculation. It is insurance we trust will never be needed—but insurance which we could never forgive ourselves for forgoing in the event of catastrophe.

Note the express rejection of the strategic implications of civil defense and the concentration merely upon insurance—if deterrence fails. This may have been a prudent thing for the President to say, but no one who knew anything about the situation and the program—neither its supporters nor its opponents—believed there was no strategic intent. The Kennedy program was described as "the initiation of a nationwide long-range program of identifying present fallout-shelter capacity and providing shelter in new and existing structures." Federal funds would be needed. The proposed shelter program provided: "where appropriate, incorporation of shelter in Federal buildings, new requirements for shelter in buildings constructed with Federal financial assistance, and matching grants and other incentives for constructing shelter in State and local government and private buildings. . . . [T]o assure effective use of these shelters, additional measures will be required for warning, training, and radiological monitoring, and stockpiling of food and medicines." The announcement to Congress indicated an intention to switch the bulk of the civil defense apparatus to the Defense Department. The existing agency would be reconstituted as a small staff agency known as the Office of Emergency Planning (OEP—"oh-ee-pea"), which would advise the President, engage in long-range planning, and at least initially deal with the issues of stockpiling and postattack recovery. Ellis was being shunted aside. He resisted as long as he could, surrendered gracefully, and was paid off with a federal judgeship. Over in Defense, civil defense was seen as primarily a political matter and therefore was assigned to Adam Yarmolinsky, who was faced with the immediate problem of staffing the effort.

Initially, nothing was actually done. No legislation was offered to Congress, no actual reorganization was accomplished, and no additional funds were expended. But international events intruded. In June, Kennedy met Khrushchev in Vienna, and it is widely reported that the Soviet boss was not favorably impressed by the young President. This is conjectural, but the best analysts of the Soviet governing class argue persuasively that the Soviet system generates, promotes, and highly values iron personal self-control; to Khrushchev, Kennedy certainly seemed to be a dissolute playboy, not a serious person, someone who could and should be pushed.

During the summit and afterward, Khrushchev insisted that the Berlin issue must be resolved by the end of the year. To show his earnestness, in July the Soviet Party leader announced that he had cancelled previous plans to cut his armed forces by a third, and instead would increase them by a third. New combat aircraft were displayed at Moscow the following day, including a new bomber.

Kennedy was hard pressed by insiders, particularly by Dean Acheson, that the United States was now entering a grave crisis, a thorough test of its resolve, and that Kennedy had to face up to it. On 25 July the President addressed the nation on television, and told of the Berlin threats and his rejection of the Khrushchev ultimatum. He announced an expansion of the armed forces, costing $3.5 billion, and:

> Tomorrow, I am requesting of the Congress new funds for the following immediate objectives: to identify and mark space in existing structures—public and private—that could be used for fallout shelters in case of attack; to stock those shelters with food, water, first-aid kits, tools, sanitation facilities, and other minimum essentials for survival; to increase their capacity; to improve our air-raid warning and fallout detection systems, including a new household warning system now under development; and to take other measures that would be effective at an early date to save millions of lives if needed. In addition, new federal buildings will include space suitable for fallout shelters, as well as normal use. In the event of an attack, the lives of those families which are not hit in a nuclear blast and fire can still be saved if they can be warned to take shelter and if that shelter is available. We owe that kind of insurance to families, and to our country . . .
>
> The time to start is now. In the coming months, I hope to let every citizen know what steps he can take without delay to protect his family in case of an attack. I know you would not want to do less.

The crisis developed dangerously. At the beginning of July, Air Force reservists were alerted for a possible recall to active duty. A week later, Khrushchev announced that Soviet reserves were being called up. Two days later, he escalated the rhetoric: "If you want to threaten us from a position of strength, we will show you our strength. You do not have 50 and 100 megaton bombs. We have stronger than 100 megaton bombs." And in the middle of August Khrushchev showed that he was not all bluff. Soviet armored divisions ringed West Berlin and gave cover to the East German security forces to begin to seal off the city. If the President's intention was to terrify the country, he was eminently successful. There was heated charge and countercharge by the two superpowers, and

Khrushchev made his point by resuming nuclear testing. After a warm-up of a mere 30 megatons, the Soviet boast of having 50-megaton weapons was made good in October. The American garrison in Europe was reinforced and the alert status of U.S. forces raised. But the crisis seemed to taper off when Khrushchev told the Communist Party Congress the Soviets would end their nuclear-test series, and let slip the end-of-year deadline for signing a German peace treaty on Russian terms.

## The Balloon Goes Up

As Kennedy's speech writer, Theodore Sorenson, put it in his court biography, "the President's aim was to bestir a still slumbering public; and it succeeded beyond his own expectations and desire. The civil defense 'balloon' not only went up, it disappeared from sight." The civil defense office was swamped with queries for information on building family fallout shelters and stockpiling food. The daily requests exceeded the monthly requests before the crisis. A public-opinion survey indicated that nearly two-thirds of the population said it had read federal CD literature. Loans for fallout-shelter financing by the Federal Housing Agency increased.

The private sector was not inactive. The sales of existing legitimate producers of protection devices such as radiation dosimeters went haywire. And unscrupulous operators were eager to pander to the public's inflamed taste for disaster. Among the scams was the mail-order offer of "survival shelters," which turned out to be a crowbar and instructions on how to lift manhole covers. Another operator sold a "man sized fallout bag" that would protect you from a limited amount of fallout, if you didn't suffocate inside. A truly ingenious hustler peddled radiation salve that would presumably repel gamma rays. Chet Holifield's House committee warned the public to beware of "fly-by-night operators with shelter-building schemes and would-be sellers of expensive or useless gadgets. . . . do not sign a contract for construction of a home shelter until you have consulted civil defense officials in your city. . . ." There were rumors of vigilante groups arming in the hinterlands to repulse the swarms of refugees that might flee the great cities. Right by Bell Labs in respectable Nutley, New Jersey, the local civil defense organization urged every

American to provide fallout protection for his family and cast doubt upon the patriotism of anyone who failed to do so.

The press hopped on board. McGraw-Hill ran a sixteen-page supplement, "Nuclear Attack and Industrial Survival," in its esteemed trade journals such as *Aviation Week* and *Oil and Gas Journal*. The most influential single voice on the civil defense front was Henry Luce's *Life* magazine, which stated casually that with fallout shelters, 97 percent of the population would survive a nuclear war. (True enough, in "a" nuclear war in which the Soviets did not attack the cities.) This optimistic forecast was preceded by a letter to the readers written specially for the issue by President Kennedy.

Congress was flooded with legislation, constructive and crackpot. After dragging their feet on civil defense for so long, the solons finally moved, but not very fast. The original 1962 civil defense bill presented in the spring had asked for $104 million; the House had slashed this to $79 million; after the crisis began, the Senate approved $95 million. The final compromise was $86 million—well above the previous year's budget, but still short of what the administration had requested before the crisis erupted. Nonetheless, the stampede was on. On 26 July, after his speech, the President asked for a supplemental appropriation of $208 million. Many congressmen were dubious, especially because the program had been given the most cavalier justification by the administration. Congressman Gerald Ford of Michigan was among the skeptics. Nonetheless, in the crisis the bill passed easily, and Kennedy signed it into law in August.

Chet Holifield helped matters along by holding additional hearings on civil defense to remind people what it was all about. McNamara, General Lemnitzer, Chairman of the Joint Chiefs of Staff, Yarmolinsky, Ellis, Jerry Strope, and Herman Kahn testified. No one against civil defense was heard by Holifield; only a few crackpot opponents were permitted to insert statements in the appendix to the committee's report. McNamara made a characteristically informed and comprehensive pitch for the program. The administration had a very thin civil defense in mind. The bulk of the funds was to survey the country to locate and mark existing shelter spaces—not to build shelters, just to label existing facilities that would be of some use, better, it was hoped, than nothing at all. These were to be marked with what became the familiar black-and-yellow shelter signs. About $60 million was for some minimal storage of equipment, food, water, tools, first aid, sanitation kits, and a stock of dosimeters (radiation meters) for the inhabitants to inform themselves of the levels of danger inside and out.

The official policy did not mention what Kennedy had told the nation about the provision of family fallout shelters. That would be off budget. In mid-August, Ellis told the National Association of County Officials that it was "the Christian thing to do, the Godlike thing," to provide your family a fallout shelter, while failure to do so constituted the "sin" of suicide. McNamara told a newscaster that "most importantly it's the responsibility of each individual to prepare himself and his family for that strike." The President's promise to tell every family what-to-do had to be met, so the new civil defense office in the Pentagon was given the job of turning out yet another booklet about civil defense. It was written by bureaucrats at Battle Creek, whose names have been expunged from the historical record, doubtless to their relief. Not only did the shelter program seem to be aimed entirely at the upper middle classes (as noted by John Kenneth Galbraith, with "a picture of a family with a cabin cruiser saving itself by going out to sea"), but the overall tone of the manual was bubblingly upbeat. It made nuclear war seem like a hike along the Appalachian Trail. The President's court historian, Arthur Schlesinger, Jr., personally had to edit the draft into a reasonably balanced account of the difficulties to be faced in a nuclear attack.

If civil defense was to be a presidential priority, the top CD post was no longer a job for a hack. Yarmolinsky was temporarily placed in charge of the program, while a permanent chief was sought. An approach was made to Oscar Ruebhausen, a New York lawyer and a Rockefeller link to the establishment liberal Democrats, who had lost a turf fight in the Rocky court to Henry Kissinger and had been posted by Nelson to the outlying civil defense beat. Ruebhausen had written the New York State civil defense plan which had failed to pass muster in the legislature. By obtaining Ruebhausen, the administration would gain a competent and well-connected man— and would defuse attacks by Rockefeller. But Reubhausen wouldn't bite. Yarmolinsky scratched his head and recalled that a few months earlier, a member of his dinner discussion club had held forth on the subject of personal survival; well, that was sort of like civil defense.

Steuart Pittman seemed perfect for the Kennedy team. The Steuarts had obtained land in Maryland in the early 1700s, which their Pittman descendants still held. Steuart was born with a silver spoon stuck deep in his throat—St. Paul's School, Yale, Harvard Law School—and acquired the most gorgeous upper-class New York accent. He was rather a sportsman and bred a large family. In every way, it is hard to imagine a man more representative of the better elements of his class. During the war he had been a Marine officer and had been put ashore on the south China coast to make it hot for the Japanese. "I always had a soft spot for terrorists," he said, having been one himself. After hearing on the radio of the Japanese surrender, Pittman's party commandeered a junk and sailed north for Shanghai to celebrate victory among the fleshpots of civilization. En route they encountered a Japanese armed junk unaware of the termination of hostilities. A firefight followed, and Pittman's crew boarded the enemy behind a barrage of hand grenades. Lieutenant Steuart Pittman, USMCR, was victorious in the final naval engagement of World War II.

After the war he returned to the practice of law, held some interesting jobs with the foreign-aid office, and joined the elite law firm of Cravath, Swaine and Moore, where he was sufficiently well regarded to earn the endorsement of Roswell Gilpatric, McNamara's deputy SecDef. Pittman was given the title of Assistant Secretary of Defense for Civil Defense, and the rest of his team was filled in by men of decent political caliber. His number two, William Durkee, was from the Agency. For advice on the research chief, Yarmolinsky called up Herman Kahn, who recommended Jerry Strope, who was immediately appointed. (With Strope gone, and with research now under his auspices at the Office of Civil Defense, the Naval Radiological Defense Laboratory was considered superfluous and failed to survive McNamara's installation cuts in the mid-'60s.)

Cool, gracious, and a quick learner, Pittman quickly endeared himself to his staff, and became, perhaps because of the increased funding, the most highly regarded civil defense chief there ever was—which is not intended to be damning with the faintest possible praise.

## The Stalling of Civil Defense

Many, if not most, of the White House staff had been wary of the civil defense thrust from the first. They were courtiers, and their king had willed the program, so they were obliged to execute it. Yet they could also drag their feet, snipe, and intrigue to reverse the policy. In November 1961, Kennedy met his advisers at the family compound at Hyannis Port to make a final determination as to what the civil defense program should be. McNamara was there, with Bundy, Attorney General Robert Kennedy, Carl Kaysen, and Jerome Wiesner. Arthur Schlesinger, Jr., had brought along an elaborate memorandum arguing that some shelters, especially community shelters, were desirable, yet were no panacea for nuclear war (a claim no one had ever made), and the administration had opened a political Pandora's box. Wiesner said fallout shelters would be obsolete in five years. (This was when the Air Force was digging in its ICBMs and the Soviets were expanding their ICBM force to root them out—and smother the nation with fallout.) Kennedy's speech writer Sorenson quoted his boss as saying, "I don't want the survivors, if there are any . . . to say we never warned them or never did anything to save at least some of their families while there was still time." Robert Kennedy was especially eager for civil defense.

To appease Wiesner, a panel on civil defense was set up under the auspices of his Presidential Scientific Advisory Council. The panel was rigged against civil defense from the start. But the White House staff made the mistake of appointing to it several people who understood the issues thoroughly, including Donald Ling of Bell Labs and Jim Digby and the economist Jack Hirshliefer of RAND. As was so often the case, when presented with the evidence, even people who approached civil defense skeptically could be persuaded if they had reasonably open minds and/or minimal intellectual standards. The Harvard chemist and arms-control activist Paul Doty was grudgingly brought on board—but the physicist Wolfgang Panofsky, although he could not counter the civil defense case, was adamantly opposed. The arguments for civil defense pushed the panel toward a recognition that, yes, modest investments in civil defense could have a rich payoff in lifesaving and national recovery in the event of nuclear war, should deterrence fail. And no one denied that there was at least some chance that deterrence would fail. These findings were reported back up, and may have had minor influence on policy. Disregarded for the traditional reasons was the suggestion that CD should be a military function. (This, by the way, was the last strategic gasp of PSAC; McNamara, Brown, and company plucked away its influence and returned defense policy to the Pentagon, where it belonged. Henceforth the organ of scientific counsel would be the Defense Science Board.)

The policy of emphasizing community shelters was forwarded gingerly. In the annual hearings for defense authorization early in 1962, McNamara laid out the program as consisting of three parts:

1. Carrying out the existing-shelter survey program;
2. A federal shelter incentive program, to create new spaces by means of new construction and modifications of existing structures;
3. Stimulation of private construction by the example of the shelters in federal buildings and technical assistance and information.

The shelter incentive program was intended to be restricted to nonprofit institutions, especially schools and hospitals. The civil defense office would pay up to $25 per shelter space, or $2.50 per square foot of actual cost, whichever was less. It was estimated that this subsidy would cover about 60 percent of actual costs. In other words, once again a major part of the cost of what were presumably national defense facilities was to be borne by the citizenry itself, not provided by the federal government, which was charged with "providing for the common defense." To be sure, it could be argued that people had incentives to save their own lives, but the budgetary considerations drove the funding level. The estimate for the next four years was $450 million a year, which would provide 100 million shelter spaces by 1967.

The Berlin Crisis was over. The Congress moved very slowly. In the House, the program was put into the hands of Congressman Albert Thomas ("doubting Thomas") of Texas, a longtime opponent, who made every effort to kill it. Thomas was open-minded enough to call in representatives of vocal anti–civil defense groups: the National Committee for a Sane Nuclear Policy, the Methodist Board of Christian Concerns, the Peace Research Institute, the

Quakers, and the Women's International League for Peace and Freedom. Except for the first, these were long-term promoters of peace through capitulation to worldwide socialism. The Senate was in no big hurry either. The opposition to the shelter program did not, for the most part, heed the rumblings from academia; rather, it reflected a combination of fatalism and a trust in the efficacy of our offensive forces to deal with The Problem. Lack of interest among America's allies was also noted. The House of Representatives cut the guts out of the bill.

The Senate at least allowed enough funding to continue the shelter marking, but was unwilling to provide for the shelter incentive program. Senator Alcott of Colorado was very vocal in favor of the program, and received strong support from Senators Humphrey and Symington, both longtime strategic defense adherents. Nonetheless, although the Senate voted almost $100 million more than the House, the compromise fell between the two, appropriating a mere $128 million, only a quarter of the administration's request.

Hardly noticed, the shelter survey went forward with deliberate speed. Thousands of civil engineers, hired through the Corps of Engineers and government arsenals and naval yards, wandered about America's cities identifying and marking fallout shelters in public and private buildings. The teams did "quick-and-dirty" surveys to see if a place seemed all right, checked off a few sheets, and provided a black-and-yellow marker of what it was and how many people might go in there. More elaborate evaluation would have been a waste of time and money; in a crisis, the public would determine for itself how many people would enter each shelter and what crowding they would endure. As for protection standards—well, any shelter was better than none at all. And although the administration had not bought the strategic argument for civil defense in its declaratory policy, anything plausibly identifiable as a shelter would be counted in the strategic balance. Almost all public officials and property owners were cooperative, and willing to devote space for the token survival supplies provided by the government.

## The Defenders' Kaffeeklatsch

A peripheral event of the great civil defense frenzy was the founding of the Hudson Institute. The tension between Herman Kahn and

Frank Collbohn, certainly exacerbated by Air Force pressure, although not directed at Herman personally, on the RAND management, led to a final split early in 1961. The catalytic events were twofold: the new Kennedy administration was receptive to elaborate analysis of military issues; and Herman fell in with Max Singer, an eager young lawyer who was a consultant to RAND. A family friend of the Singers' was Oscar Ruebhausen, Rockefeller's man. An anonymous donation by T. J. Watson, Jr., of IBM provided seed money. Charlie Zracket of MITRE provided the first contract. But the major funding was to come from Jerry Strope in the fledgling Pentagon civil defense office. The Hudson Institute was to be the RAND of civil defense.

Herman had to recruit a staff. Few from RAND were willing to abandon the beaches of Santa Monica for such a risky endeavor on the Hudson. Only William Brown came east. After he bankrupted his family firm, Bob Panero came on board. Herman gathered a new group. One of them was the amazing Frank Armbruster, a true proletarian intellectual, a railroad fireman who discovered from the Army tests that he was a genius. After the war he got a college degree on the GI bill and became an operations analyst for Boeing (Bomarc) and ITT (ARPA BMD). Because he had been a railroad man, he investigated evacuating cities by train and found that the railroads had enormous capacity, which would permit the evacuation of the poorer people who lacked automobiles. Hudson conceived of marshaling passenger and freight cars to transport the refugees by the tens of thousands. The railroad cars also offered a nice bonus in providing shelter from the elements, and even some shelter from fallout. It was a pretty scheme. Nothing came of it.

Another marvelous character was Cresson Kearny, a Texan who had gone to Princeton in the '30s, taught jungle survival school in Panama as a junior officer, served with the OSS in China, and worked as a geologist in the West in the great uranium search of the '40s and '50s. Impressed by *On Thermonuclear War,* he had approached Herman and was recognized as an asset. Kearny's specialty was not government programs, fancy plans, or advanced technology, but means of simple survival: How does an individual maximize his chances of riding out a nuclear attack? How exactly do you build a shelter? What do you do after evacuating a city, or climbing out of a shelter into an unknown and dangerous environment? Kearny was devout about his preachments; while living in a nearby motel, he dug his own fallout shelter back in the woods.

As his number two, Herman brought in Donald Brennan of Lincoln Labs, a leader in the arms-control agitation of the late '50s. Among others, Brennan recruited the young mathematician Jeremy J. Stone (son of the fellow-traveling journalist Izzy Stone, who wrote a blistering attack on the vicious influence of Herman Kahn while Jay was his employee). Jay Stone worked on railroad evacuation with Frank Armbruster. So another major source of funding was the Arms Control and Disarmament Agency, where the Hudson people dealt with a research bureaucrat named Richard J. Barnet.

The Hudson people also put together materials in ways that hadn't been done before. A very literate paper was written for ACDA about the interrelation between arms control and civil defense, which actually said that there was very little interaction, but the real point was that civil defense was a pacific measure. And Brennan suggested that the U.S. and U.S.S.R. should cooperate on civil defense—a bad idea, because cooperation meant sharing of information useful for the offense to overcome the defense. None of this research, nor any of the other civil defense research conduced by SRI and other contractors, ever amounted to anything at all, although it was intelligent and competent.

A lot more significant was the achievement of one of Herman's principal reasons for establishing his institute. He wished to initiate an educational program—not for the masses, but for the "decision makers," "analytical community," and other advisers and staff types—in how to think about thermonuclear war, other high-level military issues, and national policy issues in general. Such a program had been set up at RAND, but was necessarily constipated by too much internal bureaucracy and the steadily tightening Air Force censorship. In 1962, Herman started his seminar courses for paying guests, for invited serious guests, and for assorted freeloaders who attracted the generous patron's attention. Herman was the star attraction; with his supporting cast of briefers, he would lay out the discussion of issues of interest, always including strategic defense—initially passive defense, and as the '60s progressed, active defense as well. Because RAND had been overrun by the barbarians, Hudson was to be the Second Rome of strategic defense.

Further, the founders of Hudson created "fellow members," sort of proxy shareholders of the nonprofit corporation, who had no function except presumably to elect trustees, but who all knew that the place was really Herman's personal proprietorship. These people were garnered from Herman's cronies and acquaintances, ranging from Teller on the right to the radical cleric A. J. Muste on the left, but with a pronounced loading of what Herman referred to as the "responsible center," his catchall term encompassing liberal conservatives and conservative liberals who were concerned about the national defense, especially about strategic defense. So the list included Ruebhausen, Don Ling of Bell Labs, W. W. Kaufmann, Roger Fisher, Paul Doty, Fred Ikle, Wohlstetter, Weidlinger, Wigner, Freeman Dyson, the German Helmut Schmidt, the Frenchman André Beaufré, Charlie Zracket of MITRE, Bob Sprague (a trustee, major contributor, and fund-raiser), William T. Golden, Jack Hirshleifer, Zbigniew Brzezinski, Charlie Adams of Raytheon, William A. M. Burden, and later, after they left office, Adam Yarmolinsky, Pittman (later a trustee), Charles Herzfeld, and Johnny Foster. The fellow members could attend any seminars, and had an annual meeting of their own. The Hudson Institute became a kaffeeklatsch for strategic defense and was to remain so until Herman's demise.

## The Defenders Dig In

Congressional opponents of the shelter program charged that a damning indictment was that its administration adherents had no shelters of their own. Most of them had just moved to Washington, and either had shelters where they worked or lived so close in that fallout shelters would have been worthless, or hadn't yet had time to harden their new country homes. The White House and the Pentagon had (and still have) World War II air-raid shelters, futile against nuclear blast, but more than adequate to deal with fallout. Paul Nitze had a well-equipped shelter on his farm, complete with a footstool cover stitched by the wife of Chip Bohlen, the ambassador to the U.S.S.R. Steuart Pittman also fitted his Maryland farm with a shelter for his large family. During the RAND study, it had also been charged that none of the principals had provided themselves with shelters—but Jim Digby had a shelter, as did the house

Charlie Hitch sold to Jack Hirshleifer when he joined the McNamara team. When he came to Washington, Jerry Strope built a state-of-the-art shelter in his Virginia home.

Herman almost got a shelter too. When he came east in 1961 to set up his own think tank, John Menke offered him temporary space in the United Nuclear Corporation headquarters on an estate at White Plains, north of New York. United Nuclear made all manner of useful equipment for the Navy's burgeoning nuclear-submarine program and other military and civil atomic uses. It was a reasonable extrapolation of the established business to move into civilian atomic equipment, so Menke's firm worked up a top-of-the-line fallout shelter, the very Rolls-Royce of shelters. The purchaser would buy the structure, have it shipped to his home, and install it in an appropriate hole in the backyard or the basement. Menke proffered one of his classy shelters to Herman. Certainly, the guru of fallout sheltering ought to have his own in his suburban ranch home in Chappaqua. The hole was duly dug next to the living room, but while waiting for the shelter to be delivered, Menke demanded a test run. He insisted Herman demonstrate that he could get his 300-pound bulk through the entrance. The first try was so difficult and humiliating that Herman refused to undergo the ordeal again. Menke withdrew the shelter, and the hole was pressed into service as an enclosed heated swimming pool. Herman argued that the Hudson Institute was only twenty minutes away by road, that sufficient warning would (probably) be received, and that he was duty-bound to share the community shelter on the Institute grounds. Many family fallout shelters, either built or at least imagined with the best of intentions, went the way of Herman's. And the shelter business was a bust for United Nuclear, and everybody else.

Still, a few were dead serious about personal passive defense. The physicist Eugene Wigner, one of the three wise men from the East who had borne the nuclear-munitions message to FDR, dug himself in at his Princeton home with a 30-psi blast shelter, enough to protect from attacks on New York, Philadelphia, or McGuire Air Force Base. The Lone Eagle, Charles Lindbergh, publicly discredited by his excessive fear of the Luftwaffe but privately active in the Business, was blast-sheltered in his Connecticut country house. Perhaps the most elaborate personal fortifications were constructed by William A. M. Burden. The appellation "stinky rich" was custom-tailored for him. Burden was a Vanderbilt and a fanatic car nut. In the 1930s, it was not a great leap from cars to aircraft, so he converted his passion into a vocation by becoming one of the first aircraft-industry stock analysts on Wall Street. When Franklin Roosevelt assembled a national government for World War II by recruiting Republican patricians, Burden was made Assistant Secretary of Commerce for Air. Under Truman, he was Assistant Air Force Secretary for Research. Wearing that hat, he had viewed the 1952 Mike thermonuclear shot at Einewetok, and was petrified. While his floor-through flat overlooking Central Park was beyond defense, so his urban stock of French Impressionists would be incinerated, he directed his retainers to construct an underground apartment at his Mount Kisko estate, north of New York. Burden couldn't take it with him, but took measures to keep it as long as humanly possible.

Many institutions also dug themselves in. AT&T burrowed a bunker into the New Jersey mountains near Netcong. Rockefeller saw to it that the State of New York had its little Fort Ritchie near Albany. Massachusetts had one near Maynard. The Canadian government dug a "Führerbunker" near Ottawa. Promoters sold space to corporations to house their vital records underground. It is startling how much was accomplished, almost unnoticed and off-budget, in the period straddling 1960.

## The Ann Arbor Speech

By the spring of 1962 the McNamara strategy was thoroughly worked out. The Secretary of Defense first presented it in a classified session of the NATO ministers at Athens, and in June at the commencement exercises at the University of Michigan. "The Ann Arbor speech" is one of the great landmarks of the declaratory nuclear strategy of the American Republic. The text was reviewed by the President himself. In wonderfully clear and forceful language, McNamara argued that the security of the United States in the nuclear age relied upon maintenance of deterrence—not in crude 1950s Curtis LeMay/SAC/blow-them-all-away terms, but in Wohlstetterian means of maintaining a defendable deterrent, an offensive force that can receive any first strike laid against it and retaliate. The offensive force should be superior to that of the other side, and the policy should be to keep it superior, even to excess, if only to maintain a margin for underestimation of the enemy's capabilities.

Furthermore, the offensive force should not be used against the other side's cities, at least not at first, because that would only call attack back upon our own. Rather, a counterforce strategy was declared to be in effect: our forces should destroy his forces. Further, our forces should have a "damage-limiting" function; that is, to reduce, as much as was feasible, the damage the enemy might cause by striking first or striking back. Damage-limiting could be achieved by a combination of offense and defense: of counterforce to destroy the weapons before they hit at us, of active defense by interception of aircraft and missiles, and of passive defense of the civil population.

The solution to The Problem in Europe was labeled "flexible response." While we might blow the continent away, we would rather not. A preferred solution was to raise the escalation threshold by augmenting conventional forces. And there needed to be some sort of Euro-American nuclear force to bridge the deterrence gap between conventional defenses and strategic retaliatory attacks. While McNamara was always very careful to go over his material himself, he had found a spur and a sympathetic speech writer in the excellent W. W. Kaufmann. The Ann Arbor speech was essentially the RAND strategy, as much a *summa randiensis* as was Brodie's *Strategy in the Missile Age* or Herman's *On Thermonuclear War*. The Ann Arbor speech was the high point of American *declaratory* strategic policy, and perhaps it set the high-water mark of the American Republic as well.

## The Last Crisis

The tale of the Cuban Missile Crisis has been told often, yet the full story will take generations to unravel. Looked at from the viewpoint of the defenders, its resolution appears rather less than the glowing triumph presented by Kennedy's courtiers then and subsequently. Most of the defenders curse Kennedy's ghost for not taking that opportunity to cauterize the Cuban Communist sore once and for all. A powerful faction in the administration led by Dean Acheson and Paul Nitze advocated sending an expeditionary force as soon as the Soviet offensive missiles in Cuba were identified.

They were supported by analysis in the Building and at RAND demonstrating that the Cuban-based missilery could wipe out SAC's air bases in fifteen minutes.

The professional strategists were enthralled. At last, here was a real live nuclear crisis to observe. The pros had no doubt about the outcome. Considering the then balance of forces, the Soviets were so hopelessly outgunned that they had to give way. There was no real likelihood of war. But that view was not universally held. The telephone lines from Cambridge to Washington were burning with capitulation pleas. All too many of the best and the brightest went bonkers. Kennedy defeated Nixon in 1960, but prefigured his archival program by bugging and taping the conversations of his staff. On the transcripts they read like babbling fools; the only one who sounds competent, coolly and reasonably laying out the options, is Robert McNamara.

Of course, NORAD went on alert. That was its job; the Soviets might try to redress the adverse strategic balance by a preemptive strike. Well, it is only partially correct to write "of course." When the signal went out of Washington, it did not go out of Ottawa. Prime Minister Diefenbaker saw no need for prudent preventive measures, and his foreign minister found nuclear weapons distasteful. It took considerable cajolery by the American government, working through the Canadian defense minister, to get Diefenbaker to issue the orders alerting the Canadian squadrons of continental air defense or even the Canadian officers in NORAD headquarters at Colorado Springs. This was a lesson learned that the Americans took to heart; never again would they trust the Canadians. Every supposedly Canadian slot in NORAD has an American backup ready to fill in instantly should there be an alert and the Canadians welsh again.

And something else disturbing occurred. Herman and Frank Armbruster were flying into Boston for a meeting. As the plane landed at Logan Airport, they glanced out the window and saw there, off the end of the runway, low on its undercarriage, pregnant with death, a B-47 bomber. The Hudson people knew what that meant; SAC had responded to the alert by dispersing its bombers to civil airfields easily observed by East Bloc observers, bait to draw death on the cities. The bombers were at Newark, just across the river from New York; at Chicago's Midway, snuggled in the heart of the nation's second-largest metropolis; and at fifty-odd other airports. In order to help preserve the bombers, the cities were placed at fatal risk. The dispersion gave the Soviets more targets to hit, and it tucked the bombers inside the protective curtain of the Army's Nike antiaircraft batteries deployed to protect cities. SAC would not invest in the missile defense of its own bases, claiming to rely upon its mobility and striking power, but when the crunch came, SAC ran for cover behind the Army's missiles.

Fortunately, SAC did not have to go. The Army, Navy, and tactical air forces did a commendable job of mobilizing and redeploying American forces to Florida and the Caribbean, ready to pounce. At the height of the crisis, the President called the commander of Tactical Air Command, which would have been tasked to raid the missile sites in Cuba. Kennedy asked CINCTAC if he could be sure of taking out all the missiles. CINCTAC said he couldn't be certain. Apparently the President heard this answer as meaning that a Soviet IRBM might survive American efforts, and smash, say, Atlanta. But CINCTAC was a fighter pilot; he heard the President asking if planes would be lost to surface-to-air missiles. A more fundamental question no one dared ask openly at the time was why was the President dealing directly with a subordinate commander; why was that amateur meddling in military matters? Kennedy lost his nerve. Fortunately, the gentlemen of the Politboro accepted some surreptitious concessions—in particular, to keep hands off Cuba—and pulled their missiles out. The Soviets seemed to be humiliated publicly, but won a minor victory in the world power struggle; being serious people, they find real victories more valuable than hype.

The effect of the crisis on civil defense was just what you would expect: the civil defense offices were inundated with queries for advice. Newspapers published information about the placement of shelter areas. The Dean of the Washington National Cathedral had his Gothic basement flooded to store water for the emergency. While no hard data are available, it seems millions of individual families "self-evacuated" cities to vacation cottages or family homes in the country. Only one case can be identified of an individual fleeing the country: Leo Szilard, the midwife of the Bomb, absconded to Switzerland, to enjoy the protection of the dull shelters of the dull Swiss.

Something more relevant also happened. At the height of the

crisis, Kennedy called Steuart Pittman to his office and asked him what could be done to civil defend Miami and other Southern cities within striking range of the Soviet IL-28 bombers in Cuba. Pittman told him that what needed to be done was to execute the planned fallout-shelter program. That was not what Kennedy wanted to know. He wanted to know what could be done right then, and Pittman had no useful response. To Kennedy, Pittman's answer meant "nothing." It is obvious that much could have been done. A road map and some elementary traffic control could have evacuated Miami in a few hours. But there were no plans, so there would have been confusion, and the mess would have been labeled "chaos" and blamed on the administration—and that would never do. No one at the time realized it, but that was the last time American civil defense was given any military consideration.

## ARADCOM Opens a Southern Front

When the expeditionary force assembled for the Cuban invasion redeployed back to its bases, something was left behind: four batteries of Nike-Hercules and eight batteries of Hawks strewn along the tip of Florida from Homestead Air Force Base, south of Miami, to Key West. As a consequence of the Cuban capitulation, it was necessary to deploy a few Hawks for a continental air defense mission. The Keys air defense barrier was very good duty for the troops— empty beaches, excellent swimming, fishing, and tourist girls to service.

The gunners played games with Cuban and Soviet planes testing the defenses and the radio operators learned and named the individual voices of pilots. Once the game was in earnest: radar picked up an incoming, low and slow with the signature of a helicopter. A crew of Cubans was coming over to our side. But their Soviet adviser was loath to make the flight; the Cubans rolled his corpse out onto the tarmac at Key West.

## The Canadian Missile Crisis

Up North, the American government did not forget John Diefenbaker's attempt at waffling in the Cuban missile crisis. Recall that the failure of the Americans to deliver necessary subcomponents had killed the Arrow fighter, requiring Canada to accept Bomarcs for self-protection and CF-101s for expediency; recall that the Bomarc-Bs were designed for nuclear warheads and that the CF-101s were nearly useless without the Genie atomic rocket; note that American law forbade the handing over of nuclear weaponry to foreign governments, requiring that they be held in American custody to be released under a dual-key arrangement if war should break out; and record that John Diefenbaker, as a good Canadian nationalist, was exceedingly loath to have Americans posted permanently on Canadian soil with their grasping hands on Canadian munitions. Small wonder that he took no action to resolve this predicament. In place of their nuclear warheads, the Bomarcs had sandbags. The journalist Peter Newman described the Canadian air defense arsenal as "the most impressive collection of blank cartridges in the history of military science."

The Cuban matter brought Canada to the attention of Washington. The retiring NATO commander, General Lauris Norstad, USAF, just happened to visit Canada and pointed out forcefully that its government was not fulfilling its pledges to the common defense. His sentiments were echoed by numerous distinguished retired Canadian general officers, and the active-duty officers, while duty-bound not to contradict their government, remained mute. The officers were Tories to a man, and a chill went through Anglo-Canada.

The Liberal Party, the pro-American party, had been firmly opposed to the adoption of nuclear weapons. But its leader, Lester Pearson, was a close personal friend of Dean Acheson's, and the Liberals conveniently reversed their position. The U.S. State Department sent a strongly worded rebuke, drafted in the White House, to Diefenbaker. The Tories split, the Diefenbaker government collapsed, the Liberals won a smashing victory in the subsequent election, and the nuclear weapons were deployed to Canadian bases under U.S. military control.

The Kennedy administration could not bring down Fidel Castro, but it could depose John Diefenbaker. It was nicely done. It was a piece of imperial politics that would have done credit to Disraeli. Later that year, the Kennedy administration brought down the Diem government of South Vietnam. That was not so nicely done.

# V

## THE DEFENSE STALEMATED

*Gentlemen, countrymen, friends and my fellow soldiers: I
have brought you this day from the shops of security and
the counters of content, to measure our honour by the ell
and prowess by the pound.*

BEAUMONT AND FLETCHER

One SAC reconnaissance pilot was killed over Cuba. Another
casualty, unnoticed at the time, was McNamara himself. No one
spoke of it at the time, but when McNamara in the 1980s began to
make curious pronouncements on nuclear-strategic matters, quite
at variance with his statements and actions as Secretary of Defense,
his former colleagues began to whisper, "McNamara lost his nerve."
McNamara had cracked in the crisis. McNamara had shown in the
crunch that he was just a bean-counter, that the generalissimo of
paper could not look into the face of war.

While these slurs need not necessarily be believed, the disinterested observer can note that after the "the missiles of October" a
suspicious change occurred in the tone and thrust of the public
statements of the Secretary of Defense and his aides. The first public
break was in an interview with the journalist Stewart Alsop, but
that was in the lowly *Saturday Evening Post,* and no one noticed it.
In the spring of 1963, his former deputy Roswell Gilpatric published
a long piece in the Council's *Foreign Affairs,* an obvious appetizer
to a policy change, which cast a chill through the defenders. It argued
that a policy of better arms and more brilliant thinking could increase
your security, but not make you secure. Therefore, something else
had to be tried, and the Kennedy administration and the social
elements it reflected began to tilt toward another way of trying to

182

manage The Problem. The greater casualty of the Cuban missile crisis was the McNamara strategy.

## Arms Control

After the disappointment of grandiose schemes for international control of atomic energy after World War II, notions of dealing with The Problem pacifically were made irrelevant by the perception of Soviet intransigence. The events in Eastern Europe, especially in Czechoslovakia and Berlin, the brazen North Korean attack on the South, and the advent of the Soviet nuclear weapon made the thought of working out a deal with those fellows seem utopian. The scientists' opposition to the hydrogen bomb was not rooted in any idea of disarmament, but rather in a sentiment that these murderous innovations were already progressing too rapidly and excessively. Maybe the Soviets would not develop thermonuclear fusion, and if they did, we could match them, and in any event the United States had or would have sufficiently ample and brutal fission bombs to satisfy the requirements even of Curtis LeMay.

Yet Stalin died, and the new Soviet rulers appeared as bullies or buffoons, not the pathological mass murderer who had been their patron. There was a lot of peace gush and champagne-guzzling in Geneva, and chatter about "disarmament" was thrown back and forth. The Soviets would always counter with a proposal for complete, total, and uninspected disarmament. Nobody took them seriously. However, the "thaw" era seemed to be a ripe time for considering the possibilities for a new and prudent way to look at the issue. Sometime in the mid-'50s the term "arms control" surfaced. The center of the interest was in the universities along the Charles, at Harvard and MIT, where some very bright people had been involved with weaponry for fifteen years and liked not what they saw ahead. There had been agonizingly terrible advances in the offense, and while the defense in the 1950s seemed promising for a time, where would it all end?

Tentatively, small groups began to discuss the matters at hand. None of them were pacifists, Communist sympathizers, unilateral disarmers, or fools. None of them were sanguine about finding common ground with such an alien, despotic, secretive, and belligerent state as the Soviet Union. None of them were naive about the

internal difficulties of dealing with the American military and public.
This was just after the peak of the McCarthy craze, when self-
appointed vigilantes were sniffing about the country for real or imagined subversives. This was when SAC was flying high. So the
ur–arms controllers initially disregarded ideology and politics and
concentrated on technical and theoretical matters. What did arms
control mean? What were its goals? How did you achieve them?
How did it coincide with U.S. security?

Some of the Cambridge people had already been in contact with
the RAND crowd. In those days, any academic interested in military
affairs could obtain a consultancy or summer appointment at Santa
Monica. There they learned the elements of nuclear strategy and
tried to use that knowledge to form a better understanding of a
world in which nuclear strategy perhaps would not be as necessary.
The RAND people also took an immediate interest. In the mid-
'50s, RAND was still held on a very loose rein by the Air Force,
and the subject might be of some interest to the client. Now, the
dominant views in RAND were roughly equivalent to and heavily
influenced by those in Nathan Leites's *The Operational Paradigm
of the Politburo,* which made a painstaking content analysis of the
official declaratory policies of the Soviet Union, and concluded that
the Soviet leadership thought quite differently from the bourgeois
West. This made them intensely dangerous, although not impossible
to deal with. RAND people, reflecting the interest of the defense
establishment, concentrated on working out the operational details
of how arms control might work and what it meant to the American
military.

One of the most ingenious and useful of the RAND analysts was
the photoreconnaissance interpreter Amron Katz, who had been at
Bikini and promptly joined the United World Federalists. The events
of mid-century made him look to national solutions to security problems. Katz specialized in what came to be called "verification": how
can we know whether or not the other side is upholding the agreement? The Soviets had been granite in refusing to permit foreign
inspectors to sniff around their country. And a disinterested analysis
also would reveal the near-impossibility of organizing Soviet inspection of the United States, because most potential hiding places
are private property: what legal procedures would be necessary to
abrogate the unambiguous provision in the Bill of Rights prohibiting

"unreasonable search and seizure"? Were the KGB and Soviet military intelligence to have nationally valid search warrants to poke in every factory and basement?

A conclusive test of arms-control verification procedures had been administered in Weimar Germany in the 1920s. The Treaty of Versailles had imposed very tight limits on the armaments of Germany, and Allied inspectors swarmed over the country. The German Republic was an open society, but nonetheless the Germans—the liberal and social democratic Germans, who were naked to exposure by internal enemies of their republic—had managed to field a surreptitious army and a phantom air force. Could not the Russians or the Americans secrete a few nuclear bombs or rockets? Katz and colleagues organized arms-control games—paper competitions between "hiders" trying to hide weaponry and "finders" who tried to sniff them out. The hiders always won.

Another of the most active and productive of the RAND arms-control analysts was Fred C. Ikle, who addressed some of the most glaring negative questions of arms control. If we do catch the other side cheating, then what do we do? He asked that question in the late 1950s, and it has never been answered. All subsequent arms-control treaties have contained no provisions for redress of violations, only the implicit understanding that, as in all international agreements, a violation is proper cause for abrogation by the other parties to the treaty.

Nonetheless, most of the RAND people were sympathetic at least to the objectives of arms control. The prospect of continuing the pace of weapons development at the rate of 1945 to 1960 was truly horrendous. Herman displayed an arsenal of terrors that might, indeed likely would, appear in the next generation. A particularly nasty one was the gigaton bomb, a thousand megatons exploded high in the atmosphere, with the thermal heat frying hundreds of square miles of terrain. He also had a list of weaponry that should be available in future paper wars in 1961, 1965, 1969, and 1973; this material was intended to frighten Air Force officers who held that More is always Better. (And it did—one officer shouted during a briefing, "Herman, stop the world, I want to get off.") Later he was smeared with the charge of advocating these nasty things. Actually, as he wrote to a friend at the Berkeley Radiation Lab in 1958, "I have the feeling that there really are urgent reasons for trying to get along with the Russians and these reasons are clear to them also. An unrestricted arms race which is really unrestricted begins to look incredibly dangerous to all concerned in the '65–'75 time frame. 5–10 years doesn't seem like too short a time to try to settle things—hopefully short of war. Much has to be done now if something close to cataclysm is to be headed off."

The arms-control thrust did not, nor was it intended to, prevent the strengthening of offensive or defensive forces. Arms control was something else to be taken into some consideration in force planning. Everybody who mattered agreed with it. The only grumblers were those who thought the Soviets sat up all night, every night, thinking of ways to get us. Most such people were at the extremes of American politics in those days; the few in positions of responsibility and power, including many high military officers and congressmen, thought it best to lie low for the nonce. Perhaps they also suspected that arms control might be worth a little effort and interest if only to demonstrate conclusively to the whole world how rotten the Soviets really are. The center of right-wing arms-control research became the Foreign Policy Research Institute at Philadelphia, which held many conclaves during the '60s in conjunction with Richard Foster's Army research team at the Stanford Research Institute. (Among the gofers were a political operator named Dick Allen and a graduate student named John Lehman.) The FPRI-SRI crowd examined arms control in the spirit in which Jesuits studied Calvinism.

But the consensus in the American establishment circa 1960 was that arms control was no panacea, nor would it mean delivering the world to Communist hordes; rather, it was an approach worthy of effort, something might come of it, and we could find out only by trying. Eisenhower's people had made a few interesting, though clumsy, attempts. The Kennedy administration made an arms-control thrust a coherent part of policy.

A central concept was "stability." If you do not want to have a nuclear war, you want to minimize everybody's incentives for starting one, which means you want to arrange matters so that no one thinks he can gain an advantage from a first strike. Now, the very first thing to learn about nuclear strategy is the marvelous advantage of getting in the first punch—you take out a big chunk of his forces and lose only whatever his defenses may skim on the way in. The other side also recognizes the benefits of "preemption." This mental set is "destabilizing."

Well, it is obvious how sweetly the Wohlstetterian notion of protecting the deterrent force corrects that condition. An undefended force is a temptation for the other side to strike first, a provocation, and therefore to be avoided. But a well-defended second-strike force is stabilizing. So your top stabilizing priority is to protect your second-strike capability. And that is also the first traditional military priority—because your attack forces are your most important forces and the other side's primary target. So far, the arms-control approach reinforces traditional military thinking.

Further, you also want the other fellow to protect his forces: not so much to annul your temptation to go first as to allow him enough assurance of the survivability and reprisal potential of his forces so that *he* will not be tempted to strike first—to "use 'em or lose 'em." An unprotected attack force is therefore a first-strike force, which is A Bad Thing; while a protected force is a second-strike force— A Good Thing. Now, from a traditional military point of view, this is perverse: you want the enemy's forces aimed at you to be secure against your attack?

Next, you want to be safe from accidental or unauthorized use of nuclear forces. You do not want some crazy bomber pilot flying off on a personal crusade, or a missile fired by a short circuit. So you want "positive control": you want personnel systems that prevent unauthorized behavior, and mechanical systems that will absolutely "fail" safe—will respond to malfunction only by being disarmed, not propelled against an enemy to incite him to respond in kind. Both sides had those interests; commies and capitalists equally could recognize their benefits. The United States invested in safeguard systems: complex "dual-key" procedures and "permissive action links" made the unauthorized or accidental firing of nuclear weapons for all practical purposes impossible. Livermore and the RAND physics department were leaders in these systems. The results were deliberately transmitted to the Soviets—in general outline, so that the other side couldn't beat ours, and so that they would have to expend resources developing theirs.

Once those two objectives of a survivable second-strike capability and robust systems for control of weaponry on both sides had been achieved, nothing else should be done. Any change from this system, any innovation, would disturb the "balance of terror," would be "destabilizing" and potentially, if not actually, downright danger-ous. That should be obvious to everyone involved. After the desired stability was achieved, then one could begin to talk of arms reduc-tion. Moreover, the activity of achieving stability would mean that the hostile sides had learned the desirable habit of seeking mutual solutions to their security problems, of slowly muting their hostili-ties, of defusing the Cold War. So "the process" of arms control was also an end—and to be fair, no one thought in the '50s that it would degenerate into an end in itself. Yes, the arms controllers were an optimistic lot, very much in the American grain. They were going to convert not only the Americans but also the Russians to the correct, just, humane, and rigorous way of looking at the world as it is and as it should be.

## The Arms Controllers

Several distinguished men became involved in these discussions. It is not to denigrate the importance of any of those men to concentrate on two of them. Jerome Wiesner was from Dearborn and had a sound engineering background at Michigan. During the war he came to MIT's Rad Lab, but was posted to Los Alamos, where he worked on the electronic controls for the first bombs. After the war he returned to MIT, where he was an accomplished research manager, working his way up through the multifold systems-management jobs, gaining the respect of his superiors. He continued working closely in defense matters. The reader will recall how frequently his name has appeared already in this chronicle, especially in relation to air defense.

Perhaps no single person took the cause of arms control more seriously, and with more fervor, than did Jerry Wiesner. Perhaps one reason is that unlike many of his colleagues, he had had intense and prolonged experience in working with the military, and he liked it not. He was involved in many of the dirty squabbles in the missile wars and the haggling over air defense. By the time he became Kennedy's chief science adviser, he had pretty well made up his mind that fiddling with weaponry past the levels of safeguards and second-strike capability was just a waste of money and a threat to the nation.

His enthusiasm took him, like many others, to the Pugwash Conferences, organized by the fellow-traveling industrialist Cyrus Eaton and named for the site of the first meeting at Eaton's estate in Nova Scotia. Eaton had been sold on the naive idea that getting scientists together from different nations, especially the United States and the Soviet Union, would help to promote the cause of World Peace. Eaton was very enthusiastic, very rich, and an openhanded host, so Pugwash attendance was an epicurean's delight, not to mention its offering of the spirited conversation of bright, or at least voluble, scientists from around the world. Among the Americans who went to Pugwash in the 1950s were Paul Doty, Thomas Schelling, Lewis Sohn, Leo Szilard, the physicists Victor Weisskopf and Bernard Feld, Eugene Rabinowitch, editor of the *Bulletin of the Atomic Scientists,* Frederick Seitz, Alvin Weinberg and Eugene Wigner of Oak Ridge, Linus Pauling, David Inglis of the Argonne Labs, W. W. Rostow and Donald Brennan of MIT, and Amron Katz of RAND. Almost an American was John S. Foster of McGill.

Whatever were their motives, the Soviets also sent a handful of their science apparatchiks to Pugwash. Some of them were crude buffoons who would parrot the Party line; others, who seemed to lack basic information in their supposed specialties, were understood to be agents of the Soviet security forces; and others had the cool intelligence and suave political skills of the leading scientific managers in the United States. These last Russians were the ones whom the Americans would "educate" in the ways of achieving world stability.

A less visible figure than Wiesner, but one who was able to devote more time to the arms-control enterprise, was a young engineer named Donald Brennan. He had come out of Waterbury, Connecticut, where his father had been a stockbroker whose modest prosperity was wiped out in the Depression. Don was taken with radio, the high-tech interest of bright young men in the 1930s, and hung out at the local radio station. He was drafted at 18 into the Signal Corps. After the war, he continued his interest in practical electronics and was a licensed radio engineer. Brennan found his way to MIT, where he was found to be a prodigy, a brilliant mathematician as well as a theoretical electrical engineer. He was especially honored by being accepted as a graduate student of Norbert Wiener, one of the great minds of his generation, and one of the few who rejected a role in the Manhattan Project. In the early 1950s, Brennan followed the usual career of an aspiring researcher with a combination of academic work and odd jobs relevant to his specialty. At Lincoln Labs, he worked on the theory of long-range radio, the fascinatingly difficult problems involved in bouncing radio waves off the ionosphere, a line of research that twenty years later resulted in over-the-horizon (OTH) radar, which would extend the range of radar manyfold.

Brennan became a sort of *rapporteur* to the arms-control seminars at MIT, and rather a leader in the field. He wrote relatively little himself. Although his prose was succinct, he had trouble elaborating ideas, and it may be that however valuable he was to the whole endeavor, he was not productive of new thoughts himself. A culmination of the 1950s' arms-control seminars was the anthology he edited for the distinguished journal *Daedulus,* which was published in somewhat expanded form as the volume *Arms Control, Disarmament, and National Security,* the bible of the arms-control movement, a compendium of the heavy hitters in the field. Most of the contributors were Cambridge types. Wiesner, Brennan, and Ithiel de Sola Pool were from MIT. From Harvard: the chemist Paul Doty, the economist Thomas Schelling, the law professor Roger Fisher, Lewis B. Sohn, Robert Bowie, the political scientist Morton Halperin, the physicist Bernard T. Feld, and the international-affairs theorist Henry Kissinger.

There were some scattered people from elsewhere, such as the economist Kenneth Boulding, then at Ann Arbor. From RAND were Herman and Lewis Bohn. Some politicians were in the volume: Arthur Larson, who had worked disarmament for Eisenhower, and Hubert Humphrey, who was a vocal early advocate of arms control. For comic relief, the advocacy of unilateral disarmament was left to the psychotheorist Erich Fromm. As if to give balance, Edward Teller was permitted an essay arguing that nuclear testing was good for you and broadly implying that arms control was a waste of time. The editor did not deem it appropriate to include an exposition of the Neanderthal thesis that the Soviet Union had not the slightest interest in arms control except insofar as it might forward the interests of the Soviet state and its ruling party. The arms controllers were painfully aware that this view existed; indeed, refuting it was the implicit theme of the book, but they thought not to give such aid and comfort to the internal adversary.

But the key arms-control concepts were expressed more succinctly elsewhere by Thomas Schelling and Morton Halperin. The objectives of arms control are:

- to reduce the risk of war;
- to reduce the damage of war;
- to save money.

Brennan took this trinity to heart and preached them for the rest of his career; other arms controllers lapsed from the true doctrine.

## ACDA

In the Brennan bible, Hubert Humphrey made a pitch for his scheme for a disarmament agency. His was in substance the plan that was put into effect in 1961—but with one minor change. Don Brennan suggested that it be named the *Arms Control and* Disarmament Agency so that people would not misunderstand its purposes. Don Brennan also believed that he was the ideal person to become its first chief. To be sure, he was wonderfully expert on the subject and had been an organizer of sorts in Cambridge; but like many people of a scientific bent, he did not properly realize that knowledge of a field does not necessarily mean that one is qualified to administer an organization presumably devoted to forwarding its purposes. The top post at ACDA ("ack-dah") went to William Foster, a well-connected establishment lawyer who had been Deputy Secretary of Defense in the Truman administration. Foster had a firm policy of keeping a very low profile, which was the reason he was suitable for the job, and will not appear again in this chronicle. Under his benign supervision, ACDA was to become the center of efforts to resolve The Problem in a narrowly prescribed manner. The preferred solution of the arms controllers came from overseas and under the seas.

## The Problem in Europe

The Europeans were not ignorant of The Problem. Although the need for America to defend Europe on the cheap was, in a sense, The Problem itself, the Europeans were aware that their weakness gave them very little leverage on either side in these matters, but they did the best they could, both financially and intellectually. It was, after all, Winston S. Churchill who gave the world the phrase "the balance of terror." The Germans knew full well that their nation was on political parole, and nothing would be more injurious to German interests than for the revitalized democratic (west) German state to show the slightest interest whatever in nuclear weaponry, so they were content to follow the United States in building up their army for "flexible response" to "raise the nuclear threshold."

The French were the most ingenious of the European participants in the great debate over the implications. The Big Thinkers of the nation of Descartes and Comte took nuclear-strategic thinking to heart, and worked out The Problem to a terrifyingly logical conclusion. Because the Soviet Union could strike back at the United States if the United States struck first to protect Europe, obviously the Americans would not do so. Whereas many Americans had stated this as a possibility, or concern, or something to take into consideration, the French took U.S.–S.U. mutual deterrence as an absolute fact. This was a brazen example of strategic mirror-imaging; had the French sat in Washington, of course they would have sold out their allies.

This logic required that France had to look to its own nuclear defenses, which in those early days, because of France's late start in the nuclear-arms business, meant simple, large, inaccurate weapons that could be delivered only by bombers. This did not go unnoticed by the French Armée d'Air. But under no plausible circumstances could France possibly have for itself sufficient nuclear forces to match the Soviet Union; France was doomed to inferior force. What to do? The answer was given by the voluble air force general Pierre Gallois, a veritable reincarnation of Douhet. Gallois argued for a risk strategy: that even a puny nuclear force could do so much damage that no one would dare mess with its possessor, not even a much larger and more powerful country. To be sure, a weak power would use such weapons only *in extremis,* in the last ditch, because the retaliation would mean national destruction. Gallois presented a picture of a world of nuclear powers, all with pistols at others' temples, as a world of peace and stability. Everyone would be at the mercy of everyone else and everyone would therefore keep his place, and the peace would be kept. To Gallois, it was desirable that every country have nuclear weapons, but certainly, of course, France.

The Fourth Republic had begun an efficient nuclear-weapons program, and its heir Charles de Gaulle saw no reason to reverse this supplement to the glory of France. And to be sure, it was noticed, but not remarked openly, that the declaratory strategy took no heed of the ability of the French forces to devastate Germany. To the question "What if deterrence fails?" the French merely shrugged. The theory of multipolar deterrence was circulated worldwide, much to the horror of the Americans, who saw it as a goad to nuclear proliferation. And it trickled through RAND and international diplomacy circles into the heads of the arms controllers at Cambridge.

## Finite Deterrence

Another thread in the arms-control tapestry was spun by civilian analysts at the Naval Weapons Evaluation Group. In the 1950s the Navy had a doctrinal problem, in some sense a very positive problem, created by technology. In the late 1940s, in "the revolt of the admirals," the Navy had argued for new carriers capable of carrying aircraft that could deliver nuclear weapons, on the ground that these forces could be used against military targets in the Soviet Union, in place of the blast-the-cities policy of the mad bombers of the Air Force. The sailors were then calling SAC "the baby-burners." The Navy lost that fight, but got the supercarriers in the budget swell following on the Korean war and thoroughly equipped them with medium bombers and nuclear munitions.

But an even neater idea appeared in the Navy. There was a sub-Navy, a satrapy controlled by Admiral Hyman Rickover, a sort of blue-suited Edward Teller who charmed numerous congressmen and had much his own way with the nuclear-powered submarine program. Naval engineers ginned up the most wonderful weapon system—and this is no hyperbole—that had ever been conceived.

Combine nuclear weapons, ballistic missiles, and nuclear-powered submarines, and cement the system by a method of launching the missiles from underwater. The sea-launched ballistic missile (SLBM— "ess-el-bee-em") was the way to defend the deterrent, not by hardening or flying around, but by concealment under the zillion square miles of the world's oceans. These deadly subs conceivably might be attacked and sunk, but the record of antisubmarine warfare (ASW—"ay-ess-double-u") during the past forty years was dismal, to say the least. Submarines had been vulnerable only on the surface or when they closed in for a torpedo attack. A submarine that wanted to avoid contact was damn near impossible to find.

This concept was given the label Polaris, which had been laid on the missile itself, the boats themselves, but more properly on the whole system. In one of the most gorgeous achievements of systems management in human history, the Navy pushed through the Polaris program in forty-four months. Yes, Polaris solved the defense problem, but it needed an offensive rationale. No system is without drawbacks, and those of Polaris were considerable: it was hard to communicate with, and therefore hq could not reliably count on getting off a split-second attack order of the type that would be needed for nuclear counterforce strikes; yes, eventually the attack order would get through one way or another, but by that time all the enemy's forces might long since have been launched.

Another weakness of Polaris was that although the Navy had made an incredible technological achievement in designing the guidance system that could pop up from underwater and fly 1,500 miles to a target, despite that magical calculation, the missile was not highly accurate. Polaris could not hit a hardened target anywhere near close enough to surely kill it; Polaris could be relied on only to hit soft targets—for example, airfields. But the Soviets did not have very great numbers of strategic bombers or airfields, and most of them were far inland, out of Polaris' range (although the impending Soviet sea-launched ballistic missiles would later give SAC fits). With an average accuracy of 5 miles, Polaris was particularly suited for smashing cities.

Now, the original boats were designed to carry 16 missiles. While Polaris was a wonderful system, it was even more wonderfully expensive. Even the most flush Navy could not afford more than a few dozen of them, and even that number would threaten the rest of the naval budget—not an agreeable prospect to the "black-shoe" (surface-ship) or "brown-shoe" (aviators) Navy. A doctrine was needed to justify a relatively small number of Polaris boats. Such a doctrine was generated by NAVWEG and floated out of the Navy under the label "minimum deterrence." All we need is enough stuff to burn his cities; count up his cities, divide by 16, and the quotient is your number of strategic submarines. And—oh, yes—no strategic air force is required.

But the term "minimum" deterrence did sound rather paltry, so the phrase was presently modified to "finite" deterrence; therefore, it was easy to calculate exactly how much firepower was needed to do $x$ amount of damage, which was all that was needed to deter the other guy. Anything in excess of that was a waste of money and time and was unnecessarily provocative.

## Mutual Deterrence

Putting together the Navy's and the French schemes gave you a very clear idea of what was needed for world stability. Each side just had to have enough to do a certain amount of terrible damage to the other, and that was it. Anything in excess of that amount was "overkill." With both sides having enough, you had mutual deterrence. But—and not noticed or discussed openly at the time, but to be of absolutely central and driving significance later in our chronicle— mutual deterrence required mutual vulnerability. Vulnerability therefore was not part of The Problem; it was part of The Solution.

And in the early '60s, an engineering professor at Columbia named Seymour Melman actually went to the trouble of calculating how much we needed to kill most of the people in the entire world, if they somehow had arranged to line themselves up in such a way as to be killed with the minimal number of nuclear weapons. The notion of "overkill" was so simple and superficially plausible that it penetrated deep into the public mind; certainly it was still a powerful idea in the 1980s and could be expected to last as long as did nuclear weaponry.

Leo Szilard took this notion so seriously that he advocated a much cheaper delivery system than Polaris: that each side, to simplify the attack problem, plant nuclear mines in the other's cities. He did not ask why a nation would let the enemy plant the bombs in its own cities. But Szilard was following the logic of mutual vulnerability to a reasonable conclusion. His concept was marked by Donald Brennan and by a physicist and offhand weapons specialist named Richard L. Garwin.

Herman Kahn was fascinated by the idea, so much that he suggested a thoroughgoing *reductio ad absurdum* of mutual deterrence—the Doomsday Machine, a device that would effectively destroy the world. The possessor of the device would respond to provocation by threatening to set it off, or better yet, the machine would be triggered automatically by some unwanted act, such as the detonation of a nuclear explosive anywhere in the world. It was a bizarre and irresponsible concept; however, his bad judgment paled before the irresponsibility and bizarreness of people then accusing him of advocating a Doomsday Machine. Indeed, he was sufficiently interested in the concept, and touchy about accusations that he was being too fantastic, as to commission his RAND aide William Brown to work out some concepts of how it might be done. Brown, an accomplished weapons-effects analyst, identified a few dozen ways to destroy the world—not easily, and not cheaply, but not at impossible and unrealistic expense. To be sure, it might be difficult to get the equipment into the military budget, because destroying the world, and destroying your own country in particular, is not why you have armed forces: which was exactly the point of the parody of the Doomsday Machine, and exactly why mutual deterrence is an irresponsible and bizarre concept.

## The Rise of the Kooks

The developing arms-control movement obtained an unfortunate and in the end disastrous reinforcement as a consequence of the hydrogen bomb and the overthrow of Senator Joseph McCarthy's clumsy witch-hunting campaigns and resultant political fallout. The announcement of measurable radioactive fallout appearing in the atmosphere, not out in the Pacific somewhere but right here in North America, led to an initially small yet enthusiastic and eventually cancerous agitation. To begin with, there was a real issue: the rate of accumulation of long-lasting highly radioactive materials that could and would collect in the human body was accelerating markedly. It was also a fact, however, that this total accumulation was still, and almost certainly would continue for a long time to come to be, inconsequential. But the second fact failed to take into account the cleverly exploited public ignorance of and fear of radiation. It was poison that you couldn't see, or feel, or taste, or hear; radiation is magic. We were being irradiated, being killed slowly by nuclear weapons.

The Federation of Atomic Scientists types in 1946 had found that it was necessary to preach doom to get a hearing. That doom preached then was plausible, quite within the range of known weapons effects; the potential cataclysm of crushed cities could meet, as nearly as any forecast can, the most rigorous demands of scientific presentation. It was with the fallout issue that scientists began to lie systematically. A physicist from Colorado claimed that existing radiation levels would have permanent debilitating effects upon the populace; he neglected to mention that the "existing levels" were the peak levels immediately after a test, which quickly subsided back to normal.

The subject of the effects of fallout from the testing was being investigated carefully by the Atomic Energy Commission. Because the cumulative radiation was still at a very low level, the AEC may not have been pushing the research forward as fast as it might have been; nonetheless, there was movement, and eventually the consensus was that a continuation of the existing rate of testing of the types of weapons then being tested—that is, of hydrogen bombs which at the end of their process exploded an outer core of uranium-238, scattering radioactive debris and also contaminated dirt blown into the air by ground bursts—would indeed be unhealthful for future generations. It was inevitable that this sort of testing should be restricted, if only on the most elementary public-health grounds.

To be sure, this line was not attractive to the antitest agitators. In 1957, something was formed called The Committee for a Sane Nuclear Policy, and it flourished on into the 1960s. Most of its leaders were eminently respectable politically liberal loyal Americans. But like any mass movement, SANE had within its ranks both overly enthusiastic idealists and cynical hustlers. SANE made opposition to nuclear testing respectable, and it spread, as one would expect considering the social elements involved, through the universities—recruiting not, of course, the few serious scholars and scientists who are usually fascinated with and immersed in their work and either are loath to pretend that they have any competence in the wider world and or don't give a damn about public affairs, but rather the hackademics.

In the 1950s also were organized international groups of "scientists," few of any whom knew anything in particular about atomic energy, not to mention world affairs. Their public pronouncements displayed their incredible naiveté and ignorance of both. The worst of them was the supposed philosopher Bertrand Russell, who had in the late 1940s advocated that the United States make a preemptive strike against the Soviet Union to prevent it from gaining nuclear arms. While a few American right-wingers had muttered the notion privately, Russell was the only person in the entire world foolish enough to say such a thing openly. When the Soviets did get nuclear weapons, he then advocated surrender, and supported Khrushchev in the Cuban missile crisis. To be fair, he was then a very old man. It is not useful to name these "scientists"; most of them are long dead, and their politics and even their supposed scientific accomplishments forgotten. Nonetheless, their names gave a gloss of verisimilitude to the growing agitation. Had it merely been against the atmospheric testing of potentially dangerous nuclear weapons, that would have been quite sensible and agreeable to almost everyone, but the agitation was not so restricted; it turned against something called "the nuclear arms race" which was supposedly making the world more dangerous. (The phrase seems to have been put into circulation in a book by the British polemicist Phillip Noel-Baker.)

In 1960, at a meeting in Washington, another famous phrase was added to the thesaurus of arms control. The novelist-scientist C. P. Snow told a SANE meeting, referring to the relative dangers of trusting the Soviets compared with the threat of nuclear war, "between a risk and a certainty, a SANE man has no choice." To be fair, it was not only flaccid mannerist novelists who were afraid of nuclear war; everybody was, and the early '60s showed that they were not, in the short run, without considerable prescience.

The Brits were ahead of our thinking in many areas. In the mid-1950s, the Soviets started rattling their intermediate-range ballistic missiles at west Europe, not without effect. The kooks first appeared in force in Albion in the late 1950s. The Committee for Nuclear Disarmament was formed to advocate the unilateral nuclear disarmament of the United Kingdom. Some of the disarmers said that Britain's petty arsenal was militarily and strategically worthless (which was an arguable position) and that the United States would protect Britain in any event (probably right on the money), but many more said that the weapons were immoral (how were they more immoral than other weapons?) and that by disarming Britain would set an example that the world would imitate (absolute twaddle).

The relevance to America of the CND agitation is transparent. The threat to Britain became evident earlier than the threat to America. Her Majesty's Government, to save money, invested in "deterrence" and not in defense. Britain is much smaller than America; Britain is much closer to the Soviet Union. By 1958, Britain could be totally destroyed by a Soviet attack. The CND appeared at that time. To be sure, the British populace did not give way; to be sure, the political leadership—even the necessary cynics of the Labour Party who had to pander to its fringe elements—did not give way. When you pull hard on a piece of fabric, the weakest threads give way; when pressure is put on a polity, the weaklings crack—the weak of mind, the weak of character, and especially the weak of courage. The kooks give first.

## The Kooks Take On Civil Defense

Incredibly, the antitesting agitation in America spilled over onto civil defense. The two were almost precise polar opposites. Nuclear testing was a modest threat to public health now, while civil defense would be a considerable protection of public health in the event of nuclear war. Yet, out of the woodwork, the most perverse battery of attacks on civil defense appeared. Some lying was from expected sources; the Women's International League for Peace and Freedom whined that "it threatens our moral and spiritual values as well as our democratic heritage"—an interesting complaint from a forty-year supporter of the Soviet experiment.

Psychiatrists said that civil defense would frighten children, whereas the program, if reasonably successful, would save the lives of millions of children, who had every right to be gravely frightened under the circumstances of nuclear attack. It was argued that civil defense would "militarize" the country; presumably having fire drills in schools was "fire-departmentizing" the country. The American Friends Service Committee said that "Peace Is Our Only Defense"; presumably nonviolent shelters were too bellicose for Quakers.

Reciting the entire litany of anti–civil defense complaints would be tiresome, because in a considerable sense it was irrelevant. A clue is the complaint by a woman in, of all places, Livermore, California, who said that by resisting a local community shelter program she was opposing "the arms race." Now, digging a hole in the ground, or stacking a few cans of beans, or making plans to help people flee to the boondocks would seem but nebulously related to increasing the payload and accuracy of intercontinental ballistic missiles, but the woman was not without a point. She could do nothing about ICBMs, or submarines, or bombers—she could not even understand those things. But she understood—quite correctly—that the sum total of all those things was something potentially very ugly, and she thought that it ought to be stopped, or at least slowed, and all she could do about it was complain about, refuse to participate in, or obstruct the civil defense program in her community, which was somehow related to the entire dirty business. That may be a pathetically naive approach, but it is not insane. However, the deliberate political exploitation of those sentiments later was to become viciously harmful to the national defense.

The most powerful weapon used against the civil defense program was ridicule. The American government was thoroughly hoist with its own petard; so much had been made publicly of the power of nuclear weapons in the period immediately post-Hiroshima that it became almost impossible to convince the person with casual interest that there is any point at all to civil defense in the face of such awesome weaponry. What's the use? Now, the sentence above was deliberately written to include the phrase "with casual interest," because the evidence is that a person with some interest who was willing to devote a few hours could be convinced of the utility and desirability of civil defense. This was achieved regularly from 1955 on by many of the defenders; but few people were willing to give the time, and certainly why should anyone, excepting a crank, devote any effort to addressing a lost cause?

One particularly unfortunate minor incident in the flap was a foolish article by a Jesuit at Georgetown University who addressed the ethical question of whether a householder would be morally justified in shooting a neighbor who wished to gain entrance to his family's fallout shelter. This was blown up into a large public brouhaha in the press. Clearly, in a nuclear war the shooting of neighbors was not one of the central concerns of the nation, and individual people would make decisions on an individual basis. Alas, this would not be the first time that irrelevant ruminations of idle clergy would further muddy these murky waters.

Sometimes it seems that every Big Thinker had something to say about civil defense. For example, the anthropologist Margaret Mead (who had done some research at RAND in the late 1940s) suggested at a symposium of the American Association for the Advancement of Science that some percentage of newlyweds should spend their honeymoons in deep blast shelters so that a residue of the breeding population would be safe from annihilating nuclear war at all times.

Another plausible argument against civil defense was expressed only by very well-informed people, the highest-ranking being Kennedy's Science Adviser, Jerry Wiesner, during the cooling off of the great civil defense flap. He told his White House associates that any civil defense program could be overwhelmed by enemy countermeasures. The simplest version would be for the attacker to lay on a multimegaton high-altitude burst that would fry large areas, creating enormous fires which would barbecue people in their fallout shelters, as had happened to thousands of residents of Hamburg during the vicious incendiary attacks by the RAF and USAAF in 1943. Yes, of course, if you assumed that the enemy's objective was to slaughter your people. Also, for an attacker to make intensive efforts to kill people who were scattered out into the countryside or dug in deep would be militarily idiotic. Why waste weaponry on such attacks? Why waste resources acquiring the means to execute such madness? Why would anyone but a genocidal maniac use nuclear weapons to wipe out a scattered, huddled, and harmless population? And if the Soviets are genocidal maniacs out to eradicate the American people, how on earth does one justify high confidence in arms-control measures? (The knowledge that large parts of the population might die in the shelters was not unknown to the advocates of civil defense. Unstated in their analysis was that a nasty problem in a postattack world would be the public-health threat caused by millions of decaying corpses; better they inter themselves in shelters than die on the surface to pollute the survivors. Fred Ikle at RAND examined drugging people in shelters.)

Some of the more sophisticated enemies of civil defense saw dangers in its very strategic virtues. Just as the defenders believed that a civil defense program to reduce damage would strengthen America's will and increase its credibility to threaten a potential aggressor with nuclear attack, the opponents of civil defense saw grave dangers in this reassurance, and feared that the American leadership would use this leverage for adventurous and risky foreign policies. Ultimately, this came down to a fear and distrust of the American government. Considering the influence of SAC on policy in the late 1950s, this concern was not without some substance.

The argument is not really resolvable by professional analysis. The reader can judge as well as anyone. Would the U.S. government be more willing to go to war if it estimated its fatalities could be reduced from 120 million to 20 million? Would we, our allies, and the Soviet Union place more credence in our threats of deterrence if all knew that the Americans believed that the consequences of carrying out those threats would be reduced from 120 million to 20 million dead? That is imponderable but not unreasonable. But certainly the opposite statement cannot be reasonable—it cannot be true that the prospect of 20 million dead constitutes more self-deterrence than 120 million dead.

On the other hand, is "only" 20 million dead a tolerable outcome? Is that acceptable damage? Would an American government be adventuresome and risk-prone with a forecast of suffering only 20 million, or 2 million, fatalities? In the late 1940s and early 1950s, when the U.S. government was much more bellicose than it was circa 1960 (much less circa 1985) and when there was no chance for Soviet retaliation because the Soviets had no bombers or missiles, the United States did not push the Soviets offensively. The policy was "containment," a hard line in defense against Soviet expansionism, not a direct threat to existing areas of Soviet hegemony.

In the Holifield hearings in 1961, Herman summed up the objections to civil defense thus:

### Some Common Reactions to Civil Defense
1. Completely ineffective.
2. Too effective—will touch off a United States–Soviet Union arms race or even a United States or Soviet Union strike.
3. Both 1 and 2 above.

A few months later, at the height of the civil defense flap, an unknown wit submitted this broadside to the Harvard student newspaper:

> It has been brought to our attention that certain elements among the passengers and crew favor the installation of "life" boats on this ship. These elements have advanced the excuse that such action would save lives in the event of a maritime disaster such as the ship striking an iceberg. Although we share their concern, we remain unalterably opposed to any consideration of their course of action for the following reasons.
>
> 1. This program would lull you into a false sense of security.
> 2. It would cause undue alarm and destroy your desire to continue your voyage in this ship.
> 3. It demonstrates lack of faith in our Captain.
> 4. The apparent security which "life" boats offer will make our Navigators reckless.
> 5. These proposals will distract our attention from more important things, i.e., building unsinkable ships. They may even lead our builders to false economies and the building of ships that are actually unsafe.
> 6. In the event of being struck by an iceberg (we will never strike first) the "life" boats would certainly sink along with the ship.
> 7. If they do not sink, you will only be saved for a worse fate, inevitable death on the open sea.
> 8. If you should be washed ashore on a desert island, you will be unaccustomed to the hostile environment and will surely die of exposure.
> 9. If you should be rescued by a passing vessel, you would spend a life of remorse mourning over your lost loved ones.
> 10. The panic engendered by a collision with an iceberg would destroy all vestiges of civilized human behavior. We shudder at the vision of one man shooting another for possession of a "life" boat.
> 11. Such a catastrophe is too horrible to contemplate. Anyone who does contemplate it obviously advocates it.
>
> Committee for a Sane Navigational Policy

The great debate over civil defense soon faded, although it never completely died, because its advocates and its enemies, when active in fights over other national-security issues, maintained similar positions later on; nevertheless, the debate introduced two new elements to the American political-strategic equation. For the first time, large numbers of citizens had become mobilized and active in opposition to the strategic policy of their own government. It became acceptable, even fashionable in considerable circles, to take a position opposite to that generated by the responsible officials of the government. Never mind that the Constitution gave to the federal government the duty of providing for the common defense; never mind that the Congress was supposed to make laws to that end; and never mind that civilian and military officials were paid and were responsible to execute those laws—obviously, any professor, any professor's wife, any student in some jerkwater university knew better than those dolts.

Beginning with the civil defense debate came the debilitating notion that Everyman was a strategist, that the reader of a newspaper knew more about these matters than did people who had devoted their lives and careers to understanding them. Never mind that every side, every facet, of these issues had been thoroughly debated and worked out among people who had devoted years of effort to trying to understand them as best they could. It may well have been—it may well be—that their best is not nearly good enough; but can ignorance be better? Not only did some clowns say they knew better than the government—they said that it was A Bad Thing even to think about thermonuclear war; in other words, they knew better than the generals, politicians, and analysts because they hadn't thought about it.

Another long-lasting consequence of the civil defense debate was the introduction of a strain of viciousness into what began as a reasoned and gentlemanly discussion among well-mannered people. The opposition to civil defense turned very nasty very fast. Rarely can the birth of a political tendency be identified precisely, yet on this issue it can.

In May of 1961, a slick, well-edited, and ordinarily useful high-middlebrow magazine devoted to scientific matters, *Scientific American*, published what purported to be a review of Herman Kahn's *On Thermonuclear War* by a popular mathematical writer named James Newman. Newman had nothing in his background that would seem to give him any authority to review a book on nuclear strategy, and the review itself reveals that he had no such knowledge, which he might have obtained from reading the book, which internal evidence in his review clearly indicates that he did not. Newman accused Herman Kahn of planning mass murder and other sins. According to Newman, it was A Bad Thing even to think about nuclear war and to write about it. The review was a potpourri of brazen lies. No reputable magazine should publish such insolent tripe. That the libel was not merely a reflection of the individual views of the reviewer was evidenced by the widespread circulation of galleys with an accompanying letter by the principal proprietor and publisher of *Scientific American*, Gerald Piel, informing his correspondents of his aim of "decontamination."

The review made *On Thermonuclear War* a *cause célèbre*. Over 30,000 copies were sold—a rich sale for a work published by an academic press—and made Herman Kahn a celebrity, and earned respectable royalties for him (and for The RAND Corporation, with which he split them). But Herman had not written the book to gain celebrity, money, and least of all notoriety. He was appalled at the attack and offered to write a rejoinder for *Scientific American*. The editors turned him down flat. They refused even to publish a letter in his own defense. All that Herman could do was photocopy and circulate the correspondence widely.

Gerald Piel exposed his political colors in a radio address from Town Hall later in 1961. He made some of the standard arguments against civil defense, drooling over the harsh consequences of a nuclear attack with malicious glee, and whining that what we should be doing was working on ways to prevent thermonuclear war, not thinking about how to fight it, much less how to mitigate its consequences. Of course, he offered no practical proposals for achieving that eminently desirable end, nor was *Scientific American* ever willing or able to express any positive scientific or American solutions to the problem, except to engage in endless embittered philippics against the American defense establishment in general and any new weapons system in particular. Listening to the tape of Piel's cultured voice advocating the infantile notion of "general and complete disarmament," and the bitterness of the tone, one can sadly mark the debate about the survival of nations slipping into demagogic gutters. The psychological defense was breaking down.

The Kennedy people resolved their political embarrassment by abandoning their support for civil defense. They left their initial proposals on the table, neither added to them nor subtracted from them, and made no further push for civil defense either publicly or to the Congress. In 1962 and in 1963 the administration again formally asked for substantial appropriations for shelters in federal buildings and incentives for private shelter buildings, and each time the proposals were knocked out, in the absence of any administration arm-twisting, by the House and Senate. Steuart Pittman had to struggle on almost unaided.

## The Test Ban

In the Congress in 1963 it was claimed that the civil defense program was made superfluous by the recently negotiated partial atomic-test-ban treaty. The argument was spurious, but the success of that negotiation fundamentally affected the status of the American offense and defense. The test ban was promoted by the spreading recognition of the adverse environmental consequences of continuing atmospheric testing. It was forwarded by the carefully orchestrated thrust of the first years of the Kennedy administration, with support from most of the most thoughtful and influential elements of the Congress, with carefully prepared political and polemical tactics to outflank the presumed enemy of the thrust, the virulent anti-Communist right-wingers. Nonetheless, a catalyst on the American side, and probably to the Soviets as well, was the stark terror engendered by the Cuban missile crisis. Both adversaries agreed that it was necessary and desirable to defuse international tensions and to assure their publics that the state of crisis provoked by Khrushchev's adventurism and saber-rattling, perhaps exacerbated by the American polemics necessary to gain political support for the U.S. strategic-force augmentations in the late Eisenhower and early Kennedy administrations, required that something be done to cool off the Cold War.

Among educated Americans a ban on nuclear tests was generally held desirable, and the most ambitious arms controllers held out as long as they could for a "comprehensive" ban—of all testing of any weapons anywhere anytime. This was an unfortunate objective. The concept of a complete ban was founded upon the prejudice that nuclear tests were inherently bad, and that further testing would worsen the world's situation. This ignored the possible positive benefits of nuclear weapons for the United States, in particular in saving lots of money by obviating the need to match the Soviets "man for man, gun for gun, tank for tank." Despite the anxiety, the nuclear age had corresponded to a paucity of wars between major countries, and to an absence of major wars, not to speak of total wars. The worst conflict between major powers had been when the Chinese intervened in Korea in 1950, and they were careful to label their troops as unofficial "volunteers." The Chinese and the Americans limited the war to the territory of Korea itself, and the Americans eschewed the use of nuclear weapons. The Chinese then had no nuclear munitions, but they knew where to get them if they needed them, and we knew they knew.

More troubling was the assumption that more testing would lead to the further development of nuclear weapons and therefore to even worse horrors. To be sure, the progression from Alamogordo to Eniwetok was ugly, and Khrushchev's howling about his hyper-bombs in 1961 promised more devilish devices, not to mention the nastier concepts of American weapons designers, some of which had been listed in Herman Kahn's *On Thermonuclear War*. Fortunately, the nuclear developments during the period 1950–55 had both positive and negative effects, and the progress since about 1956 was entirely on the plus side. Whereas the original A-bombs and H-bombs were so clumsy that they could be used only to destroy cities, the general tendency since 1950 and the universal tendency since about 1956 was toward technology that was not benign, but at least offered some promise of mitigating the consequences of the nuclear age. Smaller bombs meant that they could be used without destroying large numbers of people. Cleaner bombs, that is, generating less of fallout-producing radioactive isotopes, offered relief from the plague of radioactivity. The devices conceived at Los Alamos, Livermore, and RAND in the late '50s and early '60s did not foretoken worse damage to America and to humanity, but presented an opening toward the evolution of the defense. Defensive nuclear weapons killed only attacking aircrews, and AICBM weapons didn't kill anyone—they saved lives.

### Nice Nuclear Weapons

The original notion of an ABM warhead had been simply a big thermonuclear bomb shot up to the edge of the atmosphere that would cripple the incoming by brute force—enough megatonnage would generate some combination of blast and radiation that would damage the reentry vehicle or the warhead. Better-tailored solutions were considered in the late 1950s at RAND. The Nova concept contemplated by Richard Holbrook, a chief BMD researcher, was charming in its simplicity: a 300-megaton bomb exploded at the edge of space would clean out whole clusters of the incoming RVs, and all the decoys as well. It is just as well that Nova wasn't tested, because the resulting electromagnetic pulse, then unknown, would have burned out every electrical circuit on a quarter of the globe.

Sam Cohen, also known as Samuel T. Cohen, also known as S. T. Cohen, was introduced to the nuclear business by being assigned as an enlisted man to a mysterious post in New Mexico. While awaiting his initial interview, he was left to cool his heels in the library. When asked by an officer what he thought the activity was about, Sam replied, "You are building an atomic bomb." After the officer recovered from his shock, Sam revealed that he had noticed that the Los Alamos library contained a disproportionate amount of materials about nuclear energy, and only a nuclear bomb could justify such fantastically elaborate security.

After the war he finished his education, joined RAND, quit in a huff to go to Lockheed for a time, and returned in the late 1950s when the nuclear weaponry was getting really interesting. Some scientists challenge his claim, but Sam Cohen has been recorded in history as "the father of the neutron bomb." In work with Livermore people, it was calculated that a hydrogen bomb could be so designed that a substantial part of the neutrons generated by the chain reaction would not continue the reaction, but would spread out from the weapon to hit the target directly. The neutrons from a defensive detonation would impact on the incoming warhead, disturbing the nuclear mechanism and rendering it inoperative. This brilliant concept created what was effectively an anti–nuclear bomb. Although it was pressed into use later in the ABM program, it suffered from a lack of lethal radius—it could not kill far enough away. Another of the RAND physicists had a better answer.

Albert Latter and his brother Richard were stars of the early RAND Corporation physics department, and key links to Livermore. (Dick Latter, on leave from RAND, was the original acting head of Livermore's theoretical-physics department.) Al was your typical physics-weapons prodigy, and early attracted the attention of Edward Teller. In 1958 they coauthored a popular book that purported to be a layman's explanation of the nuclear age, but was actually a transparent pitch for continued atmospheric testing. Physicists are a competitive and contentious lot, and few claims of originality are generally accepted, yet Al Latter gets universal accolades for conceiving the gamma-ray/X-ray warhead. In the atmosphere, most of the gamma-ray radiation from the nuclear reaction heats the surrounding air, creating the blast. The 1952 Lincoln Summer Study examined and rejected direct gamma-ray kill for air defense because the blast was more efficacious. In space, with careful design, the gamma rays heat the warhead itself, generating X-rays which project much farther than neutrons, reaching the incoming RV, intensely heating and distorting the nose cone, and ruining its aerodynamics, so that it tumbles or crumbles as it reenters the atmosphere. The X-ray warhead is an excellent ICBM killer.

Other nuclear AICBM ideas reportedly were considered, but none of them seemed to be as promising as the neutron bomb and the X-ray bomb. These devices were of no use to the offense, but excellent for the defense, and they needed to be developed and tested. One of the people most sensitive to this issue was Edward Teller. No one man can read the soul of another, but many people have held that Teller was gravely troubled by the consequences of the age that he had helped inaugurate by driving Szilard to Long Island to encourage Albert Einstein to write a famous letter to the American Commander-in-Chief, and by his lobbying in the Pentagon and the Congress for Super. Unlike many of the dissident atomic scientists—who sought to wash their hands of the matter or cry *Mea culpa* or try to reverse history—Teller's career post-Super exhibited a distinct pattern of trying to justify the existence of these nasty gadgets by putting them to positive uses. He was the promoter of the AEC's Plowshares project to try to find peaceful applications for atomic munitions—to blast canals, and later to drive natural gas from deep rock into wells.

Teller was an early and continuing earnest agitator for civil defense. Initially, he had been highly skeptical of ballistic missile defense. At a 1960 conference at Asilomar* on the California coast, Richard Foster of SRI brought him around with an all-day briefing. Teller and Al Latter and many other people on the inside knew full well that nuclear testing was not leading to more and more grotesque and damaging weaponry but to weapons that would be at least neutral and might well be—the most enthusiastic thought they surely would be—positive to national and global security.

Teller took the lead in the fight against the test-ban treaty. He had been a strong advocate of less stringent security regulations on scientific information. The opposition to the test ban was hobbled by the ban on openly discussing exactly what was being studied in the weapons labs and in the skies above the islands of the atomic archipelago. The testing of the '40s and the '50s had revealed that rapid nuclear reactions did so much more than merely generate big blasts and the inefficient poisons of radiation. The atomic gadgets were fascinating—they had such remarkable and unforeseen effects. So much more needed to be understood about so many of the most important of those effects:

*Blackout.* An early Nevada test was monitored by sounding rockets. The blast severed the radio controls. Further experiments and analysis revealed that an atmospheric explosion did to radar just the opposite of what flash did to the eye. The heat and pressure ionized the air, creating a fireball that diffused, absorbed, and did not reflect the radio beams. A blob appeared on the screens. Because it was extremely hot, it would quickly rise and dissipate. But while it existed, the radar could not detect whatever was on the other side of the blob. A nuclear engagement in the upper atmosphere would surely generate much "blackout" from the explosions of the nuclear-tipped defensive interceptors. And the attacker might fit his warheads with "salvage fusing"—the missileers' version of the deadman's fuse—which would ignite when an interceptor closed with it. Or the attacker might lay on a "precursor strike," a preliminary

---

*Devotees of the curious and bizarre should note that Paul Nitze upheld Kennedy's arms-control approach at this conference. In the audience was Admiral Chester Ward. Soon he coauthored several books with Phyllis Schlafly claiming that a cabal of "Insiders" was conniving to sell out America to the Communists. They fingered the Insiders' commissar—Paul Nitze.

attack intended to blind the radars to permit the main force to penetrate untracked.*

Not enough was known about blackout. More testing was needed to learn how the defense might better deal with blackout.

*Redout.* The same intense heat from a fast nuclear reaction that created the blast also affected heat sensors. An infrared detector capable of distinguishing the tiny mote of heat of an incoming from the great coldness of space could not handle the megacalories of nuclear detonation. This was precisely the equivalent of the effects of flash on the eye—temporary or permanent blindness.

Not enough was known about redout. More testing was needed to learn how the defense might better deal with redout.

*EMP.* In 1958 in the South Atlantic and in the South Pacific, the testing programs included very-high-altitude shots, at the edge of space. There was a weird output which blew out electric circuits hundreds of miles away. The effect was labeled electromagnetic pulse (EMP—"ee-em-pea"). The closest natural phenomenon is a bolt of lightning. EMP is fast and widespread, but of low intensity; it has little effect on robust electronics such as vacuum tubes, but can burn out more delicate devices, such as the microprocessors in computers and in almost all military equipment, including defensive hardware.

Ingenious methods were devised to estimate and simulate EMP, and elegant solutions were designed to shield against it. Still, not enough was known about EMP. More testing was needed to learn how the defense might better deal with EMP.

And Teller *et al.* knew that X-ray and neutron warheads had yet to be tested. And they knew that the planned defenses of the ICBMs, the hardened silos, hadn't been tested against real attacks. And they

---

*A rococo elaboration was the "ladder-down" attack. The offense would explode a warhead just inside the atmosphere to blind the defender's radar; then a second warhead would drop through the blob of the first and be fired; then subsequent warheads would repeat the sequence, climbing down to the target, which would be nailed by the final blast. Well, no attacker would believe that warheads could be located and exploded with such split-second precision at intercontinental range. Even if he could, high virtual attrition had been imposed on him. And defensive tactics were easy: Early-warning radars would identify the attack, and exoatmospheric interceptors would break it up in space. A ladder-down attack in the atmosphere could be foiled by firing an interceptor with proximity fuse through a blob to kill the successor warhead. Although taken seriously by some consultant scientists circa 1960, ladder-down tactics were merely a curiosity of the paper wars.

knew painfully well that the mirror-imaging assumption that what-ever-we-can-do-he-can-do might not be the correct formulation. The Livermore crowd knew that the Soviets had a thermonuclear bomb first, and they also knew how difficult was the Super program, how all the computers in the nation had to be dragooned into service to fix the calculations, while the Soviets had achieved their Super *without* computers. The Livermore crowd knew that the Soviets had just completed several major high-altitude test programs. Teller *et al.* feared that whatever-we-can-do-he-can-do—*first*.

It was not politic to say all or any of that publicly. The opponents did persuade the Senate Armed Services Preparedness Investigating Subcommittee, dominated by Henry Jackson, to include among its other arguments against the test ban: "the United States will be unable to determine with confidence the performance and reliability of any ABM system developed without benefit of atmospheric op-erational system tests." The opposition to the test-ban treaty had to concentrate on the narrow technical point of "verification." Tel-ler's people, and many others in the government and among its consultants, had worked out in detail how one would go about cheating on the treaty. The consensus was that exploding any weapon in the atmosphere was almost impossible without its being detected by atmospheric sampling of radioactive materials and/or by the now regularly circulating reconnaissance satellites. Further, it was gen-erally held, although with a little more skepticism, that nothing could be tested in space anywhere near the Earth without the radioactive flux registering on instruments deployed casually to record cosmic rays and other extraterrestrial phenomena.

The critics concentrated on the problem of underground testing, arguing that a cheater could get away with subterranean explosions because the Earth always has an upset stomach, is always shifting and rumbling, so a blast of significant weapons power might pass unnoticed. An easy way of cheating—which the general public could easily visualize—was the digging of a monstrous cavern to absorb most of the blast so that it could not be recorded on seismographs. This specter was sufficiently convincing to the parties involved that it permitted a compromise. The test ban was not to be comprehen-sive at all; it was to apply to testing in the atmosphere, under the seas, and in space—but not underground. The arms controllers took this as a terrible affront, yet the result had some merit.

Although the outcome was not entirely satisfactory to the promoters of security through further weapons development, it did offer them an opportunity to continue testing their devices, not only to invent weaponry for new and more desirable uses, but to do regular quality checks of existing inventory. For example, it was not entirely certain that nuclear weapons kept in storage for long periods would continue to function effectively. Because the United States was relying upon the threat of nuclear weapons to maintain the peace, and because a wide overlap existed between the arms controllers and those who believed that security was maintained by mutual vulnerability, it could be accepted that the effects of weapons should be kept highly credible in order to maintain the "balance of terror."

Senator Humphrey led the fight for the test ban on the Senate floor. The hearings gained it a long list of highly respectable advocates, pillars of the scientific, political, and military establishment. The Joint Chiefs of Staff, perhaps grudgingly but as good soldiers, went along. These were high times for the arms controllers. From Hudson, Don Brennan was priming the counsel of the Foreign Relations Committee with questions to browbeat Teller. The treaty went through very easily. The arms controllers were elated, and justifiably so, because at last an actual arms-control agreement with the Soviet Union had been signed. The two superpowers had shown they could agree on something of mutual benefit.

Why the Soviets signed on we will not know until the Kremlin archives are opened to public view. At the time, the more virulent anti-Soviet agitators asserted that the Soviets intended to cheat; over the years, as no evidence of cheating appeared, this original claim was swept into the political memory tube. Another explanation was that the Soviets had learned so much in their testing previous to the ban that they thought that they had a distinct advantage in knowledge of nuclear weaponry, especially in the area of effects at very high altitudes and at the edge of space. Another theory held that Khrushchev personally favored it because he was under increasing pressure from opposition elements within the Party to show that he was a reasonable and sensible man, not the crazed *muzhik* whose wild posturing and adventurous schemes threatened the very existence of the Soviet state, not to mention the preeminence of the Party. If the last was the case, it did him no good. Khrushchev was overthrown in late 1964 and went into forced retirement.

Like good tacticians, the arms controllers recognized that this wondrous breakthrough should be immediately exploited. The follow-up produced immediate disappointment. Attempts at further agreements broke down on the fundamental asymmetries of interest between the two countries and the asymmetries of weaponry. In commercial transactions, a common medium of exchange is money, which has been created for that express purpose. In international matters, what is at stake is power, which has no common coinage; high values of state can be traded only by barter, and all parties have the problem of deciding what is worth what to whom. It was not possible to gain agreement on other important arms-control matters for four years.

All sorts of suggestions floated. Some advocates, especially Jay Stone of the Hudson Institute, proposed that both nations destroy large bomber forces in a "bomber bonfire"; but the Soviets knew the Pentagon had already halted B-52 production and programmed the phaseout of its B-47s, so they would be foolish to barter for something the Americans were about to give up for nothing. And the Soviets had already had their own unilateral bomber bonfire when they gave a few hundred Tu-4s to the Chinese and scrapped the rest. The same difficulty arose with the earlier ICBMs that the Americans had decided to junk because they were inaccurate, vulnerable, and expensive to keep in operational trim. The newer well-defended strategic weapons, the Minutemen in the hardened silos and the submarine-borne Polarises, were recognized by the arms controllers not to be "destabilizing" but desirable at least in the short and medium run and therefore worthy to be kept in service.

And no one with a grain of mother wit would expect the Soviet Union to agree to an arms-control deal of serious import so long as the United States maintained the impressive superiority in strategic offensive forces created in the early 1960s. In 1964, President Johnson proposed a "freeze" on strategic offensive and defensive "vehicles." Given the overwhelming U.S. advantage at that time, everyone knew that the offer was puerile demagogy in an election year. Real dealing would require that the Soviets catch up; then presumably an arrangement in the interests of both superpowers and of humanity could be made in good faith and with proper precautions for both sides.

What else could an arms controller control? That the only immediate substantive controllable arms were ballistic missile defenses presently became evident, and the logic limiting them became almost universally accepted in arms-control circles. It is precisely at this time that the arms-control bandwagon broke two wheels and proceeded to run in mad circles for two decades. The arms controllers forgot the fundamental goals of arms control: to reduce the risk of war; to reduce the damage of war; to save money.

And because the theorists knew that their work would be read by the Soviets, and hoped that it would educate them, the arms controllers omitted from the conventional formulation the adjective "American." It is the function of the *American* government to reduce the *American* risk, to reduce *American* damage, and to save *American* money. It perhaps did not occur to the arms controllers that the Soviet officials responsible for the security and survival of their system would insert the appropriate national adjective in their own calculations.

To the arms controllers, the need to control arms by negotiation meant that the Soviet Union had to be essentially as strong as the United States in nuclear weaponry, thus nullifying the nuclear advantage with which the United States presumably had been keeping the peace through "deterrence" since World War II. To be sure, spiritless parallel negotiations were being conducted to try to control conventional weapons in the key theater of central Europe; but many players were involved, and the relative needs of the Western powers to defend themselves could not coherently be matched against the Soviet need to threaten the West with conventional attack and/ or to protect itself from German revanchism and/or to keep the subject nations of Eastern Europe under the Soviet boot.

To achieve arms control, the United States had to abandon a fundamental point of strategic superiority. This did not go unnoticed by the French, who pulled out of NATO and began feverishly building up their own independent nuclear force. Nor did this shift of emphasis go unnoticed by the Germans and other western Europeans, who adjusted to the changing balance of power by an *Ostpolitik* of accommodation, granting recognition to the bastard East German regime and cosseting the Russian bear with sweets of trade credits and high technology. While this erosion of the American position was occurring before their eyes, the arms controllers were arguing that nuclear superiority was worthless.

In the arms-control world, substantive controls had to wait on the achievement of Soviet parity in offensive weapons. In the meantime, nothing else could be controlled but ABM, and it had to be done fast, because the Soviets began deploying a functioning system. The other side was first.

## The Last Fight of Nike-Zeus

Meanwhile at Whippany, Huntsville, Kwajalein, and the far-flung research shops of the subcontractors, the Army and Bell Labs were soldiering on with Nike-Zeus. The process was not easy, but bit by bit the subsystems were working up to performance levels. The radars were made operational. The computers were programmed slowly. Most dramatic was the testing of the missiles themselves— dramatic because the inevitable failures in the development of missilery have a propensity to blow up spectacularly. The Army believed it had persuasive information for the Office of the Secretary of Defense and for the Commander-in-Chief, and continued to lobby hard for money to put Nike-Zeus into production.

Apparently, the pressure reached the White House. The Army's Pentagon action officer for Nike-Zeus, Lieutenant Colonel C. J. LeVan, was summoned from leave at Cape Hatteras, ordered to rendezvous at Andrews Air Force Base with his briefing charts, and flown in an executive transport to Hyannis Port in company with the Secretary of Defense. McNamara instructed him to make the best case he could for the Army's ABM system. Colonel LeVan's briefing for the Commander-in-Chief did not get far, because the President cut him short and moved immediately into the interrogatory section. The President had many questions to ask, decidedly skeptical questions. The President was not much interested in what Nike-Zeus could do to protect the country, nor in the significance of anti–ballistic missiles to national strategy. All the President's questions were negative: about the operational difficulties, about how Zeus might not work. LeVan responded as best he could to Kennedy and his cabinet and then retired to the veranda, where he shmoozed with the President's father, old Joseph P. Kennedy, while the civilian leadership deliberated behind the French doors. The R&D continued to be funded generously, but Nike-Zeus did not go into the budget that year.

The Executive is not the only power in the American polity, so the Army turned to the Congress, where it had a champion in a senator from South Carolina who happened to be a major general in the Army Reserves. Strom Thurmond was hardly at the center of the American political stage. In 1948 he had been the standard-bearer of the Dixiecrat revolt and was a diehard segregationist. Thurmond was a hero in his own state, and more broadly in the South, but not the sort to conquer the political center. Nonetheless, he was all the Army had, and in a desperation fight you use whatever resources are available.

A new approach was needed, and the Army resorted to a very old trick; calling attention to the presumed enemy's capabilities. Now, in many types of human competition, including warfare, it is very pertinent to compare equivalent items. Early in the 20th century, the maritime powers could count the other's battleships, and tally their own, and judge that their forces were superior, equal, or inferior. By the nature of its design and equipment, a battleship is not an offensive or a defensive weapon, but both; battleships fight battleships, so the number of battleships that engage in fleet actions is decidedly relevant to the outcome, and therefore to national strength, and therefore to the ability to achieve national goals through threats, explicit or implicit. The habit of counting battleships, or guns, or troops was deeply ingrained in both the military and the popular mind. It was relevant and simple to understand. Unfortunately, the convention was carried into the air age. Bombers did not fight bombers. Your number of bombers affects the amount of damage you could cause to the enemy with bombs, and the enemy's number of bombers affects how well he can bomb you. But counting bombers against bombers made no sense—it was your interceptor-fighters and antiaircraft guns versus his bombers, and your bombers pitted against his interceptors and antiaircraft. And in air defense, the intercepting weapons were less important to the balance than the sensors and communications. Counting bombers against bombers and missiles against missiles was the fundamental error of the "gaps" of the 1950s.

Nike-Zeus was an anti–intercontinental ballistic missile. The Soviets already had a handful of ICBMs and promised to have many more. It would have been proper to compare our AICBMs with their ICBMs, and vice versa. But the idea of measuring defense against offense was perhaps too complex for some minds in the early '60s (and also in the late '80s). A simpler calculation is balancing his ICBMs against our ICBMs, and his AICBMs versus our AICBMs. This was the Thurmond ploy.

## ABM on the Other Side

Already there had been a Soviet ABM flap. Aerial and satellite reconnaissance had located a series of construction sites in the northwestern part of the U.S.S.R., along principal routes of attack on the major centers of Soviet Russia from North America. These mysterious complexes were clearly intended to house something that was intended to shoot down something; there were radars and emplacements for missiles. The first of these was sighted near Tallinn, the capital of Estonia, and so the whatever was called "the Tallinn System." The Soviets built many of these, and apparently to this day no one is quite sure what they were for. It is held, with what merit cannot be said surely in this context, that these were for missiles that NATO labeled the SA-5, intended to defend against the forthcoming B-70 superbomber. Although the United States could not be certain at the time, perhaps they were intended to be ABMs, and even if they were designed against the B-70, they might have ABM potential. Technological mirror-imaging was sufficient to grant the Soviet SAMs some AICBM potential: had not the United States already in 1961 killed missiles—albeit not ICBMs—with the lowly Hawk and the middling Nike-Hercules? The theory that the missiles were intended to pot B-70s is given considerable support by the generally accepted view that the Soviets stopped augmenting the Tallinn sites when the United States terminated the B-70. But something else immediately popped up on the landscape of the northwestern frontiers of the Soviet Union.

Strom Thurmond went to the floor of the Senate and called attention to an ABM gap. The Russians, he claimed, are deploying an ABM and we are not—and why not? Senator Thurmond's intense interest in the subject prompted him to do something unprecedented in peacetime. He maintained that he needed to present such sensitive evidence that the Senate should be called into classified session. With the doors locked, Thurmond displayed Army intelligence material calling attention to indications of mysterious and threatening construction around Leningrad, construction which the analysts interpreted as the beginnings of a Soviet ABM system. Again, the Americans would fall behind the Soviet Union in prestige and in real military power, which might well be converted into Soviet aggressiveness against American interests worldwide. Of course, the military response to a strengthened defense is to augment the offense. But Thurmond's political answer to the ABM gap was that we should go ahead with Nike-Zeus.

Had the chronicler the same access to Soviet sources of information, half, indeed more than half, of this chronicle would deal with the defensive activities of the Union of Soviet Socialist Republics during its period of political strife against the capitalist West. Unfortunately, such information is not available. So the Soviet side of the great game of superpowers must perforce be handled briefly—and with megatons of skepticism. To be sure, a massive volume could be filled with accounts of what various people have alleged the Soviets were doing. Pity that most of such a book would be occupied by analysis of statements by Soviet leaders—who lie even more chronically, enthusiastically, and clumsily than their American equivalents—and with gossip and rumors about U.S. "intelligence" reports of what is supposedly going on behind the Iron Curtain and why. The intelligence is gathered by some extraordinarily elaborate and sophisticated technical means and possibly through reports from understandably anonymous persons on the scene. This information is analyzed and presented under very secure conditions to persons in the government, and a few close contractors, who presumably have "a need-to-know."

The receivers of the output are told little about the methods of the analysis and practically nothing at all about the "raw data" that are the input. What they receive goes through several filters. A finer-mesh screen is what is released openly or surreptitiously via "leaks" to the public at large. All that emerges is influenced to some degree by the political motivations of the people who let it out. This is not to say that the material is necessarily incorrect or biased; it is to say that the casual individual has no way of knowing. However, over the years there is somewhat of a correcting mechanism, as other people with other interests come to power, and as more information is gathered, and as the older information becomes less sensitive and slowly, even despite the most rigorous security regulation, oozes into the public domain. So in hindsight, even with all the caveats above, the general consensus among people who discuss these matters in a serious way is that Strom Thurmond was reasonably correct in telling the Senate that the Soviet Union was indeed building something of an ABM defensive nature in the vicinity of the fine city of Leningrad. The Senate heard Thurmond, and it heard DoD denials—not of the existence of something defensive around Leningrad, but of any great significance to this activity—and strong opposition to the notion that forwarding Nike-Zeus was the way to deal with it now. The Senate had a short debate. The opposition to Strom Thurmond was informed by other elements in the Department of Defense than the Army, and took their judgment as definitive, on the ground that the Executive Branch should be followed on such matters. The Senate deliberated and voted down Strom Thurmond by 10–86. That was the last fight of Nike-Zeus.

## Project Defender

Meanwhile, ARPA had been exploiting its mandate to investigate advanced ballistic-missile defense research in Project Defender. The initial program was rather excessively advanced, including examination of antigravity, antimatter, and force fields; those science-fiction concepts could not be defended from the scrutiny of a PSAC subcommittee under Wiesner and Brown. As in so many national-security trends circa 1960, the process was so continuous that the change of administration was hardly noticeable. The only obvious modification was more generous funding, as McNamara countered demands for immediate deployment of Nike-Zeus by supporting Defender and upgrading its priority. Whereas the Army had committed itself completely to Bell Labs, ARPA took a more catholic approach, and cast its research money wide among a plethora of contractors, who vied with each other for generating ingenious methods of killing intercontinental ballistic missiles.

Defender was a veritable research Disneyland, the greatest toy shop since the nova of frantic experimentation of the last days of the Third Reich. At its peak, $100 million per annum was budgeted for the program. Little of this largess went to actually making anything. Some of the budget was for overhead and profits, but the bulk paid the salaries of engineers and a few scientists who desired nothing more than thinking of really great ways to thwart ICBMs—not merely to help defend the country, and not merely to generate the great killer idea that would gain their firms production contracts, but to produce brilliant concepts for the most noble and perhaps the most stimulating of incentives: for their own sake. Those were great days for the concepts men.

Presiding over this cornucopia was Charlie Herzfeld, a man of marvelous breadth of knowledge and extraordinary personal charm. He was a Viennese by birth, of sound bourgeois background. His father had been an artillery officer in the service of the Hapsburgs in the First World War, and later had fought in the ultra-right-wing *Heimwehr* against the socialists in the Austrian civil war of the 1930s. But the Herzfelds would have no truck with the Nazi riffraff who seized Austria in the late '30s, and the family pedigree bore a little taint according to the racial standards of the new regime, so they found themselves in republican America, where Charlie studied chemistry, taught for a while at Catholic University in Washington, joined the Naval Research Laboratory working on solid-state physics, and later moved on to the National Bureau of Standards, then active in defense research. He earned a sterling reputation as a research manager. The Berlin crisis prompted Herzfeld to accept appointment as head of Project Defender in 1961. Much of the work was put out through, and evaluated by, the Institute for Defense Analyses, our old friend IDA. Herzfeld founded the classified *Journal of Ballistic Missile Defense Research* and moved the Defender offices to Rosslyn, just upriver from the Pentagon, and thus established that once-tacky crossroads as a center for defensive research. Rosslyn became the capital of the Beltway.

*BAMBI.* ARPA's contractors worked over hundreds of concepts of intercepting and destroying ICBMs from launch to impact. The projects ranged from the esoteric to the down-to-earth. At the nether end of the range of AICBM was boost-phase intercept—nailing the ICBMs on the way up. Their initial speed is slow as they climb into space, accelerating under the thrust of their powerful boosters and passing into thinner and thinner air. They are also stuffed with heavy fuel, which is also volatile and vulnerable. While rising, they cannot fox the defenders with precursor attacks or decoys.

One system devised by Convair has given its name generically to all of them: BAllistic Missile Boost Intercept (BAMBI—"bam-bee").

(The engineer who coined this dear label remains anonymous, deservedly so.) One of the first such schemes was Lockheed's INSATRAC, INterception by SAtellite TRACking. Already near to deployment was the Midas satellite, which would pick up missile launches by reading their heat through infrared sensors. In INSATRAC, Midas would alert a second group of satellites operating at lower altitudes which would then track the missile. The tracking satellites would alert a huge interceptor missile ground-based along the Distant Early Warning Line, which would kill the ICBM over the Arctic. It was an interesting start, but was soon shot down in the paper wars. The communications were liable to interruption, and the system could be fooled by very simple countermeasures— a slight maneuver of the ICBM would cause the interceptor to miss by miles.

A more promising approach was that of Convair's SPAD—Space Patrol Active Defense. Under this proposal, the defenders would place in space a flotilla of satellites carrying a load of small homing missiles. As the ICBM rose from Earth, the mother ship would read the heat plume, calculate the course, and launch an interceptor to meet it. The Convair engineers calculated, plausibly enough to persuade their technological judges at ARPA and IDA, that sufficient accuracy could be attained that the interceptors need not have large and expensive nuclear warheads; indeed, they need not even have conventional high explosives. As the interceptor closed with its prey emerging from the atmosphere, it would unfurl a large umbrella, a net of steel weighing only a few pounds; at the speeds of encounter, this would mangle the ICBM, destroying the integrity of its nose cone, which it needed to survive the ordeal of heat and pressure imposed by reentry to the atmosphere. The webs were cheap, but the interceptors were expensive, and the satellites were galactical in cost. The Convair design team worked out various combinations and came up with a need for a 58,000-pound satellite as one promising variant. Unfortunately, the largest American rocket at the time was the Saturn I, which could only lift 40,000 pounds into low Earth orbit. The engineers imagined cheaper ways to put vast flocks of satellites into space, and conceived of a reusable shuttle that could heave a dozen at a time.

In addition, the concept needed defensive decoys, because the satellites were an obviously lucrative target for a preemptive attack. Although they could be defended with the same missiles that were defending the homeland from attack, the loss of satellites could open up a hole in the screen which needed to be covered by other means. SPAD was worked out in considerable detail. The Convair team deserve high marks for ingenuity, but no matter how smart they were, they came up against fundamental obstacles: To maintain coverage of Soviet territory at all times, hundreds of satellites had to be in orbit. To get them up and keep them up required an amount of lift that was far beyond anything that the United States could buy in any time span even outlandishly conceivable. Yes, it worked, on paper, but the cost was exorbitant.

Another BAMBI program was TRW's random barrage system. This eliminated the mother ship by seeding space with thousands of small interceptor missiles in random orbits, each interceptor capable of picking up an oncoming ICBM. The random warhead used a shotgun load of steel pellets to kill its target.

That did not exhaust the toys in ARPA's shop. If putting the interceptors into orbit was too expensive, then why not try a ground-based system? The ARPA Terminal Defense (ARPAT) proposed a large launcher carrying smaller rockets that would spread out high in the atmosphere and would then release numerous small, light, homing interceptors. A feature of this concept was a "loiter" capability, which meant that the launcher could turn off its engines and coast for a few seconds to wait for the incoming, or to reignite, if necessary, to adjust position for a superior intercept. The ARPAT subsystems were actually tested at White Sands. A later version of ARPAT was Homing Intercept Technology (HIT—yes, "hit"), intended to be an interceptor so inexpensive that it could be purchased, deployed, and fired in such large quantities that anything that came down from space could be attacked, thus nullifying all decoys. The notion of using what came to be called "kinetic" kill—exploiting the energy in the fantastically rapid closing speed of the ICBM and interceptor—was the basis for a series of ingenious concepts. SAMBO and TAMBO were schemes to throw up a large shield of pellets in the path of an upcoming or down-dropping ICBM.

Another version of a blaster defense was HELMET, a terminal defense system, in effect a monster shotgun putting a cloud of pellets in front of the dropping warhead. This idea came out of the Canadian version of ARPA, the Canadian Armaments Research and Development Establishment (CARDE—"kar-dee"), which was the first, and so far only, contribution of America's presumed continental allies to strategic-missile defense. The Canadian analysts estimated that a defense of Toronto or Montreal by this system would cost 20 to 50 percent more than the estimated value of all the physical assets of either of those great cities.

Another project took up air-launched anti–ballistic missiles. The tests worked, but keeping the planes flying and keeping in communication with them was another budget-buster. Other ARPA work was the GLIPAR Program (GuideLines Identification Program for Anti-missile Research) which dealt with nuclear means and directed-energy ways of killing ballistic missiles. Much of this is still closely held. One notion was CASABA, a directed nuclear weapon which would squirt a hypervelocity beam of liquid or solid pellets against the incoming. These too were not deemed appropriate to push toward development.

The high weights and therefore unacceptable launch costs of the missile-armed space battle stations prompted ARPA to examine other means of killing the rising ICBMs. Early in the century, H. G. Wells had imagined a death ray in *The War of the Worlds*, and the notion of a pure blast of destructive energy had become a staple of science fiction. Early experiments had tried to turn radio energy into a focused beam or pulse to kill or disable at a distance, but the power that could be transmitted was inadequate. In the late 1950s, however, several researchers, working independently, rapidly devised a new system of amplifying energy by exciting it within a tube mirrored at either end; the energy, originally light, would bounce back and forth within the cylinder until it reached sufficient intensity to break through one end in a concentrated pulse of wonderful power.

The primitive version of this principle was the MASER; that was a warm-up to the immediately discovered LASER—Light Amplification of Stimulated Emission of Radiation. The military potential of this research was grasped instantly by everybody. The most immediate and practical employment was rather like radar itself, to illuminate a target or to aim a weapon, and such devices were used for "smart bombs" in the early 1970s. A pure energy kill was rather more difficult—but tens of millions of dollars went into the ARPA budget.

Another version of directed energy was the particle beam, which was a spin-off of theoretical work in nuclear physics. Subatomic particles could be generated in experimental laboratory particle accelerators and flung at hostile targets. ARPA also looked at the old idea of microwave weapons to burn at a distance. All these were very interesting, and of considerable promise, and worthy of continued research, but none of them could be expected to have weapons applications, especially for ballistic missile defense, within anything resembling a policy-relevant time frame—not for a decade at the very least. And for all the "exotic" schemes, the cost calculations, however crude, gave prices that would have absorbed the entire U.S. defense budget and then some. Herzfeld about BAMBI: "The scheme has the fatal flaw that at the present time and in the foreseeable future, the reliability of complicated satellite systems would be so low that one could not possibly afford such a defense system." Not only did you have to get BAMBI up, you had to keep it up. Two estimates of the cost were bandied about: one was $50 billion a year; the other was $100 billion a year. The total defense budget then was $50 billion.

When Charlie Herzfeld resigned from ARPA in 1967, Donald Brennan reminded him of one of the earliest and most ambitious of the exotic ballistic missile defense concepts. While still at Lincoln Labs, Brennan had written up a short paper advocating "Project Turnabout." The scheme was that the defending nation should ring the Equator of the Earth with powerful rocket engines. Upon warning of the enemy launch, the rockets would be fired, rotating the Earth 180 degrees, causing the ICBMs to impact on the attacker's own territory. Brennan calculated the rocket thrust required (it was considerable, but not beyond the state of the art) and made some crude "back-of-the-envelope" estimates of the "details" of environmental effects and orbital dynamics. Cost estimates were made in terms of multiples of gross world product. Brennan requested only a thousandth of the total budget for further research. The joke was also a gentle and friendly way of teasing Herzfeld about the crackpot nature of so many of the Defender concepts.

## Nike-X

The offense and the defense work together. Added to Project Defender's mandate was advanced research in penetration aids. ARPA's Project Jason part-time scientific consultants examined pen-aids in 1962. On paper, these created miserably difficult problems for the defense—that is, if the defense tried to discriminate and intercept in space outside the atmosphere (exoatmospherically, in BMD jargon). There were possible counter-counter-countermeasures, but all the fancy schemes of all the superbright engineers could not improve upon the first and the most obvious of all relevant physical phenomena: when something enters the atmosphere rapidly, it creates friction with the air, the friction generates heat, and the heat leaves a signature that can be read by radar, infrared sensors, television cameras, and sometimes even the naked eye. A meteor seen in the night sky is the track of the heat of the incoming extraterrestrial fragment.

And reentry to the atmosphere will occur at different speeds, depending upon the weight and shape of the incoming. However ingeniously designed, a decoy could not fall at the identical speed, follow the identical trajectory, and generate the identical heat pattern of the real thing, unless the decoy was exactly the same size and weight as the real thing; and then why bother with a decoy? In the mid-'60s at least, far and away the best way to beat the discrimination problem was with "atmospheric screening." This meant that ballistic missile defense had to reverse the traditional thinking of air defense, which gave great advantage to an early intercept; with atmospheric screening, the later the intercept the better; the later intercept allowed more time to examine the characteristics of the incomings, and pick out the real thing. So the way to go was an in-atmosphere (endoatmospheric) intercept.

So it turned out that the Army had been on the right track all along. Terminal defense was the best answer to the anti–ballistic-missile problem. But the Zeus program had been heading in the wrong direction by striving for more range to intercept in space. The thinking had to be turned around. An entirely new missile had to be devised. A second line of defense offered the benefits of "layering." Zeus, the first line, like any defensive device, like any equipment, could not be 100 percent effective. This was anticipated from the beginning, and the Bell Labs people had worked with "shoot-look-shoot" tactics—shoot; then look to see if you got him; if not, shoot again. But with the missile coming in at 4 miles a second, you do not get all that many shots especially if your antimissile missile is not all that fast, as Zeus was not. Better to have your second shot be something else, and something else to bedevil the enemy, to further complicate his attack planning.

The Army had a backup missile under consideration for some time, but before it even reached the drawing boards, a better scheme came out of ARPA research. The newcomer had to accelerate from its base, in order to make the intercept after waiting for the enemy to fall far enough through the atmosphere to be identified by the radars' computers, at incredible speeds. Originally called Intercept-X, the new device was quite appropriately labeled Sprint. In appearance, Sprint resembled nothing so much as a narrow inverted cone, a dunce cap. It had no guiding fins, for their drag would slow it down. The missile had two stages, the bottom half having no guidance whatever, merely blasting the bugger off the ground and dropping off, when the second stage would guide the warhead into the path of the incoming. The air friction heated the skin hotter than a blowtorch. Sprint was a brutal device, all the more so because the enormous thrust required that the fuel be laced with nitroglycerin.

Sprint was added to the program, and the contract was awarded to Martin-Marietta. For the Zeus program and for Bell Labs, it was back to the drawing boards to integrate this new layer into the calculations for battle management. Fortunately, the speed of computers was progressing fast enough to make this at least a plausible proposition.

Another breakthrough occurred outside the ABM program. An attacker will try to beat the defense by going for its soft spot. In July of 1940, the Luftwaffe very nearly knocked out British air defense with repeated raids on the radars themselves, and failed only because of a lack of persistence. Under the conditions of nuclear attack, traditional radars were pathetically vulnerable. Two pounds per square inch of blast could knock most of them over. The elaborate spiderweb of the Zeus Acquisition Radar would not last out the first barrage. The problem was addressed and partially solved, at least on paper, by phased-array radar.

From the beginning of radar, the transmitting and receiving device, the antenna, had taken the form of a large mesh screen, either rectangular or the familiar round scoop. The array of wires had to be light in order to be elevated and rotated in the direction of the target; because it was light, it was inherently soft. A better idea evolved slowly in incremental steps by Bell Labs, Bendix, Sylvania, and others: aim the radar electrically rather than mechanically. The array of receiving wires was fixed, but the screen could be made to scan by adjustment of the current through the array of wires in phases—thus, "phased-array radar."

To be sure, the radar could not scan all points of the compass: the limit was less than 180 degrees; to get all-around coverage, four such arrays had to be blocked together. It was a complex and expensive system, and initially its performance was not up to that of the wonderfully sensitive ZAR, but phased array had two advantages which drove all the other drawbacks into insignificance: Phased-array radar was much harder; it could survive a nuclear blast an order of magnitude higher than the traditional design. And phased-array could change its aim at almost the speed of light, as fast as the electricity coursed through the computers and the radar itself. Phased-array was the answer to the traffic-handling problem of hitting hundreds of bullets with hundreds of bullets. Bell Labs was slow to recognize the desirability of the innovation, but was forced into it.

The combination of phased-array radar and Sprint to defend the radar made possible such an improvement on the Nike-Zeus system that an entirely new name was justified. The newly conceived system had twin administrative effects: on the one hand, finally terminating Nike-Zeus, to the relief of the Office of the Secretary of Defense and perhaps the Army as well; and on the other hand, of providing the Army, Bell Labs, and the advocates of ballistic missile defense future with a system that looked a hell of a lot better, at least on paper. A technical committee headed by Al Latter signed off on it, McNamara was sold on it, and Zeus redux went into the research budget as "Nike-X."

## CD: RIP

In late 1963, the right-wing Republicans were aroused. Insofar as they had a coherent defense policy, it was that of SAC. Trying to thwart this tendency, John Kennedy took to the road to sell his program in the heart of the domestic opposition's country. He planned to defend his administration's defense achievements in a speech before the Dallas Public Affairs Council; but his skull was no defense against at least two 6.5-millimeter bullets. The next President had distinguished himself in support of space programs in the late 1950s, but had not shown any particular predilection for any military posture or strategy, offensive or defensive. Lyndon Johnson did display a sense of personal illegitimacy at having ascended to the presidency in such an unfortunate manner, and for a time, quite a long time, he kept Mr. Kennedy's courtiers in place. Because they looked down their noses at the Texas barbarian, this must have been rather a trial to Johnson. But no strain at all was keeping on board Robert McNamara, who had thoroughly bewitched the new Commander-in-Chief. To be sure, the President was the mikado, but McNamara was the shogun of the military establishment of the American Empire. The Kennedy-McNamara programs were continued unchanged, save one.

After the assassination, the Office of Civil Defense again presented its program for fallout-shelter subsidies to the Bureau of the Budget, had it cut some but not significantly, and then went before the Congress, where it passed the House, thanks to the recent conversion of Congressman Hebert; but the Senate stalled. The bill was blocked by inaction of a subcommittee controlled by Scoop Jackson. He told Steuart Pittman he would move the bill only when he received unambiguous notice that the administration seriously wanted it. Unlike John Kennedy, Lyndon Johnson had made no personal commitment to civil defense.

Pittman sought such a letter from McNamara and from McGeorge Bundy; Pittman says he was assured that such a letter to Jackson would be forthcoming. For whatever reason, the letter did not come into Jackson's hands. Jackson did not support the bill for subsidies for building fallout shelters; only Strom Thurmond supported it; and it did not escape from the dead file of Jackson's subcommittee.

Pittman blames McNamara and/or Bundy. But a peer of the realm such as Jackson had no need of a letter from courtiers; when he called the palace, the king himself would answer. Whether or not he called, we cannot know. Some observers have noticed that McNamara had overridden four DoD committees that had chosen Boeing to produce the TFX multiservice fighter in favor of a Texas contractor. But also worth remarking is that Scoop Jackson once said of civil defense, "Brave men don't hide in holes." Either way, he was the Senator from Boeing. And McNamara could not be made Vice President by Boeing.

Steuart Pittman resigned as Assistant Secretary of Defense for Civil Defense, the first and last man to hold that position. Then the post was downgraded to "Director of Civil Defense." Presently the office itself was cast from OSD to the administrative slum of the Army secretariat. The CD enthusiasts saw but another disappointment, not realizing that that was the end of civil defense as a serious political and military endeavor for the United States. The quality of subsequent directors was determined by Yarmolinsky's Rule. Steuart Pittman thought a major factor in the downfall of civil defense was that he beat McNamara on the Pentagon squash courts.


## Assured Destruction

Following the Cuban Missile Crisis, the tone of the declaratory strategy was modified substantially, as exhibited by an interchange McNamara had with a reporter during this period. In response to a query as to "How much is enough?" he scratched on his secretary's pad:

> Enough = the am't reqd to deter a Sov strike
> + the am't needed to minimize damage to this country
> in the event of a strike
>
> What will deter a Soviet strike? Answer: Unacceptable damage from our surviving forces.

Two new terms dominated the SecDef's rhetoric from then on—"assured destruction" and "damage-limiting." The first became immortal, and will surely be associated with McNamara forever, yet assured destruction was just another way of saying finite deterrence.

You needed to be able to reliably cause some fixed horrendous amount of damage to the other side to deter him. McNamara's apologists, especially Enthoven, claimed that he ginned up this argument not out of conviction, but out of political necessity. The counterforce doctrine preached at RAND had a little drawback for a pretentious bean-counter: To fight a war of counterforce, the more weapons you have, the better. You cannot count on launching all your weapons safely, nor can you count on nailing his weapons with only a few of your own, so you need plenty of weapons. The more the better. You cannot have enough. There was no way to analytically cap a budget.

The possibilities of this traditional military thinking had not gone unnoticed in the Air staff, which belatedly, under brighter leadership than some of the antediluvians of the '50s, saw the wonderful potential for covering the country with offensive and maybe even a few defensive weapons. The Air Force wanted thousands of ICBMs. But adopting the declaratory strategy of minimum/finite deterrence, of assuming that only a fixed set of targets must be hit, especially targets that are easy to hit and to destroy, then you can say with some crude degree of accuracy and credibility: See, this is enough. What fits that criterion is a doctrine of smashing the enemy's cities, eradicating his industry, and barbecuing his population.

Further, this destruction can be easily plotted on a curve. Ten bombs/missiles will take out his ten largest cities, the next ten will take out ten smaller cities, and so on, producing a curve of destruction that initially rises sharply and slowly turns over and flattens out. This was precisely the same kind of curve drawn in the 1950s to calculate the costs of civil-defending the population from enemy attack.

The number-crunchers in the Pentagon found that the preferred place on the curve provided for the destruction of roughly 30 percent of the Soviet Union's population and 25 percent of its industry. This, McNamara *declared*, was enough. This *should be* sufficient to deter the Soviets. This *ought to be* assured destruction. To be sure, while such horrible losses should give the screaming terrors to anyone with a grain of mother wit, there was not then, nor was there any attempt to pretend that there was, the slightest bit of evidence that this actually was the amount required to deter the Soviets. The calculation was made on the basis of what was convenient for our side.

And the calculus of death ignored The Problem: how can we threaten to assuredly destroy them if they can assuredly destroy us?

What is sad is this pit poor McNamara dug for himself with his spurious claims that the fundamental issues of national will could and should be put to rigorous calculation. Had not McNamara worked himself into his positivist frenzy, he could have merely said to the Air Force, "No, you can't have all those missiles because there are other things we want to do with the money. Why? Because I'm the Secretary of Defense, and those are orders." That is logic the military can analyze. That would have been enough.

### Damage-Limiting

"Damage-limiting" was, according to the McNamara II declaratory strategy, the second function of strategic forces. The phrase "damage-limiting" lent itself to the most elaborate analysis: how did you best limit damage; and more to the point, how did you limit the most damage at the least cost? Very early it had been noticed that "counterforce," or blasting the enemy's weapons before they were fired, and "active defense," or intercepting his weapons in transit, and "passive defense," or reducing damage after the weapons had been delivered on target, were all one and the same in their effect on you, in the other side's perceptions of the damage he could do to you, and consequently upon your perceptions of his perceptions. Destroying half of his attackers before launch, intercepting half in passage, and cutting the resulting destruction in half are all means of skinning the same strategic cat. But what was the best way? Stating the question in more professional terms, what was the best mix of damage-limiting measures?

McNamara found a useful tool in Colonel Glenn Kent. With such a stereotypical Anglo-Saxon name, he might have been a character from a popular military novel, combining the outward demeanor of a good ol' country boy with a machinelike mind. The prototypical Air Force generals had been high-flying, swashbuckling individualists; Glenn Kent was a meteorologist, but he flew computers. He loved monster computers the way Curtis LeMay loved big bombers. And he was McNamara's beau-ideal of the officer required for the new age of scientific defense management and cost-effectiveness. Kent became the Air Force's model of the uniformed number-cruncher who would match, thwart, and eventually outfly those troublesome civilian usurpers who had infiltrated the sanctuaries of the true-blue and green upholders of military virtue and glory.

Glenn Kent did not long remain a mere colonel. He had made all the right contacts with a fellowship at Harvard, and had been offered a job at the Hudson Institute. His rise to the stars was given a big boost by his successful execution of the Damage-Limiting Study of 1962–63. The measure of output employed was that adopted back in the 1950s: how many lives lost/saved under what conditions using what materials in exchange for what resources? Shortly this was simplified to lives/dollar. Just as all these types of calculations had supported a civil defense emphasis in the 1950s, so did Glenn Kent's study.

At that time the Hudson Institute was performing much civil defense research, and Herman and Bill Brown wandered into the Pentagon to present their latest findings—that even more lives could be saved at even less cost than in the previous estimates. Even though the calculations had not been done on a computer, Kent was delighted. The outcome of the Damage-Limiting Study was that the best way to invest relatively small amounts of money—meaning in the few billions—was through civil defense, not active defense. To most efficiently save American lives in a nuclear war, we invest in civil defense, not in the Army's ABM program. To be sure, as you moved up the curve of devastation, the calculations changed; at some point you needed to invest more either in active defenses or in counterforce; but at the lower cost levels, the range in which McNamara was interested, civil defense was a clear-cut winner, and ballistic missile defense a loser. But civil defense had been killed by the politicians, so what was McNamara's motivation in promoting studies that showed we should first invest in civil defense before more ambitious measures?

### The Next War in 1965

In 1965 the probable next war was seen as a complicated affair, at least in its early stages. There would be a crisis, then a show of force; then one side or the other would use conventional weapons; then one side or the other would be losing and would try to repair the failure by escalating to nuclear weapons—first tactically against armies, fleets, and aircraft, then (only *in extremis*) in a first strike against the other's strategic forces. Each side would try to restrain itself from hitting at the other's cities for fear of reprisal in kind, but neither side could be certain that the other would exercise such restraint, and neither side could be certain that it could restrain itself.

But if the war "went nuclear," the United States would win at any level or in any theater of combat. The Soviets knew this, and were not about to cast the gage. But even if the United States won, a war that escalated to city exchanges would grievously harm America. The Americans knew this, and were not about to cast the gage either. Still, the United States was better off in 1965 than in 1955. In the age of Curtis LeMay, the United States had had to strike first to surely win. As a consequence of the programs begun under Eisenhower and brought to fruition under McNamara, the United States could surely win by striking second.

"Win!" with such terrible losses? Yes, winning is getting what you want from the war. No one thought you could win a world war and get off without blood.

## The Army Gets Reinforcements

The final defeat of Nike-Zeus demonstrated that the Army needed analytical reinforcements. The material was immediately at hand. One of the largest of the postwar "think tanks" was (and is) the Stanford Research Institute. But SRI was not a coherent whole, an intellectual warehouse like RAND or IDA or Hudson; rather, it was more of a bazaar or flea market, wherein individual entrepreneurs set up their own shops to sell their own research wares, and prospered and expanded, or failed, on their own abilities. One of those entrepreneurs at SRI was Richard B. Foster. Dick sprang from a long line of Congregational ministers. An ancestor had been a supporter of the strategic offense of John Brown against the slave-ocracy. At college in the late '30s, Dick had shown the same sort of restlessness of intellect and character that characterized his near-contemporary Albert Wohlstetter. Young Foster studied both engineering and philosophy at Berkeley. During World War II, he had a series of jobs in production engineering at several different aircraft companies. There always seemed to be some difficulty that made it desirable to move on. One of his positions was at the Convair bomber plant at Wichita Falls punching out heavy bombers for the Army Air Forces, where he was persistently bedeviled for numbers, for more and more numbers, for more and more elaborate numbers, by a staff officer at Wright-Patterson Field with an insatiable appetite for numbers—a Major McNamara. Late in the war Dick was at Douglas Aircraft, where he was involved with a small group doing long-range planning in R&D, as they called it then, "r an'd"; he did not remain in Santa Monica long enough to see that egg fertilized by the sperm of the Air Force.

After the war Dick Foster became engaged in politics. He was stricken by the atrocities of the Third Reich, and devoted time and effort to raising money for gunrunning for the Jewish Haganah militia in Palestine. At that time also word reached the West of the incredible crimes perpetrated by Stalin's Soviet Union. Dick Foster was by no means the only American who saw the struggle against Soviet Communism as directed against the same forces of evil as National Socialism, merely flying a different flag.

In the early '50s he found his proper milieu. He built at SRI a small air defense study group that supplied analytical aid to the Army's burgeoning air defense command. This grew, if only because he took it very seriously. Foster was very bright and very persistent, with great respect for the very special duties and obligations of the military in giving and taking life. By the mid-1950s, as RAND's interest in air defense was declining, and as the Charles Gang were moving from concepts into hardware, Dick Foster's SRI operation was beginning to hit its stride. The group devised an elaborate scheme for continental air defense of covering the nation with short- and medium-range surface-to-air missile batteries—Army weapons.

The Foster team was also distinctly different from its contemporaries in the emphasis it gave to the other side. The technical folk in Massachusetts assumed away any special characteristics of the Soviet Union, and merely took for granted that the Soviets also would follow the inevitable consequences of whatever technical capabilities were put on the line. And the RAND types, while in no way sanguine about the Soviets, believed that they would necessarily be forced by threats and counterthreats to behave in a reasonably prudent manner. At SRI the view was rather more severe. They saw the Communist Russians as Communists and as Russians and held that they would behave accordingly. Communism was a vicious and criminal doctrine, and Russians were crude and brutal people.

While Dick Foster and many of his colleagues were liberal Democrats, their view of the nature of the threat coincided more with that of the Army than with that of the other services. The land soldier, the mud soldier, cannot afford the virtue of imagining the prospective enemy to be merely another calculator and an operator of military machines. The land soldier has to get down in the dirt and in his own blood to fight against the other side. It is good for morale, perhaps necessary, to have a sense not of "the other side," but of "the enemy." This view of the Soviets necessarily led the SRI people into alliance with the right-wing foreign-policy analysts who strongly and credibly argued that the very nature of the Soviet Union and its leadership required "a protracted conflict"; that the Soviets were out to get us, and we had better shape up to that fact in the short, medium, and long runs. The most visible center of this view was at the University of Pennsylvania's Foreign Policy Research Institute (FPRI—"fip-ree") of the ex-Austrian Robert Strausz-Hupe and Professor-Doctor-Colonel William R. Kintner, USA (retired).

The Foster SRI team particularly specialized in evaluating the future threat in terms of what the other side would want to do and could do with what technology would be available to them and how long it would take. This was economic work, and Foster's principal lieutenant was Frank Hoeber, a most improbable high-flying hawk— a gentle man, an Antioch graduate. The name of Foster's shop evolved to the "Defense Analysis Center" to the "Strategic Studies Center." About 1961, the Army had belatedly followed the Navy in creating its imitation RAND Corporation, the Research Analysis Corporation (RAC—"rack"), about which the less written the better. RAC was predicated upon the premise that the Army wanted numbers crunched to tell it that it had been right all along. So the Army required a better-quality advice, higher-quality analysis, more sophisticated advocacy, justification, support, and even a little careful challenging of Army assumptions. In the early 1960s, Foster's shop had become so valuable that the Army demanded that part of it relocate from Menlo Park, next to Palo Alto, to the precincts of the Pentagon to provide continuous input to the staff officers. (The Air Force already had this capability, and RAND had avoided day-to-day firefighting by the founding of the Analytical Services

Corporation, or ANSER—"an-sir"—another of the unfortunate acronyms and contractions circa 1960.) So SRI moved to Rosslyn.

The Strategic Studies Center shifted, as did the Army, directly from air defense to ballistic missile defense. The questions were not difficult to ask, and not, it turned out, terribly difficult to answer either. The original objective of ballistic-missile defense was identical to that of continental air defense: to kill all the incomings; yet even if one doesn't accept the more pessimistic assessments of how easily the attacker could thwart the defenses, only a nut would claim that the defense could be sure of perfect success in blocking the offense. Therefore, if an imperfect defense is inevitable, what sort of imperfect defense should one build, and why?

Foster and colleagues gave the answers, with not a little help from Albert Wohlstetter and Herman Kahn. The answers were very similar to those of civil defense: BMD was insurance if—God forbid—deterrence failed. BMD was humanitarian; it kept millions of people from being killed. BMD was no direct threat to the enemy, because it was strictly defensive. And SRI scrutinized what the Soviets said and did, rather than forming theoretical constructions of what they should do, and noted an interesting peculiarity in Soviet doctrine and force deployments. The Soviets seemed, much more than the Americans, to be absorbed with the defense, with protecting Mother Russia/The Socialist Fatherland from attack from without.

SRI's interest in air defense led naturally to examination of what little was known about Soviet PVO Strany, and an impressive achievement it was, if not in capability, at least in effort. The Soviets kept their antiaircraft guns in service long into the 1960s, and had planted SAM batteries over the countryside like tulips in flower beds, and had fighter-interceptors swarming like mosquitoes on a summer day in the damp mountains. The Soviet SAM deployments of the '60s bore a startling resemblance to the heavy SAM cover that SRI had recommended for the United States in the early '50s. Dick Foster had a remarkable talent: he thought like the Russians.

How effective was the Soviet air defense system? We don't know. We do know that many informed and disinterested people in the Business were skeptical that our bombers could penetrate in the mid-'60s. We do know that the Strategic Air Command was sufficiently impressed to discard a forty-year tradition of bombers flying higher and faster, in favor of new tactics and equipment to fly lower and foxier. The B-52 crews trained to go in on the deck to get under Soviet radar coverage. New radars were devised to permit low-level flying in all weather conditions. Stand-off missiles were designed to enable the bombers to kill targets without risking their point defenses. Wonderfully ingenious radar-jamming measures were developed. All of this, of course, reduced the effectiveness of the offense by cutting speed, range, and bomb loads—the Soviets had achieved virtual attrition against us.

Soviet air defense was a problem for the Air Force, and not for the U.S. Army, but it nonetheless was an encouraging phenomenon. What if the Soviets invested in defenses and we also invested in defenses? What would that mean for the world? But the immediate problem for the Army was not the Red hordes, but McNamara's skeptical bean-counters in the Pentagon. The Army complained bitterly about the results of the Damage-Limiting Study, and McNamara, who was always open to intellectual opposition, which he was confident he could overcome, agreed to consider an Army version of the same material, the Threat-Assessment Study.

The bulk of the Army's top-level analytical research was done by SRI, and commendable work it was. But for whatever reason, perhaps the diffuse organization of SRI itself, or perhaps Foster's irascible personality, or perhaps its perceived extreme views of the Soviet threat, his shop never had either the numbers or the quality of people of RAND in its heyday or of Herman's Hudson Institute. The Army shortly decided it needed reinforcements. And about 1963, all was finished between Albert Wohlstetter and The RAND Corporation.

From now on RAND will hardly appear in this narrative, and then tangentially and covertly. Jerry Strope solicited Santa Monica for more civil defense research, and management quashed it. The leading ballistic missile defense people, Ben Alexander and Dick Holbrook, left to form the Defense Research Corporation (later GRC), a Defender consultant. Between 1960 and 1965 almost all of RAND's stars departed, each, it seems, for an excellent independent reason. Some went to the Pentagon; others established their own businesses. But it looks as if there was, if not a purge, at least intolerable pressure laid on RAND. At the time when exRANDites in OSD were shooting down the Air Force's high-flying systems, the Air Force was taking reprisals at a lower level. The prime victim was Albert Wohlstetter.

Albert was invited to join the Hudson Institute—significantly, by Don Brennan, not Herman—and knew it couldn't possibly work. Instead, he signed on with SRI. The association was abortive, because Albert had no respect for Foster, and Dick was not suave enough to caress such a difficult character, and Wohlstetter's product was less than his best. When civil defense collapsed, so did its research budget, and so nearly did the Hudson Institute. Herman signed on for Army BMD strategic research, but not in volume— Dick Foster was not Herman Kahn, but he was more careful and thorough with the numbers so dear to McNamara, and was doing a very good job. For example, SRI did most of the work in the thirty-three-volume Threat-Assessment study, nominally headed by Major General Austin W. Betts, the Army's research chief (and the first temporary head of ARPA). For a time, Colonel C. J. LeVan had Herman, Albert, and Dick in his Army staff stable, and he would throw the strategic stars together, like a redneck hurling a piece of raw fish among three alley cats.

## The Thin System

Out of this turmoil, generated by the necessary logic of the situation, the concept surfaced of a "thin" defense. A "thick" defense would *almost* defend the entire nation against attack. But "almost" was incredibly difficult and impossibly expensive, certainly much too costly to advocate for deployment in one fell swoop. A thin defense achieved other desirable objectives. It did not so much defend against a full attack by the Soviet Union hurling its entire missile force at the United States in a SAC-like wargasm—that horrid eventuality was countered by the threat of a reprisal in kind. A thin system took for granted the existence of mutual vulnerability, and concentrated on defense against other threats, identified in the paper nuclear wars that had been generated in the fervent imaginations of the strategic analysts.

A minor threat, but one that had gained widespread public attention and was worthy of inclusion in a complete list of advantages of a thin BMD, was the interception of an accidental launch, a missile that went astray through some malfunction or screw-up. The primary protection against this menace had already been worked out in considerable detail in the late '50s and early '60s, especially at Livermore, through the invention of elaborate procedures of dual-key operations and "permissive-action links" which would prevent the use of nuclear weapons unless they were handled just so, by just the right number of people, with just the right amount of information. Nonetheless, as is widely known, no system, however ingenious, is perfect, and a missile just might get loose. A related function of a thin system was dealing with "the crazy colonel"— some screwball officer or terrorist who had illicitly obtained a weapon. These two capabilities were admitted by everyone to be useful, if only as insurance, but not in the wildest imagination did they justify the deployment of a multibillion-dollar anti–ballistic missile system. They were a bonus.

A more promising justification for a thin system was defense against a lesser ballistic missile attack. The Soviets had other options than throwing their entire force against the United States; under certain circumstances, the preferred attack might be a lesser strike—they might wish to strike tactically to eliminate an American force buildup, say, against Cuba. To be sure, a limitied nuclear attack was stratospherically risky, because it could provoke a full American response, but if that in return would surely earn a full Soviet response, perhaps the threat of reprisal was not entirely credible, so the Soviets might think they could get away with a smaller attack.

Another use for a thin system was to defend the command and control system. It was recognized that Cheyenne Mountain, Omaha, Washington, and Fort Ritchie were a very small group of targets. A very sensible action for an enemy in a nuclear war was to attempt a "decapitation strike"—to chop off the head of his enemy to prevent him from striking back. A thin defense merely of the command centers would blunt this possibility. The enemy could eventually penetrate the defense, but the time it would take would give the defenders sufficient leisure to process and execute the counterattack orders. Much thought was given to the defense of the National Command Authority (NCA—"en-see-ay"; outside the Business, this is usually called "wah-shing-ton-dee-see"). The passive defenses there were almost nonexistent—the shelters in the basements of the White

House and the Pentagon left over from World War II would be popped by the most minor attack.

Another version, one favored by Herman, was protection against a demonstration strike by a single missile or a small salvo, just to show that they were serious, to encourage us to do things their way in some crisis or they would throw in the whole nut. A thin BMD system could handle that. Still, that was not an entirely plausible scenario. The risks for the Soviets were fantastically large.

Not to be disregarded was a function that thin BMD shared with thin air defense. The defense made the attacker build up his force to be certain of penetration. The larger attack force was easier to detect, and therefore could more probably be detected earlier. Especially in a layered defense, an early thin screen could force an enemy concentration that could alert the terminal defenses, and the reprisal forces.

Another justification for a thin system advocated by Herman was postattack recovery. Even a miserable defense that was over-whelmed might be able to save a residue of the productive power of the nation to assist in the postwar recuperation. This was a carry-over from civil defense thinking. Indeed, almost all concepts of thin BMD paralleled passive defense—passive defense is inherently thin. No one can imagine a perfect passive defense.

## The Nth Power

Most of the theoretical thinking about nuclear war had taken for granted the existence of two sides, and some imaginative number-crunchers had tried to reduce this polarity to mathematical nota-tion—"game theory," which was taken seriously by academic critics of strategic analysis, not by anyone in the Business. Nonetheless, the two-sided U.S.–S.U. formulation was stuck in everybody's mind. A topic more of interest to arms controllers was the notion of the Nth power, the next power that might get nuclear weaponry.

Already a third power had appeared when the British joined the nuclear club in the 1950s, but their forces were tiny, and it was unthinkable that they would take any sort of independent nuclear action that would directly threaten the United States. In the event, the Americans had the British political system covered and penetrated, and the fear of an "independent" British force died in 1962 when the Brits accepted the American Polaris system and thereby tied their strategic rowboat to a line towed by the American ship. As the fourth nuclear power, the French were a dim possibility as a potential enemy; while the insolent rhetoric of de Gaulle was annoying, no one took them seriously either. And the French nuclear testing in the atmosphere—and above the atmosphere—could not but be noticed by American weapons-effects specialists.

The paper concept of the Nth power was brought to life in 1964 when the People's Republic of China exploded a nuclear device. While the post-Khrushchev Soviets seemed, at least in their rhetoric and actions, to be growing a little decrepit, Mao Tse-tung's China assumed the pure, fire-eating, belligerent Communist revolutionary mantle. The Chinese sounded nastier than the Bolsheviks ever had. Bloody accounts came out of China. Bit by bit, reports of the Chinese revolution had come to light, and it was calculated that the Chi-Commies had butchered even more people than had Stalin and Hitler combined. Worse, in the mid-'60s Mao incited "the great cultural revolution" and started slaughtering the remnants of the bourgeoisie, the intelligentsia, and anyone else who seemed to lack a thoroughly revolutionary fervor. It was Stalin's great purges of the 1930s all over again. And the Red Guards exceeded the NKVD by shutting down the universities and forcing the professors to work for a living.

Worst was the official stated doctrine of the People's Republic that nuclear war would not be so bad after all. So what if China lost a couple of hundred million people, so long as the Revolution was pure and the inevitable progress toward the victory of Marxism-Leninism-Stalinism-Maoism went on unimpeded? In the Korean war, the ChiComs demonstrated their willingness to take on the Americans without nuclear weapons. In the late 1950s, the Soviet Union had rejected Red China's requests for aid in building its own nuclear force, so the Chinese went ahead on their own.

The United States was reasonably well informed about the quality of the talent in the Chinese nuclear and rocket establishments. Some of their top scientists had studied and worked in America. One of the achievements of the great American Red hunt of the early '50s was to force them from the United States. They were known to be competent men. So it became necessary to face up to what the Chinese nuclear threat might mean, and how to deal with it.

While China was a primitive country, it had immense resources, and even greater potential ones. The Soviets had handed over a few hundred Tu-4 bombers. Well within the bounds of reason was the scenario of Communist China's gaining a substantial strategic stockpile and developing at least simple rockets to deliver them against the United States. Deterring them by threats of reprisal seemed to be at least somewhat nullified by the Maoist rhetoric, by the lack of major industrial centers, by the vast and scattered population, by reports of an enormous civil defense program, and by a widespread belief that Oriental leaders valued life more cheaply than Westerners. American targeters were faced with the prospect of killing hundreds of millions of Chinese in minor hamlets. This was gruesomely unpleasant, expensive, and wasteful of weapons better aimed at Soviet targets.

Furthermore, the strategic analysis led to the same sort of thinking as had long been applied to west Europe. The initial Chinese nuclear arsenal would probably be primitive intermediate-range ballistic missiles or bombers that could not reach the United States, but could do foul work on Taipei, Seoul, Saigon, Bangkok, or Tokyo. If the United States tried to provide an umbrella of protection by threat of reprisal, The Problem again arose: what good was the U.S. nuclear threat if the Chinese could respond against the American homeland? In Asia there was no possibility of the supposed European solution of "flexible response" to block, at least initially, the oncoming Red onslaught with conventional forces. There was no single concentrated major front, as in central Germany. The Chinese could attack in many directions and against India in 1962 demonstrated their ability even to operate over the Himalayas. And not even the most enthusiastic promoter of conventional forces was willing to face up to the prospect of having to match the Chinese man for man. The U.S. Army had gotten a bellyful of Chinese hordes in Korea in 1950–53 and wanted no more tangling with that formidable light infantry.

The elaborate analytical apparatus available to America's defense decision-makers worked through every conceivable variation. A very promising idea, given serious consideration at the time, was to abort the Great Beast in its womb, to lay on a preemptive strike against the embryonic Chinese nuclear establishment. The locations of the key labs and test grounds were known, and a very small strike could have destroyed them and killed most if not all of the key personnel. Reportedly, the Soviets made some helpful hints along these lines—which helped stimulate American hopes for détente. But, it is said, McNamara finally rejected the preemptive-strike option in conference in his plane on the runway at Omaha, for the reason that the fallout on Korea and Japan would be excessive. The analysis inevitably worked its way around to an ABM defense capable of dealing not with the principal and concrete threat of the Soviet Union, but with the secondary and constructive threat of China.

## Defending the Deterrent Redux

Another, entirely different line of analysis was defense of the strategic forces. In the mid-1960s, the Minutemen were going into their hardened silos and would be secure for some time; but American accuracies were improving, and it had to be expected that the same was true for the Soviets. It was possible to estimate, within much narrower ranges than most strategic calculations, how accurate a missile was required to mangle a silo, and how many attacking missiles were necessary to kill almost all of an ICBM force with a disabling first strike. Further, it was believed at the time that the limits of the practical possibilities of hardening had been achieved (perhaps because Paul Weidlinger had become bored with digging weaponry and turned his consulting toward the more conventional work of bridges and buildings). Sometime in the future, the not-too-distant future, the Soviets would achieve the ability to threaten the American ICBMs. Passive defense—hardening—would no longer be sufficient to defend the deterrent. What to do?

*Hard-Point Defense.* The Aerospace Corporation devoted some modest efforts toward this end. It had no mandate to defend the country, only for the defense of the Air Force's own offensive forces. As a response to the ever-increasing speed of combat aircraft, which promised to quite outrun the rate of fire of the long-established Maxim-principle machine gun, in the 1950s the General Electric Company, dipping into the weaponry of recent antiquity, resurrected the principle of the first machine gun, that of Dr. George

Gatling of Indianapolis. The new/old Vulcan device had many rotating barrels, but rather than being cranked by a burly gunner, was
spun by a GE electric motor. A battery of guns emplaced on the
ground around a small target could put incredible volumes of lead
or small cannon shells into the air. If the target was small enough
and if you knew the general direction and angle through which the
attacker would fall—"the threat tube"—you could fill it with lead
and presumably have a high probability of killing it, and thereby
presumably dissuading the attack.

How would the attacker counter? The gatlings had an effective
range of about 8,000 feet, so the offense could put in a precursor
attack with salvage fusing, exploding his first missile at 10,000 feet.
The blast from a modest-yield-weapon air burst at 2 miles' distance
would mangle the guns, immobilize the turrets, and flatten the radars. So much for that idea. The gatling guns were cut down in the
paper wars.

Another idea, to be expected given Ivan Getting's Raytheon background, was to defend the ICBM sites with batteries of Hawk missiles—Minuteman-Oriented HAWK: MOHAWK. Remember they
had been successfully tested against short-range ballistic missiles by
the Army in 1961. While an ICBM was a more demanding target
because of its much higher speed, that you are merely defending a
tiny area such as an ICBM field, or perhaps just a single silo, simplified the interception problem. The defender knows, within narrow
limits, the threat tube, so it could concentrate its attention on that
tight avenue of approach. While the Hawks were also soft and easily
taken out by a precursor strike, they would complicate attack planning. And the defense did not have to last long, just long enough
to launch the retaliatory missiles. And the defense did not need to
successfully protect all the ICBMs—if some of them got off, that
was curtains for the other side. The Air Force called this "point
defense." The Army called the same concept "site defense." At the
time, it was thought they meant the same thing.

*O/D*. That did not exhaust the bright ideas of the Air Force.
Another version of Air Force ballistic missile defense was a retrogression to Wizard days—a very-long-range interceptor using the
Minuteman as booster, with a nonnuclear warhead as a first layer,
backed up by the Army's radars and Sprints. This avoided radar
blackout. Using Minuteman saved money on development costs.

Nonetheless, the only distinct advantage of the scheme was the possibility of deceptive basing. Offensive and defensive Minutemen looked identical, so the attacker would have to go for all of them. The greater reach than Zeus' was worthless because Minuteman lacked the acceleration to get out to its maximum range within the warning time made available by the radars. It could work only with earlier warning—by satellite over Soviet territory. And it still had the decoy problem to deal with. Not a good idea—nowhere near as good as the Army's ABM. It didn't even pass recruitment examination in the paper wars.

The Navy also weighed in, with the seaborne anti–ballistic missile intercept system (SABMIS—"saahb-miss"). The label tells the concept: put a ballistic-missile defense system on ships. Float the radars, computers, and interceptor missiles. A noticeable plus is the ability to move the defense—in peacetime to complicate enemy planning, and in wartime to thwart his attack on the radars. But the drawbacks were numerous. The ship would have to be as large as a cruiser— an expensive and visible target for air or submarine attack. Obviously, shipborne systems could not give terminal protection to inland cities, so the missiles would have to be long-range area-defense weapons. If located far forward—say, in the Arctic—they would have to reach the ICBMs near the top of their trajectories, requiring a rocket with as much thrust as would be required to reach the ICBMs' launching sites. The Navy's planned Poseidon missile would have the punch and the reach, but was very expensive.

The Navy also considered SABMIS in submarines (then how would you tell it to fire in the few seconds of attack?) and SABMIS under the polar icecap (then how would the interceptors punch through the ice?) and SABMIS in the Great Lakes (then how would you keep the enemy from swamping it with a not-so-near miss in shallow waters?). SABMIS was sunk from the start—it didn't have a chance in the paper wars; fortunately, only a few dollars were spent on the concept.

ARPA had still more ideas. Sprint was a slowpoke to the ARPA engineers ambitious to really advance the state of the art of acceleration. ARPA supported the HI-g Boost EXperiment (HIBEX— "high-bex"). Whereas Sprint jumped up with a force of 100 gravities, HIBEX went up at 400 gravities. Weight is the enemy of acceleration, and fuel is weight, so HIBEX could not carry much fuel;

and at those speeds HIBEX would devour its fuel immediately, so its range was necessarily limited. No matter, because the scheme was intended for a last-ditch, low-altitude (20,000 feet) defense of hardened missile silos.

At an altitude of 20,000 feet, an ICBM is closing at 10,000 feet per second. Not only did the booster have to be fast, it had to get started fast. The design provided for an exit from the launch silo in $\frac{1}{4}$ second, and the gyroscopes necessary to provide stability had to be activated in a fraction of that time. ARPA solved that problem with a laser-activated gyro. The missile was matched to a special HArd Point Demonstration Array Radar (HAPDAR), whose name should be self-explanatory. It had to be hardened against the blast of the missiles it was controlling. Seven HIBEX boosters were tested at White Sands. The experiment was a great success, realized on schedule and almost within budget, reflecting well on ARPA and the Boeing systems engineers. Vic Kupelian, the project leader, received a commendation medal from McNamara. Although it was merely an experiment to demonstrate the potential of hyperaccelerating missiles, HIBEX was to play an important background role in the politics of ABM.

## Fireworks at Kwaj

Meanwhile out at Kwajalein, the ABM development team settled in. Schools were added. The island was small enough to make bicycles the principal form of transportation. Somehow space was found for a nine-hole golf course. And there was a military-style commissary of adequate but limited stock derisively nicknamed "Macy's." A deprivation for mid-century Americans was the lack of television—fear of antitrust action had obliged AT&T to withdraw from the t.v. business.

The first attempted launch of Zeus was made in December of 1961, but the effort failed after eleven seconds. The first shots were flops. But failures had to be expected in testing of new high-performance systems, and the work went forward. In March of 1962 was a successful Zeus shot against a spot in the sky. Failures followed in the ensuing months. And in April the ZAR transmitter antenna caught fire and a section of it was destroyed. Prompt repairs were organized from Whippany, and the radar was back in service in time for two more failures, the one in June especially disappointing because a real Atlas ICBM had been fired from Vandenberg, and its breakup and splash was hard evidence of the failure of the Nike-Zeus.

Matters turned out differently in midsummer. On 19 July 1962, the seventh Zeus shot successfully intercepted the nose cone of an Atlas ICBM. A delighted observer in the command bunker was Charlie Herzfeld. Less impressed was his boss Harold Brown, the Defense research director, who considered the intercept merely an expected milestone in the development program, and not significant for an operational ABM system to repel a barrage attack. The Zeus–Atlas encounter was announced to the world. Further shots later in the year and in 1963 went just as well. Later in the year the system was worked up to two-missile-salvo shots with equal success.

Progress on ballistic missile defense was diverted slightly by a new mission assigned to the Pacific Missile Test Range by the Secretary of Defense. After the successful Nike-Zeus shot, McNamara asked if the system could be used to shoot down satellites. Obviously it could, because it was designed to intercept objects at the edge of space, and most early satellites, especially reconnaissance satellites, were in very low orbits. And like all the Nikes, Zeus was command-guided, ordered to a spot in the sky where the computer calculated it should be. Calculating a satellite orbit is a snap.

McNamara asked the Army's research people what it would cost to give Zeus an antisatellite mission. The estimate was about $20 million. McNamara told them to go ahead. The Army complained of having no authorization or budget. The Secretary scratched on his note pad, "I owe the Army $20,000,000," tore off the page, tossed it over the table, and ordered them to get on with it. Apparently the administration was afraid that Khrushchev would put a monster hydrogen bomb in orbit to threaten the United States, not so much as a real weapon but as a publicity stunt like his super-duper bomb of 1961. By activating Nike-Zeus as an Anti-Satellite (ASAT—"ay-sat"), the government could assure the nation and the world that the United States had a riposte to the Red Devil's terror device.

By the purest chance, the Army was perfectly set up to handle the mission. Low-flying satellites execute many orbits a day. The earlier Army radar tracking station at Ascension Island, in the South

Atlantic, was almost exactly on the opposite side of the world from Kwajalein. The radar on Ascension would pick up a satellite and transmit the orbit data to Kwajalein. The Kwaj radars were superfluous; with the tracking information from Ascension, Nike-Zeus could be fired at the precise time to nail a satellite coming over the horizon. The warhead had been fired in space in the last test series over Johnston Island in 1962—and was ready to go. The nuclear warheads were surreptitiously brought onto Kwaj and stashed away. In May 1963, the ASAT was in service. And just to let Khrushchev know, a stray Soviet booster was potted in space.

But note that Nike-Zeus was still under development, still in the hands of the contractors. No one in the Army yet knew how to operate it. The only people who knew were the engineers and technicians of Bell Labs and Western Electric. Thenceforth, in addition to their development duties, the AT&T personnel manned the American antisatellite defense. Like a crew of antiaircraft gunners, the engineers performed interminable firing drills, until they reduced the interval between the go order and firing to under an hour. Unlike their distant cousins at Peenemunde, Ma Bell's brightest boys did not understand that war was necessarily only for the soldiers. To be sure, this was a temporary expedient, and toward the end of 1964 the mission was handed over to an Air Force crew, with a different jury-rigged ASAT system using Max Hunter's Douglas Thor missiles, based on Johnston Island to the east. Meanwhile, throughout Middle America, parents were responding to queries about their sons' occupation, "Oh, he works for the telephone company."

In late 1963, Jake Schaefer took over as the station director at Kwajalein, and soon thereafter Bell Labs began the shift over to Nike-X. The computer was designed with Univac. It had to be integrated with the new phased-array Multifunction Array Radar (MAR—"mahr") by GE. Land on Kwajalein Island was exhausted so more of the lagoon was filled in. Yet this landfill still was not sufficient for the swelling activity, so the eyes of the planning staff turned their attention to Meck Island, 19 miles north, an islet previously untouched by all the wars and all the paper wars at Kwaj. As the firing from across the Pacific accelerated, precautions against shorts had to be escalated. The remaining natives scattered on the small islets stretching northward had to be relocated to the Micronesian ghetto on Ebeye Island.

The new accelerated program demanded all manner of odd an-
cillaries that no one would have anticipated earlier. The need to
pluck ICBM debris from the lagoon required the acquisition of a
small boat for the divers. As the operation became more sophisticated, a tiny two-man submarine was commissioned from the Ken-
tron Company: the Army had its own navy. Flying out of the airstrip
on Kwajalein was a modified Lockheed Constellation, a converted
Navy radar search plane, flown by a Douglas Aircraft crew and
operated by a team from AVCO-Everett Labs, the reentry-vehicle
specialists. A local newspaper was founded, and as the staff grew,
all the social structures of suburban life proliferated—athletic teams,
square-dancing and chess clubs, Boy Scout troops, even (as one
would expect) a yacht club—although the Bell people were outdone
by Ed Rosenthal, the Huntsville civil servant, who was so taken by
the qualities of the native proa that he commissioned one to be laid
down by the last native boatbuilder, which was the last proa that
was ever made or ever will be made, unless the white man's outboard
motors are destroyed and the natives relearn the old skills after a
nuclear cataclysm. One can wonder where they found the space for
it and how they got it to Kwaj, but there was also a Nike-X Flying
Club, which operated a small Cessna aircraft.

In 1964, two substantial changes happened to Kwajalein—one of
ownership, the other of time. The Army had long been annoyed at
having to hold the island by leave of what was effectively an absentee
landlord, the Navy, and agitated for a change of control. McNamara
agreed, the Navy did not resist ferociously, so the transfer was made
and the Army had its own island. Of more practical importance was
the solution to the annoyance caused by the location of Kwajalein
just west of the International Date Line, and therefore on a different
day from Whippany, Washington, and Vandenberg, causing endless
confusion. This was not merely a problem of dating correspondence;
the workweek on Kwaj did not jibe with that of the continental
United States, so it was resolved to effectively bend the International
Date Line around the island to put Kwaj on the same time as CONUS.
This necessitated adding an extra day to the year 1964. The period
selected was between October 31 and November 1. But what day
was it? October 32 would never do. So they called it "Kwajalein
Day" and made it a holiday, with appropriate celebrations.

Fortunately, one problem that was feared by the Bell Labs management never materialized. At the time, thirty women on the island were pregnant. Imagine the dastardly life facing an unfortunate infant born that unique day. Fancy the responses to a personnel interview:

"And where were you born?"

"Kwajalein."

"Where the hell is that?"

"It's an island in the Central Pacific. My father was working there at the time."

"Is that U.S. territory?"

"No, it was U.S. trust territory."

"Come on, is it U.S.? Were you born in the United States or weren't you?"

"No, Kwajalein was not U.S. sovereign territory, but both my parents were American citizens, so I am a native-born U.S. citizen."

"Okay. Now, your date of birth?"

"Kwajalein Day, 1964."

Fortunately, no baby sprang from a womb that day, so the nightmare scenario was not realized.

The command of Kwajalein, not a demanding job, passed on to an Army colonel, yet the real control was through the representative of the systems engineers, the field-station director of Bell Labs, ably assisted by his colleagues and the representatives of the other contractors. Another 1964 innovation was the institution of a ferryboat to transport the native workers over from Ebeye each day. The ZAR radar was shut down and torn down, and work went forward. The Zeus missile itself survived the shift over, but only for a time, because of a decision that a longer-range missile was desirable, and this appeared on Douglas' drawing boards dubbed the DM (Douglas Missile) 15X-2 in 1965. This was to carry the warhead that came from Albert Latter's bright idea. Zeuses continued to be fired off for testing purposes. A total of 61 were launched from Kwaj in addition to those at White Sands and Point Mugo.

An airstrip went in at Meck to shorten the 19-mile trip up from the main island. And the construction crews, engineers, and technicians commuted by Canadian De Havilland Caribou aircraft, made for bush flying in the Arctic, yet eminently suitable for equatorial hops. Meck Island was to be the site of the forthcoming Missile Site Radar (MSR—"em-ess-are"), which represented a great advance over the three radars of the Nike-Zeus system. MSR was phased-array, each face with 5,000 elements. The prime subcontractor for this chunk of the system was Raytheon. The power of the radar was driven by a new transmitter and enormous klystron tubes provided by Varian. These main power tubes were ripe for a B-grade science-fiction movie—they glowed, sputtered, and arced most impressively.

The other principal component of the full Nike-X system was the ZAR replacement, the phased-array Perimeter Acquisition Radar (PAR—"pahr"); this, however, was not erected at the missile site at Kwajalein, because the prototypes developed there could be used as proxies for the final system. The Nike-X plan provided also for the MAR, but that came to be deemed an unnecessarily complicating component, and later was scrubbed; its functions were plugged into the PAR and the shell of the MAR structure abandoned uncompleted at Kwaj.

The design work was well enough along and many of the components had been checked out, but the new long-range Zeus variant and the Sprint had not been successfully tested, nor had any of the actual radars been built and tested, nor did the computers exist, not to mention their software; and to be sure, the entire system could not be tested against even the simplest simulation. Nevertheless, the people who were building the system had confidence in it, and all the numbers checked out. Nike-X, the judgment was, would be a successful ABM system, under certain circumstances and with certain limits.

## Passive vs. Active Defense

Up until early 1964, the arguments against an ABM system were almost always couched in entirely technical terms. The high officials of the Department of Defense who argued against deployment invariably remarked that a ballistic missile defense would be desirable, if it worked, but the present concepts, although progressing nicely, did not yet hold out sufficient promise to justify going into production at the projected costs. In retrospect, these arguments were impeccable. The proponents of later more advanced ABM systems granted the validity of the earlier negative judgments by calling attention to the improvements over the prior systems, often admitting openly that the earlier systems which they had supported had been inadequate. This line did not increase confidence in their new judgments. Up until about 1963, the OSD leadership always had a good case on technical grounds.

In 1963, the technical case became a little too good. Early in the year, McNamara told Congress that Nike-X could not be deployed because the nuclear warheads needed to be tested against real targets. In the summer, McNamara told Congress that the test-ban treaty was no impediment to Nike-X deployment. In the short interim, nothing objective had happened that could have changed the SecDef's technological judgment.

Beginning in early 1964, the terms of the debate changed, shifted in a very ominous direction. That year McNamara began to argue that there was no point in building an active defense system unless the Congress also passed a civil defense program. Again, the case was valid and unexceptionable. The Pentagon's own Damage-Limiting Study, as had all studies, showed that civil defense was the better buy at the bottom of the spending scale. A new argument against ABM and for civil defense appeared publicly. The enemy could beat any city defense system by merely exploding a ground burst upwind of a target city, and inundating it with the resultant fallout. In order to protect the urban population from this sort of environmental attack, massive fallout shelters were necessary.

This notion had come out of WSEG at the tail of the Eisenhower administration. It is a damned strange concept. The "upwind" attack is a poor alternative to a direct attack on a city which would destroy it and its inhabitants by blast, fire, and direct radiation. Not only did the upwind attack leave the city intact, but the time for the fallout to become lethal offered the inhabitants space to flee or get under cover. The attacker could not be sure of the direction and speed of the wind, and in any case, they might shift. Several missiles would be necessary to be certain of taking out the city. By forcing the offense into an upwind attack, the ABM defense would greatly downgrade the effectiveness of the enemy attack; the ABM imposed plentiful virtual attrition on the offense. Forcing the enemy to switch from direct to upwind attack would justify ABM in and of itself. The upwind scam is the equivalent of saying you shouldn't fireproof your house against arson because the arsonist can always smother your family with smoke by burning your garage. Furthermore, the Zeus-upgrade DM-15X missile had longer range and therefore defended a much greater area, providing a larger "footprint" of defensive coverage, making the upwind attack inordinately more difficult.

And what was very peculiar was that McNamara and the administration had abandoned all but *pro forma* attempts to get a serious civil defense bill through Congress. Given the lead times to build an ABM complex, a deployment decision would have required at least the simultaneous initiation of a serious fallout-shelter program, which would have cost a fraction of the price of the ABM, not to mention many other major weapons systems. If the lack of civil defense was an objection to ABM, why was McNamara failing to push hard for civil defense as well? This contradiction was noticed by members of Congress; McNamara responded that the administration had repeatedly asked the Congress for very modest civil defense funding and had been turned down, so it had given up all together. Again, not an unreasonable position, but many supporters of strategic defense were beginning to believe that perhaps this was a red herring, and that McNamara really wanted no kind of defense at all, and was merely grasping at thinner and thinner straws to block deployment of an ABM system that was beginning to persuade his own number-crunchers.

A sort of punctuation to the Kennedy civil defense surge, rather on the order of a postscript, was a feeble attempt to revive Johnson administration interest in civil defense by means of a letter addressed to the President in 1966 and, of course, widely circulated. It gave a tidy summary of the arguments for civil defense, and with a few interesting twists: "A rational United States Government enhanced our national security by demonstrating its willingness to risk nuclear war in October, 1962. Chinese testing has drastically reduced chances of confining nuclear weapons to a few responsible powers with the technology to minimize accidents and miscalculations. In the face of these facts, the comforting dogma that nuclear war is impossible cannot be the basis for public or official attitudes without undermining our security."

Then the letter cited McNamara's damage-limiting studies and, in reference to Pittman's problems and McNamara's waffling, pointed out that civil defense was caught in a Catch-22 situation because the Senate had said that completion of a shelter program must await a decision on ballistic missile defense, while "The Secretary of Defense has said (and still says) there will never be a Nike-X decision until Congress provides assurance that the shelter system will be completed."

The letter was written by Pittman and signed by such civil defense stalwarts as Herman, Wigner, Teller, and Oscar Ruebhausen, as well as William A. M. Burden, Robert Goheen, the president of Princeton, General Gruenther, and Frederick Seitz, a physicist and president of the National Academy of Sciences. Also signing were two men lately escaped from the Pentagon: Charlie Hitch and Adam Yarmolinsky, both of whom demurred from a section advocating missile defense and at least insinuating support for immediate deployment of the Army's Nike-X research system. The letter was passed down to Secretary of the Army Stanley Resor, who issued a polite reply. Nothing was done, and civil defense continued to be cut in the later McNamara budgets.

## Defense Is Offensive

If McNamara's intent was to stall ABM, his job was eased by the appearance of the first scattered opposition to ballistic missile defense from outside the government. Hardly was civil defense beaten down when ABM became the target of real and self-appointed experts. One of the most vocal was the physicist Hans Bethe, who as early as 1962 had argued that ballistic missile defense was A Bad Thing: it could not work because of the usual problem of discrimination and decoys, and it should not work because the other side would always take steps to outstrip it. These people like Bethe did not speak from ignorance, because they were involved, at least on the periphery, with the continuous discussions of ballistic missile defense among sundry study groups and consultants to ARPA, IDA, and other government agencies. And no one had ever claimed that hitting thousands of bullets would be easy. In 1964, the Federation of American Scientists came out against both ballistic missile defense and civil defense on the ground that "a civilian population would have to be trained, to some extent regimented, and taught unquestioning obedience to authority." This was a complete reversal of its original position.

Perhaps the most effective of the skeptics was Freeman Dyson, the national chairman of the Federation of American Scientists. He was involved in IDA's Jason studies of BMD, which was a nurturing ground for scientific skeptics. Yet he wrote in 1964 that the central argument against BMD was not technical but strategic: any BMD deployment threatens to upset "stability"; reducing a nation's vulnerability to an enemy counterstroke will tempt its leaders to attempt a first strike, and will provoke the other side to preempt—to go first in a crisis. This position was becoming the conventional wisdom among the arms controllers.

Dyson was another foreigner, raised and educated in Britain, where he had served as an operations analyst for the RAF's Bomber Command during World War II. Dyson's war experience illustrates the cruel choices faced by defense analysis: Bomber Command was suffering terribly from the German air defense. Losses could be reduced by tighter packing of the formations to better concentrate the firepower of their defensive guns; but bombers flying closer together have more collisions. The natural tendency of the flight crews was to accept losses from enemy action as necessary wages of war, but to consider deaths from colliding with their comrades as intolerable. Dyson and his ground colleagues had to coldly calculate the trade-off point at which reduced combat losses from packing the bombers closer equaled the increased losses from in-air collisions. The calculations were made, accepted by the air marshals, and imposed upon the crews. More collisions occurred, but fewer bombers were shot down by the Luftwaffe interceptors, and total losses were sharply decreased. This experience had a lasting effect on Freeman Dyson in another way: because he had been employed by the offense, he was made painfully aware of the puissance of the defense.

Following World War II he emigrated to the United States and was welcomed at Princeton's Institute for Advanced Studies, where he became a highly regarded member of the American scientific establishment, although considered a bit fey. He had opposed civil defense on the ground that hardening our country would increase the worldwide fallout caused by the other side's heavier attack on our defenses. With Brennan, he worked out a parody of nuclear-strategic thinking: The megatonnage required to destroy a country was measured by the unit "Kahn" and the unit of measure of the megatonnage that would kill the population of a hemisphere was a "Beach," after Nevil Shute's imaginative novel. Better passive defenses would increase fallout, ultimately raising the Kahn to the level of a Beach.

However, Dyson was always somewhat idiosyncratic. He recognized important strategic differences between the United States and the Soviet Union, and argued that the Soviets were inherently more defense-minded, both because of their history and because their traditional military thinking tended to emphasize a doctrine of a "long war," whereas the United States had a "short war" theory. Dyson's analysis was particularly persuasive to many people because it did not "mirror-image." He concluded that the Soviets were likely to develop and deploy an ABM system, but that this should not disturb the United States because it merely reflected their out-of-date military doctrine. The American response should be to reinforce our offensive forces, through improvements in penetration aids to get through whatever defenses the other side might deploy.

Also appearing in 1964 was an ominous augury of the future in a *Scientific American* article by Jerome Wiesner, who had bailed out of the White House, and Herbert York, Eisenhower's last DoDR&E chief. The pair had worked together in the killing of Nike-Zeus in 1959. They said ABM couldn't work, which was A Good Thing, because it would be disastrous if it did work. They argued against BMD deployment because "the practical fact is that work on defensive systems turns out to be the best way to promote invention of the penetration aids that nullify them." In other words, if you build a defense, that would merely encourage the offense to try harder. What an idea! Don't put locks on your door because that will encourage burglars to pick your locks. Don't lock your car because that will encourage thieves to break your windows. Don't avoid dark streets at night because that will make the muggers operate in the daylight. Presumably serious people, holders of high position in American academia and government, were arguing in terms of a world absent change, competition, and conflict. This infantile concept may be some dim recollection of the security of personal infancy. Putting an end to "the arms race" became the conventional wisdom of academia, nicely mirror-imaging the world-view of tenured faculty: nations have no tenure; social classes have no tenure.

Advocates of BMD granted that defense might provoke the offense, but it was by no means certain that a good defense could be totally counteracted by the offense. Yes, the defense against high-altitude air attack led to an offensive response of going in at low levels, but the defense had exacted something from the offense, which had to invest more resources and downgrade its capabilities in order to meet the defense. Any measure that makes the enemy adjust his attack, reducing its effectiveness by 50 percent, has exactly the same effect as a defense that would shoot down half of his attackers. Virtual attrition is perfectly understood by the military, and is central to all army thinking on antiaircraft defense. The purpose of air defense is not to shoot down enemy planes, but to keep enemy planes from attacking the field army. The perfect air defense system is the one that dissuades the enemy from ever trying to bomb your tanks or strafe your troops.

Furthermore, if the defense makes the enemy try to overcome it with better offense, this forces a diversion of money, men, and materials—in war or in peace. From this thinking came the notion of the "cost–exchange ratio." How many dollars would it cost our offense to offset the cost of his defense, and vice versa? To take an extreme case, $100 billion worth of defensive investment that could be offset by $1 billion of his offensive investment did not look very attractive, while the inverse was a great deal more favorable.

It was possible to make a virtue of even an unfavorable cost–exchange ratio. General Earle Wheeler, the Chairman of the Joint Chiefs of Staff during the mid-1960s, argued that a spending race with the Soviet Union in strategic weaponry might be a positive competition, because our country was so much richer than theirs that we could pour in money faster, and peacefully break them. This was a doubtful proposition on several grounds: in peacetime, no nation has ever made anywhere near a maximum effort, and can always try harder; the Soviet Union had often exhibited its willingness and ability to devote high levels of resources to the "steel-eaters" of heavy industry and the military; and the Soviet Union had tough internal discipline to prevent the public from rebelling against the sacrifices imposed upon it by the military requirements. In Donald Quarles's terms: the United States may have a stronger wallet; the Soviets have a stronger stomach. And the Soviets, like all traditional military types, know that conflict, hot or cold, is at bottom determined by will—not beans, but balls.

General Wheeler apparently had forgotten his experience as a staff officer in the 1950s, when President Eisenhower had concluded that the health of the American economy required limitations on defense spending. Eisenhower might or might not have been right, but the attitude that high government spending had adverse effects upon a capitalist economy was not limited to a single disillusioned general. Oddly, the notion of a spending race against the Soviet Union coexisted with opposition to Big Government among American conservative elements into the 1980s.

In the mid-'60s, the analysts and other number-crunchers in OSD, in the Army and Air Force, and in all the think tanks and contractors elaborated cost–exchange ratios ad infinitum. The method grew more and more sophisticated, disguising the fundamental fiction of the output. While we could crudely estimate how much a ballistic missile defense system might cost us, we had only a very vague idea of what the other side's offensive costs would be to overcome it. And while we could calculate very closely the cost of our additional penetration aids to get through the Soviets' defense, we lacked the foggiest notion of what those defenses were costing them. Worse, the most elaborate and sophisticated analysis with the most enlightened analytical capabilities and the most advanced computers could not tell anybody how much the Soviets or the Americans were willing to spend on what.

And in 1964, President Johnson proposed an arms-control program, including "a verified freeze on the number and characteristics of strategic offensive and defensive vehicles." But no public fight over ABM occurred in that election year. Nike-X was not far enough along in development for the Army to justify trying to push it forward at that particular time. The bill for a national deployment of Nike-X was estimated at $30 billion.

## The Budget Bleeding Ground

Early in his regime, the positivist enthusiasm of McNamara led him to believe that he could calculate the defense needs to within a billion dollars, or so he told the Congress. As the decade of the 1960s drew on, another demand was placed upon the defense resources of the United States. One of the challenges that America "would pay any price, bear any burden," as President Kennedy said at his inaugural, was the threat of the steady erosion of the Free World through Communist-sponsored or -supported "wars of national liberation." The testing ground, the battlefield, was to be Indochina. The defense of South Vietnam seems a digression from the defense of the American homeland—but it was to have a decisive effect on strategic defense.

In the early 1960s, the U.S.-supported Republic of Vietnam began to suffer badly in its civil war with the Viet Cong opposition supported, supplied, and directed by North Vietnam. Money was needed for the South Vietnamese forces, as were increasing numbers of American "advisers"—not merely to advise and train, but to provide the necessary staff work down to operational fighting units. This was land warfare, so the main burden fell on the U.S. Army, which accordingly needed to find people to send to South Vietnam. In 1962, the military advisory group to South Vietnam was reinforced. Where was the Army to get the men? According to a general staff officer, "to be perfectly frank, we plan to get those 7,000 spaces out of ARADCOM."

For political reasons, Kennedy's successor believed that public support for the U.S. effort in Vietnam was insufficient to expect sacrifices by the American middle class. It was not considered desirable to call up the reserves or National Guard, because political heat would be increased and also because the units had been rather less than elite troops during the mobilizations in World War II, Korea, and the Berlin crisis in 1961. Furthermore, Lyndon Johnson, apparently fancying himself a reincarnation of his youthful mentor, Franklin Delano Roosevelt, determined to have his own little New Deal in The Great Society, which would be created by The War Against Poverty in response to The Crisis of the Cities. The economic progress of the country under Kennedy and Johnson had been exemplary, one of the greatest prolonged booms in American history. Modest inflation with fixed progressive tax rates increased the federal revenues faster than the GNP; but still not enough was available for all demands. McNamara was instructed to hold the line on other defense spending in order to shift resources to fight the war in Vietnam.

Programs were scrubbed right and left. The Air Force's Dynasoar, which was to carry the aviators to aerospace, was scrubbed, and the light-blue-suiters again cursed McNamara. A hold had to be imposed on the expanding strategic force. McNamara determined that limits had to be placed on the number of ICBMs and ballistic-missile-launching submarines. The older bombers were taken out of service and not replaced. The supersonic B-58 bomber was considered too expensive to operate and was junked. The thrust of American military interest and funding went from high-tech gadgetry to small-arms ammunition, jungle fatigue uniforms, and helicopters for the air-cavalry tactics employed against the elusive partisan enemy in the paddy fields and mountains of Southeast Asia.

The buildup in Vietnam redirected the interest of the American uniformed military. This was no push-button thermonuclear holocaust, no paper war fought with computers, but a real war, against a live enemy, fought with bullets and with blood, an opportunity for honor and courage. A real war was something an ambitious soldier needed to have on his service record; it offered opportunities for achievement and promotion. A real war was why a nation had a military. Everybody who wore a green or blue suit wanted to be out in the western Pacific, and was glad to put aside the bookish things of the nuclear age.

In the early '60s, the best brains in the Army addressed themselves to the elaborate preparations for the invasion of North Vietnam, and when this was nixed by their superiors, to the war theater in the South. The Army received the bulk of the resources and took the brunt of the combat. Fighting the experienced and superb Viet Cong, shortly reinforced by first-class North Vietnamese regular troops, the Army faced difficult tactical problems, requiring valor and ingenuity, and the Army addressed itself competently and commendably to its duty. Casualties were high, and there were the frequent blunders as in every war, but the Americans never lost a battle above the platoon level. There were none of the horrid debacles that had afflicted American forces early in previous wars. No one even dreamed of using nuclear weapons in Vietnam. Against what? A battalion of troops that might or not be in that patch of jungle? Against some crummy town in North Vietnam which was not supplying the forces anyway?

The Air Force also shifted its emphasis. The fighter-bombers operating out of South Vietnamese and Thai air bases had a wonderful time with close air support of the Army troops and interdiction strikes against North Vietnam. There had been some foolishness among the political leadership circa 1965 to the effect that the mere display of U.S. force would signal the other side that America was serious. The other side was not convinced. The Vietnamese Communists knew the Americans were fighting a limited war, while they were fighting a total war and were prepared to go on indefinitely.

The fighter jocks had their own way against the feeble numbers of the old MiGs of the North Vietnamese, and could shoot up the country at will—until the other side began to paper the country with automatic antiaircraft guns, and early in 1966 began to install Soviet-supplied surface-to-air missiles. The first American plane was lost to a SAM in July 1966, and thereafter the Vietnamese gave the Americans a little lesson in air defense. (The high-tech Americans thought to crush the air defense by taking out the radars with Shrike homing missiles. The enemy had cunning countermeasures: peasant eyes to see the Shrikes being launched, and prole hands to switch off the radars. The Americans responded to the SAM menace with a brilliant use of sensors and computers: pilots' eyes to see the rockets coming up and pilots' brains to direct frantic evasive maneuvers.)

Of course, SAC had to get into the act. The great lumbering B-52s intended to carry the H-bombs and short-range attack missiles to Soviet targets found themselves sallying from Guam to plaster jungle areas with bushels of small bombs. Curtis LeMay's crack SAC had become a long-range artillery bombardment force. Privately, the air generals grumbled at not being able to throw everything in, to smash North Vietnam with a decisive air offensive. But no one else in the government believed the official propaganda that the insurgency in South Vietnam was entirely a consequence of Northern invasion. The total destruction of all the cities of North Vietnam would doubtless have helped, but could not possibly be decisive. Viet Cong arms came from China and the Soviet Union. The principal assets of the enemy were not his factories, but his dogged troops and the indomitable will of his cadres. The war could not be won in the air; it had to be won on the ground. The war would take time. The war would take men. The war would take money. The money had to be found elsewhere in the budget.

Although the Vietnam war is vulnerable to many criticisms, on the whole the American military did not do badly in the field. But the war had a debilitating effect on the soldiers. Before the intervention, the Joint Chiefs had told the White House that it would take a million men five years to secure Vietnam. They were told to make do with much less than that. They were ordered to tell the nation that the war would be won soon. They were ordered to produce numbers for McNamara which demonstrated that the war was being won. American soldiers are taught from kindergarten to obey civil authority. So the soldiers lied—or convinced themselves that the lies were truth—and discredited themselves. When the crunch came, when the lines could no longer be sustained, the politicians, most of whom had supported the war effort, dumped the buck onto the military, who had to salute, and say "Yes, sir," and eat the shit of Vietnam.

The think tanks were also drawn into the war. A right-wing mythology was later generated that their delicate concepts of gradual escalation were responsible for getting us into the quagmire, but that was false. Nobody at RAND, or SRI, or MITRE, or Hudson knew enough about Vietnam to offer a judgment of what it would take to break the will of the other side, but nonetheless, after the war was on they were brought in. RAND and MITRE advised the Air Force in operations, as was their function. ARPA was properly tasked to supply high-tech to the matter, and Charlie Herzfeld set Hudson loose. Herman's fixes were low-tech: Simple compasses so the troops wouldn't get lost in the jungles. Rural constabulary, as had worked earlier in the Philippines.

The Vietnam war had other fundamental effects upon the fortunes of the defenders of the nation. In the short run, the antiwar agitation drew attention and talent away from the resistance to strategic defense. The principal aim of the "antiwar" agitation was to harass, cripple, and eventually destroy the defenses of the Republic of Vietnam, the Kingdom of Laos, and the Kingdom of Cambodia. Ultimately, this was a complete success, but it required a long war of attrition against American morale. While inflamed agitators were howling against tactical bombing and the use of traditional infantry and counterinsurgency tactics, the more important strategic defenses of the nation and of the American *imperium* gained a brief respite.

But not for long, because the antiwar agitation built up a substantial cadre of individuals, mostly from the children of the privileged classes, to whom it became *de rigueur* to oppose the national-security policies of the United States, and even to cast America as the source of all evil under Heaven. This was a charming inversion of the old American arrogance, that the capital of Virtue was the "city on a hill" which was to be a beacon to the world; the Amerika of the 1960s was the city in the sewer. The agitation rejected all the dominant aspects of American life in the mid–20th century—not merely U.S. military puissance or the forward defense against the Soviet Union, but technology as well. Many younger college professors joined the movement, and others, higher up in the academic pecking order, senior professors who had been actively engaged in defense research and policy in the 1950s, exhibited intellectual and moral cowardice. If anything, the administrators were still more culpable. When terrorism first appeared on the campuses, groups of students immediately organized themselves against it, but were not supported by the constituted authorities, which capitulated most contemptibly. The Stanford Research Institute was pushed off-campus and became SRI International. The Columbia Electronics Laboratory was pushed off-campus and became the Riverside Research Institute. The young stalwarts of the Right, of the Center, and of the (social) democratic Left shortly concluded that the riffraff of the establishment were not worth defending. During the 1960s such young men and women were ignored by their elders and by the press (only radicals were "youth"); but they would come into their own later on.

### Cambridge's Last Defense

Many academics considered even the feeble bombing of North Vietnam to be an excess. Roger Fisher, the arms-control lawyer from Harvard, suggested as an alternative that the United States attempt to seal off the interdiction routes on the ground. This coincided with a notion of McNamara's to investigate high-tech fixes for the Vietnam problem. Adam Yarmolinsky was an organizer. An IDA summer study was held in Wellesley in 1966. Among the participants were Kaysen, Kistiakowsky, Wiesner, and Zacharias.

The result was a scheme for littering the border areas of South Vietnam with lines of sensors that would record and report truck and troop movements—and call in air strikes, artillery bombardments, and disruptive troop raids. The plan was enthusiastically embraced by the Secretary of Defense, who ordered General Albert Starbird to take charge. His number two was David Israel of MITRE, which performed the systems engineering. The result, officially labeled Igloo White but better known as the McNamara Line, was partially built and operated at a cost of a billion dollars a year—but with partial success. The insidious enemy deployed a countermeasure unanticipated on the Charles: water buffalo.

The perceptive reader will notice the parallel with continental air defense a decade earlier. Again, Cambridge scientists tried to divert offensive operations by proposing a defensive alternative. That was to be Cambridge's last defense. And it must be remarked that they did not insist that the defense was dangerous if it was not perfect. Alas, for their efforts, the planners of the McNamara Line were branded as war criminals by their "idealistic" students.

A curious by-product of the air war over North Vietnam and of the McNamara Line was an institutional change in the Air Force. The strategic forces, both offensive and defensive, were stagnant, while the tactical forces required improved sensors to locate the enemy, precisely aimed munitions to kill him, and complex $C^3$ to link all together. So the fighter jocks became the emerging high-tech leadership of the Air Force.

## The Bleeding of NORAD

As the budgeteers looked for the places in the military to cut, their eyes naturally fell upon NORAD. The initial late Eisenhower freeze was now reversed. Not only was there not to be more money for continental air defense, there was to be less. Hardly was the conversion of the city-defending missile batteries from Ajax to Hercules completed when the numbers began to be chipped away. The maximum deployment was 143 batteries in 1963, and money was saved by transfer of many of them to the National Guard, and the forcing through of an absolute reduction. In 1966 the Herc batteries were cut to 121, in 1969 to 96, and to 82 in 1970. The battalions were combined into air defense artillery groups. Some cities were denuded entirely. Dallas and Cincinnati were stripped of their defenses. The few defenses at SAC bases were among the first to go. The National Guard converted units to "internal security" battalions to defend cities from black insurrection.

Easier to take was the stripping out of the Bomarc squadrons. At the beginning of the decade, McNamara had scorned them, and left them in service merely because they were so cheap to maintain. Like automobiles, missiles need more maintenance as they get older, and even those few tens of millions of dollars became too much. The remaining Bomarc-As were cast away in one fell swoop in 1964. The number of Bomarc-Bs was reduced in a sensible way by cannibalizing of old discarded missiles to keep the remainder operational. Between 1963 and 1970, the squadrons were shrunk from 8 to 5, and the missiles from 383 to 140.

The interceptor force went on the same downward slide. With a real air war over North Vietnam, no fighter jock wanted to be on a field defending Plattsburg. The talent in the Air Force found its way across the Pacific. Again, some interceptor squadrons were shifted over to the Air Guard, and the reduction in force took out the older planes first. The number of squadrons dedicated to continental air defense gradually ran down through the '60s, at a rate of about 10 percent per year. The 1,700 interceptors in 1961 were cut to fewer than 500 in 1971. But the average quality of the aircraft greatly improved as old Air Guard F-86s and F-89s and the regular F-101s and F-104s were scrapped; by the end of the decade, the smaller force came to be made up exclusively of ANG F-102s and regular F-106s, the last and best of the interceptors. In 1969, for the first time, more Air Guard than USAF squadrons protected the nation from air attack.

The radar sets also were reduced in number, again bit by bit, incrementally, saving the best. And as the air defense network shrank, one by one the SAGE centers were shut down. Their AN/FSQ-7 computers were already obsolete, the tubes long since superseded by transistors and even more compact devices for processing information, but there was no budget to replace them, so the old units were cannibalized to keep the survivors operating.

The Air Force resorted to dispersion for defense of the air defense. In the early '60s, with MITRE and RAND counsel, they established BackUp Interceptor Control (BUIC—yes, "buick")—auxiliary control centers colocated with the radars. This was a grotesque retrogression. It assumed that the SAGE centers would be taken out and the system would have to continue to fight on a decentralized basis. So BUIC meant that they were back to 1951 again. And the Soviet bombers had not disappeared; quite the contrary: the medium-range jet "Badgers" were a graver threat than the Tu-4s they replaced. Thanks to Kennedy and company, the Soviet pilots could hit their targets and seek refuge in Cuba. Yes, Cuba would cease immediately thereafter to be the pearl of the Antilles, but a lot of good that did us.

The Canadians took the same tack, although it could not be said that their defense budget was strained by involvement in Vietnam. (The Canadian contribution to the Vietnam war effort was surreptitious and inexpensive.) Canada had concluded that it was not to be a superpower in the British model. And Canada belatedly noticed that the United States was no longer a threat which required appeasement. The dominant elements among the Canadian ruling class determined that their principal problem was national unity—how to accommodate a newly secularized, prospering, and restless Quebec. The solution was for the country to de-anglicize itself and be bilingual and bicultural—not French, not British, not American, but Canadian.

It was deemed necessary to purge the antique British elements of Canada. The Liberal government of Pierre Trudeau struck at the core of British symbolism in the country: the Union Jack was taken off the national flag. As much as possible, government institutions were stripped of the label "royal." The most visible sign of the old British–North American Canada was the military. The Royal Canadian Air Force was annihilated, along with the Royal Canadian Navy, and the army. In their place was erected a defense hermaphrodite called "Canadian Forces." The military was bitter. Many members resigned. Others ostentatiously raised the Ontario flag on their front lawns—unlike the Maple Leaf rag, the provincial banner still bore the Union Jack. Unhappy men appeared at their stations at NORAD headquarters in Colorado Springs no longer bearing the exotic RAFish ranks of air vice marshal, wing commander, group leader, and the like, but as ordinary generals and colonels; and no longer in light-blue uniforms but in green. Among the aviators, many took early retirement and settled in Colorado Springs—to hunker next to a real air force, far from the frogs in Ottawa.

To be sure, official numbers ill reflect the Canadian contribution to continental defense. While tens of thousands of well-publicized U.S. draft-dodgers fled north, unrecorded more tens of thousands of Canadians swarmed south to join a real navy or a real army or a real air force in a real country. The bulk of these men sought to fight in the real war in Vietnam, but surely some found their way into the ranks of CONAD.

The second element of Canadianization was less visible but more significant. Trudeau's political economy was northwest European–style social democracy, with a very large and active government maintaining social peace among the disparate and far-flung provinces by an elaborate and complex system of high taxes, cross-subsidies, and make-work jobs. Canada was in a sense Massachusettsized, the capital holding the country together through payoffs. These came out of the pockets of the Canadian taxpayers and out of the defense budget.

This meant that Canada could not afford a new interceptor, and it could not buy new American interceptors because they were not being produced. So the Canadian Air Defense Command soldiered on with the decaying CF-101s, treating them as the Americans had the F-106s, slowly losing planes one by one through the inevitable accidents and attrition of peacetime operations, and cannibalizing the older planes for parts to keep the remainder flying. Slowly the number of air defense squadrons shrank. The Mid-Canada Line, the nation's most ambitious unilateral contribution to continental air defense, was stripped out in 1965.

Every five years the NORAD agreement came up for review for renewal. Whereas most Americans were ignorant of its existence, and whereas the U.S. military considered it to be a minor sideshow, to the Canadians, petty as it was, NORAD was an important aspect of Canadian national defense, which generated elaborate discussions among the corporal's guard of Canadian international-affairs specialists and defense analysts who had nothing better to talk or write about. NORAD was always renewed.

But . . . the elaborate sensing and communications apparatus of NORAD was employed to keep track of the developing U.S. and Soviet space programs. BMEWS had been wired into Cheyenne Mountain from the beginning. Over the 1960s, as the air defense role waned, the space attack assessment and warning role waxed. NORAD was on its way to becoming the North American Aerospace Defense Command. Yet ballistic-missile warning and space tracking and recon were no part of the U.S.–Canadian bargain, so the Canadians *officially* were cut out of more and more of NORAD's operations. After 1967, the Canadians were not *officially* given access even to NORAD's official history.

## The Defense That Never Was

On paper, continental air defense did not die. The U.S. Air Staff and OSD continued to consider ways of keeping it alive and refreshed, if only until the Soviet bombers finally were all junked. The intelligence estimates had always been that the Soviets would take their bombers out of service, as the Americans had their older bombers; but the Soviets never did. Soviet long-range aviation stuck at about 200 Tupolev-95 turboprops (NATO-designated "Bear") and Myasishchev ("Bison") jet bombers. Many of the Bears were belatedly converted to air-to-air refueling, and many more became long-range reconnaissance planes, and the bomber force slowly shrank through the inevitable attrition of operations. But it never declined as rapidly as American intelligence forecast. Many suspect that the primary objective of the Soviet bomber force was NORAD; that it existed for the purpose of making the United States spend money on air defense. But we could not be sure, and even with the growing Soviet ICBM and SLBM forces, those few hundred bombers remained a threat, ready to strike over the Pole if and when the Soviet high command gave the "go" orders. New plans for continental air defense were drawn up and given serious consideration by the now more experienced number-crunching officers, as well as the systems analysts in OSD. Four elements were to be central to the continental air defense of the 1970s.

• A new interceptor would be needed, if only because the F-106s would sooner or later fall apart. It took the Air Force a long time to learn that the successor was not to be. In the mid-'60s the SR-7—successor to the U-2, a high-altitude, high-speed reconnaissance plane, a scout for SAC, to help the offense, not the defense—was considered for interceptor configuration as the YF-12. But the project could not penetrate the review process of the Pentagon. Innumerable concepts were tried out, and oddly, it was found that the most completely different ideas were almost identically cost-effective: it was possible to take a big slow plane, even a large jet transport, and load it with long-range air-to-air missiles and fly it up to the polar region at slow speeds to intercept, and that turned out to cost just about as much and work just about as well as short-range interceptors with short-range missiles based on dispersed fields.

• On paper, the fundamental radar drawback—the conflict between the curvature of the Earth and the line-of-sight projection of radio waves—was solved by over-the-horizon (OTH—"oh-tee-aich") radar. Just as radio waves could bounce between the ionosphere and the Earth itself and gain global range, so could radar transmissions and reflections. It is easy to write down the principle, and it is equally easy to comprehend what an incredibly complex technology is involved in applying the principle. The ionosphere is hardly a shiny mirror; rather, it is a diffuse region of the atmosphere which reflects some radio waves and scatters all that it reflects. Worse, the target reflects the waves back again to the ionosphere and scatters some back to the receiver. From this mess of data the equipment is supposed to identify the target.

Small wonder that the OTH radar was rather delayed in going into service. The first effort was the late-'60s over-the-horizon "forward scatter." Transmitters in the Far East projected radio waves forward, westward across Eurasia to ricochet between the ionosphere and the earth of Mother Russia, in passing through encountering aircraft, which would be recorded by the receivers in Europe. How wonderful to be able to track aircraft and missiles in Soviet airspace. The effectiveness of the system is conclusively exhibited by the decision to shut it down in the mid-'70s. Back to the drawing boards.

• A third element, to spot low-flying planes as well as to minimize the maintenance of far-flung, fixed, and vulnerable radar sites, was airborne warning and command systems (AWACS—"ay-wacks"). A Boeing 707 transport would be festooned with radar sets and stuffed with data processors and consoles, turning it into a cruising SAGE that would fly its circuits, detecting and identifying intruders and transmitting the information to the ground operators and to the interceptors. The Air Force particularly liked this system because it could be used in theater operation as well as continental air defense. AWACS was expensive, but a lot cheaper than having ground radars everywhere. AWACS could be hit on the ground or in the air, but all ground radars could be nailed on the ground at any time. The Air Force wanted plenty of them, and got a few.

• The Army's contribution to continental air defense was to be the successor to the Nike-Hercules, which, despite continual upgrading, was expected to be obsolete in the early 1970s. The follow-on was labeled Surface-to-Air Missile—Developmental (SAM-D—"sam-dee"). Thoroughly immersed in the Nike-X project, Ma Bell did not deign to compete for the successor to its Nikes. The initial contract went to Raytheon; the SAM-D concept was in effect an elephantine Hawk, with semiactive radar guidance and a command-guided first stage to give it a multifold advantage in range over its fledgling. Sometimes it was called SuperHawk. Like the Nikes, SAM-D was to defend both the field army and the continental United States; yet it had a third function in mind.

The 1946 defense concepts heard so skeptically by General Eisenhower with his "bullet-hitting-a-bullet" summation slowly evolved in Army circles. Sooner or later, there would be a requirement for something to block "tactical" ballistic missile attacks upon the field army: ATM ("ay-tee-em"; later ATBM—"ay-tee-bee-em"). In the 1950s the Army developed its Honest John, Redstone, and Pershing battlefield ballistic missiles. Prospective enemies would surely do the same (and they did), so the Army should be prepared to counter this threat. In the 1950s, minor research contracts were awarded to the Cornell Aeronautical Labs to work on something code-named Plato; this, however, was unpromising, especially compared with the Nike-Hercules, which without any intention had better ATM performance in reality than did Plato on paper, so the Cornell project was scrubbed.

In the 1960s, as tactical missiles began to be deployed to the Soviet forces in Eastern Europe, the requirement for a defense was pushed up in the Army's priorities under the rubric Field Army Ballistic Missile Intercept System (FABMIS—"fahb-miss"). Much SRI analytical work dealt with this topic. The early-'60s test successes of Hawks and Hercs in meeting ballistic missiles inevitably suggested that the Army regress to the original Nike-II formula of having a missile that was capable against both high-performance aircraft and ballistic missiles.

Now, although dealing with a short-range ballistic missile is considerably easier than with an ICBM, the problems are not essentially different. Remember that the SAM-D semiactive-radar concept should have been able to fulfill the simple requirement of meeting a falling ballistic missile, which is much simpler than intercepting a maneuvering aircraft. With a long-range early-acquisition radar, such as the PARs under design for the Nike-X system, and decent computers such as Bell Labs was working up for Nike-X, SAM-D could well have been fitted as at least a backup for U.S. strategic ballistic missile defense. The research contracts for SAM-D were put out in 1967.

## Nike-X Reaches Adolescence

Still, despite the increasingly constrained budgets and the slackening enthusiasm of the Army, the technology of Nike-X was making rapid progress. As the research was circulated within the technical circles of the Business, more and more scientists and analysts became converted, if not to the desirability of the system, than to its practicality. Those who were hostile on technical grounds became less so, those who were skeptical became less so, those who were modestly skeptical became waverers, waverers became modest proponents, the proponents became believers, and the believers reinforced the ranks of the original enthusiasts.

On paper it looked as if Nike-X would work. Furthermore, the strategic analysis of the subject, principally the work of Dick Foster and his crew, had convinced more and more people of the strategic utility of having such a system. It seemed to provide at least a partial solution to The Problem; and if not, a ballistic missile defense system was at least an indication to America, the Soviets, and the world that the United States was aware of The Problem and was making serious attempts to mitigate it. The notion of a thin system spread throughout the Business. The Joint Chiefs of Staff were brought on board. To be sure, unqualified support for Nike-X was certainly promoted by the special pressures they were under. A commonplace of international political analysis is that fundamentally hostile powers are united by the threat of a common enemy. All the armed services were under attack by McNamara's muftied minions, and the loss of their privileges and monopoly of military expertise led dark blue, light blue, green, and olive green to join forces against

OSD. McNamara sought unification of the services; they united—against him. The Air Force was still fundamentally opposed to ABM—but military solidarity won out. In any event, the longer-range ABMs that would protect America would also protect the Air Force.

The inability of Nike-Zeus to give full coverage of the nation without an exorbitant number of batteries provoked the consideration of a longer-range missile. In addition to the considerable cost savings from reducing the number of missile sites and missiles, discussed and analyzed at some length in the Pentagon was the notion of a "preferential defense." Missiles with sufficient range to cover several targets could concentrate their fire to protect specific targets, just as fighter-interceptors could be concentrated to shield some places more vigorously than others. Because the enemy would not know in advance which targets would be most staunchly defended, he would have to assume that the full weight of the defense would be thrown around whatever target he selected: if he spread his attack equally, part of it would be blocked by the heavier defense; if he focused his attack on weak points and penetrated easily, he would waste weapons, and the rest of the country would escape unscathed; if he concentrated on the defended places, he would lose most of his force against the defense and the rest of the nation would get off; if his attacks against the defended places were insufficient, the entire attack would fail.

Preferential defense was an elaboration of the Air Force justification for the long-range Bomarc, and not a bad argument it was—except that it meant the defense had to write off some part of the country in advance, so the internal discussions could never get outside the Building. The idea had to be *officially* rejected, although there is considerable reason to believe that preferential defense remained the operational ABM plan—after all, you cannot design a defense to defend everything identically.

An alternative scheme for an "equalized" defense was a grotesque example of how analysis can run amok. The notion was that the price of attack entry should be made proportional to the value of the target. Assuming that population is value, then a city of 10 million is made ten times as difficult to kill as a city of one million—or stated another way, the enemy should find it equally difficult to kill 10 million Americans by hitting one city of 10 million, ten cities of a million each, or 100 cities of 100,000 each. This concept nicely fits American egalitarian ideology, but is militarily nonsensical. Are the Soviets so irrational that they are thirsting to butcher any Americans—if they cannot get New York and Los Angeles, they will blast Bakersfield, Schenectady, and all the Springfields? This notion was properly buried in the circular grave for losers of the paper wars.

In the mid-'60s, McNamara's Pentagon was being hassled by complaints that no new weapons systems had appeared lately. Compared with the plethora of ingenious gadgets that had flourished in the late Eisenhower era, McNamara's people looked miserably unimaginative and unproductive. Never mind that many of the Eisenhower-age schemes had to be junked either just before or just after they went into service, such as the odious Snark and the clumsy Atlas, or took years of reworking, such as Bomarc and the F-102/106. McNamara's people were being given a hard time because they had stained the Pentagon corridors with the blood of butchered weaponry, but had failed to show the nation any new whizbangs of their own.

Actually, new strategic weapons were coming out almost monthly, but the new stuff had the same names as the previous equipment. The B-52 bombers were being constantly modified by the addition of new attack missiles and new radars and electronic countermeasures in hopes of overcoming the ever-thickening Soviet air defense. Minuteman was actually three different missiles. Hardly was Minuteman I sunk into its silos when it was supplemented by Minuteman II, which, although also made by Boeing, was a new weapon, and hardly was it in place when the also-new Minuteman III began to appear to replace the Minuteman II.

Progress was even more rapid with the Navy's Polaris. Initially clumsy gadgets, they were treated by the Navy engineers and their contractors to a long series of improvements in accuracy, range, and throw weight. But all of them were called "Polaris," so cynical or ignorant critics could smear the "do-nothing" Johnson-McNamara Pentagon. Cognizant of this unsystematic, unanalytical approach to defense politics, Alain Enthoven wandered down to the Navy staff and asked the responsible captain to rename the latest Polaris variant. The salt took but a second to imagine an exquisitely appropriate name for a naval weapon: another god, Poseidon.

The Army also learned this lesson. Nike-Zeus had become too much of a political football. The interminable development prompted some weary officer to suggest the name Marathon. The extended-range Nike-Zeus became the Spartan—not a Greek god, but close enough. Pentagon cynics sneered that the new name was an acronym for "Superior Performance And Range Through Advanced Nomenclature." Whether or not DM-15X was such an improvement upon Zeus as to warrant a new name is a pointless question. Spartan it became and stayed.

But who was to design the warheads? A genteel little squabble broke out between Los Alamos and Livermore, which had to be resolved by the Atomic Energy Commission high command in the sort of sensible compromise easily accomplished by scientists outside universities: Los Alamos did the neutron warhead for Sprint, and Livermore did the X-ray warhead for Spartan. The chief Spartan designer, William Lokke, was a cheerful young man who looked like a junior high school teacher you would meet on a hike. He and his colleagues and their Los Alamos equivalents did their work well.

The ABM effort received an appropriate reinforcement. At the end of World War II, Oswald Lange, the promoter of the patriarchal Wasserfall surface-to-air missile, did not come to America with the Braun team, but attempted to remain in eastern Germany. It was an exceeding unpleasant milieu (about this period Frau Lange is quite hysterical—something about what the Russians did to a niece using a stick). So Lange, the outsider, signed on with the British and worked on air defense systems design for the Royal Aircraft Establishment at Farnborough. In the mid-'50s he belatedly rejoined his erstwhile colleagues at Huntsville. The Army's rocket command was just like the good old days at Peenemünde: the enemy was still the Russians—and the Luftwaffe.

When the Braun group was sent to NASA, Lange did important systems work on the Moon-expedition planning, and then returned to the service of the Army. Frau von Braun was incensed at this defection and snubbed him; but Lange, after twenty years of digression, was back in strategic defense work as the chief scientist for the ABM project (while his Americanized son was fighting in Vietnam, in the Signal Corps). He disapproved of Spartan on aesthetic grounds—the modification to add range to Zeus was a far less than optimal solution (Max Hunter had left Douglas for NASA)—but what was done was done. He was very favorably impressed with the quality of Bell Labs people—the best systems engineers he ever encountered in the service of three empires. Their thoroughness and competence made the twilight of his career comfortable.

## The Conundrum of Arms Control

The arms controllers had the problem of identifying arms to control. There was a serious problem of asymmetry: the Soviet Union and the United States had quite different armaments, and it was exceedingly difficult to balance one arsenal against the other. A forward-looking approach was to limit the missile forces then being installed by both sides. Again, asymmetry tipped the bargaining table; the U.S. had many more ICBMs, and the Soviets certainly could not be expected to accept limitations until they had caught up.

The air defense of both sides had a different asymmetry. The United States was shriveling its defenses, albeit at a snail's pace, so why should the Soviets abjure their defense if they would have a free ride against ours anyway? And the United States maintained a large bomber force. The Soviet Union also needed a thick air defense because its strategic air defense was also its tactical air defense—unlike the United States, the U.S.S.R. was surrounded by enemies: not merely the various and sundry imperialists, but also the schismatic Chinese Communists.

All that was accomplished between 1963 and 1967 was some hand-waving called the "outer-space treaty," which in retrospect must be seen as evidence of growing impatience on the part of the American government. The treaty specified that weapons "of mass destruction" not be placed in outer space, in orbit, on the Moon, and on "other celestial bodies." It seems commendable on paper and was acceptable to the military of both sides at the time because the only weapon that anyone could conceive of placing in outer space at the time was an orbital bombardment system (OBS—"ahbs"), a device placed in orbit and brought down from orbit by rockets slowing it so that gravity would pull it back to Earth. OBS was considered in detail, and some sort of primitive fractional orbital bombardment system (FOBS—"fahbs") was tested by the Soviets in 1966 and a handful deployed; but this method of delivering a nuclear weapon was so much more expensive and less accurate than an intercontinental ballistic missile, and OBS was so vulnerable to attack in space versus the security of the down-to-Earth, down-in-earth, snugly hardened ICBM in its reinforced-concrete silo, that it had no point at all. Although, as has been related, the threat of OBS imposed a curious footnote on the defense.

So the treaty on outer space was duly signed, with appropriate celebration by the arms controllers. Alas, it failed to adhere to one of the crucial principles early in the arms-control movement: it could not possibly be verified. The United States had to take the Soviet Union's naked word that the treaty was being adhered to. The increasing sophistication of the space programs of both superpowers, joined by modest efforts by Europeans and the Japanese, was filling near space with orbiting devices. Many of them, indeed most of them, were transmitting precious information to the ground. These could be detected and located by monitoring signals, but there was no way, nor is there now any way, to determine that the satellites are not also, or predominantly, or only, deadly weapons of some sort. Only the growing impatience for an arms-control deal can explain such an unfortunate slip, and a failure to work out in detail its possible consequences.

## The Other Side Goes First

Practically nothing is known in the West about the origins of the Soviet ballistic missile defense technology. We can only mirror-image and conclude that the Soviet technicians, analysts, and soldiers thought about the problem and exercised the technological options along the same lines as the Americans. We do know that the Soviets in the post–World War II era have taken defense rather more seriously than have the Americans, both in their military writings and in their deployments. The United States established a continental air command; the Soviet Union created a separate air defense service, coequal with the army and the navy. The Americans began and almost completed an elaborate air defense network; the Russians began one, completed it, rebuilt it, and rebuilt it several times again. American strategic writing concentrated on the offensive one-shot war and the offense in general; Soviet military writings present a balanced view of the whole spectrum of warfare, both offensive and defensive.

The Soviets had captured many of the German scientists and had quickly adopted their infant rocket, radar, and infrared technology and elaborated on it. The Rosenberg spy ring had shown a special interest in early air defense technology. In 1960 the Soviets humiliated President Eisenhower by plucking a U-2 down from the edge of space with a very-high-altitude SAM. An earlier U-2 flight had noticed something even more forward-thinking. Near Sary Shagan, in central Asia, the Soviets were constructing their own combined White Sands and Kwajalein. And one shot during the sudden Soviet nuclear test series in late 1961 was particularly interesting: a multi-megaton device was exploded at a height of 40 miles. Shortly rumors swept through the Business that it was an intercept of an ICBM by an AICBM. If so, that was the first such intercept, and the Soviets deserve credit. But an intercept at 40 miles up reveals how primitive was Soviet AICBM technology. Forty miles is not high enough to get in another shot, but too high to take full advantage of atmospheric screening.

This crude ABM seems to have been the basis for the system the Soviets began to install around Leningrad which attracted the concern of Strom Thurmond. The following summer, Khrushchev proclaimed that the problem of ballistic missile defense had been solved, that the Soviet Union had the technology to "hit a fly in outer space." This was at almost exactly the same time as the first live test of American Nike-Zeus, so the American intercept over Kwajalein and the Soviet assertion in Moscow may reflect either remarkably parallel development or, more likely, that the Soviet announcement was bluff. By then the United States had its own bluff—the vaunted reconnaissance satellites were few and crude, but the Soviets could not be sure; now they had to consider the American "overhead." Hardly had Strom Thurmond given his last appeal for Nike-Zeus when the Soviets began to strip out the Leningrad system. The Soviets hate to throw anything away—so it must have been prodigiously awful. Back to the drawing board.

Apparently a parallel design team was working up the mystery Tallinn system, and there was also a Soviet ballistic missile early-warning effort, whose timing suggests that it was begun in imitation of the American effort. The delay was beneficial to the Soviets because it gave them the opportunity to venture into phased-array radars. When the overhead picked them out, an anonymous photo-interpreter noticed that they resembled chicken coops, so they were labeled "Hen House" radars. (A later peaked radar structure became "Dog House," followed inevitably by "Cat House.")

Something else appeared near Moscow in the mid-'60s, with lots of soft radars. And at the celebration of the October Revolution in 1964, the Soviet Union paraded canisters through Red Square and announced that these contained anti–ballistic missiles. Following the NATO parlance used to label Soviet surface-to-air missiles, the device was given a "G" name, Galosh, but no one in the West actually saw one, nor is there any public record of anyone on our side having seen one to this day. Perhaps it is mirror-imaging, but the radars and the missile were not unfamiliar to the Americans— it was Ruski-Zeus.

In 1966, the Soviets began to build something around Moscow that was interpreted by the most skeptical people as the beginnings of an ABM system. This was not like the misunderstood bomber and missile gaps. We could see this abuilding. For the first time the Soviet Union had clearly taken a lead over the United States in strategic armaments. And it had taken a lead not because of technological advantages, but because political and budgetary decisions in the United States had retarded production and deployment.

## Arms Control Through Defense

Not everyone thought that the Soviet ABM deployment was an ominous event. Don Brennan was delighted. In the mid-1960s he had staked out his own idiosyncratic arms-control position. Elaborating an old idea of Herman's, he argued for arms-control-through-defense. The first step in the reasoning was that defense was inherently desirable because it was humanitarian: it hurts no one and saves lives in the event of a nuclear war. This was an argument for civil defense carried over intact to ballistic missile defense. Next, the United States should not take umbrage at the other side's equipping itself with defenses, because we ought not to want to hurt it any more than was absolutely necessary, especially its civil population. The United States ought not to be eager to kill Russians, Ukrainians, Estonians, and all the rest of the tribes of the U.S.S.R. Brennan's emphasis was on population defense and on maintaining national economic and civil cohesiveness.

Compared with the terrible potential costs of nuclear war, the economic costs of building defensive systems were hardly worth counting. Each side, and everyone, should welcome security that could be bought at the pinchpenny price of some tens of billions of dollars. Next, while it was true, as the vulnerability advocates claimed, that one side might respond to the other's defenses by augmenting its offense, that was not a drawback of the defense, that was an argument for restraining the offense. To Brennan, the object of all arms-control efforts should be the control of offensive arms; defenses should be encouraged to expand—even uncontrollably. Security would be bolstered by an arms race—a defensive arms race.

Furthermore, thick defenses made arms-control negotiations and agreements more practicable. If a side was well protected from enemy attack, it didn't make as much difference how many weapons the other side had and of what sort, and therefore you didn't have to be so cheese-paring in negotiations. Even if he cheated substantially, it hardly mattered, so why not cut an agreeable deal?*

Brennan was not thoroughly obsessed with the defense; he did not deny the desirability, if not the inevitability, of substantial offensive reprisal forces, nor did he oppose the improvement of the passive or active defense of those forces, nor did he object to effective counterforce weapons; but he insisted that the proper direction was away from "deterrence" toward a regime of damage-limiting, preferably by active defenses. Further, Brennan had spent much time shmoozing with the Soviets at various arms-control conclaves, and he had concluded that they were reasonable fellows. He was struck by the quality of Soviet strategic and arms-control writings, which, among other features, emphasized the defense. He became rather a Sovietophile, recanting his previous view that Americans should educate Russians in arms control. Quite the reverse.

His erstwhile friends and coworkers in the arms-control community thought the new Brennan position incredibly bizarre—so much so that they attributed his conversion to his having sold out to the Pentagon. After all, he was Irish—Tammany Hall and all that. There seems to have been no attempt by any of them to refute

---

*Another advantage is the ability of a heavy defense to thwart a bolt-from-the-blue strike. Because of the experience of Pearl Harbor, American soldiers and analysts were obsessed by that contingency. For the 1958 Geneva Surprise Attack Conference, the U.S. delegation drafted a proposal that both sides deploy BMD to provide reassurance. The conference broke up before any concrete proposals could be formally presented. Brennan did not use this argument because he, like Herman, pooh-poohed a thermonuclear Pearl Harbor.

Brennan point by point; they merely reiterated the themes that ABM wouldn't work because it wouldn't provide a perfect defense, and that any defensive attempts would be more than swamped by the other side's eagerness to maintain an assured-destruction capability. In other words, they argued that the Soviet Union, with whom we intended to deal for mutual security, had a raving homicidal urge to do us in, no matter what. They had implicitly adopted the old Air Force doctrine. "Assured destruction" meant that the role of U.S. strategic forces was to "deter" aggression by threatening to incinerate all of the enemy's cities; this was a regression to the flush times of SAC. Curtis LeMay was redeemed. Omaha had conquered Cambridge. But that comparison slanders SAC. The most primitive Neanderthal in a sky-blue uniform never imagined that a situation with both sides primed to destroy each other, like two men holding pistols to each other's head, was a situation of "stability," of "progress toward easing world tensions." The view of the newly-civilized Air Force was succinctly expressed by Glenn Kent: "I'm all for Doomsday Machines—if they work."

To be sure, the dominant arms-control position was not opposed to all defense. The theory of mutual vulnerability required that the forces primed to destroy the other side be as nearly invulnerable as possible, to be proof against temptations toward a preemptive first strike. So it was considered okay to defend the deterrent, to harden the silos or build submarines. Nor did the arms controllers object to improving command, control, and communications, so that reprisal systems could survive "decapitation" strikes. Nor did the advocates of mutual vulnerability object to all types of BMD on principle. Defending the offensive retaliatory forces was consistent with the theory. A BMD system that intercepted half the incomings aimed at ICBMs was in theory the same as a passive defense which saved half the missiles that were attacked. This position was logically impeccable, and Don Brennan was naive enough to believe that its advocates were sincere. So was Henry Kissinger.

## McNamara's Last Defense

In the 1966 election, the Republicans recovered from the Goldwater debacle of two years earlier and regained most of their lost seats in the Congress. Johnson, McNamara, and their associates had had things all their own way for three years, but now the opposition was resurgent, looking for national-security issues with which to assault the Democrats. ABM looked ripe for it. In 1960, the Democrats had dished the Republicans with the Missile Gap; an Anti–Missile Gap would be delicious political recompense.

Immediately after the election LBJ's high command held a conference in Austin. Among the topics on the agenda were the prospects for Nike-X. During the flight down to Austin, the Army Chief of Staff, General Harold K. Johnson, ostentatiously reviewed some analytical charts in his seat. McNamara saw them, as was planned, and in a fury tore them from the General's hands. A major breakthrough had occurred in the Pentagon. Dick Foster and the Army analysts had persuaded Alain Enthoven that a strong case could be made for the Nike-X system.

Perhaps it is needless to write that General Johnson held a set of duplicates of the papers that McNamara seized, and presented them to the President. It has been suggested that this incident may have been the last straw: at that point LBJ concluded that McNamara was not reliable, that his whiz kid had gone sour. That is speculative. What is not speculative is that when, early in the following year, the Republican National Committee, reportedly under the impetus of Congressman Melvin Laird, put out a thoughtful discussion of the ABM issue, there was a flood of leaks of the Army's studies.

Nike-X had been getting better and better on paper. And the case for a thin defense was becoming stronger. At one meeting in the Pentagon, Dick Foster was making the case that an exchange calculation based on the Soviets' throwing their whole force at our cities made no military sense; rather, they would concentrate their attack on our ICBMs, so the city defenses need only deal with whatever the Soviets would have left over from their counterforce strike, which wouldn't be much, considering the projected numbers and accuracy of their missiles. In a nuclear war, the Soviets could not risk letting our strategic forces live. McNamara demurred: "If I was a Soviet general and I faced this need to attack the United States, I'd put more of my force on your cities and wipe you out." Don Ling of Bell Labs whispered to Cy Betts, the Army research chief, "If I were a Soviet citizen, I'd take Dick Foster as my general." Apparently McNamara had forgotten what the RAND people had taught him about counterforce and avoidance of cities.

For the first time, the Joint Chiefs of Staff unambiguously endorsed a full deployment of Nike-X in a closed session of Congress (and this was shortly leaked). The Congress voted money for pre-production purchases of long-lead-time items necessary to deployment of a full national system of city protection. When the political process came to its inevitable conclusion, cynics called the result "the anti–Republican-missile" system. Yet the issue could not have come up when it did, the way it did, unless there was something substantive to advocate and present. Nike-X was a system that was credible—on paper.

The principal credit for selling the system, of course, rests with its designers, given considerable support by the intelligent and articulate chief of Bell Labs' military research, Donald J. Ling. The Army itself seems to have orchestrated the politics in concert with sympathetic members of the Republican opposition and the Democratic hawks who were becoming disabused of their sometime enthusiasm for McNamara. The underlying analytical work strategically justifying the system must be credited almost in its entirety to Dick Foster's crew at SRI, with a modest supporting role by Herman Kahn's Hudson Institute, and a key intervention by Albert Wohlstetter.

In his early 1967 Posture statement, McNamara exhibited a peculiarly convoluted table, constructed in terms of how many Americans the Soviets want to kill. Here are McNamara's numbers presented in terms of how many Americans an ABM system could save, of a then population of 180 million:

| Level of U.S. Fatalities | Cost–Exchange Ratio |
| --- | --- |
| 40 million | $1 S.U. to $4 U.S. |
| 60 million | $1 S.U. to $2 U.S. |
| 90 million | $1 S.U. to $1 U.S. |

At the high levels of killing, where national survival was at stake, the cost–exchange ratio was unity. We needed only match them dollar for ruble to maintain national survival. ABM was winning the paper wars fought according to McNamara's own rules of engagement. ABM had won the battle of the numbers.

The exploits of the victors enthrall the popular mind; only the military cognoscenti celebrate the great losers. Devotees of strategy can appreciate Bonaparte's writhing 1814 campaign to delay the inevitable Allied triumph after the debacles of Moscow and Leipzig, or "retreating Joe" Johnson's inch-by-inch fall back from Chattanooga to Atlanta before Sherman's superior force. We should add Generalissimo McNamara's last defense against ABM. It was heroic. He had to fight on several fronts at once. Most of his energy was devoted to Vietnam—and it was going badly. Although he had flattened the Air Force, it retained sufficient vigor to gnaw at his ankles. The military was conducting a surreptitious mutiny. European allies continued to resist his efforts to promote "flexible response." The French were especially insubordinate. He had lost the full confidence of King Lyndon. Oh, yes—there were the Soviets; but they were a minor annoyance.

The quality of his lieutenants had collapsed. Charlie Hitch, Harry Rowen, and Adam Yarmolinsky had bailed out—not over Vietnam, to be sure (in the Business, as in all businesses, serious people never let it be known that they have resigned for cause; they always have something better to do). Nitze was restless, and was too powerful to cross, so he was given the Navy secretaryship, and sailed through the Vietnam war defending the Navy from McNamara's minions.

At ISA, Nitze was replaced by John McNaughton, a thoughtful man, highly regarded in academia and the think tanks—which illustrates his weakness. His deputy and successor was a cynical lawyer named Paul Warnke, who in turn was backed up by Mort Halperin, one of the very, very clever Harvard fellows. Harold Brown was promoted to Secretary of the Air Force, and was succeeded at DoDR&E by yet another Livermore alumnus, one of Teller's boys, John S. Foster, Jr.—"Johnny" Foster, son of the John Foster of the McGill Fence: a Canadian, who had been born in New Haven during his father's graduate studies at Yale. Alain Enthoven manfully stayed on—but as we have seen, while he dutifully crunched the numbers McNamara desired, he did have high standards, and such men are not to be trusted. Traditionally, the number two job in the Pentagon actually ran the Department; McNamara was his own Mr. Inside, so he left the deputy secretaryship vacant—with Cyrus Vance. For the Army secretaryship, he had an amiable Republican, Oscar Ruebhausen's law partner, who cheerfully served his client's case, regardless of its merits. Stanley Resor represented the Army, so he was for ABM; he represented the SecDef, so he was against ABM.

According to McNamara, the only people in the Pentagon opposed to Nike-X were himself and Vance. Understandably, the leaks became a torrent. The X-ray warhead was leaked to William Beecher of *The New York Times*. The MIRV was leaked. Classified testimony of the Joint Chiefs and the service secretaries in favor of ABM was leaked. The oddest leak was a superb piece delivered by a Republican political operator to the extreme-right-wing Roman Catholic magazine *Triumph* by "Xenophon," immediately reprinted by *U.S. News*. (Charlie Herzfeld says he never even heard of *Triumph*.) And the well-connected Republican journalist Richard Whalen published some very well-informed pro-ABM material in *Fortune*.

In December, McNamara tried to outflank the military by dealing directly with the telephone company. He implored AT&T executives to cooperate in designing a cheaper ABM deployment. He imposed three rather tight conditions: a given enemy threat, an up-front cost limit of $5 billion, and an Initial Operating Capability (militarese for when you can start actually using it) within four and a half years. In early 1967, McNamara organized a seance for Johnson—all the past and present heads of the Presidental Science Advisory Council and all the past and present directors of Defense Research and Engineering—old friends by now, including Killian and Wiesner of MIT, Kistiakowsky of Harvard, Herbert York, Harold Brown, and Johnny Foster. None of them approved of ABM. Each was asked for his views, except Foster, who was prudent enough not to volunteer his own. It was reported that the "experts" were unanimous against ABM. Still, McNamara stalled. His final position was the arms-control card—we must wait for the Soviets to respond to our initiative to control offensive and defensive weapons. But the Soviets wouldn't play. At the meeting with Premier Kosygin at Glassboro in 1967, McNamara attempted to persuade the Soviet boss that defenses were A Bad Thing; Kosygin reacted to the notion as if the man were daft.

Much of McNamara's annual appearances before the Congress was devoted to fighting off ABM proponents. He presented the usual numbers to show how the Soviets could overwhelm our defenses. The Army and the Joint Chiefs let the crudest outlines of the planned Nike-X deployment ooze out. The entire country would get a thin Spartan coverage, backed up by Sprint coverage of the Spartan sites and radars, and also of major cities. The Army had worked hundreds of possible ABM deployments, yet only two produced by OSD were presented to the public in 1967. "Posture A" provided for Spartan area coverage of the entire continental United States and Oahu, plus Sprint point defense of the radars, doubling up with terminal defense of 25 major cities. Sprints covered the 16 largest metropolitan cities: greater New York, Los Angeles, Chicago, Philadelphia, Detroit, San Francisco, Boston, Pittsburgh, St. Louis, Cleveland, Baltimore, Washington, Minneapolis, Miami, Houston, and Buffalo. Most of these also had major defense production centers, military installations, and/or ports. Also on the list were the smaller cities of Seattle, Denver, Atlanta, New Orleans, Portland, Oregon, Honolulu, El Paso, Charleston, and Albany, Georgia. All these were important cities, but they were on the list because they were well located to be bases for the wide-area coverage of the Spartans.

Posture B was to be 52 sites—adding, among others, Milwaukee, Dallas, San Diego, Cincinnati, Kansas City, Providence, Louisville, San Antonio, Columbus, Indianapolis, Dayton, Memphis, Norfolk, Birmingham, and Rochester. While military considerations were obviously taken into account, the population defense objective was paramount—consider some places lacking Sprint defences: Omaha (SAC hq.), Colorado Springs (NORAD), Albuquerque (Sandia), and Tucson (Titan ICBMs). Some knowledgeable participants believe that the two postures were deliberate straw men, designed to discredit and defeat ABM.

The preproduction money for Nike-X deployment went through Congress with little difficulty, although Senator Joseph Clark of Pennsylvania was bitterly opposed on the grounds that not all cities in Pennsylvania would be defended by Sprint, and also because no city would be defended because the ABM wouldn't work.

### Robert McNamara's Strategic Defense Initiative

Through the spring and summer of 1967, McNamara stalled, but he was forced against the wall, apparently under direct orders from Johnson. Before a meeting of the editors of United Press International at San Francisco, McNamara delivered an extraordinary speech. He laid out in unexceptionable rhetorical terms the complete case for "assured destruction"—that all the United States really needed was a nuclear force able to impose unacceptable damage upon the Soviet Union, to smash its cities under any circumstances. Conversely, an assured-destruction capability was all the Soviet Union needed against us, so our posture should ensure the defense of the offensive force necessary to impose unacceptable damage upon them. And we ought not to be surprised or greatly troubled that the Soviets will try to defend the force that is intended to deter us by threat of smashing our cities. But any attempt to defend Soviet cities would and should be countered by a U.S. augmentation of offensive forces to overwhelm that defense. This was not a theoretical construct, because McNamara spoke in full knowledge that the United States was prepared to reequip its missile forces for exactly that function should the appearance of a serious-looking Soviet defense seem to require them. Word of the multiple independently-targeted reentry vehicle (MIRV) was leaked at the time.

Conversely, McNamara argued that any attempt by the United States to reduce damage from Soviet attack would merely stimulate the Soviets to increase their offensive forces to overwhelm the defense. McNamara called this the "action–reaction syndrome" that "fuels" the arms race. The draft of the speech was written by Morton Halperin, a veteran of the Harvard-MIT arms-control kaffeeklatsch, and the final text was worked up by McNamara's top staff around the secretarial dining room table. The words were carefully drafted. Note that McNamara did not say that the "action–reaction syndrome" *causes* the arms race; merely that it *fuels* it, a formulation that no reasonable person would deny, although one may argue its relative importance. Later vulgarizers of the syndrome thesis would be much less careful in their language.

To the assembled editors and to later readers of the speech, it was evident that the Secretary of Defense was making a strong case against ABM, but then he seemed to reverse his tack, as if adding an appendix peripheral to the text. He announced that the administration, at long last, after nine years of research, development, and agitation, would deploy an anti–ballistic missile defense system. The ABM was justified on three grounds:

1. A nationwide thin area defense would thwart any Chinese missile attack that was conceivable within a decade. (Earlier in the year Alain Enthoven had set Albert Wohlstetter to lay this theme heavily on McNamara.)
2. The same system could also deal with accidental and unauthorized launches of ballistic missiles.
3. The system could be expanded to provide for defense of the retaliatory force, of the missile fields and silos.


McNamara emphasized that none of this was aimed against the Soviet Union. Indeed, insofar as the San Francisco speech was coherent, it said that not to defend against the Soviets was more important than defending against anything.

And there were some minor oddities in the San Francisco speech that went unnoticed outside the Business. McNamara said that the estimate for a thick defense was $40 billion—but earlier he had reported an estimate of $20 billion which would likely cost twice as much because of overruns. Well, overruns had been studied to death in McNamara's Pentagon, and the SecDef knew perfectly well that Bell Labs' estimates for its Nike systems had been right on the money. And he said that $40 billion or more could be borne cheerfully for "a genuinely impenetrable shield," which, alas, was not possible. Well, this was a perfect straw man—no one was silly enough to consider a perfect shield.

The Joint Chiefs of Staff and the Army did not agree with McNamara's analysis and policy. Privately and publicly, they still held out for a fuller deployment against a Soviet attack. But orders are orders, and half a loaf is better than none—and what is now thin can later be made thick. Subsequent releases and congressional testimony—in which McNamara's new Deputy Secretary, Paul H. Nitze, took the lead—described the outlines of the deployment. Sentinel, so labeled by Secretary of the Army Resor, was a deployment plan, not a system; the system was a production version of the latest variant of Nike-X. The hardware of the system was the radars, missiles, communications, and computers on which Bell Labs, Western Electric, Raytheon, Douglas, and so many other subcontractors had labored for many years.

The Sentinel scheme was based upon a concept labeled Plan I-67, prepared in 1966. The scheme included 480 Spartans and 455

Sprints—325 for Minuteman defense, the rest for defense of the main PARs. In the final plan, the Sprints were reduced to 220, with an option to add 208 Sprints for better Minuteman site defense if desired later. Twenty-eight Sprints would be in the Hawaiian battery and 192 would defend Alaska and CONUS.

The central feature of Sentinel was 16 Spartan missile sites. Their 460-mile range created enormous, overlapping "footprints" that would give light area coverage to the entire United States. Because ICBMs would attack from the north at a shallow angle, the footprint of coverage was a giant elliptical egg, with the narrow end to the south. Each Spartan site was associated with a Missile Site Radar to control those missiles. The CONUS Spartan sites were to be near Boston, New York, Washington, Detroit, Chicago, Albany, Georgia, Dallas, Salt Lake City, Los Angeles, San Francisco, and Seattle; and to cover the heartland, at Whiteman Air Force Base in Missouri, Warren AFB in Wyoming, Malmstrom AFB in Montana, and Grand Forks AFB in North Dakota. Thirty Spartans were assigned to each site.

To provide the early warning to alert the system of attack, the long-range Perimeter Aquisition Radars were also to be installed at the sites along the northern border of the United States—Seattle, Malmstrom, Grand Forks, Detroit, and Boston. Because the PARs were the vulnerable point in the overall defense scheme, each of these was defended by the short-range hyperspeed Sprint missiles. Malmstrom and Grand Forks were Minuteman bases, so the Sprints defended them as well, and Sprints were also planned for the other ICBM bases at Whiteman and Warren.

In addition, Alaska got a complete set of PAR, MSR, Spartan, and Sprint near Anchorage. The Alaskan PAR would provide continental early-warning attack from the northwest. Hawaii was provided only with MSR and Sprints, because the area of Oahu was so small that it could be completely covered by the shorter-range missiles.

In sum, the nation was defended by the Spartans and the MSRs; the PARs warned the entire system, and the Sprints defended the PARs. Although national coverage was provided, the system was less thin in the industrial Northeast and Pacific Coast. The ICBMs were defended best of all. It is well to keep in mind that the principal cost and complexity was not in the missiles but in the radars, communications, and computers, and that many more missiles could be added in the future, although there was a limit to how many could be handled by the data-processing equipment at a given time. Nonetheless, the initial Sentinel deployment was to have been for only 700 anti–missiles, a number far short of Soviet ICBMs and SLBMs in 1967, and a fraction of the Soviet strike forces that could be expected by the time the system was completed. Unless the defensive arsenal was enormously expanded, Sentinel could be used only to blunt a very light attack indeed. Truly was it "thin." However, the planned Sentinel deployment was to be accomplished at a decent speed. There was no point in a partial area defense of the United States. Sentinel was to be all or nothing.

## The Building of ABM

A weapons system is not put into service by someone's making a speech and punching budgetary buttons. Deployment means that the real military gets to work. McNamara picked to oversee the entire operation the man he thought the best program manager in the military, Lieutenant General Alfred Starbird, who, despite his exotic name, was a down-to-earth, steady, dedicated, serious, exemplary officer of Engineers. He had been the chief of "military applications" at the AEC and headed the research for the McNamara Line. Starbird's title was Sentinel Systems Manager. To get the system operating, the Army created the Sentinel Systems Command at Huntsville, commanded by Brigadier General Ivey Drewry, who was also Starbird's deputy.

Installing Sentinel was an entirely different job from continuing the development of Nike-X. This was left under the control of Army Research and Development through Missile Command, which really meant Bell Laboratories. The Nike-X project would continue to develop the ABM system, while General Starbird was overseeing the building of the sites and buying and installing the equipment. As part of the reorganization, Project Defender was cut out of ARPA and handed over to the Army as the Advanced Ballistic Missile Development Command. This was strongly opposed by the ARPA chief, Charlie Herzfeld, who didn't get on all that well with Johnny Foster anyway, so he quit and went to ITT as its technical director.

Constructing military facilities is the job of the Corps of Engineers. The first duty of the Corps was to select the sites for the radars, the missile silos, the headquarters, and all the ancillary paraphernalia needed to maintain a body of troops performing any military function—the barracks, mess halls, infirmaries, and dependents' quarters. The Engineers got the specifications from the Sentinel systems people, who got them from Missile Command at Huntsville, who got them from Bell Labs and Western Electric. Although the Corps had much relevant experience from the previous construction of the Nike antiaircraft batteries, the ABM complexes generated more elaborate problems. The radars required enormously large and heavy structures, which could not be placed just anywhere. Ground conditions had to be stable enough so they would not sink into the soil. The missiles would be emplaced in hardened silos to provide safety for the surrounding area (after all, they did have nuclear warheads) as well as from direct enemy attack and fallout. Because the silos were underground, care had to be taken about the groundwater level.

All the fighting units had to be linked together by underground cabling, and tied to NORAD headquarters. MITRE was a major subcontractor for the communications designs. The electrical requirements, especially to drive the radars, were considerable. Because power lines could be severed by enemy attack, huge auxiliary generators had to be installed near the sites. Although an ABM site was not a single place, but many places scattered over many square miles of countryside, an ABM complex was a fortress. Fortresses had not been built in America since the flush times of coastal-defense artillery.

Sentinel was to be an enormous undertaking, and because the equipment was to be identical throughout the country, the Corps decided that the traditional pattern of having installations conducted by regional engineering districts was not appropriate. A single nationwide command was a superior institution. Because the Corps was traditionally divided into districts, the organization was called a "district"; because of its link to Missile Command at Huntsville, it became the Huntsville Engineering District. There was a precedent for a national single-purpose district—the Manhattan Engineering District—and Major General Rip Young, the first commander of the Huntsville District, had been one of General Groves's brightest young officers.

That did not exhaust the organization the Army needed. Massive amounts of matériel had to be obtained to build the ABM complexes. So yet another command was established, a Sentinel Logistics Command. And the the crews who would operate and possibly fight in the ABM complexes needed also to be selected and trained. This was a reasonable extension of the existing continental air defense artillery function, and was handed to the ADA school at Fort Bliss. When completed, Sentinel would be handed over to ARADCOM for operation under the overall command of CONAD and NORAD. The ARADCOM officers were delighted. They had experienced the waning of the continental air defense; ballistic missile defense was the future—their future. The National Guard made plans for manning ABM sites by Guardsmen/ "civilian technicians." Monitoring this activity as agent and adviser to the Army Chief of Staff was General C. J. LeVan. The soldiers were delighted to finally get the ABM deployment going—the damned politicians had delayed the defense for more that ten years.

# VI

# THE DEFENSE DEFEATED

*The old idea of the Pythagoreans, that the world is ruled by numbers, may be especially applicable to war. First, in the number of battalions. Then the value of ordnance is expressed quantitatively: in the number of cannon, their range and accuracy. The moral qualities of the soldiers are expressed in their ability to endure long marches, to hold out for a long time under enemy fire, etc. However, the further we penetrate this field, the more complicated the question becomes. The amount and quality of the equipment depends upon the condition of the forces of production of the country. The composition of the army and of its commanders is conditioned by the social structure of society. The administrative and supply apparatus depends upon the state apparatus, which is determined by the nature of the ruling class. The morale of the army depends upon the mutual relations of the classes, upon the abilities of the ruling class to make the tasks of war the subjective aims of the army. The degree of the ability and talent of the high command depends in turn upon the historical role of the ruling class, upon its ability to concentrate the best creative forces of the country upon their aims, and this ability depends again in turn upon whether the ruling class plays a progressive historical role, or has outlived itself and is only fighting for its own existence.*

LEON TROTSKY

In two short years, from mid-1967 to mid-1969, the American polity flip-flopped on the ABM issue. The national security establishment began by fighting off formidable internal forces that favored deployment and ended by resisting ABM opponents. Of course, those were disturbing years. The urban rioting had discredited the Great Society. The campuses were aflame with dissent. Most commentators would agree that the focal event was the Tet Offensive against the South Vietnamese cities in February 1968, which failed in all its objectives and expended the Viet Cong cadres, yet put the lie to government promises of enemy exhaustion and speedy victory. The psychological defense had broken down.

Yes, but also in this period, unheralded and unnoticed by the American public at large, the Soviets at last achieved what had been dreaded for a generation: the other side had the ability to totally destroy the United States. The Soviet Union had ICBMs and SLBMs of sufficient accuracy and yield to put America out of business in half an hour. This raw fact, the chronicler believes, demoralized the people in the Business who knew of it. This awareness generated that peculiar hash of wishful thinking and appeasement labeled "détente."

### Anti–ABM

Hardly was the San Francisco speech printed when the opposition pounced. The opening salvo was fired in a *Look* magazine article by Jerry Wiesner. A major broadside in the fight against ABM was the first widely circulated popular account of the relevant technology and strategy in Gerald Piel's *Scientific American* by Richard Garwin and Hans Bethe. An odd fish was Bethe. Another foreigner, a physicist fled from Nazi Germany who for a time headed the theoretical department at Los Alamos. Everyone agreed that he was a genius physicist, and thoroughly deserved his Nobel Prize. But not everyone was convinced of Bethe's political judgment. Geniuses are not necessarily smart. Bethe's particular weakness seems to be that he was too much swayed by other people.

His assistant at Los Alamos was Klaus Fuchs, a Soviet spy. After the war, a member of the Rosenberg network pointed to Bethe and his Cornell colleague Philip Morrison as possible recruits; but evidence of active contacts is nil, despite Morrison's deep involvment in the fellow-traveling Progressive Party of 1948. During the fight over Super, Bethe vigorously resisted fusion weapons in a widely discussed *Scientific American* article. When the project was started, he made valuable contributions to the H-bomb. When arms control was in preliminary discussion, he objected to the emphasis on verification, on the ground that it was insulting to the Soviets.

In the early 1960s, Bethe was a consultant in the development of the radiation weapons for the ABM warheads. He took an early position of laying out in detail the ingenious possibilities for offensive penetration aids, which were not his specialty—they had nothing whatever to do with nuclear physics—but could be understood by anyone with knowledge of ballistics and the Newtonian laws of motion of physical objects. In an early 1962 Cornell lecture he listed some tactics of the offense: saturate individual targets, saturate radars, and lay on decoys. "For these reasons I believe there is no effective AICBM system. But I believe that this is good because after all we want the stable deterrent to remain stable." He said this between the Berlin crisis and the Cuban missile crisis.

An overly charitable explanation is that Bethe's access to information about penetration aids must have dried up about 1964, because his public discussions through the ABM debate five years later disregarded the progress the defense had made in dealing with that problem. As the Army's chief research general, Cy Betts, wrote at the time, "Garwin and Bethe are apparently not very well informed about the tremendous advances we have made in ballistic missile defense technology in the past ten years."

While there is no evidence of any nationwide organization, the opposition to ABM sprang up in academic centers. An early focus was the Argonne Research Labs, the heir to the University of Chicago's Metallurgical Lab where Fermi, Wigner, and others had put together the first nuclear pile, the necessary precursor to the atomic bomb. The chief instigator at Argonne seems to have been David Inglis, former chairman of the Federation of American Scientists, sometime Pugwash attendee—and, incredible to note, author of a precursor of the Kahn-Brennan "arms control through defense" concept in a mid-'50s article advocating halting nuclear testing and building up strategic defenses.

Among Inglis' objections was that deploying ABMs near Chicago would make the city a target for Soviet ICBMs—ignoring the fact that not only was Chicago almost certainly already a target, but according to assured destruction theory, Chicago *should* be a target. Chicago's suburbanites soon became incited by the frightening notion of nuclear weapons just down the block—never mind that nuclear warheads had been neighbors to crabgrass since the Nike-Hercules batteries had been installed a decade before.

It was symptomatic of the political naiveté of the Corps of Engineers that it chose Boston for the lead ABM site. Eight locations in a fan roughly following Route 128 were examined. Preference was to be given to government-owned land, and the Massachusetts National Guard's Camp Curtis Guild was appropriate for the Missile Site Radar and for the missiles themselves. The site selected for the initial Perimeter Acquisition Radar was at Sharpner's Pond, near North Andover, 20 miles north of Boston and Cambridge.

An Engineer officer who specialized in real estate acquisition came up to explain to the locals how the Army would go about buying the land. He was received courteously by the citizenry. But the second Army visit followed Wiesner's article, and the unsuspecting officer was beset by a gaggle of MIT professors who grilled him about, among other things, the strategy of ballistic missile defense— about which he was unqualified to speak—and about the constitutionality of building fortifications within the Commonwealth of Massachusetts—about which he knew nothing—and treated him with the coarseness, arrogance, and bad manners that had become a mark of high-mindedness at America's leading centers of scholarship. Present and accounted for were Richard Goodwin, a sometime Kennedy speech writer, Provost Jerome Wiesner and Professor George Rathjens of MIT, and law professor Abram Chayes of Harvard.

It is perhaps most instructive of how detached were the good Engineers from political reality that planning of the San Francisco defenses led to consideration of a site first in Berkeley and then radical-chic suburban Marin County. In Seattle they ran into a little trouble because the first proposed site was on Bainbridge Island, a tony summer retreat for the better sort in that territory; Washington's Senator Henry Jackson showed some concern.

Ferocious opposition appeared in the United States Senate. A large band of liberal senators vociferously opposed the ABM system. The point was taken by Senator Joseph Clark of Pennsylvania, whom the reader may recall as a supporter of civil defense and of the Gaither Committee but who had become almost manic about all types of defense spending, attributing it to the nefarious influence of "the military-industrial complex." His opposition to ABM was frantic, but he opposed every new weapon system, and there was no limit to the peculiar arguments he would employ. For example, he complained that the planned ABM deployment did not defend the smaller cities of Pennsylvania—in contradiction to his overall position that no cities should be defended.* The anti–ABM forces in the Senate mustered almost exactly a third of its members, all of the most liberal Democrats and Republicans. Nonetheless, the pros, led by members of the Armed Services Committee, fought off repeated attempts to delete the ABM funding from the budget, and the work progressed.

Early in 1968, McNamara, thoroughly demoralized and discredited, was pushed out of the administration with a golden parachute into the presidency of the World Bank. His successor, Clark Clifford, an accomplished political operator quite ignorant of defense matters, was Johnson's man and continued the policy. The day-to-day operations of the Department were left to his deputy Paul Nitze. Public advocacy of ABM went to Paul Warnke. The ABM work went forward.

ABM was not an issue in the 1968 presidential election. Although Nixon made a few perfunctory comments about the subject, he had better sticks with which to beat on the beleaguered Democrats. Hubert Humphrey was the most beleaguered Democrat of all, buffeted between Johnson's policy of sticking it out in Vietnam and the peaceniks/arms controllers, so he sensibly eschewed the ABM subject altogether. (After the election, Humphrey expressed great skepticism.) The public at large was not exercised over the issue. Many polls conducted during the 1960s showed overwhelming support for ballistic missile defense—and the same polls revealed an equally overwhelming belief that the United States already had a ballistic missile defense in place.

At the beginning of 1969 it was clear that ABM was in big political trouble. The defeat of the Democrats in the presidential election released them from any partisan obligation to support the administration's program. Worse, the pols who had hitched themselves to the Kennedy entourage, only to be twice thwarted in their ambitions by assassins' bullets, regrouped around the presumed leadership of

---

*Clark was up for reelection that year, and was soundly defeated, but not by "the military-industrial complex." He was a vocal advocate of the Gun Control Law of 1968; in Pennsylvania, deer hunting is a religion, and the National Rifle Association easily shot him down.

Edward Kennedy. Early in 1969, the Kennedy gang planned a violent barrage against ABM.

## Richard Nixon's Strategic Defense Initiative

Few in the Business were much impressed with Richard Nixon. He won in 1968 by default, because poor Humphrey had chained himself to Johnson's cart for too long, and because George Wallace—not to mention his running mate, Curtis LeMay—was impossible. Still, Hubert looked rather the wimp, and Nixon appeared tough by comparison, so he had the support of most people in the Business. Nixon, however, had run on a platform of national conciliation, and came to power painfully aware of how thin was his margin of victory. He had won only a bare plurality of the vote and faced a Congress firmly in the hands of the opposition. Nixon knew he had no mandate. At the time, few noticed a postelection interview with Richard V. Allen in *U.S. News.* Allen was nominally Nixon's campaign defense-issues adviser, yet actually little more than a political errand boy—good reason to recognize that he would not have volunteered this view of U.S.–Soviet relations on his own: "There are areas of mutual interest where agreement would be good for both sides. Agreement to stop development of antiballistic missiles is one such issue."

Immediately after the change of administration, there was a defection from the Sentinel cause. The Joint Atomic Energy Committee put out a paper announcing its opposition to any type of city defense in lieu of a hard-point defense of the missile silos. The most important figure on the committee was Henry Jackson of Washington. He had supported Sentinel publicly, but in mid-'68 he pointedly asked Johnny Foster how much it would cost to delay the deployment a year. On February 6, the new Secretary of Defense, Melvin Laird, ordered a freeze on Sentinel construction pending a review of the situation.

Everyone in the Business was startled when Henry Kissinger was named Nixon's National Security Adviser. Henry, it was understood, had belonged to Nelson Rockefeller. It was certainly ingenious to pluck this accomplished courtier from the ranks of the liberal opposition. Henry Kissinger was not known for expertise in military ·and nuclear-strategic matters, but he was as knowledgeable in foreign affairs as could be expected of a professor, and his selection could not be faulted after the experience with McGeorge Bundy and Walt Rostow.

Kissinger did know politics, however, and he moved quickly on the ABM issue. His erstwhile colleagues at Cambridge were ferociously hostile to city defense, but had granted that an ABM might be desirable in defense of the deterrent. This opening was quickly exploited. But what was peculiar was who worked it. Mort Halperin—who, perversely, was a Republican—had come over from the Pentagon to the National Security Council staff; but already, it seems, Kissinger didn't trust him, so another young NSC staffer just transferred from the Systems Analysis office was put on the case — Lawrence Lynn, who had worked sealift and such in the Building, and knew nothing whatever about ballistic missile defense. Nonetheless, Lynn was set to turning Sentinel into something politically tolerable. Lynn moved rapidly to get information from the Pentagon, and discovered that among the myriad schemes for ABM deployment were some that changed the emphasis from area defense of the population and cities to defense of the missile silos.

As the debate over Sentinel on Capitol Hill heated up, Henry was designing a political penetration aid to order for Nixon. In March, the new ABM was announced. Instead of the 17 sites proposed by McNamara, the Nixon version would have a dozen sites, with the radars and the mix of the Spartans and Sprints rearranged to concentrate the defense on the missile silos. Ignorant cynics have claimed that the new scheme, labeled Safeguard* by the White House, was merely Sentinel under another name. This is false. The equipment was the same; the radars, computers, rockets, and structures were still Nike-X. What was changed was the system's primary strategic function; therefore the deployment was modified. Because Sentinel had a secondary mission of missile-field defense, the Safeguard deployment had no need for radical revisions.

The new deployment deleted the New York and Salt Lake City sites and combined those of Chicago and Detroit. Without an explicit function of protecting against a Chinese threat, the Alaska and

---

*An anecdote serves to illustrate the vaunted thoroughness of General Starbird. When Safeguard was announced, the ABM program manager was concerned that the name might be a registered trademark of an underarm deodorant, so he dispatched his staff to determine the legality of the Army's use of the name. This was during a weekend, so no one was available at the copyright offices. (In Washington, only people in the Business work on weekends.) Shortly it was decided that "Safeguard" was sufficiently generic to be safely used.

Honolulu positions were also abandoned. The political heat was reflected in the vague designations given all the proposed sites other than Washington and the missile fields; instead of Boston there was "southern New England area"; instead of Chicago or Detroit, "Michigan/Ohio area"; instead of Seattle, "upper northwest area"; for San Francisco read "central California"; Los Angeles became "southern California." Later, when the issue cooled, then it might be possible to specify exact sites. In the meantime, the Army Engineers had to lie very low.

The contractors at Sharpner's Pond, near North Andover, had cleared the area, begun bulldozing the terrain into the proper contours for the radar site, and started digging the hole for the enormous PAR structure. Orders came down from Huntsville to halt, to cancel the contracts, and to fill in the hole. Sharpner's Pond lies stripped and deserted to this day, used only for the nocturnal trysts and illicit off-the-road races of the local punks. There is no historical marker.

In the hassle over Safeguard that followed, it was often ignored that a more significant change than the design of the deployment was the *rate* of deployment. Instead of asking for money for the beginnings of the nationwide Sentinel system, the Safeguard request was initially for only two sites to be funded. In theory, this made a certain amount of sense, because a partial national area-defense system to minimize Chinese threats was pointless, but a system of defense of missile silos need not defend all of them. To defend the deterrent, you do not have to protect all the offensive forces, so two defensive positions around the four major U.S. land-based ICBM fields was reasonable. Also, it stretched out the budget.

And the incremental deployment had very interesting implications for arms control with the Soviet Union.

The shift of emphasis away from the presumptive Chinese threat was not without objective merit. In March of 1969, the long-dreaded war between nuclear powers broke out: China and Soviet Russia clashed on the Manchurian border. To be sure, the war was as limited as a war could be—fought with clubs and rifle butts. As in the overused analogy: nuclear powers made war as porcupines make love—*very* carefully. Although it was not noticed at the time, downplaying the China threat indicated that Henry Kissinger had some other means in mind of dealing with Chicom hostility than building ballistic missile defenses.

The Safeguard system was heaved like a dead cat into the middle of the ongoing ABM debate. An emphasis on defending the missile fields should have changed the minds of many of the most adamant arms controllers. Of course not. They turned out to be just as vehemently opposed to the "stabilizing" defense of the missile fields as to the "destabilizing" defense of the cities. Poor Henry had spent all that time in Cambridge in vain. He had not appreciated how utterly devious his academic colleagues could be (perhaps because he believed that he was the only thoroughly devious person in academe).

To tempt "the scientists," Henry dangled before them the bait of a revival of the President's Scientific Advisory Council. Recall that McNamara had stripped away its military influence—but McNamara was out, as was Nitze, and the new SecDef, Melvin Laird, didn't know a klystron from a cuckoo clock; his deputy, Dave Packard, was competent but necessarily overworked; Johnny Foster was okay but no Harold Brown; and the new ARPA chief was—well, who was he? The structure looked like Ike Redux. Surely those boob Republicans would heed the counsel of the brilliant brains from Cambridge.

So Kissinger pretended to pay attention to the views of the scientists. They wouldn't play his game. When asked for options on MIRV, they delivered one: no MIRV. Worse, PSAC members took public stances against the administration. Worse still, they leaked stuff all over Washington. Henry gave up the charade, and embittered the aspiring successors to Killian. A few years later he threw away the empty shell of PSAC.

Melvin Laird had been selected because his long experience in the Congress was supposed to have given him competence and credibility in dealing with his erstwhile colleagues. Immediately, he demonstrated that however skilled he might be at cajoling in the corridors, he was insufficiently conversant with the issues to handle hostile and well-briefed committees. He had to hand over the substantive material to his deputy, David Packard, of Hewlett-Packard. Packard supervised the Pentagon switch-over from Sentinel to Safeguard and took the point on this issue.

He presented charts supposedly illustrating that the Soviets were augmenting their offensive forces at such a rate that they would soon have missiles that could be justified only if they were going for a "first-strike capability"; that the only rational reason for such large numbers was to be able to take out our ICBM force with a preemptive strike. Therefore defense of the ICBM silos with ABM would become necessary.

Senator Albert Gore of the Disarmament Subcommittee was ready to fight back. He too had a set of charts, prepared by his staff, showing that the United States, no matter what the Soviets did, would have huge numbers of surviving offensive weaponry, more than enough to devastate the Soviet cities after a first strike. It was the same old finite-deterrence argument rehashed. One of Gore's charts was even labeled "overkill."

## The War Against ABM

The spurious complaints against ballistic missile defense seemed limitless. One "expert" pointed out that an ABM might blow up in its silo, disregarding the intricately elaborate precautions against such an eventuality, not to mention the decade of experience with Nike-Hercules warheads. In opposing Sentinel, Jack Ruina of MIT took a few minutes to complain that there was no point in having an anti–ballistic missile defense against China, "for the simple reason that they do not have any intercontinental ballistic missiles." To be sure, the United States did not have any *anti*–ballistic missiles either. Of course, our deployment would take several years to accomplish, and was intended against the expected Chinese ICBMs when it was completed.

The old McNamara specter of ground-bursting bombs killing with fallout was raised, as was the fear that a late intercept with a nuclear warhead could threaten people on the ground with blast and heat. Both the upwind-attack objection and the collateral effects of late-attack objections were handled by missile and weapons design. The Spartan was given longer range to provide such a large "footprint" that the whole nation could be covered, so that the enemy could not be sure of getting a missile down to the right spot on the ground to scatter a rain of deadly dust; and the neutron warhead for the Sprint made a very-low-level intercept a safe proposition.

One Ernest Sternglass published calculations supposedly showing that the fallout from ABM intercepts would be sufficient to bring about human extinction. Sternglass was a complete crank about radiation, and his calculations were easily shown to be weird, but he had a hearing in the *Bulletin of the Atomic Scientists* and later in *Esquire*, while the refutation by Edward Boylan and Sanford Aranoff of Hudson was buried in an obscure anthology.

A peculiar side fight broke out over the ability of the ABM computers to handle the data processing necessary for battle management under heavy attack. No one seems to have doubted the ability of even a simple ABM system to block a very small attack, because the trajectories of missiles and the interceptors were easily calculable and predictable. The complicating factors were sorting out the reentry vehicles from the decoys, and handling monster attacks of hundreds if not thousands of warheads simultaneously—an extraordinarily difficult problem.

There appeared something called "Computer Professionals Against ABM" who asserted that existing computer technology could not possibly handle the complexity of the problem. These people were experienced in operating existing civilian computers—very impressive devices by the standards of the '40s and '50s, but not the machines that were being planned for ABM calculation and control. They had no way to know how severe the problem might be and how the data might be analytically simplified before being churned in the computers. In fact, Bell Labs was already working up an entirely new way to configure computers and programs far in advance of civilian applications. Bell Labs had devised an ingenious method of multiplying computer capacity by "parallel processing"— the feeding of data through eight computers at the same time through a clever system of computerized switching. Needless to say, this work was highly classified, so the defenders could respond to the computer critics only by saying that the matter was being handled. This was not the first time, nor was it to be the last time, that the people in the Business were at a disadvantage because of superior knowledge and security classification.*

---

*One of the peculiarities of security regulations is that a person with information that he has received from a classified source cannot reveal that information without violating the espionage laws and at the very least losing his clearance. He can, however, disclose inaccurate information. In other words, it is legal to lie but not to tell the truth; many of the opponents of defense who had clearances fully exploited this paradox. To his credit, Edward Teller has always recognized this difficulty, and has always argued for more openness in discussing the technology relating to military matters. He argues that the Soviets either have, or can independently derive, the same knowledge that we can garner, so our security gags only muzzle ourselves. On this issue, he is right on target.

The Committee for a Sane Nuclear Policy jumped into the fray with a charming newspaper ad picturing a gaggle of frenzied generals playing with toys, and the caption "From the People Who Brought You Vietnam: the Anti–Ballistic Missile System." An upscale variant of this was published the following year in a book by Herbert Scoville, illustrated by the delightfully vicious anti-American cartoonist John Osborne. Wiesner exposed the obscenities of ABM in *Playboy*.

The ABM fight generated a new hustle: In Cambridge was organized The Union of Concerned Scientists, of course mostly of MIT professors and their wives, and headed by a visiting professor from Cornell, a colleague of Bethe's named Kurt Gottfried. These "scientists" said that the explosion of Spartan warheads above the edge of the atmosphere would blind people on the ground who were looking right at it; this too was false, and even if true was rather to be preferred to having an enemy hydrogen bomb explode just above the ground.

The most dangerous notion of the anti-Safeguard elements reflects either an impossible irresponsibility or real gutter cynicism: that rather than try to defend our missiles, we adopt a firing doctrine of "launch-on-warning." When the ballistic-missile early-warning system picks up incomings—or rather, when the other end of the communications system, buried in Cheyenne Mountain, has information that indicates incomings—the reprisal force should be launched then and there. This was proposed by the same people who claimed that ABM wouldn't work, and who sneered at the technical competence of our equipment. This criminally stupid nuclear hair trigger was to surface again.

The anti–ABM forces also charged that the rationales for a thin defense were spurious. The ABM system was really the thin end of the wedge, the first step toward getting a full national urban protection system. This charge was not vigorously rebutted, because it was correct. The Joint Chiefs of Staff, the Army, Donald Brennan, and Freeman Dyson, among others, favored exactly such a policy. This was why the Spartan sites had been located close to cities—so that the Sprints could be put in later to thicken the coverage. Indeed, from the point of view of the advocates of population defense, the justification of ABM in terms of missile-site defense weakened its appeal, because what the public really wanted was a system that would protect the public—people, not hardware.

The more-or-less-credible opposition concentrated on two issues. The physicist Wolfgang Panofsky pointed out that city defense and missile-silo defense had rather different design criteria (true), and the extant ABM system was a city defense system (not true). As the reader knows, ABM began as a city defense system, with phased-array radar and Sprint added to harden and defend the radars; nevertheless, the hard-point defense function of Sprint could be just as well applied to a missile field as well. And the longer-range Spartan missile provided part of a "layered" defense to make the attacker's problem more difficult. To be sure, had the military been planning a hard-point defense from the beginning, and had all the difficulties of in-space interception been anticipated, another system would have evolved, quite different from that worked out by the Army. Panofsky and other critics with access to classified information knew all about HIBEX and other late-intercept schemes. But the money had been invested, and ABM would work well enough. Indeed, the arguments that Safeguard would fail in the missile defense role, although continued in the vulgar anti–ABM agitation, disappeared from the rhetoric of the "experts" who testified on Capitol Hill. No one doubted that Safeguard would work well enough to delay a Soviet attack long enough for ICBMs to be launched in reprisal.

So the anti–ABM case had to refute the need to defend Minuteman fields. It is worth elaborating this subject because these are themes that would be heard over and over again for the next twenty years. The opposition claimed that the need to defend the Minutemen was illusory because the United States had other reprisal forces that would survive even the destruction of the entire ICBM force—the bombers and submarines. But the area defense capability of Safeguard would help give some cover to the bomber bases and submarine ports as well.

A more dangerous line was that the survival of Minuteman didn't matter. In either case, then why have Minutemen in the first place? And once you grant that, then you admit that the other side's first-strike capability has made you surrender a force in advance. He has won a battle in the nuclear war without firing a single missile. Few people were willing to make such a statement openly at that time.

A more positive approach was taken by those who argued that the Minuteman force would not be threatened by a Soviet first strike during the relevant time frame. This led to the second battle of the numbers.

## The Defense of MIT

Jerome Wiesner was meant to take the lead in the anti–ABM fight, but was distracted by the need to defend his home base. The Charles River Gang was fighting on two fronts. Over the winter of 1968–69, as they attempted to block ABM, they were engaged against infantile leftism on their own turf. To a large degree, the anti–ABM agitation was an attempt to divert the lefties from attacks on defense research more vital to America's leading institutions of learning. The Lincoln Labs were bringing in $67 million a year, and the Instrumentation Labs earned $55 million (triple for mid-'80s dollars), with MIT raking a respectable amount off the top for "administration." James Killian was then MIT's chairman of the board. The president was Howard Johnson—no kin, but inevitably called "HoJo" by insolent students. Wiesner was the institute's "provost" with unspecified duties, because writing down the job description of the chief political operator would have been imprudent. The vice president for military research was Jack Ruina. These worthies had little time for the tiresome detail of fighting ABM in Congress. So the point was given to George Rathjens, a chemist and old WSEG research hand, who a decade earlier had written the best single advocacy of "minimum deterrence."

The assault on MIT began in earnest when Kurt Gottfried arrived as a visiting professor from the Bethe cell at Cornell, bringing with him two SDS goons. It was demanded that MIT get out of the defense-research business and cease and desist from contributing to the imperialistic resistance to those nice Soviets. On March 4 a big talk-in was held to head off a strike. Bethe was brought in to harangue the mob. His case was that the opposition of people like him to ABM was a justification for people like him to participate in defense research. Attention was successfully diverted to the Instrumentations Laboratory. Lincoln Labs had long since moved up near Hanscom Field, while the Instrumentations Lab was right there in

Cambridge. Furthermore, Lincoln Labs was a fuzzy operation, with anonymous leadership and unknown functions, while the Instrumentations Lab, the personal vehicle of the redoubtable Charles Stark Draper, was the great center for improvements in inertial guidance of ballistic-missile warheads and was then finishing off the breakthroughs for MIRV.

Draper told the radicals to stuff it—and his engineers and technicians armed themselves in self-defense. The MIT high command determined to jettison the Instrumentations Lab, which was reorganized as a nonprofit corporation named for Draper, and henceforth the MIT party line put more emphasis on the evils of missile accuracy and multiple warheads. Thus Lincoln Labs was saved for MIT. It played no public role whatever in the great ABM debate—although it was a leading center of advanced ABM radar research, regularly feeding data into Raytheon, GE, and other radar developers.

Although the accession of the Republicans to power cut off his political influence, Wiesner became the next president of MIT. Certainly the appointment was richly deserved. Although rioting, bombings, and sabotage carried on at MIT long after they faded at other institutions, MIT ranks to this day toward the top of defense-research contractors.

## The Defenders Organize Themselves

The support for ABM was concentrated among those elements who had been supporters of civil defense, but not exclusively. Of course, Brennan, Herman, Jack Hirshliefer, Wigner, Teller, but many more: Frederick Seitz, the president of the National Academy of Sciences, took a leading role, as did Lawrence O'Neil, a radar man who was chief of Riverside Research, Columbia's former electronics lab, which had been driven off-campus and converted into his personal fiefdom. Bob Sprague reappeared, took a quick look at the issues, and concluded that nothing had changed since Gaither Committee days.

Initially, Brennan was the intellectual leader. He was then at his peak. He had just married a congressional staffer; the best man at their wedding was Scoop Jackson's protégé Congressman Thomas Foley. He became the principal public supporter of ballistic missile defense, writing in *Foreign Affairs*, debating against Wiesner, Bethe, and Rathjens in various forums, and appearing on television. But he wanted all-out population defense. Sentinel was okay as the thin edge of the wedge, but Safeguard was a bit too skinny for his taste. Defending the deterrent was to him a tedious "engineering issue." So he was thrust aside by an important recruit, a man who had previously kept in the background, a man who long had been the quintessential insider, who went to the point in the ABM fight— Albert Wohlstetter.

Political leadership of Safeguard defense was seized by the former Deputy Secretary of Defense of the outgoing administration, Paul H. Nitze. Apart from individuals who had been held over by the new administration, most notably Johnny Foster, the Defense research chief, and Stanley Resor, the Secretary of the Army, Nitze was the only member of the team that approved Sentinel who had anything to say about Safeguard. Johnson, McNamara, Warnke, and Enthoven were mute. When he saw his name on a list of ABM supporters drawn up by Don Brennan, Harold Brown sharply demanded it be deleted. Nitze was not so much concerned about the benefits of ABM, but rather sought to block an out-of-control movement to weaken the United States relative to the Soviet Union. Nitze's concern was the overall strategic balance, which he wished to keep tipped in favor of the United States. Parity and sufficiency were anathema to him. He knew that the U.S. position on Eurasia required being able to credibly threaten the Soviets with a U.S.-initiated nuclear war, and that required at least some semblance of superiority.

Nitze also knew something of the requirements for purposeful political action. Early in May he contacted Wohlstetter, and the pair put together an ad hoc group that they called The Committee for a Prudent Defense Policy.* Nitze's mentor, Dean Acheson, was the figurehead. Don Brennan was immediately brought in to suggest other members. Charlie Herzfeld was a key player. The draft of the initial letter of solicitation was written by Nitze and fleshed out by Albert and Roberta Wohlstetter in their suite at Washington's

---

*At the same time, a parallel Republican political operation was organized under the auspices of the Baroodys, which gained a long list of distinguished Republicans to support the President's policy, including John Wayne and its promoter, the lawyer William J. Casey. (After 1969, the two lobbies were folded together into a paper organization run out of the office of a professional lobbyist.)

Shoreham Hotel. In the end, they accumulated a considerable list of reputable Americans. In addition to those named above, there were the Princeton physicist John Wheeler; a few early Kennedy appointees, including Chip Bohlen (whose wife had stitched a footstool cover for Nitze's fallout shelter) and Livingston Merchant (our man in Canada when Diefenbaker was brought down); some liberal academics who were just about to be labeled "neoconservative"— Irving Kristol, Aaron Wildavsky, Ernest Lefever, and Morton Kaplan; the theologian Paul Ramsey, chaplain of the hawks; and Peter Clark, the learned proprietor of *The Detroit News*, which published a pro-ABM feature by Herman.

The organization was minimal, but even a shoestring operation requires flunkies. Wohlstetter engaged a young man just out of graduate school, whom he had first met many years ago when his daughter had tutored him in high school and had learned that the young man had been much taken by Wohlstetter's "Delicate Balance of Terror" essay. The young man was Richard Perle. He brought along another graduate student, his erstwhile roommate at the London School of Economics, a wandering military scholar named Edward N. Luttwak. The strategic flunkies were paid $15 a week for their services to the defense.

One of the ploys used by those arguing that Minuteman needed no active defense was the presentation of materials purporting to show that the number, yield, and accuracy of expected Soviet missiles would not be able to take out most of the hardened Minutemen, as was claimed by the administration. Thus the opposition was saying that the administration and its supporters were either incompetent or lying. That was a monstrous mistake, because they were challenging Albert Wohlstetter, whose virtues did not include tolerating criticism or suffering fools. He was well prepped for the encounter. In the early '60s, he had become annoyed at the amateur meddling of "the scientists" in strategic matters. He had analytically spread-eagled "the scientists" on his observation table, examined their intellectual entrails, and discovered them stuffed with putrefying excrement; he had then sought their logical testicles and calculated that the probability of their existence was so infinitesimal as to approximate zero. Wohlstetter was primed to pot "the scientists."

The Senate Armed Services Committee had come under heavy criticism for presenting only ABM advocates the year before, so it extended an open hand to critics in 1969; indeed, it received them with a great deal more respect than the anti–ABM Senate Foreign Relations Committee under the painfully ill-bred chairmanship of William Fulbright accorded ABM supporters. The Armed Services Committee chairman, Senator Stennis, was troubled by the great variance between the numbers presented by the two sides on what should have been a fairly precise technical issue. The final showdown had two champions for each side, one presumed strategist and one presumed scientist. For the pros, of course, it was Wohlstetter, backed up by Larry O'Neil, of the Riverside Research Institute. The anti side was held up by George Rathjens and Wolfgang Panofsky of Stanford.

This was a very foolish thing for Rathjens and Panofsky to do— they were fighting Albert Wohlstetter on his own turf, on his almost patented turf. Wohlstetter asked Rathjens how he had come to his conclusions, and Rathjens was fool enough to let him know. Wohlstetter pounced. Now, the second battle of the numbers is of more than merely prurient interest. It was the ABM numbers battle which circulated the unfortunate notion that Everyman can be his own nuclear strategist if he merely has command of a simple little formula to calculate how likely it is that an attack will destroy a force of ICBMs on the ground. The terms of the formula represent real-world phenomena: the success of an attack is indeed a function of the reliability of the attacking missiles, the number of attacking warheads, the yield of those warheads, their accuracy, and the hardness of the defenders' silos. If you have all those numbers, you can calculate the probability of kill of ICBMs and the assurance of making a disarming first strike.

Fortunately or unfortunately, nobody knows those numbers, or even decent approximations. Certainly no one on our side knows the reliability of Soviet missiles in a mass attack under combat conditions, and certainly the Soviets do not have that number either. Nor do we know how many missiles they have, although we can count holes in the ground that look as if they have missiles in them. Nor do we know how many warheads their missiles have, although we can calculate maxima on the basis of how many warheads they test on what missiles. Nor do we know what will be the yield in megatons of Soviet warheads. Nor do we know the accuracy of their missiles fired in concert in combat, although we can observe their tests and roughly estimate how accurate they seem to be. Nor do we or the Soviets know more than crudely the hardness of our silos, because they have not been tested in combat conditions.

Professionals working very cautiously and elaborating their assumptions within what seem to be reasonable ranges, and paying especially careful attention to the maximum practicable enemy potential, can make some rough estimates of such "exchange calculations." This can be accomplished by people like Albert Wohlstetter. And once they've been taught by someone like Wohlstetter, it can be done by people of commonplace talents as well, by people like George Rathjens, provided they have not been befuddled by the cynicism of a political debate. It turns out that Rathjens' numbers were fiddled just a little bit, just enough to make a difference between the Minutemen's surviving and not surviving a hypothetical Soviet attack in 1975.

Rathjens was an angel compared with some of the other "scientists." In *The New York Times Magazine* the longtime nuclear polemicist Ralph Lapp wrote something really stupid. He learned somehow that because of concerns that a missile will not be entirely reliable, attack calculations customarily assume that two missiles are fired at each silo. He concluded, therefore, that a Soviet missile force of 1,700 would have to be fired at 850 silos, leaving the 150 remaining Minuteman silos unattacked and ready to reply. Obviously, the Soviets would not allow some missiles a free ride by concentrating their attack on the others. Albert tore him up, down, and sideways, and perhaps that is a reason that Ralph Lapp will disappear from this chronicle. Another screwball exchange calculation was circulated privately by a member of the President's Scientific Advisory Council, Richard Garwin.

The Committee for a Prudent Defense Policy was gravely crippled when Nitze, having demonstrated his utility to the administration (and probably at the insistence of Scoop Jackson), was named the Department of Defense representative on the negotiating team for the forthcoming Strategic Arms Limitation Talks. The committee tottered on for a bit, then folded, because its sparkplug had been screwed out, the immediate cause for its existence was a moot issue, and Wohlstetter found another vehicle to support his support of the defense. But to be sure, the notion of a committee of right-thinking patriotic folk of both parties was not forgotten by Paul Nitze.

The battle of the books was joined when the Kennedy forces prepared a comprehensive "independent" study of ABM edited by Abram Chayes and Wiesner. The "Chaysner" book (so labeled by Donald Brennan), *ABM*, included an introduction supposedly written by Edward M. Kennedy and began with an intelligent and concise summary of objections to ABM signed by Chayes, Wiesner, George Rathjens, and an MIT physicist named Steven Weinberg (but from internal evidence, especially the lucidity of its organization, probably principally drafted by Rathjens). Most of the rest of the book was flapdoodle, mostly written by people with no correct information and no special qualification other than being public names. Perhaps the most disgraceful performance was by Hans Bethe, reprinting from the *Scientific American* article he had coauthored with Richard Garwin, in which he fell back on the old standby of beating the defense with decoys—decoys that the ABM design had already learned to beat, as Bethe should have known at the time. He also raised the issue of "blackout," impressing the ignorant reader with an elaborate formula, but not mentioning that the production of so much blackout by the offense would require an enormous and incredibly well-coordinated attack, far beyond the then capabilities of the United States, much less of the Soviet Union, not to mention China. He then implied that this great obstacle to radar would be created by explosions of defensive missiles in the atmosphere, which was not true, and failed to mention the rather obvious fact that such an intense concentration of heat in the atmosphere would very quickly rise and dissipate because of convection, but perhaps that was too ordinary a physical phenomenon to attract the attention of a Nobel Laureate.

Steven Weinberg, a veteran of early Jason pen-aids studies, claimed that the Safeguard was an inefficient swindle because most of its expenses were devoted to area defense, not to the missile-site defense. He achieved this conclusion by attributing most of the costs of the perimeter acquisition radars and all the costs of the long-range Spartan missiles to area defense, blatantly disregarding the utility of the PARs in alerting the site defense and the employment of the Spartans as the first layer of the layered defense of the missile fields.

Another MIT professor named Licklider made a tidy little list of the difficulties of previous weapons systems, which was not exactly news. He neglected to mention that most of the trouble-plagued systems he listed were products of the 1950s, which had been rushed to production before the sort of development that the ABM had experienced; perhaps we can all sympathize with his understandable failure to mention his own involvement with many of those systems. The MIT physicist Bernard Feld argued that it would be a bad idea to start ABM because this was a good time to start arms-control talks. He did not ask why the Soviets should bother to negotiate arms control if the United States was unilaterally controlling its own arms. The highly regarded China expert Allen S. Whiting wrote that deployment of missile defenses might make the Maoists even more hostile to bourgeois America; Whiting is an intelligent man—it would be disgraceful to accuse him of actually believing that. JFK's speech writer Sorenson wrote that the Europeans didn't like ABM, but failed to say why they didn't.

Carl Kaysen again demonstrated his competence. Arthur Goldberg pointed out that other countries didn't want the United States to defend itself, without mentioning that they would win a war that devasted the United States and the Soviet Union. Jay Stone pitched in with an irrelevancy about how good were our satellite inspection systems, mentioning in passing that we could monitor future arms-control agreements with the wonderful eyes of our reconnaissance, closing with the observation that we could identify new offensive missiles just as accurately as we could pick up the "precisely seventy-two interceptor missiles" around Moscow; later reconnaissance discovered precisely 64 such missiles. An especially irrelevant little piece was contributed by Adam Yarmolinsky, roasting the supposed military-industrial complex. He soon thereafter wrote a book-length diatribe on the subject without specifying how it was that America was to have arms to defend itself without having experts in those arms and organizations that had an interest in manufacturing them.

How and why it was decided that Bill Moyers, Johnson's press secretary, belonged in this compendium is a minor mystery. An essay on command and control under his name whined that an ABM with nuclear warheads required that the President delegate nuclear-weapons release authority to military commanders. This was A Bad Thing. This was also downright silly. If an attack was under way, a nuclear war had already begun, and it had long since been arranged that authority for nuclear release could be accorded subordinate commanders in the event of nuclear war. Did anyone imagine that under a nuclear barrage, the President would or should have to order the use of each and every nuclear weapon? In particular, release of defensive nuclear weapons had long since been granted to the commander-in-chief of NORAD, and ABM was to be under NORAD's command and control. But it is unfair to entirely attribute this inanity to Moyers; the piece was ghostwritten by Yarmolinsky, former assistant to the Secretary of Defense.

All in all, Chaysner was a disgraceful performance. The book was widely circulated and became the standard popular text for ABM opposition. So from the viewpoint of its authors, it was a success— that is, in the short run. The long-run objectives of the book were, to be sure, not achieved; but domestic affairs are as imponderable as foreign affairs, and none of the ambitious authors could have anticipated that their return to power would be detoured.

When a manuscript of the Chaysner book was obtained at the Hudson Institute, Brennan was appalled at how one-sided and devious it was. Around the luncheon table, his assistant, the conservative economist William Schneider, Jr., pointed out that there was enough material in house to do a better ABM book. He had a willing coeditor right at hand. The Norwegian social democrat Johan Holst had a special interest in collaborating in an anti-Chaysner effort because he had been approached by the Cambridge people to write on Europe and ABM, but found a total collapse of interest when they learned that he favored ABM for arms-control-negotiating reasons.

It was easy to put a book together rapidly. Brennan's piece in favor of population defense from *Foreign Affairs*; Herman's in favor of a thin defense from *Fortune*; Wohlstetter's statements supporting a point defense before the Senate Armed Services Committee, plus serious essays on ABM and China by Frank Armbruster and on other aspects of the problem by Raymond Gastil and Michael Sherman. Other than Wohlstetter's, the only contribution from outside Hudson was a charming and persuasive essay by Charlie Herzfeld. He was supposed to write about the technical aspects of ABM, which he couldn't do because he knew too much about it on a classified level, so he sidestepped by making a strategic virtue of ignorance on both sides: Because the defender cannot be certain ABM will work, he must be very cautious—"defensive-conservative." Because the attacker cannot be sure that ABM will fail, he must also be very cautious—"offensive-conservative." A window of uncertainty is opened, and both sides are deterred from untoward acts.

Perhaps the most ingenious and useful essay was by Herman, who concluded the book by discussing not strategy but the sociopolitics of the ABM dispute, noting that the fight over ABM was not really over ABM at all, but came out of an elite academic milieu opposed to technology, the military, and the United States government. This, to him, was the real issue, not counting warheads. He had always seen nuclear strategy as a question of national will, and he saw academia cracking. As if to confirm his thesis, an unnamed professor presently said, "If I were at Harvard and coming up for tenure, it would be harder to come out for ABM than if I were working for Herman Kahn."

Although *Why ABM?* was prompted by the desire to counter the one-sided Chaysner, many people at Hudson were uneasy with the book because it was one-sided on the opposite side. Proper Hudson practice was to display all sides of an issue in a coherent and empathic manner. Herman said that he considered writing the anti-ABM position himself, but abandoned the idea, fearing he might have been too persuasive.

That little paper was Herman's only public contribution to the 1969 ABM debate, because he was devoting most of his energy to selling the new administration on his proposal to extricate the United States from Vietnam, through a concept he called "Vietnamization." But he did talk on the subject at one of Hudson's regular seminars, and he displayed a chart of arguments against ABM:

I.   It won't work.
II.  It will work too well.
III. Both.

Jane Kahn watched the unfolding fight with growing outrage: "Why, it's civil defense all over again; but then *some* of the scientists were lying, and now *all of the scientists are lying.*"

Down in Washington, another countersalvo in the battle of the books was being organized by Dick Foster. Using William Kintner of the Foreign Policy Research Institute as a front, Dick put together

Brennan's *Foreign Affairs* article, Wohlstetter's testimony, some SRI pieces, and some statements for and against ABM by administration officials and congressmen. It was useful to publish this material, but the ensuing product, *Safeguard: Why ABM Makes Sense,* was inferior to the Hudson effort.

As if in deliberate demonstration of Herman's thesis, the Chaysner book was widely reviewed and circulated and published as a Signet paperback, while the Hudson and SRI efforts were financial fizzles, although *The New York Times* put *Why ABM?* on the front page in an article by William Beecher, who thought highly of Herman. And to the credit of the *Times,* it placed back on page 13 Edward Kennedy's foul calumny that the book had been bought by Pentagon money. The *Washington Post* editorial writers had some fun with a Chaysner publisher's ad comparing ABM to civil defense—the *Post* jabbed that many of the authors had been deeply involved in JFK's civil defense initiative.

### The Soiled Victory of ABM

Probably more decisive than any of these maneuvers was that the President put his full support behind Safeguard. He had just been elected, and even in those dismal, demoralized days, a glimmer remained in the Senate of the notion that the Commander-in-Chief was most responsible for directing the national deefense. Most of the wavering senators fell on the side of Safeguard. In late June, the Senate Armed Services Committee voted out Safeguard by a 10–7 majority—a weak endorsement by that hawks' nest, but enough to get the bill to the floor. In July, the Senate held a closed session, apparently with no effect. Two extraneous events occurring in July may have influenced a few votes on the margin. There was a success and there was a failure. The success was that the Apollo mission commissioned by John Kennedy achieved its objective of landing Americans on the Moon, demonstrating America's ability to achieve wonderfully difficult technological tasks. The failure was of the guidance of an Oldsmobile automobile detoured by the blackout of Edward Kennedy's personal command and control at a bridge at Chappaquiddick, which had the unfortunate effect of somewhat distracting the Senator and his smart lawyers for a few days.

After nearly a month of debate, ABM finally came to a vote on

6 August, and the Senate split 50–50. The vote was along almost perfect liberal–conservative lines. For ABM, as one would expect, were Alcott, Russell, Stennis, Sparkman, Hollings, Jackson, Goldwater, and Thurmond. The Vice President, Spiro Agnew, broke the tie for the administration, and ABM was approved. Victories so narrow are little better than defeats. ABM had a bad launch.

## The Other Side Falters

How enlightening it would be to be a fly on the wall of the Soviet bureaus that are tasked to figuring out what the Americans are up to. To the apparatchiks in their disciplined hierarchies, the capitalist bastion must seem like bedlam. One of the tricks of our analysts is to try to determine the Soviet's views from what they write about us. Remember, the Soviets publish almost nothing about their own equipment and plans, and much of what they write is obvious nonsense, although which is nonsense and which is not is the subject of intense debates among the Kremlin-watchers of assorted intelligence interests and political preferences. A Soviet convention is to write with contempt of American strategic writing, pointing to it as evidence of the irresponsible aggressiveness of the imperialists and/or the inevitable degradation of degenerate bourgeois ideology. (To be sure, the Soviet analyses are not always without considerable objective merit.)

An intelligence analyst's trick is to notice when the Soviets do not merely bludgeon the Western ideas, but go to the trouble of rebutting them, or merely sneer at them and say nothing more; the latter is interpreted as a signal to the Soviet reader that this is something worth taking seriously. The American debates of the mid-'60s were reported fitfully by the Soviets, and always with contempt heaped upon the ideas of limiting war in any way through counter-force targeting, limited strategic strikes, or even assured destruction. Official Soviet doctrine was that nuclear war would be total war—a doctrine consistent with the Leninist view of the totality of political endeavor. In a nuclear war, everything would be thrown in all at once.

Yet one aspect of American strategic thought was not rebutted—the writings about strategic defense. Initially the Russians were extremely hostile to the notion that defense was A Bad Thing. At

Glassboro, Kosygin heard McNamara's pitch for voluntary mutual vulnerability with apparently genuine incredulity. Earlier he had made remarks in London about the latest fantastic idea of the imperialist ideologues.

Apparently, and this is speculative, the Soviets began to change their mind, when better information about American penetration aids reached them. The ballistic missile defense complex being built around Moscow was slowed, and eventually halted at 64 missiles, and the effort was not replicated anywhere else. The only rational explanation for this start-and-stop is that the Soviets had put the system into production and deployment on a crash basis, as the U.S. Army had recommended for Nike-Zeus, then decided that it was inadequate. The usual American description of this system is that it greatly resembled Nike-Zeus. Perhaps Nike-Zeus might have been upgraded to Nike-X specifications, and perhaps the Soviets eventually might have been able to do the like with their ABM. But in the late 1960s, it appeared that the Soviets had made a bad play. They could see the Americans going forward with a far superior system. The Americans, once again, were playing catch-up ball, catch up and go ahead, with a vengeance. The Soviets indicated that they were willing to treat.

But the Soviets considered other matters of state more vital than arms-controlling with the Americans. The epidemic of infantile leftism sweeping the bourgeoisie of the West had spread its virus across the Iron Curtain and had infected Czechoslovakia in 1968. Therapy was necessary, so an expedition of Soviet troops to Prague suppressed the outbreak. It is symptomatic of the quality of illusions of the 1960s that Western elements were surprised at the Soviet reaction. Still, while the West was already so demoralized that there was nothing like the radical reaction to the original Communist takeover of Czechoslovakia twenty years earlier, the response was sufficiently negative that further arms-control talks with the U.S.S.R. became impolitic. In the jargon of arms control, relating negotiations over arms to other political issues is called "linkage" and thoroughly muddies the water. If we can't trust them, how can we deal with them? But if we're dealing with them, doesn't that indicate that we think we can trust them? Or what?

Not until the next American administration was the annoyance of the West cooled enough for the negotiations to go forward. To be sure, nothing had changed in the interim—Soviet troops remained in Czechoslovakia, and the Soviet Union had not changed either—but the "public opinion" of the West could not focus on one subject for more than a few months at a time.

## ABM Goes Forward

During these political shenanigans, the ABM systems command and its contractors were laboring to make the device work. As expected, because it was an upgrade of the thorougly tested Nike-Zeus, the McDonnell Douglas* Spartan missile was successfully fired in March 1968. It was not thought necessary to test the missile against an ICBM until more of the components of the whole system were put together. Also in 1968, the prototype missile-site radar was turned on and began to be matched by satellite link to data at Bell Labs' central computing facilities in New Jersey. An ARPA/IDA study in 1966 concluded that blackout would seriously degrade Very High Frequency (VHF) radar performance, so Ultra High Frequency (UHF) was recommended. Nevertheless, in the initial design the frequencey was held down to save money, with provision to go up-frequency later if need be. It was not until the end of 1969 that the MSR could actually track an ICBM.

The second layer of the defense was also well on the way. Because of its shorter range, Sprint could be tested in CONUS. The first shots were at White Sands in 1965, and the Army continued to run tests with this nearly impossibly demanding missile for some time. (One Sprint later blew up right over its launch station at Kwaj.) Nonetheless, the development went forward, and a crucial test at White Sands in June 1967 showed that the Martin engineers had solved the central problem of designing a casing that could withstand the incredible heat, pressure, and vibration generated by its fantastic thrust up through the atmosphere. Indeed, that test was one of the factors in driving the Pentagon decision that the ABM system was ready to go. In all, 42 Sprints were fired at White Sands.

Kwajalein was experiencing a population explosion through immigration. In 1968 the first Martin Marietta employees arrived. To

---

*Independently of its missile work, Douglas went bust because its commercial airliner business was wiped out by Boeing's bomber-derived jets. It was taken over by McDonnell, fat from its worldwide F-4 fighter sales.

answer the housing shortage, house trailers were barged in, and part of the garrison was reduced to proletarian living. The leading-edge activities moved to Meck Island, where a test missile-site radar and missile launch complex was being laboriously constructed, while the main island of Kwajalein became a preserve for laboratories, offices, equipment, and housing. The testing was not without incident; the booster of a Spartan fell back to earth and buried itself in the coral. The last missile shot at Kwajalein Island was in December 1970, with perfect results.

At Meck, the firing of a Spartan in the spring of 1970 was a failure, but a June mission hit the right spot in space, and in August a Spartan directed by the MSR intercepted an ICBM nose cone. In December, a Sprint was lauched from Meck under MSR control against an ICBM, and killed its prey. To be sure, the "kill" was measured by how closely the anti–missile passed the missile—real tests with real nuclear warheads were prohibited by the Test Ban Treaty—but the lethal range of the warheads had been calculated closely from the tests under the Nevada desert. The engineers and technicians set themselves progressively more difficult tasks. A salvo of a pair of Spartans was fired in early 1971, one of which got an RV, the other a pseudotarget in space. A little later, two Sprints were fired off together. In April, Spartan intercepted an interme-diate-range ballistic missile fired from Johnston Island, and Sprint did the same the following month.

By the end of 1970, Kwajalein had achieved its maximum pop-ulation, nearly five thousand souls. The firings were, of course, dramatic, but the vital work did not show — it was the system integration, the linking of the pieces, and in particular, the pro-gramming of the monster computers. A major event was converting the system from what was coded M-1 to M-2 software, correcting what might have been a crippling glitch, and permitting much more elaborate tactical possibilities. The rate of firing increased, some-times to as many as two shots a week.

The test operations spread farther out in the atoll. Part of the layout of an ABM site was the dispersion of many of the missiles several miles from the main missile-site radar location to reduce their vulnerability and enlarge their footprint. So a prototype Sprint launch facility was constructed on Illeginni Island, north of Meck. The first shot there was in March of 1972, and that Sprint also took out an ICBM. Illeginni was too small for an airstrip, so the firing crews and mechanics commuted in by helicopter. The testing at Kwaj continued; but the attention of both the Army and Bell Labs was turning elsewhere—the Army to the operational missile sites, and the telephone company to a fundamental change in its way of doing business.

## The Conduct of the Allies

America's allies were fervently indifferent to the ballistic missile defense of the United States. At Endicott House in 1962, the most ambitious of the strategy conferences, the European participants had yawned at Glenn Kent's recital of the effects of nuclear weapons and nearly dozed off when Charlie Herzfeld made a pitch for BMD. As the 1960s wound down, the indifference became dogmatic. The reasons were not entirely disreputable. Not only were the allies also suffering from the inflated expectations for "arms control," but they had much more practical reasons for their opposition. Already the United States was bleeding its European garrison to support the effort in Vietnam, and stuffing arsenals with tactical nuclear weapons, while simultaneously nagging its allies into endorsing the declaratory strategy of "flexible response," supposedly increasing reliance on conventional forces, left over from the Kennedy days. One solution to The Problem was to fight to the last European.

Existing ABM systems would seem to be capable only of protecting the United States, and not its allies, although the Army and SRI had worked out ambitious paper plans to cover Europe and Japan, and Hudson was particularly interested in Japan, a country ideally suited for BMD. Certainly many of America's friends realized that the forward defensive posture of the post–World War II period was an aberration in American history; they had always been nervous that the Americans might attempt to fall back to a "fortress America" bastion and leave the forward positions and client states to their fate.

But another reason for the allies' position no one dared state openly: that mutual vulnerability of the U.S. and the U.S.S.R. was a winning strategy for the rest of the world. As long as the missiles did not go off, everyone was fine, especially because the U.S. and S.U. were paying for the missiles; and if—God forbid—deterrence failed, then the United States and the Soviet Union would mutually destroy each other, and the rest of the countries of the world would shed a tear or two and enjoy the fruits of restoration to their previous prominence before the rise of the upstart superpowers.

The Canadian performance was particularly disreputable. When the NORAD agreement was renewed in 1967, the Liberal government of Lester Pearson, with the full approval of the former Tory leader John Diefenbaker, put in a rider that cooperation on continental air defense in no way spilled over to ballistic missile defense. The Liberals cannot be accused of ingratitude—they would not have dared raised the issue without the connivance of the U.S. administration. Canadian airspace was not needed for a U.S. ballistic missile defense, and Canadian space would be used without asking. A Spartan fired from the proposed Safeguard site in North Dakota could have intercepted an ICBM right over Diefenbaker's parliamentary district.

## The Reconstitution of the Think Tanks

During the ABM fight, George Rathjens compounded his error by continuing to dispute Wohlstetter in the letters-to-the-editor columns of *The New York Times*. Albert demonstrated that he was a bad man to contradict, and the worst man to accuse of giving skewed and interested analysis. Picking up on a suggestion made years before by C. P. Snow that a dispute on a technical point of air defense between Tizard and his rival Lindemann could have been presented for resolution to a committee of the Royal Society—a suggestion that Wohlstetter had earlier ridiculed—Albert searched for an appropriate tribunal to weigh his dispute with Rathjens *et al.* He hit upon the Operations Research Society of America (ORSA—"oarsah"), of which he was not a member, nor were his opponents. Most of the ORSA was middle-grade professional number-crunchers. The leaders of the society were rather less than major figures; flattered perhaps by the commission to judge their betters, they became referees of the third battle of the numbers.

Rathjens and company denied the competence of the technical court and refused to participate, so inevitably the matter was examined on Wohlstetter's terms, the adjudicators concentrating on the calculations of the presumed vulnerability of the Minuteman force according to the assumptions available at the time. The ORSA jury labored for nearly two years over what could have been resolved in about a week by any normal analysis shop, and in a day at RAND or Hudson, and issued a complete vindication of Wohlstetter's position. They found that he had properly used the appropriate available materials and had made proper calculations, whereas the anti–ABM forces had used unclassified materials that went counter to classified materials to which the opposition had access and that resulted in quite a different answer. In addition, apparently to give an appearance of political balance, the ORSA panel slammed some funny studies by the American Security Council, a haven of retired bloody-fanged generals, and rapped Johnny Foster for an analytical misdemeanor.

The guilty and their cronies were thoroughly incensed, denying, as they had from the beginning, ORSA's jurisdiction, because they were not members. (William Beecher of *The New York Times* had the wit to call up Alain Enthoven out in Palo Alto and reported his apposite remark "It was rather like Linus Pauling claiming that the American Medical Association had no business evaluating his theories about vitamin C because he was not a member of the AMA.") Appropriately for Massachusetts folk, they resorted to the old Sacco and Vanzetti ploy—when the evidence shows you are guilty as hell, claim that the court is biased. Rathjens, Wiesner, and Weinberg accused ORSA of violating their civil liberties. And they said Minuteman defense was a phony issue: the real issue was whether Minuteman needed to be defended at all, considering the plenitude of reprisal forces the United States had to hurl back at the Soviets—which was not, of course, the topic to which Wohlstetter, Rathjens, and the rest had been invited to dispute before the Senate committee: it was precisely the issue of Minuteman vulnerability.

Among those who took the anti-ORSA side was Richard Garwin, who announced that he had not been a participant in the ABM debate. Apparently he had forgotten that he was then a presidental science adviser but had circulated a personal paper on ABM that made very curious calculations. And the Federation of American Scientists was sufficiently incensed to devote an entire issue of its newsletter to the flap.

In the end, the third battle of the numbers was rather like the Senate ABM vote. Wohlstetter won the battle, but looked petty and vindictive—and so lost the war. Later Rathjens casually admitted minor errors, and nobody cared.

During the congressional debates, the enemies of ABM made sweeping charges, or by innuendo implied, that all ABM supporters were hirelings of the military-industrial complex. This seems to have been mostly a classic example of "mirror-imaging." The reality was much more complex and interesting. Recall that almost to a man, the prodefense analysts and scientists had always been liberal Democrats. The defection of their faction to neoisolationism and unilateralism was deeply troubling to most of then, and also disturbing was the coming to power of a Republican administration suspicious of the lot of them. They had to demonstrate that they were loyal and useful to the new dispensation. Not that this made any of them modify their position; to the contrary, everyone who publicly advocated ABM debate supported it before Nixon presented Safeguard; but the desire to ingratiate themselves with the new administration may have prompted more visibility than might otherwise have been the case.

For example, Congressman Bingham of Westchester County, New York, noticed that whenever he debated ABM, he faced Hudson Institute people. It happened that almost all of them favored ABM strongly, and that Herman Kahn had set up Hudson precisely for the purpose of public education, unfettered by the institutional constraints of direct government control that had finally muzzled RAND. By the late 1960s, the conventional wisdom of the vocal elements of what Professor Galbraith labeled "the educational and scientific estate" was almost uniformly opposed to government policy. So Hudson people found themselves in great demand for public appearances. Typically, some public-spirited organization such as the League of Women Voters would hold a session on a public-policy topic. The program would be almost firmed up when a cryptopatriot would suggest that the speakers were rather one-sided. Shouldn't someone represent the forces of evil—that is, the position of the U.S. government? So Hudson folk would be out defending the war in Vietnam, or American foreign policy in general, or ABM. And the defense was never one that a public official could make or support, because the Hudson people proffered their own views, which were usually critical of current programs. None of them really liked Safeguard; they all wanted more ABM than that.

Still, survival was an issue at both Hudson and RAND. Herman openly courted Laird and Kissinger. His Hudson Institute was small and a personal vehicle, so he could and did move it to business-forecasting work. RAND, however, had graver difficulties. It was known to be a nest of liberal Democrats, and some elements in the administration were sympathetic to the old-line military types who had deeply resented the "whiz kids" meddling in the prerogatives of the brass. When a latecomer to RAND, James Schlesinger, was named a deputy director of the Budget Bureau, he was identified as "the only Republican at RAND." (Fred Ikle had left earlier.)

Harry Rowen sought to rectify that. He had been brought back from the Pentagon to be RAND's new president after the retirement of Frank Collbohm in 1966, and sought to restore its golden age. Rowen seemed the perfect choice because he had been a competent analyst and had the agreeable (and painfully rare at RAND) quality of getting along with everybody. His program for reconstitution concentrated on individuals. When Schlesinger left, Herman's old friend Andy Marshall was made head of the strategy section. Wohlstetter returned to the fold as a consultant. And Fred Ikle was brought back as head of the social-science department. Because Ikle was not believed to be a good administrator, Frank Hoeber was spirited away from SRI to be his deputy.

## ABM Staggers On

As if both sides were exhausted, the great ABM fervor subsided after the squeaker vote in the Senate. Although a hard core, the same as in 1968, continued to resist further funding of ABM, the money got through the Congress with little trouble. By postponing the urban deployments nearly indefinitely, the Nixon administration had defused the local oppositionists, because it was hard to get suburbanites aroused over military construction out in the Great American Desert. Certainly a related factor was that the social elements mobilized against ABM were not sufficiently disciplined to conduct a long-term campaign. The arms-control negotiations with the Soviets certainly swayed many votes in the Congress—the notion of ABM as "a bargaining chip" was acceptable and natural to the parliamentary bargainers of the Congress. Without an ABM, how could we bargain ABM with the Soviets? And it was whispered by the administration that the ABM chip might buy more than ABM from the other side.

Hardly aware of these intrigues, the Army and its contractors soldiered on. The Engineers changed direction fast. When the Sharpner's Pond work was suspended in 1969, the emphasis shifted west to the Plains. The preliminary surveys had already been made, and land acquisition began in 1970. "Grand Forks Air Force Base"* as a term for the North Dakota Safeguard site is a misnomer. It was not at Grand Forks, or a single site at all, but rather a scattering of individual locations over a wide area. The PAR was on a 279-acre plot 90 miles northwest of Grand Forks, while the 433-acre MSR site was 25 miles away. In addition were four remote Sprint launch sites of about 40 acres each dispersed around the Missile Site Radar.

The region was closer to the Canadian border than to Grand Forks, snugged up against the Manitoba line, in rich and dull-flat farmland hardly inhabited. The nearest big town was Langdon, the county seat, population 2,151. The building of the Safeguard complex would draw in construction crews and other contractors, increasing the area's population by a third, requiring aid to public schools, the building of temporary housing, and elaborate negotiations with local trade unions. The construction contracts were put out to open bids, and the winner came in with $140 million, the largest award ever made by the Corps. Ground was broken in April 1970. The ABM debate and the switch from Sentinel to Safeguard had cost the government a year's delay.

Even then, sundry "concerned" and "sane" groups held mass demonstrations and threatened sabotage. A group of radicals organized a "festival of life and love" that milled about the site, flew kites, bounced to rock music, and got high on marijuana and worse. Their avowed plan was to fill in the hole being dug for the Missile Site Radar building, but this idea was abandoned—it would have been a backbreaking amount of real work. And North Dakota was too far from civilization and too distant from the major media centers to be convenient for the Defense of Life against the evil forces of defense.

The second ABM site was also misnamed. It was scattered northwest of Malmstrom Air Force Base, north of Great Falls, Montana,

---

*Earlier, Grand Forks AFB was one of the SAGE sites colocated with a SAC base.

also up toward the Canadian border, almost exactly duplicating the layout of "Grand Forks." Although the area was politically more conservative and not troubled by political activity, it was close to the mining regions of Montana, long a hotbed of flaming syndicalism. Labor trouble bedeviled the Malmstrom complex from the beginning. Nonetheless, ground was broken in early summer of 1970.

At both Safeguard sites, the Engineers and their contractors had to work to tight schedules; the winters on the northern plains are almost arctic in their intensity, so the construction season is short. Great holes had to be dug for the PAR and especially for the Missile Site Radar building, most of which was an underground bunker—it was designed as a concrete iceberg, only its tip exposed and the rest hardened by earth and concrete to 25 psi. The complex was cushioned from shock by elaborate springing of components, and was guarded from EMP by complicated metal shielding to draw off and ground the crippling pulse.

In addition to the conventional civil-engineering concerns about soil suitability and water availability, the Safeguard complexes presented special problems. They had to be designed to be "buttoned up" against radiation. Domestic enemies also had to be taken into account—Environmental Impact Statements had to be filed with the EPA. The federal air-quality laws required that the building have towering smokestacks to carry off the exhaust of the auxillary diesel engines—which would run continuously only if the power lines were severed by Soviet nuclear blast. The EPA was defending the nation from atmospheric diesel particulates during thermonuclear war. A lesser construction problem, but only by comparison, was the silos for the missiles. Both the Spartans and the Sprints were to go into reinforced-concrete bunkers. Only slightly behind schedule, the bitter winter required that construction be shut down and the uncompleted structures winterized late in 1970. Enough structural work had been accomplished at Grand Forks to provide shelter to permit the continuation of work inside the shells of the buildings over the winter. A combination of factors, not the least of which were inflation and labor trouble, started pushing costs up ahead of estimates. Endless labor difficulties slowed the construction in Montana to a crawl, putting the program eleven months behind schedule. But the delay of Malmstrom was planned, because word had been sent down from the top of the Pentagon to tough it out with the unions to delay progress.

In 1971, the administration requested ABM funds to defend a third Minuteman field at Whiteman Air Force Base, Missouri, and to begin site preparation for a fourth at Warren Air Force Base, Wyoming, as well as for preliminary work at four area-defense sites, including Washington, D.C. The Senate Armed Services Committee, strongly by influenced by Scoop Jackson, chopped out the money ($10 million) for preparation of the area-defense sites, but let the rest go through, and it was approved by the entire Congress. But the funding required a construction slowdown. In 1972, Congress also approved most of the requested money, but this time rejecting the administration's request for an optional choice of the fourth Safeguard complex to be either at Warren or at Washington. Congress took the Washington option out of the bill.

The warhead designers were on schedule. With a yield of less than a kiloton, Sprint neutron warheads could be easily tested in holes under the Nevada desert. But the 5-megaton X-ray Spartans were too fierce neighbors even for the devoted gamblers of Las Vegas. The Pacific atolls were too small and their coral construction too fragile for underground testing. So the Atomic Energy Commission went north to Alaska and added Amchitka, in the Aleutians, to the atomic archipelago. The AEC dug a hole a mile deep, planted the warhead and the instrumentation to record its effects in the millisecond before they were vaporized, filled in the hole, and probably evacuated the air to duplicate the vacuum of space.

The "Cannikin" shot provoked an uproar among the disarmers. The usual crowd tried to kill it in the Congress. The environmentalists said it would be a disaster—or at least, it would bother the sea otters. Jay Stone showed up in Anchorage to block it. Wolfgang Panofsky opposed it. George Kistiakowsky and Bernard Feld said it was the "potentially most destructive man-made underground explosion in history." The governor of Alaska thought it a smart idea to challenge the AEC chief, James Schlesinger, to personally attend the test if it was as safe as was claimed. He appeared, bringing along his wife and two daughters. Cannikin was fired on November 7, 1971, with perfect results. The island trembled. "It was kind of like a train ride," said nine-year-old Emily Schlesinger. The comments of the sea otters are not recorded; perhaps they are less neurotic and mendacious than "scientists."

## SALT

The story of the Strategic Arms Limitation Talks has been well told elsewhere, and need not be related in detail here. There is no quarrel over what happened, and the why will perhaps be forever disputed. The United States entered the negotiations continuing the position of the Johnson administration of a zero option on ballistic missile defense—none at all. The American negotiators seem to have been in near-perfect agreement that BMD was not worth having. The central difficulties in the negotiation concerned limiting the offensive arms, because of the asymmetry of the two superpower's weapon systems, the ubiquitous verification issues, and the steady Soviet deployment of more and more missiles.

After months of internal haggling, the United States proffered the Soviets a limitation of a single ABM site around the national capital. The Soviets grabbed the offer. The Americans then offered the Soviets a choice of no ABM or national-capital defense ABM. The Soviets replied that they had already accepted the offer of national-capital defense. The Americans then offered the Soviets no ABM, national-capital defense, or Soviet capital defense and four U.S. ICBM-site defenses. The Soviets reminded the Americans that they had already agreed to the national-capital site for both sides.

So the Soviets immediately granted in principle the desirability of limiting ballistic missile defenses to at least trivial levels, so the only issue was how many. This turnaround by the Soviets in no way startled the U.S. negotiating team because it took for granted the obviousness of the undesirability of defenses, and merely nodded that the Soviets had finally wised up. To American advocates of the offense, the Soviets' agreeableness was evidence of their recognition of the puissance of MIRV; to advocates of the defense, Soviet acquiescence proved that Galosh was a turkey, and that the American ABM system appeared effectively ominous to the other side.

The offensive limitations were the major issue, because selling defense restraints to both polities would have been difficult without

limiting offenses as well. The negotiations were painstaking and tiresome, because the Soviets played their conventional games of secrecy, propaganda, and peevishness, which may have worn down
the American side. Whether or not the final deal was equitable is
disputed. At the time, the issue was whether the United States was
justified in abandoning its twenty-five-year advantage in strategic
offensive forces. The domestic opposition to SALT, the "hard-lin-
ing" "hawks," complained against granting the Soviets at least parity; even parity was bad enough. By abandoning superiority, the
American government was admitting *de facto* that our vulnerability
to a Soviet counterthrust made quantitative and qualitative superiority meaningless. Under harassment by the hawks, exhausted
from a long trip, Henry Kissinger, the genius of the negotiations,
blurted out at an airport, "What in the name of God is strategic
superiority? What is the significance of it at these levels of numbers?*
What do you do with it?" He was later to recant, but was widely
praised at the time by the arms controllers.

The SALT result looked skewed on the offensive side: the Soviets
were permitted to have more missile launchers than the United
States; but this simple counting was misleading. Bombers were not
counted, and the Soviets made the considerable concession of disregarding U.S. "forward-based systems." Because nuclear weapons
based in Europe, Japan, and Korea and on ships at sea could smash
the Soviet Union, the other side had not unreasonably defined them
as "strategic." To be sure, forward-based systems were inherently
more vulnerable than were CONUS or submarine-based weapons
because of their proximity to the Soviet Union. Yet the Soviets
conceded this advantage to the United States.

At the time, the United States had many more MIRVed missiles
than did the Soviets, so it had a clear lead in total warheads. But
this advantage was recognized by everyone to be temporary, as the
Soviets began to MIRV their forces with them. A troubling issue
to a few specialists was the fact that Soviet missiles were on the
average much larger than their American equivalents, so they had
greater "throwweight." When the Soviets installed lots of MIRVs

---

*The second sentence, ". . . at these levels of numbers," is deleted when quoted by Henry's
critics. Nevertheless, the answer is unchanged: strategic superiority is the ability to impose
more harm than you receive; what you do with it is threaten the other side and reassure your
side.

and achieved better accuracy and more efficient warheads, they could outnumber the United States as much as U.S. strategic offensive forces had outnumbered the Soviets in the 1950s. That little detail, however, was put aside in the general rejoicing that at last significant arms control with the Soviet Union had been achieved.

Actually, the arms-control agreement failed to control, not to say reduce, offensive arms. The "interim agreement" merely limited the number of ICBM and SLBM missile launchers, not the number, yield, or accuracy of the warheads which did the killing. The United States had already determined unilaterally to freeze the numbers of its launchers, and the Soviets had probably done the same. SALT was the equivalent of Cadillac and Lincoln agreeing to limit stick-shift transmissions on their cars. It was a fraud.

The only arms that were actually limited were defensive arms. Both sides were permitted two anti–ballistic missile defense sites, each with not more than 100 interceptors and with tight limits on the number of radars that could be built. One complex could be centered on the national capital, as was the Soviet's Moscow installation; the other could contain ICBM silo launchers, as did the lead American unit in North Dakota. The treaty gave some advantage to the Soviets, because "the national capital" also covered dozens of ICBMs in the Moscow region, while it was doubtful that the Americans would go ahead with defending Washington, and placing ICBMs in Maryland and Virginia was out of the question. The advantage to the Soviets was small, probably without strategic significance, but did reveal that the Americans were so eager for an arms-control agreement that they were willing to concede less than equality; it may be presumed that that did not go unnoticed by the Soviet Union.

Oddly, the SALT treaty did not just restrict the existing ABM systems, but banned any system that might be developed in the future.

There was somewhat of a squabble over Senate approval of the SALT agreements, but mostly about the offensive forces. Scoop Jackson and his increasingly visible aide Richard Perle led a minor guerrilla war against the administration. Very little dispute about the defensive side of SALT appeared. Strom Thurmond expressed some skepticism: "Is there a good reason why we should forever preclude the possibility of a truly effective defense of our cities if

our technology should make one available?" He specifically mentioned lasers. The testimony in the treaty hearings was almost uniformly positive. Of course, one of its negotiators, Paul Nitze, appeared
for it. Edward Teller testified in favor of SALT. Only one serious
person held out to the bitter end against signing the treaty, Donald
Brennan:

> The argument can reasonably be made that although both
> agreements represent important failures, the best course of action
> in view of current political realities is simply to accept them.
>     I am sympathetic to this argument. I also doubt very much
> whether any recommendations of mine will alter the expected
> acceptance of these agreements. But it seems appropriate that
> someone should say, unambiguously and on the record, that both
> of these agreements are wrong, that the United States ought not
> to be in the position these agreements will leave us in, and that
> the country would ultimately be best off by rejecting them both
> and then doing what is right. I hereby take this position.

When the treaty came up for Senate approval, only two senators
were present and voting against it: James Allen of Alabama, the
senator from Huntsville; and James Buckley of New York, whose
defense aide was William Schneider, Jr., Don Brennan's protégé
from the Hudson Institute.

## The Twilight of ABM

On Kwajalein, the ABM development work approached its final
phase. Sprints were being fired regularly. The last tests of the system
against flurries of decoys were especially demanding. To the inhabitants of Kwaj, the early '70s were a period of decline. Although
videotapes belatedly brought some television to the island, the recreational assets had been greatly reduced when the wreck of the
*Prinz Eugen* was declared off limits after the unfortunate deaths of
two Western Electric employees while diving there. The size of the
garrison began to shrink steadily; by 1974, AT&T employees were
only a quarter of those of the peak. To some degree, they were
replaced by subcontractors who were preparing to take over the Bell
systems work. At the end of 1974, major modifications were made
to the Missile Site Radar, and the program had to be fixed up. A

last set of test firings was made to try out the modifications in April 1975. As the North Dakota site went operational the development work was accomplished, so Bell Labs and its subcontractors pulled out, leaving on Kwajalein a residue of the Army and of ARPA and a new set of contractors.

The work on the Malmstrom site was canceled immediately upon signature of the anti–ABM treaty, and the Engineers put out contracts to tear it down. Of course, the preliminary work on the other Minuteman defense sites was also terminated. Apparently nothing was ever done about building a defense of Washington, D.C., beyond paper studies of the PAR at Fort Meade to the north and Sprint batteries at the Old Soldiers' Home and at Bolling Field. A D.C. defense was militarily difficult and politically impossible. Unlike Moscow, Washington is not far from the ocean, and can be popped in a few minutes by sea-launched ballistic missiles from submarines. The congressmen would not dare go back to their constituents with the news that they had provided for their own defense and not that of their fellow citizens. Fortunately, for reasons that are obscure, the Soviets decided to let us off the hook on this issue by agreeing in 1974 to a protocol to SALT reducing the number of deployment sites to a single one. The best explanation is that they had no intention of trying to defend a single ICBM site, and they wanted to kill off any hope of an American national ABM system, yet wished to keep their Moscow cover against China, Britain, and France.

Construction of Grand Forks did go forward on an unhurried schedule. The PAR structures were finished and the radars and computers erected. The missile silos were planted in the North Dakota soil, and the missiles flown in by helicopter and inserted into the ground. The software was installed and endlessly modified. This was to be the last contribution of the tireless engineering talent of Bell Labs.

The intensity of feeling among the dominant elements of America against the military and defense contractors had taken its toll on AT&T. No longer was Ma Bell generously contributing to the national defense; now Ma Bell was seen as participating in a ripoff. It was even argued that the reason for the ABM was to fill the coffers of Western Electric. The telephone company, as always, considered itself almost a government agency, very sensitive to "public opinion," and circa 1970 determined to disengage from the military—not quite totally, but to reduce its exposure by slashing the man-hours of Bell Laboratories devoted to defense research from the established 10 percent to less than 3 percent. That continuing work was to be quiet and uncontroversial—the hush-hush SOSUS underseas surveillance work for the Navy, for example; but projects such as ABM were just too visible. Ma Bell surrendered.

The entire Bell Labs ABM operation was shut down. A priceless national asset was torn apart and thrown away. These were the people who knew the most in the whole world about ballistic missile defense. The plans for upgrading Nike-X equipment, such as the Improved Spartan with loiter capability and a lighter warhead, were scrapped. The last job of Bell's ABM manager, Cliff Warren, was to find jobs elsewhere in the organization for his nine hundred crack engineers; then he took early retirement. Systems engineering for the vestigial rump ballistic missile defense follow-on work was handed over to lesser firms.

### ABM's Last Stand

As the development work was phased out, the operational side of ABM was phased in. The Army had established a Safeguard systems training school for the people to actually operate the Safeguard sites at Fort Bliss, the Army's air defense training center, then commanded by Major General C. J. LeVan. A wooden mock-up of a missile launch structure was constructed for training mechanics and electricians. The operators of the computers and the scopes were brought up to operational skills. The ABM school attracted the brightest young officers and NCOs of air defense artillery. Teaching troops to run the system was painless, because it had been so well designed. While ABM was still in development, GI operators had been put on the prototype MSR on Meck Island, and it was learned that ordinary soldiers with minimal training could watch the radar screens and could discriminate the real missile from the decoys. These fellows were commonplace young Americans just out of high school, not Nobel Laureate physicists who said it couldn't be done.

On 1 April 1975, exactly five years from the go-ahead, the Safeguard complex at Grand Forks, North Dakota, was operational. The radars were turned on, the computers working, the missiles primed and ready to go. After twenty years of effort, America finally had a ballistic missile defense—but not much of one: only 30 Spartans and 70 Sprints. It gave two layers of protection of the ICBM missile field at Grand Forks, and a single ultra thin layer of area protection of the northern Plains, hardly the most valuable area of the United States. Strategically, the complex was of trivial value. Even had it worked perfectly, the Soviets would have needed to add only 100 warheads to their attack on the Grand Forks field, a piddling fraction of their growing inventory. With its expected 75 percent kill rate, Safeguard would have extracted even less cost from the offense. In 1973, as forecast, the Soviets tested their first MIRVed missiles. To get more benefit from the complex, the Army indulged in contemplation of a curious retrograde step: to give the ballistic missile defense some air defense functions. The radars were rather good.

The Safeguard site did have considerable curiosity value: it was one of the two operating ballistic missile defense sites in the world; the other was around Moscow and not open to visitors, so various firemen stopped by Grand Forks, including the chief of staff of Japan, a nation ideally suited by geography for ballistic missile defense, and a high Swedish official, an old friend of Herman's from the passive defense days. While the site was under construction, Henry Kissinger had the gall to drop in and make some diplomatically apologetic remarks about killing ABM.

The Safeguard site was an excellent facility, a tribute to American engineering genius, but it was essentially useless and was expensive to operate, and worst of all, it was a symbol of defense and of the political defeat of a senator's clique. Again, the saga of strategic defense cannot be separated from other political events. Early in the Nixon administration there were leaks of the SALT bargaining position to right-wing elements, and the White House was furious. Feeling beleaguered and distrustful of the permanent bureaucracy, the White House staff fudged an amateur counterintelligence bureau to plug the leaks—"the plumbers." (One of the characters in this chronicle was "fluttered" by E. Howard Hunt.) As a consequence of their subsequent efforts in his behalf, Mr. Nixon felt obliged to resign, to be replaced by Gerald Ford, who promptly pardoned him for any real or presumed transgressions, to the considerable annoyance of a good part of the American electorate, which responded in 1974 by electing in droves all manner of marginal leftish Democratic types, bitterly opposed to the military-industrial complex and all its works. That crowd greatly influenced the composition of the Congress that first sat in 1975, and its potential was perceived by the advisers of Edward Kennedy.

In late spring, flushed with victory from the annihilation of Indochina, Kennedy proposed that funding for Safeguard operations be deleted from the defense budget. Kennedy was weakly resisted in the Congress and by the administration, which was entirely on the political defensive. The Army itself, while proud in a narrowly professional way of having carried out its orders to get the Safeguard site operational on schedule, was obviously worn down and sick and tired of the entire ABM affair. Its venture into atomic-strategic manners had been nothing but an enormous headache. The Army was infinitely more concerned with reconstructing the field army— the real army—from its post-Vietnam blues and converting to the "all-volunteer force" mandated by Nixon and his advisers. The best response the Army could make was to propose saving a few bucks by putting Grand Forks on a forty-hour week so that it would remain operational in semireserve and could be brought up to round-the-clock operations in crisis. About all that could be said for continuing to run the system was the experience that might be gained, which the Soviets presumably were acquiring in their complex around Moscow. But this would be of little value without targets to test against and without funds for continual upgrade—neither of which were available in northern North Dakota or in the Washington budget in 1975.

The only vocal opposition to Senator Kennedy was from James Buckley of New York, still advised by William Schneider. Buckley raised the old bugaboo of the ABM potential of Soviet surface-to-air missiles. In the end, a crumb was thrown to the defense. The complex would be terminated, except for the Perimeter Acquisition Radar, which had value as an early-warning radar of Soviet attack. Although not designed for that role, PAR was more advanced and much better hardened than the three BMEWS radars in the Arctic. The naked PAR was politically acceptable because it would only help to warn and trigger the offensive forces to strike back in reprisal for a destroyed nation.

At the end of the year Grand Forks was shut down. The highly trained crew supervised the evacuation of the missiles and warheads by Army helicopter, and proceeded to tear the guts out of the Missile Site Radars and the elaborate communications to the missile silos. The site was paved over, and the ABM missiles put in canisters in cold storage in Alabama.

## The Defeat of NORAD

While the ABM wars were being fought, NORAD was defeated by a single aircraft. On 5 October 1969, a fighter pilot, recently rotated home from raids over North Vietnam, was circling to land at Homestead AFB, south of Miami, and noticed something familiar. He reported to the tower, "There's a MiG in the pattern." The visitor made the signals of noncombatancy by lowering his landing gear and waggling his wings, and duly landed at Homestead. Sitting on the runway was USAF C-135 *Air Force One,* which had just carried the Commander-in-Chief to his vacation retreat at nearby Key Biscayne.

The intruding pilot was Lieutenant Eduardo Guerra Jiménez, who wished to join the exodus of his countrymen from the sunny socialist paradise. He was granted political asylum. His old MiG-17 was of no interest to air intelligence and was promptly returned to its owners. Many people wondered how it was that a Cuban MiG was able to arrive over Homestead unnoticed and unchallenged by the North American Air Defense Command. Florida's congressmen wondered most of all. It was simple. Lieutenant Guerra had merely flown in under the radar. He had crossed the Florida Strait just above the waves. Could not the entire Cuban air force come across in the same manner? Yes, of course, anytime Fidel told them to go.

The Air Force responded with a pitch for the latest goodies it wanted—especially for the new AWACS planes—some of which might be used for continental air defense. The congressmen were not impressed. How much had we spent on continental air defense for how long? Jay Stone of the Federation of American Scientists helpfully suggested converting to a "coast guard of the air."

Further slashes were made in NORAD. More radars were torn down, more SAGE centers shut down, more interceptor squadrons deleted. The Bomarcs had departed in 1970. Oddly, however, one method of paring away at NORAD actually increased its effective-

ness: to save money, fighters and air defense missions were trans-
fered to the Air National Guard, which turned out to be better than
the regulars. The Guardsmen were pilots who liked to fly and mechanics who worked on only one type of airplane and were superior
to the regulars in their performance. And as in the 1960s, the shrinking of the fighter force improved its quality. The remaining planes
were the best ones. Even Canada got better planes when the remaining original CF-101s were supplanted by 66 less worn replacements in 1972.

But those cuts were minor compared with those which hit the
Army. *All* the remaining Nike-Herc batteries were taken out. The
regular and National Guard units were shut down. The Nike crews
were given the tearsome task of tearing out the equipment they had
so lovingly maintained for so long—in some cases almost twenty
years. Helicopters carried away the nuclear warheads. The excuse
here was entirely parsimony—since the Soviet bombers, although
they had never reached the inflated expectations of the 1950s, were
still there, and could still attack, and could still wreak terrible damage; but why bother to defend against them if we weren't defending
against the missiles? The estimated saving was $130 million per year.
Certainly more pressing on DoD and the Army was the need for
bodies—those troops and Guardsmen were necessary to man the
shriveling ranks of the field army.

ARADCOM was eradicated, shut down totally and completely.
There trickled on a residue of ground-based continental air defense
in the Nike-Hercules and Hawk screen from Miami to Key West.
However, these were considered theater air defense against Cuba.
So the United States was defending itself against Cuba, but not
against the Soviet Union. And there were Herc and Hawk batteries
with the divisions of the field army in CONUS, but these were
intended to deploy with their parent formations, were located in
such worthless places as backwoods North Carolina and Georgia,
and were not tied into the continental command and control net.
And there were a few Hercs and Hawks in Alaska, defending Anchorage better than Albany or Albuquerque.

Although the Hercs and Hawks were kept current with repeated
improved versions and upgrades of ancillary equipment, they could
not be expected to provide air defense for the field army forever.
The development of the Raytheon SAM-D went forward at a snail's

pace, in order to keep the short-term budget down. One design criterion was deleted—the anti–tactical ballistic missile capability. Members of the Congress were quite insistent on this point. After all, if SAM-D had ABM capability, it might be deployed in defense of the continental United States. This design cutback was not a direct result of the SALT treaty, because SALT was just that—*strategic* arms limitation, and not by the wildest imagination could it be interpreted to mean a ban on tactical ballistic missile defense of field armies, of airfields overseas, or of ships.

It is almost not worth mentioning, but completeness requires note of the Nixon administration's contribution to civil defense. The shelter-survey money ran out, and the Army's Office of Civil Defense was dead in the water. Remember that the Kennedy reorganization had left a residue Office of Emergency Planning in the White House. What, if anything, it did is a mystery. The Nixon people cut it into pieces and distributed them to various departments, hoping they might sink without a trace.

## The Academic Strategy

While emasculating the defense was given preference, everything was being cut in the early 1970s. Had not the Vietnam war demonstrated that having an expeditionary and counterinsurgency capability meant that such forces were dangerous? Did not mutual-assured-destruction theory mean that we should not invest in more accurate attack forces? (Senator Jackson's aide Richard Perle wrote in 1973 that "Large-scale programs of population defense coupled with highly accurate or high-yield ballistic missiles may threaten the opponent's retaliatory capability, and because they admit of possible differences between the consequences of striking first and striking second, are highly destabilizing.") Did not the existence of the SALT treaty show that the Soviets were being more reasonable, that "the Cold War was over," that we need not keep our guard up the way those frenzied hawks had been yowling for a generation?

The supersonic transport was shot down. The space program was emasculated post-Apollo. Only the reconnaissance, strategic offense, and command and control were kept up. The overhead became more effective. MIRVing went forward. The C3 became more elaborate. Deterrence would preserve the country—on the cheap.

Nixon and Ford were Stanley Baldwin all over again. America lacked a strong stomach and a strong pocketbook.

The situation in the early '70s was rationalized by a widespread vulgar set of precepts which came to be accepted as dogma among the academic rank-and-file, pretentious journalists, and that immense repository of the fashionable wisdom, their "concerned" wives. The chronicler has never been able to identify any real strategist who believed all of this syndrome, but there were many who held university posts and wrote about strategy. So let us label this syndrome "the academic strategy." Like any mass ideological syndrome, it lends itself to a few simple, easily recited incantations:

> Arms Race Bad—Arms Control Good
> Defense Bad—Offense Good
> Defending People Bad—Defending Weapons Good
> Counterforce Bad—Countervalue Good
> First Strike Bad—Second Strike Good
> War-Fighting Bad—Deterrence Good
> Limited Nuclear War Bad—Cataclysm Good
> Action–Reaction Inevitable and Bad
> Escalation Inevitable and Good
> Assured Destruction Inevitable and Good

And like any mass ideological syndrome, it relieves its adepts of the unpleasant necessity of thinking.

### The Next War in 1975

Apart from the vestigial civil defense capability, the handful of SAM batteries in southern Florida and Alaska, and the shrinking squadrons of NORAD, the United States in 1975 remained completely defenseless against strategic attack. For strategic defense it was complete, utter, total defeat.

Yet the American offensive forces were still intact, well defended, and growing, although not as rapidly as the Soviets'. In the next war, both sides would be obliterated—if the Americans had the stomach to fight. The next war was fought in Angola; the Americans caved in without fighting. The next war was fought in Nicaragua; the Americans caved in without fighting. The next war was fought in Afghanistan; the Americans caved in without fighting. The next war was even fought on Kwajalein; the American government incited the docile natives to discover grievances, so that the Americans could cave in without fighting.

## The Defeated

Defeat is not necessarily destruction. And defeat is not decisive unless the defeated side abandons the will to fight. Most of the defenders turned their attention elsewhere—if only by necessity, because men have to live, and pay mortgages, tuition, and club memberships. The '70s were lean times for the defenders. Those who flourished were those who made themselves useful to other interests and institutions.

Thank God for the Arabs. The energy crisis was the "moral equivalent of war," and it provided research contracts for many in the Business. Wohlstetter's early assistant Fred Hoffman, having done a tour in the Pentagon, returned to head RAND's energy department, but also went out soon after Rowen. MITRE also did some energy work in collaboration with Hudson and independently.

As part of the reaction against the military-industrial complex, Congress in its wisdom decided to fission the Atomic Energy Commision, putting the bulk of it, including the weapons work, under something called the Energy Research and Development Administration (ERDA—"ur-dah"). When the energy crisis broke in late 1973, the scientists were eager and willing to devote their considerable talents to the new field. "Atomic energy" became just plain "energy," and marvelous new opportunities were available to push its presumed benefits. The same bright people could work on oil, gas, coal, solar, and wind. To the east of Livermore—Teller's temple of strength through science and technology—the mountains were littered with a forest of windmills, evidence of American truckling before Arab power.

The early '70s were mean lean years for the soldiers. As the Vietnam war was wound down, budgets were slashed, slashed again, and reslashed. The abolition of conscription meant that much higher wages had to be paid to keep the forces up to even three-quarters of the pre-Vietnam levels. Programmed weapons systems were chopped out or were stretched out to reduce their budgetary impact in the short run, resulting in fewer weapons at higher costs per weapon. The bombers ran down, the fighters ran down, the ships ran down, the tanks ran down, the guns ran down. Perhaps the missiles ran down as well, but we cannot know; but probably not, because money was always to be found in the declining budgets to reinforce the offensive forces, particularly for the MIRVed missiles in the submarines.

The Army reorganized itself for defense—against the civilian leadership of the nation. The Army took steps to ensure that it would not be stuck with the rap for another Vietnam. Toward this objective, the "Total Army" was invented—the regular Army integrated itself so thoroughly with the reserves and the National Guard that a large expeditionary force could not be dispatched without dragging along the reserve components, which could require a mobilization. In other words, the Army would go to war only with a national commitment.

What happened to the Air Force is sadder. Early in the 1960s, the Army research chief, General Art Trudeau, sneered that the Air Force would become "the silent silo-sitters of the seventies." Sure enough—without new production, the bomber force ran down, so SAC became a force of missileers, of long-range artillerymen. The old blow-'em-all-away bomber pilots were retired, to be replaced by men and women carefully selected to hunker in silos waiting to push a button. SAC lost technical leadership to Vietnam-exercised TAC. The "airmen" were blue-suited number-crunchers and project managers—and cool Pentagon politicians. The Air Force had squadrons of suave operators of the quality of James McCormack and Glenn Kent.

To those who know of the Golden Age of The RAND Corporation, its history in the 1970s is inexpressably sad. RAND's Air Force budget was butchered. The attempts to diversify into "social science" research revealed that the analytical techniques perhaps useful for aiding the judgment of decision-makers in disciplined organizations such as the Air Force were of little or no utility in dealing with the essentially psychological and political difficulties of cities and of poverty. The disciplines of the social and management sciences could not manage social indiscipline. Under the leadership of the Latter brothers, the physics department defected *en bloc*, took the AEC nuclear-weapons-effects work with them, and founded

R and D Associates (RDA—"are-dee-ay"). In 1971, Daniel Ellsberg, an analyst whose considerable promise never quite worked out, went to the Xerox machine and copied a Top Secret Pentagon study of some decision-making of the war in Vietnam and circulated it to the press, and apparently deliberately did it so clumsily that he and RAND were easily fingered.

In consequence, Harry Rowen was out. Those old-timers who had survived the purge of the early 1960s retired or lay even lower, and thenceforth Santa Monica was staffed by impotent quasi-academic crunchers supervised by soft-stepping apparatchiks. Sam Cohen was fired; such a maverick was out of place and potentially disturbing to the cautious and unpresumptive new order. There was even set up a "graduate school in policy studies" to teach more elaborate and spurious number-crunching. As if to signify the revolution, The RAND Corporation became the Rand Corporation—perhaps "the rand corporation" would have been appropriate.

Albert Wohlstetter was also finished at Rand, and formed his own personal consulting firm, PanHeuristics, which was nominally an affiliate of GRC, then of SAI, and later of RDA. The great strategist found himself, among other things, lobbying for aid to Turkey. Because the Turks beat up on the Greeks, Congress cut off their aid, so the Turks shut down our snooping posts, invaluable for monitoring Soviet testing. Also in consequence of some nonproliferation work he had squeezed out of the AEC and ACDA, he found himself in northern England, testifying against the construction of the Windscale nuclear breeder-reactor on behalf of the Friends of the Earth.

Alain Enthoven dropped out of the Business altogether, devoting himself to another unanswerable how-much-is-enough—medical financing. And not a peep was heard from McNamara.

The Strategic Studies Center of SRI fared even worse. In the budget cutbacks of the early '70s, Dick Foster had lost his key contracts as the Army, the slowest and squarest of the services, adopted to the new order of numeracy. The soldiers wiped the mud and blood of Vietnam from their boots and sat down at computers and thought it wonderfully advanced to be green-suited clerks. The Strategic Studies Center had to stagger on one leg, subsisting on petty military and civil defense contracts and support from right-wing foundations to hold interminable conferences on this and that, published as subsidy books that no one read. A combination of circumstances led to "regional" studies, particularly in the Far East— and Foster's (and the Army's) legitimate fears of the adverse consequences of withdrawing the garrison from Korea earned him the (expensive) emnity of Carter's SecDef, Harold Brown.

Foster was ably assisted by a nominal consultant—Frank Hoeber was pushed out of RAND and returned to Washington.

One of the few benefits from détente was Army contracts to shmooz with the Soviets, but this was also expensive for Dick. One of his erstwhile colleagues accused him of trafficking with the enemy. To be sure, the lady may have had a personal motive for the charge, yet it was annoying, time-consuming, and expensive for Dick to beat the rap. To compound his difficulties, he was rear-ended while driving in the District. The offender turned out to be the chauffeur of the Soviet ambassador, with diplomatic immunity, so Dick could not collect for the whiplash injury to his neck.

Hudson fell on lean defense times also. There was always a scattering of minor work to be done, some of which was interesting, but Herman had long since taken its major effort into nondefense matters of studying the future for large corporations and various other ventures, such as refuting Jay Forrester's crazy computer models of impending ecological doom, a particularly fashionable fantasy of the 1970s. Although Herman had long since lost interest in strategy, Don Brennan soldiered on. He maintained his interminable correspondence with others in "the strategic community," and worked fitfully on minor continuing Hudson advisory contracts for DoDR&E and ACDA. Again, there wasn't much strategy to do because the principal enemy was no longer the Soviet Union; rather, it was the internal opposition to means of dealing with The Problem. The ABM war had scarred the man badly. He engaged in the most pathetic philandering. He had been betrayed by the other side's abandonment of ABM, and he became bitterly anti-Soviet. Because the arms controllers, his erstwhile friends and colleagues, had resorted to the most odious demagogy, something needed to be done to counter it.

These institutions have been emphasized because they nurtured the next generation of defenders. Through Dick Foster's shop passed many people as staff, consultants, or affiliates at Kintner's Foreign Policy Research Institute—including Leon Schloss, William Van

Cleve, William T. Lee, Harriet Fast Scott, Kenneth Adelman, Edward Luttwak, and Benson Adams. They shared a contempt for the pseudoscience of counting the uncountable, a healthy fear of the Soviet Union, an even healthier respect for Soviet strategic writing, and a penchant for taking the defense seriously.

Hudson was less productive of talent—because the institute was in a downward spiral, because Herman Kahn had given up on grooming bright young men, and because Don Brennan acquired such a pathetic need to be adored that he repelled all but sycophants. Nonetheless, Bill Schneider continued to work for Hudson part time, and the Institute helped keep the network of the defenders intact.

Albert Wohlstetter ran the great school for strategists. Not so much in his formal position at the University of Chicago, but rather like a medieval schoolman, he gathered young scholars around him, attracted by his reputation and his widely known contacts. For his students, Albert's greatest fault was a virtue; his towering aversion to contradiction meant that his acolytes learned not only extreme rigor of analysis and argument, but also methods of presenting them to the Great Strategist with exquisite tact. These are invaluable skills for dealing with the megalomaniacs of Washington. Wohlstetter's students and apprentices had an intensive course in the art of the strategic courtier. Among the Albertites who benefited from the regime were Richard Perle, Paul Wolfowitz, and Donald Fortier. These men were too cool and careful to be uncritical enthusiasts for the defense—except, of course, the unalloyed Albertine defense of the deterrent—but neither were they inherently hostile.

The civil defense people also were active. About the formal American civil defense apparatus in the 1970s, perhaps the less written the better. CD accomplished some useful service in floods and storms, and was manned by decent and sincere people, but inevitably any organization whose purpose is deemed futile will lose people of quality and be a refuge for time servers. The federal bureaucracy in the Department of Defense slowly eroded. The same happened in the state civil defense bureaus. Most of the city and county civil defense offices were wiped out in budget cuts at various times.

The shrinking band of civil defenders were unified in the American Civil Defense Association, and constantly exhorted by its *Journal of Civil Defense*. The association's leading light was its long-term secretary, the grand seignior of CD, Steuart Pittman, who was adored by the rank-and-file of the ragged remnants of the civil defenders. He had captained their team in the brief days of glory under Kennedy.

Somewhat of a club of the old-timers was the American Strategic Defense Association (ASDA—"as-dah"), organized in 1971 by Jerry Strope, then still the civil defense research chief, but already anticipating retirement after the completion of his minimum thirty years of government service. ASDA unified support for active and passive defense. It goes without saying that among the founders were Don Brennan and Eugene Wigner. ASDA was nothing more than a paper organization run out of a Jerry Strope file drawer. Its principal services and minor influence were in reminding each adept that the others existed, and producing a sharp newsletter in the highest tradition of personal journalism, by Jerry himself. After retirement, Strope briefly signed on with SRI, then became a principal with the small Center for Analysis and Planning, where he was joined by John Devaney, and the pair worked as a quick-reaction research team for the civil defense office.

The torch of civil defense was being kept alight in the mountains of Tennessee. As the Kennedy civil defense program ran into trouble, Eugene Wigner had decided that he was the man to redeem it. He was then at the height of his prestige, having just received the Nobel Prize, and organized yet another summer study, "Project Harbor," on Cape Cod, where many of the same old civil defense crowd appeared—among them Fred Ikle and Herman. The reports repeated what had been said before: that civil defense could not save everybody at any reasonable peacetime cost, but it could save many millions and was therefore worth doing.

Wigner thought that better research would promote the civil defense cause. He had powerful influence at the Oak Ridge National Laboratories—rather resembling that of Edward Teller at Livermore—and his friend Alvin Weinberg was the director. The wonderfully courtly Wigner, like many physicists, combined unworldliness and occupational arrogance. During the war, he had been the most pessimistic about the prospects of a Nazi bomb—because he knew how smart were the German physicists. He had annoyed General Groves at the Manhattan Project by claiming that the contracting of plant construction to Du Pont was unnecessary: 50 physicists could design the entire operation; it was mere engineering. Under Jerry

Strope, the Office of Civil Defense was sponsoring fine work—but Jerry was just a naval architect and most of the research contractors were economists, engineers, and worse. (Herman wasn't a real physicist either—his RAND work had been in applied mathematics.) So Wigner saw to it that a civil defense research program was instituted at Oak Ridge.

One recruit was Cresson Kearny from Hudson, the specialist in personal survival, who was interested in published Soviet CD manuals. Kearny, a delightfully practical man, built emergency shelters from the Soviet plans and found they worked (although some of the designs made inadequate provision for ventilation, so the the occupants might have died of heat prostration—unless the shelter was intended for use in the Siberian winter). He also built some of the shelters recommended in American official pamphlets, and found that some of them had been designed without testing; some of the "expedient shelters," as they were called, would have collapsed under their own weight had they—God forbid—had to be used.

Another stalwart was Carsten (miserably nicknamed "Kit") Haaland, who commended himself to Wigner's attention by publishing an odd paper advocating the use of space-based microwave weapons to blast enemy missiles. This was hardly civil defense, but it was strategic defense, and it showed an interesting mind that cared about the right sort of things, so he was brought on board. Unfortunately, much Oak Ridge work was simply more detailed cookie-cutter calculations of how many people would be killed by such and such a strike under such and such circumstances, but it did keep the CD flame alive, and the Oak Ridge base gave it prestige.

Without denigrating the enthusiasm of the civil defenders, worth noting is the fate of their personal shelters. They were left untended in the basements. Gradually, wives pressed them into service for storage. Jim Digby's became a wine cellar.

## The Next Generation

So far, almost all the characters of this chronicle had had the atomic age thrust upon them. About 1970, the action began to shift to those who were children of the atomic age. Amoretta Matthews was a faculty brat, daughter of an English professor at the University of California at Santa Barbara. Most of the girls of Santa Barbara specialized in surfing and tennis, but Ami ("ah-me") was bookish. And not everyone in Santa Barbara was a rich sybarite. Already the place was becoming a suburb of the Business, as contractors began to creep up the Coast from Los Angeles, drawn by the missile activity at the Navy's Point Mugu and the growing Air Force test installation at Vandenberg, to the north. From the hillsides of Santa Barbara one could see the missiles go up, climbing toward space on their way downrange to Kwajalein.

Ami was a good scholar and went to Stanford (where a classmate was one Rosemary McNamara), and needed a job when she graduated in 1963. A professor suggested she try up the road at the Stanford Research Institute, where she met an older man, very gentle, distraught at the recent loss of his wife in the most tragic manner possible. Ami was a protofeminist, but the times then were not quite ripe, so she became Ami Hoeber and labored in Dick Foster's SRI shop with Frank—and with Albert during his brief SRI stint—until she defected with him to RAND.

The change of climate from Washington to Santa Monica must have been salubrious, because she became pregnant, yet bore their son in enough time to return to Washington to be part of Wohlstetter's backup in the ABM fight. The RAND team worked out of the Pentagon basement in what they called "tranquillity base." With a handful of other analysts, Ami labored in primitive surroundings, washing her hair in a men's-room sink, feeding Albert the numbers and references needed to hold up the defender's side of the debate. It was a good education. She was a liberal Democrat and active in party politics in California—but like all of her ilk, was forced out by the New Politics crowd in the early '70s.

When Frank returned to SRI, she worked at GRC and later at SPC. With the nuclear business off, she turned her attention to another Bad Thing—CBR: chemical-biological-radiological warfare, a topic of great interest to the Soviets.

When the Zeus warhead burned the ionosphere over the Pacific in 1962, a young summer student sitting in a trailer in New Jersey watched the needles bounce off the dials of the instruments. Sociology is an undesirable way to describe individuals, but Bill Schneider exemplifies the new breed that came to uphold the defense. He was not of the old established Protestant or later Jewish stock. His name indicates one strain, and his red hair the Irish line—Roman Catholic, of course, of a lower-middle-class background, his father a contractor from the unfashionable ticky-tacky South Shore of Long Island. A shy, solitary type, he had been a radio ham as a boy. William Schneider, Jr. went to NYU, earned his doctorate in economics, and was recruited to Hudson.

Schneider also devoted much time to politics. In the 1960s, the Republican Party of New York was one of the lesser holdings of the Rockefeller interests, and those exalted precincts had no place for the likes of Bill Schneider. He gravitated toward a political sect organized by the Buckley family—the Conservative Party of New York—devoted himself to the apparently futile agitation of that loser party, and gathered contacts among younger men in the far right of the national Republican Party. Incredibly, in 1970 the liberal vote was split between the Democrat and a flabby liberal Republican candidate, and because the national party withdrew its support of the Republican, the senatorial candidate of the Conservatives was elected by a plurality. When he went to Washington, James Buckley took with him as his chief defense aide Bill Schneider.

There Schneider fell in among other young men (and increasing numbers of young women) of like social background, with similar political histories, usually as undergraduate flunkies in the Goldwater debacle of 1964, and nearly identical political aims. They came to be called the "New Right," combining the disdain of the old right for the New Deal and all its works with a parvenu's resentment of "the liberal establishment." Most of then had been treated contemptuously by liberal professors, sometimes suffering blatant political discrimination.

Bill Schneider was one of their leading defense lights. Few of them knew anything more about defense than that "America has to be strong" and that the Soviets were The Enemy. Bill Schneider agreed with both those propositions—but as a trained and accomplished analyst, knew that those principles had to be translated into policy, which requires making choices. From a political point of view in the early 1970s, the policy for a right-wing nationalist in the Congress was simple: to resist the unilateral disarmament and appeasement of the liberals. Politics requires choosing what to fight for with one's limited political resources. In a holding action, when being beaten back by superior forces, one has to decide where to concentrate defensive efforts. Bill Schneider stood firm for the strategic defense.

In particular, he mustered his limited forces in defense of a very small item on the budget, something left over from the ABM debate and SALT. The crumb that had been thrown to the defenders was the retention of some modest research and development in ballistic missile defense, for several minor but useful national-security functions: principally, to continue to give information to the offense. The offense and the defense still worked together. The defensive research would better inform the designers of America's offensive forces about what obstacles the Soviets might in the future throw in the path of "the deterrent."

Second, the BMD research might provide some other information, and in any event was a hedge against Soviet breakthroughs. Third, and this was not a priority item officially but was of central interest to Schneider and like-minded people, the research might produce something that could reverse the verdict of SALT. So in the early and mid-'70s, as the total defense budget was being cut, the petty BMD research budget was held firm, thus modestly increasing its percentage of all defense spending. The amount was so small in the budget that the achievement was practicable with the limited political clout of Schneider and his friends.

Buckley was beaten in 1976, and Schneider transferred his allegiance to a rising conservative star, Congressman Jack Kemp, and continued to labor in the vineyards of the right. Circa 1977, one of the young men, Ed Feulner, took over the moribund Heritage Foundation and converted it into the spearhead of the New Right. In the late '70s these young congressional staff ideologues began to meet regularly in a private dining room in the Madison Hotel, and were shortly labeled "the Madison group."

Another of the group was Angelo Codevilla. He was from New Jersey, son of an Italian restaurateur who had immigrated after World War II; he had gone to school at Rutgers—The State University, and served briefly as an officer in naval intelligence. He attached himself to Senator Malcolm Wallop of Wyoming, whose state contained the largest of the missile fields and had been scheduled for the fourth of the Safeguard BMD complexes. Codevilla briefly had some sort of consulting arrangement with Brennan at the Hudson Institute.

Codevilla was a Straussian, an adherent of a peculiar academic sect which had rediscovered medieval scholasticism and addressed themselves with Talmudic intensity to Aristotle and the like, and were wholly ignorant of the elements of modern natural science and technology. Nonetheless, he embraced the cause of lasers for space-based defense, a possibility that was showing promise under DoD sponsorship. Codevilla became convinced that this was the philosophers' stone of defense. This, the reader will remember, was BAMBI-laser, a concept considered and rejected by ARPA's Project Defender as a budget breaker and technologically far in advance of the state of the art at that time. But Codevilla took up the notion with the fanaticism of a new convert and pressed it on his patron Wallop, who thought a political issue might be made of it.

Another defender was Benson Adams, who was not related to Charles Francis Adams or to any other Adams except his parents, who had thought Adams a nice American name to adopt. He had grown up in Kensington, the Bronx of Philadelphia, and he never forgot the local antiaircraft guns that defended the Frankford Arsenal. Ben Adams attended Penn in engineering, fell in with the Foreign Policy Research Institute crowd, met Dick Foster, and wrote his political science dissertation on the ballistic missile defense controversy. He went into the State Department, then switched over to DoD, where he worked his way up through the research bureaucracies—never having an opportunity to work much on strategic defense, because not much work was being done, but nonetheless keeping the flame alive by attending conferences, putting out a little bit of research money, and in the early '80s writing several interesting pieces in support of strategic defense.

John Bosma was a product of the 1960s. Of a Dutch family from Salt Lake City, he had a peripatetic background—undergraduate in history, attendance at a seminary in Connecticut, working as a fisherman in Alaska, then with some "agrarian reform" sect in Washington State. While at the seminary he had become interested in arms control and had been impressed by the Hudson *Why ABM?* volume. At a Seattle strategic-studies seminar he met Raymond Gastil, one of the authors, who had since joined the Batelle Institute.

Gastil put him in touch with Don Brennan, who tried to get him into Hudson, but Herman forgot about making an appointment for an interview.

So Bosma attached himself to another member of the seminar, T. K. Jones, and went into Boeing as a junior political operator active in the rearmament network of the late '70s. Although Boeing remained committed to the offense, the defense heresy was penetrating the company. Of particular interest to Boeing was the defense of MX; but Bosma went far beyond that to promote broader strategic defense and civil and military uses of space.

Most of this agitation in the 1970s was mere nagging. Candor requires presentation of this excerpt from 1976 hearings on "the quality of life" before a subcommittee of the Senate Public Works Committee, John Culver (Democrat, Iowa, and Kennedy clone) presiding:

> MR. BRUCE-BRIGGS . . . What the Government should do about the quality of life depends upon the view of what it is . . .
> However, were I to make a priority list, it would include the following: A. Prepare better defenses against nuclear attack . . .
> SENATOR CULVER. . . . You say we should prepare against nuclear attack . . . We have mutual assured destruction in the strategic balance right now . . . What would you specifically suggest we do now in terms of our nuclear inventory, our nuclear policy, in order for people to sleep better each night?
> MR. BRUCE-BRIGGS. . . . it would seem to me it would be good policy of the United States to have mobilization-base science for serious nuclear defenses of an active and passive sort. Active defenses are antiattack systems, passive defenses are civil defense schemes—not necessarily, as I said, this year, we are talking in this committee about looking way ahead into the future.
> SENATOR CULVER. Are you talking about any refinement of our active arsenal? We have 8,700 nuclear warheads now.
> MR. BRUCE-BRIGGS. Active defenses are antiattack forces.
> SENATOR CULVER. You mean the ABM?
> MR. BRUCE-BRIGGS. ABM.
> SENATOR CULVER. You mean to reactivate the ABM? You want to break the ABM treaty with the Soviet Union?
> MR. BRUCE-BRIGGS. It is the interest of both the United States and Soviet Union, again looking ahead, to both defend themselves against other powers. It would seem to me this is in the common

interest; ABM reconsideration could be a contingency. We are talking about thinking ahead.

SENATOR CULVER. If you are asking me to vote for the American taxpayer to go bankrupt with more ABM systems, with respect to this threat, I am saying, in the interest of the taxpayer, we ought to examine other means.

MR. BRUCE-BRIGGS. If you believe that is the gravest threat to the nation and spending this money would mitigate the threat, it would be a reasonable investment and the taxpayers would not object. I don't think the taxpayers would support it this year; I think you are absolutely right. But we are talking about the eighties.

SENATOR CULVER. We had better start now if we are going to do that. We spent 10 years deciding it was a waste of time to spend $10 billion on the ABM. We lost by one vote in the Senate . . . Consequently we built an ABM system that we did not need.

We are all agreed that our security in the strategic exchange scenario is greatly enhanced as a result of having that ABM treaty. It has reduced the costs and risks.

MR. BRUCE-BRIGGS. Just for the record, not everyone agrees with that, as you know.

SENATOR CULVER. You don't agree with that? I think it is uniformly agreed. I really do. That is not a hawk–dove issue at all.

MR. BRUCE-BRIGGS. It is not hawk–dove. It is a technical issue among the people that study these matters.

Improve the quality of life with strategic defense! Some people are shameless.

## The BMD Underground

In terms of money and in terms of mission, the most important segments of the saving remnant were in Rosslyn, Huntsville, and Kwajalein. The Army was left with the mission of continuing ballistic missile defense research. While SALT forbade development and testing of tactical components, people could not be stopped from thinking about ballistic missile defense. Remember that the establishment of the Sentinel program had provided for an organization to build and deploy the operational ABM system, and another to take over the Project Defender research from ARPA. When the Grand Forks site was completed, the Safeguard Systems Command finished its assignment. The research arm, the Army Advanced Ballistic Missile Defense Agency (ABMDA—"ah-bim-dah"), soldiered on—without Oswald Lange, who retired.

With Bell Labs out, major systems engineering was done by Teledyne Brown, the successor to a local Huntsville firm which had pried its way into contracting for Missile Command. The withdrawal of AT&T and the shrinkage of ABM budgets had led to brutal fights among the contractors, and between the ex-ARPA people at Rosslyn and the Huntsville gang. As the most talented ARPA engineers drifted off to more promising ventures, Huntsville gradually won that war. ABMDA research was under two rubrics—the advanced-technology program, looking at emerging research that might be useful to BMD, and the systems-technology program, which was responsible for having in hand a system that could be ordered developed and deployed if the strategic and political situation changed—a hedge, a mobilization base.

The first systems-technology product was Site Defense, a further trimming of the existing ABM system to save money and to optimize, as the label indicates, site defense of ICBM fields. The system was little more than the Nike-X stripped of the PARs and the long-range Spartan missiles, leaving only the MSR and Sprints. With only one set of missiles to control and with no early-warning radar to prime it, the computers had to be completely reprogrammed. The missile was to be an upgraded Sprint with some Hibex input, labeled Sprint II, of even higher performance than the original. It was only a paper missile—no specimens were ever built. As the program developed, it was relabeled "base line terminal defense system" and was modified to delete the single Missile Site Radar of Safeguard to a better-protected method—"netted radars"; that is, instead of a single radar which the enemy could kill, the netted system has many radar sets connected in parallel so that the system can continue to track and fight after losing several radars. This was made possible because the very late terminal intercept did not require long-range, high-powered, huge radars. The smaller netted radars could be hardened underground to pop up when needed.

The system was tested, without missiles, against ICBMs at Kwaj in the late '70s. Indeed, as the concept evolved, it was determined that the improvements in computer technology already had progressed so swiftly that there was really no point in adapting the elaborate Bell Labs computers to the modified mission. Buying and programming an ordinary commercial computer was cheaper and easier—of course, drawing upon the previous experience with ABM. Whether the commercial computer would have been able to handle a mass attack is problematic, but didn't much matter, because site defense existed only on paper.

A follow-on concept was a conceptual breakthrough: again, the concept was for the defense of an ICBM field, but instead of relying upon modified Safeguard components, the system was conceived of from scratch. It was intended entirely to be a very late terminal defense, relying almost exclusively upon atmospheric screening to separate out the decoys. It was labeled Low Altitude Defense System (LoADS—"low-adds"). The problem of very late terminal defense was a relatively simple one by BMD standards because not only had the decoys been filtered out by the atmosphere, but late in an ICBM's course, its trajectory could be very simply computed, and the atmosphere had dragged the speed down. Elaborate discrimination and computation techniques were superfluous.

Also, because the concept provided for a very late intercept over hardened missile fields, there was little or no concern about the collateral damage on the ground caused by the explosion of the warhead of the interceptor or of possible salvage-fusing of the ICBM. In BMD jargon, the "keep-out" zone was small. And the great weakness of late intercept—that a failure to get the incoming with one shot means the target is lost—did not matter much with ICBMs; the enemy had to kill most of them, and the defense did not have to defend all of them, so a deceptive preferential defense deployment was practicable. A few ABMs could defend a lot of ICBMs because the attacker could not know which were being defended. LoADS was conceived as a limited number of self-contained units, each large enough to hold an individual radar and an interceptor missile, small enough to be mobile. As we shall see, LoADS had a very specific defense in mind.

ABMDA's second mandated research field was "advanced technology." The Army's BMD program did not ignore the possibilities of optical sensors. On paper, concepts were worked up for a pop-up scheme which would put the sensor into the upper atmosphere upon warning to detect the incoming and guide the interceptors. Another variant was an airborne version which would fly above the cloud to pick up the incoming.

Neither did the Army neglect laser research. This was—and is—tested at the White Sands Proving Ground under very private conditions, because the Army was interested not merely in lasers as a missile-killing device, but in air defense and tactical warfare as well. In the short run, the first military applications of lasers were as range finders and fire-control directors—rather an optical equivalent of radar. The intense laser beam would "illuminate" the target and the weapon would home in on the brightness of the image.

Perhaps the Army experiments were somewhat inhibited by an especially nasty consequence of introducing laser weaponry. Before tanks or missiles, or even people, could be burned by lasers, it was far more likely that the heat of this potent new weaponry would first be felt by a much more sensitive organism—the human eye. A laser beam sweeping over a battleground would burn out the eyes of all who looked at it, leaving the fields strewn with blind men. This was not what men had put on green uniforms either to impose or to suffer.

Not everybody bailed out of the defense. With the limited funding provided by the Congress, a few civilian employees and a few contractors persevered. Without denigrating others, clearly the most perceptive was the engineer Clifford McLain. His background was terrific: MIT, military service with the Ordnance Corps, then Chrysler's rocket program, then Huntsville, and on to the Building. His political skills were finely honed. When he took over the rump BMD program, he understood that his task was not so much technical as "to provide a basis for political acceptance of ballistic missile defense." Toward that end he signed on as consultants Dick Foster, Richard Garwin, and Herman Kahn. Garwin told him that the problem was technical, to come up with "something that works," and offered his bright ideas, described elsewhere. Herman took quite the opposite tact—he saw the difficulty as entirely political, and shook the worldly McLain with the admonition, "What you should be doing is planning how to spend a hundred billion dollars." McLain was an ambitious man and couldn't wait for the gravy days forecast by Herman.

He was replaced as the chief BMD political operator by Bill Davis, an old-line civil servant who had been a sergeant in the Signal Corps during World War II, obtained his engineering degree, and gone to work for the Navy before switching over to the Army in 1954, working on Hawk before initiating high-energy laser research at Huntsville. In the late '60s he participated in Minuteman defense schemes on his way up the ladder, from director of the Huntsville office of ABMDA to chief of the BMD advanced technology center, and finally to deputy ballistic missile defense program manager, the number two man to the nominal uniformed chief. He had to supervise the civilians and the few soldiers who were involved, monitor the contractors, and act as a center for ballistic missile defense promotion, among other things, organizing conferences and seminars to keep the issue alive.

The decline of the SRI Strategic Studies Center was paralleled by the decay of its ally the Foreign Policy Research Institute. In the mid-'70s, its most promising analyst, Robert Pfaltzgraff, split off with a good chunk of the funding to establish the Institute for Foreign Policy Analysis (IFPA), which took the lead in the right-of-center conference businesss. It got some money from ABMDA and other defense sources, and shortly established a reputation for high-quality publications.

Still, however devoted and commendable were these enthusiasts in keeping the flame of strategic defense alive, they at best constituted a minor strategic sect, almost a cult, of mostly marginal people, peculiarly reflecting their opposites at the other end of the spectrum, the unilateral disarmers. The defenders, at least, had a dim vision of the hope of future technology to support them, while their opposites had only the fading light of utopian expectations that the other side might respond to our openhanded initiative. And a few Americans, far from Cambridge, gave up altogether and cracked into fragments.

## The Survivalists

The weakest threads in a fabric are not physically or morally weak. The weakest do not necessarily live in Cambridge, Ithaca, Ann Arbor, Madison, and Berkeley. The weak may be merely simple and single-minded. There are in America millions of people to whom the frontier is a living memory transmitted orally by their grandparents and kept aflame by commercial mythology.

These people see the wider world through the twisted lens of television. And in the late 1960s and 1970s, they liked not what they

saw. They saw mobs looting and burning, with the police standing
by, with the National Guard standing by, with the Regular Army
standing by. They saw young adults—whom they knew to be the
children of the upper classes—cursing the American system, burning
the Stars and Stripes, and hoisting Red flags.

They saw a half-assed war being fought—and apparently lost—
with a dip-shit little country they had never heard of. Their friends
came back from that country in bags. Later they saw their country
groveling before a pack of dirty Arabs. And they heard that the
country was open to Soviet attack—and nothing was being done
about it.

These people saw their meager wages and modest estates being
eroded by inflation. They heard their children being taught degen-
eracy in the schools and sometimes even from the pulpit.

And they found nothing and nobody in the national leadership
who offered the dimmest hope of repair. Only some preachers—on
television or in prefab churches—seemed to talk to their concerns.
And the preachers preached from the Prophets, and from Matthew
24, and from the Apocalypse—of how fire and ruin come down on
the ungodly, and of the Last Days that will presently follow on the
restoration of the Jews to Jerusalem. How could anyone disregard
the eschatological import of thermonuclear energy?

Some of these people became moral revolutionaries. True-blue
Americans gave up on the American system and turned to their
own resources for the survival of themselves and their families. They
gave up on the U.S. currency—and bought gold. They gave up on
the American economy—and bought land, and polished their ar-
tisans' skills.

In the late 1960s there was a minor eleemosynary hustle called
"social indicators"; had it been genuine, its practitioners would have
pondered the significance of escalated sales of firearms, and of ammunition, and of brass casings, and of gunpowder, and of books
and pamphlets on how to make munitions. And there were books
on how to survive under primitive conditions—reprints of military
books and some specially commissioned for the audience.

Any market will draw purveyors to fulfill its needs—or pretend
to. Radiological dosimeters were sold by mail order—or what purported to be dosimeters. Other survival supplies, some genuine,
some fake, also found a wide market. Many of the books were

phony; one that was real was the treatise on emergency shelters Cresson Kearny wrote at Oak Ridge. Because it was produced under government contract, it was in the public domain and could be reprinted freely. An outfit on the West Coast reprinted it—with garish blurbs that it had been suppressed by the U.S. government and that a preface was copyrighted by Kearny. (He asked his lawyer to enjoin this hustle, and was advised that the courts were unlikely to find that the reputation of a civil defense expert had a value that could be damaged.)

A very few of the survivalists did not merely avoid taxes in the time-honored America way, but refused to pay altogether. A very few supplemented their rifles and shotguns with machine guns and explosives. And a very very few, the weakest of the weak, turned to conspiracy theories to explain the collapse of the American Republic. Of course, hustlers provided the tried-and-tested international-Jewish-bankers prescription. A few dozen went into armed resistance to the national government; they chose to become mad dogs, and as such were hunted down and killed by the security forces.

Extremists rarely represent anyone but themselves, yet they are a symptom of which way the wind is blowing. America could be blown away.

# VII

# THE DEFENSE COUNTERATTACKS

*To adopt a defeatist attitude in the face of such a threat is inexcusable until it has been definitely shown that all the resources of science and technology have been exhausted.*
FREDERICK LINDEMANN

Hardly was the ink dry on the SALT treaty when the defenders attempted to strike back hard. The leader was Scoop Jackson. The Senator from Boeing did not strongly object to abandoning defense of the nation as a whole—merely to not defending the ICBM silos, which he considered the vital element of the strategic balance between the United States and the Soviet Union. Other means, especially bolstering the offensive forces, would serve just as well, even better. As payment for his support of the SALT limits of the offensive forces, he succeeded in squeezing from the administration and the Senate a provision that no further treaties would ratify imbalances between the United States and the Soviet Union. He was ably backed up by his glib and aggressive aide Richard Perle.

Although Nixon won a smashing victory over George McGovern in 1972, the Congress remained in Democratic hands, and Nixon desperately needed Jackson's support, especially to execute the fighting retreat from Vietnam. Jackson had the administration by the short hairs—and he pulled. For several years Jackson had a *de facto* veto on major Defense Department appointments and policies. He was most dissatisfied with the Arms Control and Disarmament Agency and mandated that it be cleaned out. This was a miserable injustice— the ACDA people were dutifully jumping through hoops held by Nixon and Kissinger. An appointment acceptable to Jackson was an experienced ex–RAND analyst who early in his career had made contacts with Southern California politicians in consequence of having joined a Los Angeles Republican club to pick up girls. He later found his wife at SRI, but in the search came to the attention of Lyn Nofziger, a shrewd Republican political operator. During the 1960s he lay low at MIT and made no enemies. So Fred C. Ikle became head of ACDA. He was not a strong administrator and perhaps insufficiently ruthless, so an aggressive and ambitious veteran of the FPRI arms-control seminars of the 1960s was appointed his deputy—John Lehman.

At a higher level, Jackson insisted on nominating the Secretary of Defense as well. Here his choice was a man who was experienced in administration and in defense matters and from Jackson's point of view had a commendably dour view of the Soviet threat. So James Schlesinger became the Secretary of Defense. Paul Nitze had soldiered well on SALT, so an attempt was made to make him Secretary of the Air Force. The appointment was not consummated, supposedly because the Air Force and its congressional supporters had not forgiven Nitze for his anti–air-power heresies in the Strategic Bombing Survey and the right-wingers still saw him as a subversive, but perhaps Kissinger had not forgiven Nitze for scorning his jejune strategic analysis of the 1950s.

The change in personnel may have slowed the rot somewhat, but could not reverse it. It was these men who presided over the gutting of America's defenses. They could not restrain the congressional push to cut, cut, cut again, and cut even more. Their few successes were with the offenses and the passive defenses of the offensive forces. The multiplication of Soviet missile warheads required that the deterrent be secured.

## Defending the Deterrent Without ABM

Having forgone the active defense of its strategic forces, not to mention its cities, the United States was obliged to rely entirely upon the reliability and survivability of its offensive forces to threaten reprisals. The Soviet ICBMs could arrive in half an hour, and the sea-launched ballistic missiles in twenty minutes or less, and then a few hours later the bombers might show up, if the Soviets cared to dispatch them. Only a few minutes would be available to execute the launch orders, and it became crucial to national survival that the means of executing those orders be secure, and that knowledge of the security be known to the Soviet Union.

A credible substitute for Safeguard was a major upgrading of the Minuteman silo hardening. The SLBMs had a more dangerous defense. It was whispered about the Business that the American ballistic missile submarines were operating on "fail-dangerous" orders—that the loss of all communication with their base should be interpreted as evidence that their bases no longer existed, and they should dump their loads upon the designated Soviet urban/industrial targets. Short of that horrible expedient, secure communication links from the early-warning sensors to the Commander-in-Chief to the reprisal forces were vital. The ballistic-missile early-warning radars to the north were squishy soft and vulnerable, but their destruction would be sufficient to give a high level of warning. It was desirable to be able to evacuate the Commander-in-Chief and perhaps other high officials to Fort Ritchie or elsewhere; no one was entirely sure that it could be done. A mobile command post was put aloft, a Boeing airliner stuffed with commo, the National Emergency Command Post (NECP—"kneecap").

The vestigial interest in civil defense turned to "continuity of government" (COG—"cog"), keeping the government alive under attack, at least long enough to strike back, and preferably long enough to be able to deal with the other side to stop the war before all was lost, and perhaps to reconstitute the polity in the postattack environment. Dick Foster's shop took the lead in this work. Their reports reflect their true love of the American system of government, an affection that might not be shared by the survivors after deterrence failed.

The American "overhead," which had been mostly a bluff in the 1960s, became a reality in the 1970s. Wonderfully sensitive sensors, photographic, radar, and infrared, were put into orbit. The first effective uses of the over-the-horizon radars were in the units snuggled up to the Soviet borders in Norway, Turkey, Iran, and Japan. The infrared got very good indeed. And there were other means of detecting phenomena of vital interest to American military planners. Now, all this was a marvelous technological achievement, but the information the United States gathered by these means was rather inferior to that which the Soviet Union could obtain from reading congressional testimony and subscribing to *Aviation Week* magazine.

We were spending tens of billions of dollars to gather what the other side could get for a few dollars' subscription and postage. The Soviets also invested in attack assessment and in command and control, but not nearly so much, the published reports suggest, as the United States, for the very practical reason that the Soviets had no theory that the United States would strike first without substantial provocation and significant warning.

Under the leadership of Bob Everett and his longtime associates, MITRE continued to expand steadily in the business of command and control, helping the Air Force's swelling Electronic Systems Command to develop more and more elaborate means of warning and communicating with the strategic forces. $C^3$ overlapped offense and defense. It could have been that the information gathered on the assessment of an attack would be conveyed to defenders, as had been the intention of the SAGE system, but the same information could just as well, and did, go to the offensive forces primed to hit back in retaliation. Just before his retirement, Curtis LeMay heard a MITRE briefing on the elaborate plans, and remarked wearily, "Just leave *something* for the weapons."

In the absence of a defense, the control task became both more difficult and more vital. The enemy attack would come right in unimpeded, with naught to even slow it, so the communications had to be split-second. The communications themselves were defended only passively and were faced with the ever-increasing numbers and ever-improving accuracy of Soviet warheads. Control had to be reliable, and had to be perceived as reliable by the other side to dissuade him from attempting a "decapitation strike."

The emphasis on communications was also politically expedient: everyone on the responsible strategic spectrum could agree that highly reliable, highly survivable command and control was necessary to maintain a credible force for "assured destruction" or for more ambitious nuclear-strike postures. The engineers of MITRE easily recruited establishment worthies for their trustees, from MIT and elsewhere, ranging from Bob Sprague to Jack Ruina.

Hanscom Air Force Base became the locale of a fantastic military facility. As the site of Electronic Systems Command—the Air Force's Signal Corps—it was littered with office buildings and ringed by the labs of its contractors. The fighter-interceptors had long since been withdrawn, and the airfield handed back to civil aviation. So the base commander could look out on his flight line packed with squadrons of the Cessnas and Beechcraft of his vendors.

Among the few defenders that profited in the 1970s was Raytheon, which had always successfully avoided being too exclusively a defense contractor. Its diversification was bankrolled by the steady profits on worldwide sales of Sparrows and Hawks. (Iran was an eager client.) The engineer Tom Phillips presided over expansion and earned a well-deserved presidency and chairmanship, following right behind Charlie Adams. ABM may have failed politically, but it left Raytheon supreme in advanced radars. Lincoln Labs also prospered, as did many of the contractors swarming around Route 128. Although most Massachusetts pols were vocally antidefense, one was not: the congressman from Cambridge, the Speaker of the House of Representatives, Thomas P. O'Neill.

Cambridge's Draper Labs also weighed in for the defense. The offense and the defense are the two faces of war. ABM's historical and analytical Janus was the Multiple Independently Targetable Reentry Vehicle (MIRV—"merv"). And the defense post-1965 cannot be understood without careful consideration of the activity of the offense.

There are two versions of the origins of MIRV. The first is a morality tale of what horrors the defense can incite. In the paper wars of the late '50s and early '60s, the paper offense devised more elaborate means of decoying to fox and bewilder the defense. The paper defense responded with more sophisticated discrimination techniques, and the paper offense answered with superior decoys. Well, the defense always had an inherent advantage, because the decoys were not the real reentry vehicle and therefore would not reflect the radar like the real thing and would not track like the real thing because their weights and shapes were different. So the paper warriors of the offense imagined decoys more similar to the real thing. Inevitably, some bright person—and many, including Richard Garwin, claim to have been that bright person—said in effect, "Hey, instead of making the decoys like the real thing, why not make them the real thing? Why not load a whole bunch of reentry vehicles on the same missile?" So American anticipation of Soviet ballistic missile defenses incited escalation of the arms race.

A pretty tale, and widely believed by impartial and informed people—and incorrect. The origins of MIRV are mundane, coming from nuclear-weapons effects and solidly based bean-counting by the designers of the offense. The Polaris sub-launched-missile system was a superlative technological achievement; that it could work at all was a wonder. So it is no ill reflection on the designers that the missiles were imprecise. The estimated average accuracy was a miss of 5 miles, which means that half the missiles would be more than 5 miles off target. Soviet cities do not sprawl as do American cities. A clever engineer thought of fitting the Polaris reentry vehicle with "the claw"—three warheads with a spring between them, to push them apart slightly, to give a spread of more than 5 miles so that a miss would still kill the target with at least one warhead. The multiple reentry vehicles (MRV—"em-are-vee") would spread out slightly as they dropped through the atmosphere, widening the spread of lethality, correcting for the errors of accuracy. And smaller warheads laid on a city would do more damage than one big warhead—for example, three 1-megaton warheads blast away a larger area than a single 5-megaton warhead.

It did not take long to notice that the same guidance systems that adjusted for errors in the trajectory of a single reentry vehicle could be employed for multiple reentry vehicles as well, and those adjustments need not all be the same. Each warhead could be independently targeted in the same general region of the enemy's territory. MIRV was not without cost: some flexibility in targeting is lost because you cannot spread out the MIRVed warheads as widely as separate missiles, and you must buy the "bus" that carries the MIRVs. But MIRV meant that the Navy needed not purchase as many missiles and as many missile-launching submarines to get the same punch. The same factors applied to the land-based ICBMs of the Air Force: with MIRVs, fewer missiles were necessary, and more important, fewer missile silos. The hardened silos and command centers cost more than their missiles; the submarines cost more than their missiles. *The main advantage of MIRV is to cut the costs of defending the offensive forces from attack.* MIRV technology evolved, was tested, and eventually was ordered put into service late in the McNamara regime, principally as a consequence of intelligent bean-counting, to save money. It is a myth that MIRV was invented to overcome the ballistic missile defenses of the U.S.S.R.

Much has been made of an alleged defensive drawback of MIRV: a successful preemptive attack on a MIRVed missile can destroy all its many warheads with one or two fairly accurate missiles. This makes some people nervous because they fear that such a situation encourages first strikes and is "destabilizing"; they forget that MIRVing also means that every missile the attack fails to take out on the ground will deliver many warheads in reply.

MIRV would have been placed in service whether or not the Soviets had installed Galosh around Moscow; it was officially announced right after McNamara's San Francisco speech. That was, as the Marxists say, "no accident." Attempts to block it on arms-race grounds were fitful and in the end ineffectual. Don Brennan was hostile, but acquiesced on the ground that a MIRV ban could not be verified. To Scoop Jackson *et al.,* the ABM brouhaha was a useful diversion from an arms innovation that really mattered.

## Building the Next Offense

The MIRVed Poseidons and Minuteman IIIs went into service, and the numbers of American warheads skyrocketed. There was great R&D progress in the weapons concepts first formed in the late McNamara era—the planned follow-ups to the developing systems of the late '50s that went into service in the '60s: the B-1 bomber to replace the aging B-52s, the undersea long-range missile system (ULMS, soon to be titled Trident) to replace the Poseidons and Polarises in the submarines; a new ICBM; and the cruise missile, a gorgeous example of the possibilities of resurrecting an archaic system with the synergisms and serendipities of new technology.

The original guided missiles had been ludicrously inaccurate. The German V-1s had trouble hitting London at a range of 100 miles. An Air Force Navajo had gotten away from Cape Canaveral, was last seen heading south past Trinidad, and probably crashed in the Amazon jungle, where perhaps a cannibal tribe is worshiping it as a fiery god. The ballistic missile completely superseded the guided flying bomb. But an extraordinary combination of technological breakthroughs completely revised the guided-missile equation. Terrain-hugging radars had been invented to permit tactical and strategic bombers to penetrate enemy airspace at treetop heights to avoid radar and SAM defenses. Reconnaissance satellites provided exquisitely detailed information about enemy territory, which could be reduced to a picture embedded in the microchip brain of the missile.

A wild card, not anticipated by anyone in the Business, was an outgrowth of the automotive gas-turbine research of the Chrysler Corporation in the 1950s. One of its engineers, Sam Williams, set out on his own to make tiny turbofan engines with high power-to-weight ratios and parsimonious fuel consumption, permitting a tiny flying bomb with little fuel to fly hundreds, even thousands of miles. The device, labeled the "cruise missile" to distinguish it from its pathetic ancestors, was to the V-1 as a machine gun was to a blunderbuss. It was slow, and might be nailed by a fortunately placed antiaircraft gun, surface-to-air missile, or idling interceptor; but it could be produced in sufficient numbers to penetrate enemy airspace and follow a preprogrammed zigzag path, checking itself against the terrain it was supposed to traverse, and upon closing in on its assigned destination, climb sharply and dive to the death of the target. While the cruise was soft on the ground, it was so small that it could easily be defended by dispersion and concealment. It could fit in a garage. It was a nice weapon—and a spur to revive air defense. Of course, cruise development went into the budget.

The most visible strategic-force modernization program was the Missile Experimental (MX—"em-ex"), eventually to replace the aging Minutemen. The missile itself had the advantage of being able to heave a dozen MIRVs, compared with three for Minuteman III. But the major advance was in the reentry vehicles, incorporating the latest inertial guidance system from Draper Labs, and with advanced aerodynamics to close with a target at higher speeds than its predecessors. With its accuracy and plentiful warheads, MX was an estimable first-strike weapon, capable of squashing Soviet missile silos and leader bunkers, and chopping command-and-control links. MX gave substance to notions of counterforce and to limited strategic war. This was held in some circles to be A Bad Thing. Worse was the difficulty in securing it from preemptive attack. The search for a way to provide a "credible basing scheme" for MX—which is to say, a plausible way to *defend* MX—would embroil the American nuclear-strategic polity for more than a decade.

American satellites and electronic stations along the fringes of the U.S.S.R. were monitoring Soviet MIRVing and the rate of improvement of its guidance systems. It could be confidently forecast that the Soviets would be able to take out Minuteman in a few years. If MX was based in Minuteman-equivalent silos, the new missile was no improvement from the point of view of defense.

Perhaps a more dramatic account would hold this point to the last, but it should be put right up front that the MX-basing hullabaloo was entirely the consequence of SALT I. Had the United States been able to provide for active defenses of MX, the matter would have been easily resolved from the beginning. The fairly simple Aerospace Corporation schemes of the mid-'60s would probably have been sufficient to delay and confuse an attack enough to dissuade the other side from trying. But this option was closed by the treaty, so other means had to be found, and the concepts men had another toy shop to play in.

## A New Intelligence

In the late 1960s, those who believed that the Soviet Union would recognize the good sense of restraints on nuclear forces were somewhat supported by the official national intelligence estimates of the Central Intelligence Agency (*the* Agency). The generals would howl of some Soviet abomination, and the cooler minds of the Agency would rebut them. A group of people sought to take this tendency apart.

One of the first to try it was Dick Foster, but he ran into a little trouble. It is well to keep in mind that while most of the Business is paper wars, and about play wars, and about political wars, at bottom the Business is about real wars; the Business is about killing—and no one should be surprised that some people in the Business are killers. The word was passed to Foster that he ought not to be meddling in the Agency's mission of analyzing Soviet capabilities and intentions.

The CIA's military rivals had been discredited by the "gap" projections of the 1950s and by suspect Vietnam war numbers in the 1960s, so a more credible DoD source had to be established. The lever to create a new institution was the plausible idea that the proper way to evaluate the other side was in comparison with our side. Instead of assessing the gross forces available to the U.S. and U.S.S.R. together, one should look at the relationship between the two, to make a "net assessment." The new twist was devised by Herman

Kahn's old friend Andy Marshall, one of the few RAND leaders of the 1950s who had survived in the '60s by taking a very low profile, concentrating on "black" intelligence work. He was appointed Director of Net Assessment in the Pentagon in 1973.

Wohlstetter made a major contribution with a set of articles dissecting in detail claims that the United States had consistently been overstating Soviet capabilities. He contrasted the official intelligence estimates of the 1960s with the later appraisals of those forecasts and found a consistent strain of understatement. Unstated in his analysis was the obvious explanation: just as air intelligence in the 1950s had mirror-imaged Soviet intentions from their own strategic view, the CIA analysts of the 1960s had projected their moderate, increasingly academic worldview on the Soviet. The facts, as best we could see them, were that the Soviets were continuing to expand their force, perceptibly more rapidly than would be necessary to maintain merely an "assured destruction capability."

In 1975 the CIA Director, George Bush, ordered an independent evaluation of the intelligence materials at hand. The alternative group was labeled the "B-Team" (there was no "A-Team"—merely the regular Agency analysts). Dick Foster helped recruit the team. Its nominal chief was a Harvard history professor with no experience in military affairs—but a bitterly anti-Russian Pole. Paul Nitze was a member, as was the Albertite Paul Wolfowitz. The evaluation was determined by the composition of the B-Team. Their analysis concluded that the Soviets were striving for a first strike.

The skeptical wording does not mean to imply suspicion that their analysis was incorrect; but it suggests that it followed from their personal views, although it could be legitimately read from the data. The B-Team effort was largely an artifact of intelligence analysis as internal propaganda. According to traditional canons, the A-Team/B-Team dispute was irrelevant—military intelligence properly dealt with capabilities, not palm-reading about intentions. The undisputed fact was that the Soviets could blow away the United States. To the degree that the Soviets could blow away America's reprisal forces first, to that degree the Soviets could blow away America and get off clean.

In 1975, Paul Nitze wrote another version of the first-strike scenario in a *Foreign Affairs* piece. He used Boeing calculations from T. K. Jones that the Soviets would soon possess a force capable of executing a disabling first strike against our ICBMs, bombers, and submarines, leaving the United States with such a ragged force that it would not dare to strike back in the face of Soviet defenses. With the knowledge of this situation, the United States would have to knuckle under to Soviet demands. This notion was shortly labeled "the window of vulnerability," because the forecast of the rate of expansion of Soviet forces indicated that they would be able to knock out the American ICBM force in the early 1980s. Critics said that the concentration on the ICBMs was a grave analytical flaw—forgetting that the Soviets already had the capability of taking out most of the bombers and a good part of the submarine force in a first strike. And what was closely held was that the Soviet navy was becoming frighteningly adept at tracking our ballistic missile submarines.

Related to the battles of warhead-counting was a long, drawn-out fight over comparative U.S.–U.S.S.R. military spending. Intelligence analysts laboriously estimated how much the Soviet military machine would cost the United States, and then fought over their estimates. Of course, the Soviet Union is a socialist dictatorship, relying heavily on coercion rather than capitalistic bribes. A major contributor to the Soviet spending buildup was the Republican political operator Martin Anderson. He persuaded Nixon to abolish conscription and rely on a mercenary force. The effect was a much smaller military with much higher pay. Because U.S. costs were mirror-imaged on the Soviets, the other side's costs were inflated. Trying to put Soviet costs into American dollar values is absurd on the face of it—glaring evidence of how far pseudoscience had diverted responsible Americans from reality. The issue was not what the Soviets' forces cost them; the issue was what they had bought. And the bottom line was what the Soviets could do with what they had bought.

### The Ideology of Defense

In the circles of the defenders, a counterstrategic doctrine evolved from long-held principles, which opposed the academic strategy on almost every point. Some called it "war-fighting," apparently from Herman's RAND thermonuclear-war briefings which contrasted "war-fighting" with "war-avoiding," later relabeled "deterrence-only," strategies. Pity Herman didn't relabel the other also, because "war-fighting" was decidedly politically embarrassing. Dick Foster tried "assured survival," but it didn't take. So the defenders' strategic position was never given a name. And the chronicler can do no better: he can but limn its outlines.

To begin with, the defenders' position should be distinguished from the vulgar hawkish position (although there was considerable overlap in some individuals). Oddly, a group of supposed "strategists" appeared in the 1970s whose intellectual repertory consisted only of these points:

- *The Soviets are out to get us.* Often proclaimed loudest by those who knew the least about the U.S.S.R.
- *There is a swelling Soviet military buildup.* This is firm ground. Yes, there was a Soviet military buildup.
- *The Soviets are cheating on arms-control treaties.* Herman Kahn characterized the published alleged violations as "chiseling." Had the Soviets been seriously cheating, they could be stashing away thousands of hidden weapons. And maybe they were—we could count submarines, bombers, and holes in the ground, but not missiles; not warheads.
- *We must have whatever new weaponry is being advocated.* And, unstated, never mind the cost or the relative utility.
- *We should heed the counsel of the military.* Never mind that the various factions in the military would have us get more missiles, airplanes, aircraft carriers, submarines, tanks, and so on.
- *We should compare weaponry—type against type, offense against offense, defense against defense.* That is, compare numbers of submarines, ignore antisubmarine systems; compare numbers of tanks, disregard antitank guns. "Warhead-counting" is the appropriate sneer at this approach.
- *Systems analysis is A Bad Thing.* Unstated was an alternative means of choosing among complex systems concepts without making paper calculations. But the misuse of systems analysis by McNamara and company and Scoop Jackson's hostility led to the OSD office of Systems Analysis being relabeled "Program Analysis and Evaluation" (PA&E—"pea-ay-'n-ee").
- *McNamara exemplifies all that is wrong with American defense policy.* Here the bomber generals were supported by Dick Foster,

who had a classic love/hate relationship with McNamara. Eisenhower's DoD centralization was falsely attributed to McNamara. The early McNamara was conveniently forgotten, as was the McNamara who manfully stuck it out in Vietnam—and the oddest psychological phenomenon was relegating to the memory tube his ABM deployment. However, one attack on McNamara was unanswerable. His guilt could not be denied. For example, the brilliant Edward Teller, briefing the esteemed trustees of the reputable Hoover Institution, hissing, "Robert *STRANGE* McNamara."

• *The U.S. Strategy is Mutual Assured Destruction.* Here the writer must insert himself in to the chronicle. Circa 1970, the Hudson Institute had a contract from a division of Hans Mark's Ames Research Center to help analyze priorities for future space missions. The conclusions were that the flush times of U.S. space exploration were over, and that NASA could barely survive as a welfare program for aerospace engineers if it could keep some minimal manned space effort going. This line of thinking led James Fletcher to go ahead with the space shuttle. The clients were intelligent and pleasant, but, as the chronicler thought it witty to remark in cocktail-party chitchat, "Those NASA people are great engineers, but they have no political or literary sensibilities, or they wouldn't have called their shop the 'Mission Analysis Division'—it lends itself to an unfortunate acronym."

McNamara had pronounced "assured destruction" as the minimum strategic posture. Long previous to that had been the terms "mutual vulnerability" and "mutual deterrence." "Mutual assured destruction" was a reasonable combination—although never used by McNamara and his associates—and MAD the correct acronym. Donald Brennan seized on the acronym. In his Senate testimony against Salt I, he said:

> We and the Soviets have agreed not to defend ourselves, not only against each other but, interestingly, against anyone else, either. I believe that at least on the American side this agreement stems purely from a sophomoric ideology and fashion. Let me elaborate on this point.
> The idea has taken hold in the United States that the best route to nuclear peace and security resides in a strategic posture in which

we and the Soviets maintain a capability to destroy a large fraction, say, one-quarter to one-half, of each other's population and
cities and in which no attempt is made by either side to interfere
with the assured destruction capability of the other. Such a posture
is often called a "mutual assured destruction posture." It has the
property that the obvious acronym for it—MAD—provides at
once the appropriate description for it, that is, a "mutual assured
destruction" posture as a goal is almost literally mad.

Brennan labored the acronym as if it were intellectually relevant,
and he succeeded in making the smear stick. Never mind that the
American strategy was not MAD and could not be MAD. The
American Association for the Advancement of Science might advocate MAD, professors at Cambridge might argue that it should
be MAD, but no public official could take steps to design or im-
plement a strategic posture intended to destroy his own country.
Such is plain and simple treason.

And in fact the American nuclear forces were not designed only
for an assured-destruction role as described by McNamara or advocated by "overkill" enthusiasts. They were far in excess of what
was necessary to burn major Soviet cities, and were being steadily
augmented in both numbers and accuracy. Furthermore, an assured-
destruction posture placed priority on defense of the "deterrent"
force against attack. And not only had the ABM Minuteman defense
been liquidated, but not enough was being done to bolster the survivability of the offensive forces to withstand the growing Soviet
threat. The submarines were growing older as the Soviet antisub-
marine-warfare capability was improving. The bomber fleet was
shrinking, concentrated on fewer fields and more vulnerable to attack, especially by the growing numbers of Soviet submarine-launched
ballistic missiles which could squash everything on an airfield within
twenty minutes of firing. The only substantial defense investment
of the 1970s was the rehardening of the Minuteman silos, but that
would presently be outstripped by Soviet ICBM upgrades.

The actual strategic posture of the United States in the 1970s was
not MAD, yet was nothing that anybody would design deliberately.
It was in a sort of strategic limbo, if anything evolving toward an
early-1950s situation wherein both sides had enormous arsenals that
could do each other damage and could take out some of the other's

offensive forces—but certainly not all of them, and perhaps not enough to matter.

To be sure, there were some MADdening tendencies—the liquidation of ARADCOM, the shriveling of NORAD, and the emasculation of SAM-D. Assured-destruction theory also held that counterforce was as destabilizing as population defense—we shouldn't try to destroy his weapons that might destroy us. And some efforts were made along this line. A leader against improved missile accuracy in the Congress was Senator Edward Brooke of Massachusetts. And reportedly there were feeble efforts in the Executive Branch to restrain the progress of missile accuracy in the early '70s; but the responsible officers and civilians down the line properly disregarded such foolishness. The most promising development was superaccurate sub-launched missiles. The MADdest notion was that the Navy should try to design antisubmarine warfare that would work against Soviet torpedo-armed attack subs which could sink our ships but not against missile-armed strategic submarines which could sink our cities. This is rather like trying to equip policemen with revolvers to shoot burglars but not mass murderers. It was taken seriously only along the Charles River and its academic tributaries.

• *The civilian strategists almost uniformly believe in MAD, which came from RAND.* This dogma of the defense ideology was a complete fiction. The canard seems to have been first floated by a British academic named Colin Gray, and was circulated by Edward Luttwak, who, we recall, had worked for and with Paul Nitze, Albert Wohlstetter, Don Brennan, and Dick Foster, and the mythology was promoted by one Richard Pipes, a Harvard professor and supposed Soviet expert, who charitably might be said to have been describing the hot-air bags along the Charles, not the professional strategists.

As far as the chronicler has been able to determine, every individual advising or making American national strategy has favored U.S. possession of capability of *at least* assured destruction of the Soviet Union, and *no* such individual has favored assured Soviet destruction of the United States. Continuing Brennan's SALT testimony: "Many nuclear strategists, including those who have achieved the greatest prominence in the field, do not believe it is true. The prevalent popularity of this theory can only be described as a fashion. Yet the government is apparently prepared to gamble that the theory is true and thereby commit us to a MAD posture indefinitely."

To be sure, many people understood that vulnerability to nuclear attack was a fact, and/or the costs of reducing it to tolerable levels were too astronomical to bear, and/or there were better ways to spend military money, and/or attempts at defense would be beaten by the offense. Wernher von Braun said of ballistic missile defense, "It will never work." Hans Mark of NASA was persuaded of ABM's impracticality. Amron Katz of RAND never could make up his mind. Bernard Brodie, who had done some BMD work at the height of confidence in penetration aids circa 1962, was negative. Thornton Read, the house strategist of Bell Labs, believed the 1968 version of Nike-X had fatal flaws. A leading designer of the ABM warheads shared doubts about the computing capability of the system. Informed skepticism is always appropriately applied to expensive systems, and a negative technical evaluation of ABM was not an unreasonable position. But the people listed, and many more in the Business did not shout, did not lie, did not maintain that the system could not be fixed, did not claim that no system could work, and did not say that *no* defense should work. That position was left to independent professors, to high-minded scholars, to scientists and humanists concerned with Peace.

Brennan put it well in his testimony against SALT I:

> If technology and international politics provided absolutely no alternative, one might reluctantly accept a MAD posture. But to think of it as desirable, for instance, as a clearly preferred goal of our arms control negotiations, as the proposed ABM Treaty automatically assumes, is bizarre. . . .
>
> It is possible to make a technical case—I personally do not believe it—that it would be unwise to use currently available ABM technology in conjunction with cuts in offensive forces to begin to move away from a MAD posture. However, there is no such technical argument to be made about all possible future systems of missile defense, of whatever effectiveness and other characteristics, yet all future systems are prohibited by the treaty.

As for the charge that MAD came from RAND, that seems to have been fabricated out of ignorance or mendacity. None of the stars at RAND in its golden age believed in or advocated mutual vulnerability—not Herman Kahn, nor Albert Wohlstetter, nor Andrew Marshall, nor Bernard Brodie and Alain Enthoven. They disagreed on many emphases, but generally supported not only a well-defended second-strike capability, but also as much counterforce first-strike and population defense as was practical and affordable— all primarily for deterrence, and mostly for extended deterrence against Soviet expansion in Eurasia.

* *The Soviets had not adopted MAD, did not place arms control at the top of their strategic priorities, rather had doctrine and forces to wage nuclear war, to win if necessary.* On this issue, the hawks had a better case than the arms controllers/MADniks, whose desperate attempts to extract a smidgen of the academic strategy from Soviet writings and actions are amusing. The only piece of concrete evidence was SALT—both the signing of the anti–ABM treaty and the failure to expand the Moscow Galosh defenses to the 100 interceptors allowed in the treaty. The Soviets did invest in defending their strategic forces by hardening their ICBMs and putting more missiles out to sea—but they did not go nearly so far in that direction as did the Americans.

What analysts called Soviet "military doctrine" was published works by Soviet generals who held slots that would have been occupied by civilians in the United States, and who were afflicted by a need to publish-or-perish. Much of this product was about as believable as the output of American academics. But it consistently advocated the need to defend the Socialist fatherland and to win nuclear war if need be. It could have been intended to bolster morale. It could have been at least partly intended to be read abroad to threaten the enemies of the U.S.S.R. Yet most it was sensible, honorable, and professional—much more so than the waffling declaratory political statements of America's defense establishment in the 1970s. Small wonder that so many Americans became Soviet-strategy fans. People would pontificate about Soviet strategy who could not read a single Cyrillic character.

* *The Soviets are going for a first strike.* Observation and monitoring of their testing showed steady gains in accuracy. In 1973, as an-

ticipated, they tested their first MIRV, and that was troubling, because whether by accident or design, their missiles were much larger and could carry many more warheads. As Brennan put it in 1972:

> The payload capacity, or throw weight as it is often called, permitted the Soviets in their ICBM and SLBM forces is perhaps four times ours. The throw weight of a strategic force is unquestionably the most important single parameter for characterizing the potential of that force, even though other parameters—notably the number, yield and accuracy of warheads that can be delivered—are of more immediate importance. If the Soviets choose to do so, they can deploy as many warheads per ton of throw weight as we can and since they are permitted roughly four times as many tons, they can ultimately deploy roughly four times as many warheads as we. They may not choose to do so; they may choose some other way of using their payload, but the important fact is we have signed an agreement that says, in effect, that we have not only become but are willing to remain the second nuclear power.

"Throwweight" became central to the defenders' critique. The Soviet had built a force of much larger ICBMs than the Americans. The Soviets could "fractionate," or load their missiles with many times more warheads than the Americans. They could take out our ICBMs and everything else on the continent, and retain enough to dare us to hit back at their cities. Would we dare? How would we react to a threat that they could take out our ICBMs and everything else? How would our allies react? Did we want to find out?

## The Morality of Defense

In other testimony, and his writings and lectures, Donald Brennan also laid out a moral case for the defense. Not only was it foolish and vicious to leave the country open to destruction, but it was evil to rely upon threats of city-busting for "deterrence." Of course, morality must be sensible—application of "the golden rule" of turning the other cheek would be suicidal—so Brennan never thought to eschew threats of retaliation altogether. But he argued that it was wrong for the United States to rely excessively on "assured destruction" of innocent Soviet citizens when other alternatives might be available.

As an interim stage he proposed "the brass rule"—we should threaten to do unto the Soviets as they would do unto us, but no more. This was another case where he was elaborating on a peripheral idea of Herman's: as an alternative to "massive retaliation," Herman proposed adoption of the Old Testament "an-eye-for-an-eye," with emphasis on *no more than* an-eye-for-an-eye. Applied to doctrine, force structure, and strategy, this meant counterforce, selective response, and secure withheld reserves.

Brennan also held that we should prefer live Americans to dead Russians. So we should prefer to invest in the defense. He had converted Freeman Dyson to this position, and Dyson carried it to an extreme—an extreme consistent with Protestant morality. Dyson preached that we should try to save American lives; indeed, the technical issues in which he had engaged in the early '60s were irrelevant. Trying to save lives was a moral end in itself, regardless of whether it worked or not.

During the ABM debate, Dyson responded to a solicitation from JCS Chairman Wheeler for support of Safeguard. His statement never saw the light of day, surely because he favored reduction of military expenditures and scorned administration claims that the Soviet ICBM force had first-strike potential, but in his list of comments he put first:

> 1. Morality. I believe that there is an important moral distinction between defensive and offensive weapons. . . . To use a defensive weapon in response to attack is always morally justifiable. To use an offensive weapon is sometimes morally justifiable and sometimes not. If we have only offensive weapons we are denied the possibilities of making a moral choice. . . . I am amazed at the cheerfulness with which some of my scientific colleagues, arguing against the deployment of ABM, speak of our ability to launch a preemptive nuclear strike against China. . . . Precisely to enable some future president . . . to resist pressures to make a preemptive strike in a moment of desperate crisis—this is to my mind the main purpose of ABM deployment. It is not so much to save our skins as to save our souls.

Still, the exploitation of the moral argument by Brennan was not so much positive as negative, and not so much active as reactive. Into the faces of those who whined about the morality of nuclear weapons, Brennan hurled back: MAD IS IMMORAL.

The Brennan-Dyson position was idiosyncratic. Moral issues were of marginal interest to the bulk of the defenders. They were devout secularists, concerned with maintaining the national interest. While political necessity pushed them into uncomfortable alliance with the vulgar hawks, their strategic doctrine remained unchanged. It has been described many times herein: assured second-strike capability, credible first-strike capability, counterforce preference, strategic-nuclear options, substrategic nonnuclear flexible response capabilities, and damage-limiting through active and/or passive defenses—all for deterrence of Soviet expansionism, and for improving the outcome, if—God forbid—deterrence failed. It was the RAND strategy.

## The Real Action

As the established think tanks declined in the 1970s, a group of more aggressive private research corporations moved to the fore. Collectively they were branded "the Beltway Bandits." (The very term reflects demoralization—the term "the Business" also surfaced in the mid-'70s.) Selecting any one for special notice is misleading, because no single firm had the importance and influence of RAND in the '50s. Yet of particular interest to a chronicle of strategic defense is the Systems Planning Corporation (SPC—"ess-pea-see"). It was a child of the SALT negotiations. Many of its key people were on the staffs of the delegations and the myriad technical panels that endlessly cogitated the significance of the verifiability of the proposed force levels.

The parentage of the firm is revealed by the source of the seed money, the Riggs National Bank, one of whose directors was Paul H. Nitze. The high hawk maintained his personal office in SPC's quarters on Wilson Boulevard in Rosslyn (although not on the Beltway, Rosslyn is its capital). The headman was Ron Easley, an experienced Pentagon hand. Another key man was Sid Greybeal, a former Agency man. A rising star was the talented E. C. "Pete" Aldridge, a veteran of Enthoven's systems-analysis shop in the Pentagon, who had been involved in digging the Safeguard plan out of the files for the edification of the Nixon administration; he too had worked on SALT. Another recruit to SPC was Ami Hoeber, who became assistant to Joe Douglass, a right-wing "strategist" close to Sam Cohen. Later Cliff McLain came on board. Many other senior and junior people also passed through the organization.

SPC competed successfully for numerous Pentagon research jobs, largely in the "black" areas of reconnaissance/intelligence, and also in arms control. In the early and mid-1970s, most serious strategic research was conducted under these two rubrics. When ACDA was kneecapped after SALT, most of the real arms-control research went over to the Building. SPC also did a respectable amount of the very limited strategic-defense research that was conducted during the 1970s—it was involved in the analysis that helped to produce Carter's civil defense program and the plans for the upgrading of continental air defense. At a conference on ballistic missile defense at Harvard in 1979, Aldridge offered an intelligent paper.

The SPC approach was competent, rigorous, and tough-minded, taking the Soviets very seriously. For one contract about the significance of laser BMD, Hudson had been drawn in as a subcontractor to provide scenarios. During a meeting, Nitze remarked to the effect that "Isn't one scenario missing?—that the Soviets have been lying low for thirty years to lull us into a sense of security."

But not much ought to be made of the strategic defense work; there was simply not all that much to it. The best people go where the action is. The real action in defense research and engineering moved away from strategic defense, and from strategic offense as well. While the Draper Lab continued to work wondrous improvements in missile accuracy, this was not the central interest. The big money and the big brains were devoted to reconnaissance, command and control, and advanced technology that was weapons-relevant but not functionally specific—research, not development. Although ARPA (officially become DARPA) had been stripped of the Project Defender operation, it continued to explore technical areas relevant to strategic defense, offense, and everything else. While the Army's ABM testing was terminated at Kwajalein, ARPA continued to work its magic at Roi-Namur, at the other end of the atoll.

In the 1970s, Over-the-Horizon-Backscatter (OTH-B) radar was finally made operational. Unlike forwardscatter, which would bounce between the ground and the ionosphere from transmitter to distant receiver, backscatter had to bounce out, identify a target, and bounce back again. Sorting target information out of that mass of messy data is a fantastically difficult task, absolutely impossible to achieve without high-speed computers. Much of this work, though certainly not all of it, was achieved by intelligent and diligent research at Lincoln Labs. And Raytheon, just down the road, built on its ABM Missile Site Radar work to become the nation's leading constructor of long-range high-performance radars. In the 1970s the new radars went in for coverage of Soviet missile testing and for early warning of offshore sea-launched ballistic missiles. For the early '80s it was planned to install OTH-B radars on the east, west, and southern coasts of the United States to be able to pick up incoming aircraft and cruise missiles at ranges many times the distance of the old line-of-sight radars. (No such plans can be made for the northern approaches because the effect is jammed by the aurora borealis.) And replacements for the now-antique BMEWS radars went into the plans. By 1990, the military would have the capability to collect detailed and exact information that the United States would immediately be destroyed. That information might also be put to other uses.

While radar is familiar to the public because of many civilian applications, the sensing of heat at long distances remains almost entirely military. A skeptic might claim that infrared is a technology, like improvements on the bicycle, which has a great future and always will. In 1930, the rocket pioneer Robert Goddard speculated on a surface-to-air semiactive guided missile that would home in on heat projected from the ground, reflecting off a metal aircraft, and detected by a heat sensor on the homing missile. One of the issues in the fight between Lindemann and Tizard in the British Scientific Committee on Air Defence was precisely over whether emphasis should be on radar or on infrared. The Germans made major breakthroughs in the technology during the death throes of the Third Reich.

Actually, what made infrared detection practical was the jet engine, producing exhaust heat hotter than the lukewarm piston engine. Recall the Sidewinder antiaircraft missile. Subsequently the world's armies were equipped with hand-held short-range air defense infrared missiles such as the American Redeye and the Soviet

Strella. The quality of the sensors gradually improved as new materials were identified and put into practical service. But inherent difficulties remained. In order to be detected, the target had to transmit or reflect heat. An ICBM is a generous heat sink. When climbing, the rocket leaves a "plume" behind its exhaust which can easily be detected from space. Once in space, the missile begins to cool, but it remains hotter than the ether behind it, and as it returns into the atmosphere, the friction heats it extremely hot.

However, because infrared detection is passive it receives a continuous wave of heat, so it can record the direction of the target, but unlike radar, it cannot give the range without triangulation. And there must be a difference in intensity between the source and the sensors. For this reason, the best infrared sensors are artificially cooled to increase heat contrast, requiring time and continuous energy input. Because there are trivial civilian applications for infrared, little has been published openly about the technology. Some sense of the progress is revealed by the fact that infrared in the '30s could not identify the exhaust of a propeller-driven plane beyond 500 feet, while attack helicopters of the 1980s have special exhaust pipes to diffuse the heat that otherwise would surely draw death to them.

But the principal gain in infrared detection was not from the sensors themselves but from the same source that produced near-miraculous improvements in radars and sonars—the computers. Any sensor, especially very sensitive sensors, will deliver a big mess of information, mostly "noise." A great asset of the multichannel computer is that it is perfectly stupid and cannot be distracted from paying attention to whatever detail it has been instructed to monitor from all that jumble. The other asset is speed. One estimate of the 1970s was that a thoroughgoing continental ballistic missile defense would require processing of 40 million instructions per second; the Cray scientific computer could handle 100 million. And computers were shrinking in size and plummeting in cost. Remember that SAGE was so huge that men could walk around inside it. Lecturing in the late '70s, Herman would hold up his Texas Instruments T-50 pocket calculator, remarking that it had more computing capacity than all the monster computers he had operated for the Super program.

The most famous and visible of the new basic weapons-relevant technology was the laser. Much of ARPA's laser work was done through Lincoln Labs, which had moved a long way from its original mission as an air defense research center. It shifted over to sensors of all kinds, principally radars, but also laser sensors. Lasers were also potentially good for communications because, unlike radio, their narrow beams could not be easily jammed or intercepted. And they served for location and range-finding by bouncing the beam off the target in active or semiactive systems like radar.

But weapons-quality laser research was not neglected. A major breakthrough was in ARPA work at Avco-Everett. The engineer Kantrovitch first successfully demonstrated the gas-dynamic laser in 1968. The Air Force and Navy also contributed to laser research. In 1973, an Air Force laser burned a drone out of the sky. There seemed to be no end to the new ways of "lasing"—ruby, carbon dioxide (first demonstrated at Bell Labs), holmium, hydrogen fluoride, excimer, free-electron. You could have subscribed to a Laser-of-the-Month Club. The world was still long short of the death ray— yet the development was moving precisely as imagined, albeit not at breakneck speed.

According to one authoritative source, the laser was not the only death-ray candidate. In 1977 Brennan invited General George Keegan, USAF (retired), to brief the Hudson Institute. He was received with cordial hostility because of his reputation. He had been one of the perpetrators of the "bomber gap" back in the 1950s and was reportedly forced into retirement from air intelligence because, among other things, of his peculiar view that "the Zionists" were out to get him. Keegan was decidedly wary because the Hudson Institute was a notorious Zionist nest. (It is a tribute to Brennan's naiveté that he did not know that Hudson was known to be a notorious Zionist nest.)

Keegan's pitch was that the Soviets were working diligently on particle beams, the projection of subatomic particles for weapons effects, and this might give them a decisive advantage. None of his listeners was competent to judge whether he had accurately interpreted the intelligence data available to him. It was known that the responsible authorities in DoD were rather less than convinced, but they were also known not to be so infallibly correct. The problem with Keegan's presentation was that he exhibited almost a caricature of the paranoia ascribed to so many intelligence officers. But even a paranoid can have real enemies, and although Harold Brown suggested that his leaks were "advance flackery for the new science-

fiction movie *Star Wars,*" it turned out later that Keegan was substantially correct.

Particle beams have been downplayed in comparison with the
sexier lasers, because they would appear to have no civil applications
and their weapons potential is problematic. The bits of an atom are
the turf of physicists, and most of the relevant research has been
done in the weapons labs and in universities with government-bought
monster atom smashers. One of the first programs of the newly
formed ARPA was Project Seesaw at Livermore, an attempt at
projecting electrons, sort of artificial lightning, which was funded
modestly and shut down in the early '70s. And not a lot of enthusiasm
could be generated by the research.

To be sure, there is no such thing as a subatomic "particle." This
is a metaphor used by physicists to try to explain phenomena in a
realm of existence beyond the reach of our comprehension of a
palpable world. Still, these "particles" appear to have some attri-
butes of real things. Most of them behave as if they had magnetic
charges and were nearly weightless. So they are easily deflected by
the Earth's magnetic field—not exactly a desirable characteristic for
a weapon that you wish to aim in an exact direction. Worse, particles
with like charges repel each other, consequently spreading out—
not exactly a desirable characteristic for a weapon to concentrate
energy on a target.

But in theory, neutrons—by definition without magnetic charges—
could be projected. Recall that the neutron warhead fitted to the
Sprint ABM was a device for projecting neutrons by a thermonuclear
reaction, and those neutrons could make a nearby nuclear warhead
inoperative; the Sprint warhead was truly an antinuclear weapon.
In the laboratory, subatomic particles are manipulated by magnetic
fields, and because neutrons have no magnetic charge, accelerating
and projecting them is more than a trivial problem. Again in theory,
one could accelerate a charged particle of neutrons-plus and strip
off the charged plus at the "muzzle" of the projector, letting the
neutrons go on their merry way.

Keegan's complaints spurred the U.S. particle-beam research. For
once at least, we were able to play a game the Soviets had long
been winning—the United States was able to piggyback on published
Soviet research. Los Alamos got deep into the matter; yet the particle-beam concepts were lumped with lasers and modest microwave

research under the rubric "directed-energy weapons" (DEW—"dee-ee-double-u"), and the lasers got the big bucks.

## The Other Side in the 1970s

In the 1970s, the Soviet Union continued the 1950s and '60s development of its forces, both conventional and nuclear. The air defense apparatus was regularly upgraded with new and better radars and interceptors, and continuous augmentation of SAMs. The numbers of planes declined, but whether in response to the reduction of the U.S. bomber force or to the escalating costs of aircraft is impossible to say. Nevertheless, the Soviet air defenses were many times more ambitious than the American. The Tallinn SA-5 missiles continued to proliferate and to bedevil American intelligence analysts. What were they for? Some 18,000 high-altitude air defense missiles, when the United States had long since shown that it would send in its bombers on the deck? Or were they intended for "upgrade" to ballistic missile defense capability—but if so, why did the radars seem too thin to track incomings?

The anti–ballistic missile complex around Moscow held at 64 Galosh, and scuttlebutt was that it had been put on a part-time operating basis, as the U.S. Army had advocated for the Safeguard remnant. No one in the West could ever figure out why it stuck at 64 instead of the SALT-permitted 100 antimissile missiles. During its construction, intelligence evaluation from the overhead judged that it would reach 128 missiles. It was built up of pairs of batteries of eight missiles each, so it could easily have gone up to 80 or 96. To be sure, the 64 exactly matched the maximum number of missiles in the British strategic force, which was assigned a minimum criterion of taking out Moscow; to be sure of getting Moscow, the Brits worked up a maneuvering reentry vehicle—Chevaline. But nobody in America believed that that was more than a coincidence, and nobody working the American offense was much troubled by Galosh. The ABM defenses of Moscow were three sets of 16 antimissile missiles each; a single Poseidon submarine carried 14 warheads on each of 16 missiles.

Another form of Soviet strategic defense came to be a bone of contention. The other side seemed to be substantially upgrading its civil defense capabilities, with new organization and apparently in-

creased resources. Reports circulated in the West of compulsory
civil defense training for all schoolchildren and factory workers.
Calculations were made that the Soviets could exploit this potential
to greatly reduce their casualties, to chop them from tens of millions
to "only" a few million. If true, this put existing U.S. calculations
of "assured destruction" at risk. With their emerging ICBM strike
force, the Soviets could, in crisis, strike first against our forces,
evacuate and go undercover, and take our second strike with severe
but by no means crippling damage. In other words, the combination
of the buildup on the offense and the supposed buildup on the
defense meant that the Soviets could have a war-winning capability. And Soviet military writings all along had argued that nuclear
war would be like any other war in the past, that the nations involved would suffer terribly, but the bravest and toughest and
smartest would prevail and win.

This was much discussed in the West. It could not be disputed
that these Soviet capabilities existed on paper; but were they genuine, or just the same sort of baloney as the American civil defense
plans quoted by the Soviets? Visitors returning from the Soviet
Union would report that their contacts laughed at the civil defense
apparatus. But were those individuals of the Soviet public willing
to talk to Westerners skeptical and antisocialist, or were they government shills? The disinterested observer can note the high cor-
relation between belief in the efficacy of Soviet civil defense and
advocacy of the desirability of American civil defense, and vice
versa. One story circulated through the Business about an arms
controller who reported seeing no signs of civil defense preparations
in the U.S.S.R. He passed around some snapshots. Someone squinted
at a photograph and asked the arms controller what was that little
white structure in the background. He replied that he wondered
himself, because structures like it were all over Soviet Union. The
little white thing was the entrance to a shelter.

The Soviets had agreed to the SALT treaty in May 1972. They
had upgraded the administrative status of civil defense in October
1972. Five months seems about right to redirect resources in the
clumsy Soviet bureaucracy.

However, most American attention was directed toward the expansion of the Soviets' offensive forces. They built their submarine-
launched ballistic missiles up to the levels permitted by SALT I, as

expected. They MIRVed their warheads, as predicted, and they produced a large number of new ICBM types—some would say an unseemly number. A little model was circulated in Washington showing how few new missile types the United States had and how many new types the Soviet Union had. This display was supposed to impress the gullible with Soviet progress and prowess; actually, it indicated ferocious competition between the Soviet rocket-design groups and/or egregious inefficiencies and failures.

Nonetheless, the result was a formidable force. What had been heralded by Safeguard advocates and denigrated by opponents in 1969 came to be seen as a reality: the possibility of a successful first strike against the U.S. ICBM force. Moreover, the Soviets' expanded sea-launched-missile force gave them capabilities of knocking out bombers on the fields and strategic submarines in port, and retaining considerable reserves to destroy the United States and several other major countries. The advocates of SALT had said that the anti–ABM treaty would inhibit the Soviets' incentive to expand their offensive forces. Perhaps so—but not noticeably so. The Soviets were not heeding the academic strategy. The arms controllers were disappointed.

And still the Soviets continued to build. Harold Brown is a dour man who chooses his words carefully and is not much given to hyperbole, yet he produced a single sentence that summed up the reality of the action–reaction syndrome: "When we build, they build; when we don't build, they build." The Soviets were not responding to American initiatives. Perhaps the Soviets had never built because we built. Perhaps the Soviets were building because we were not building. In 1976, the USAF antisatellite system at Johnston Island was shut down, and the Soviets' reaction was to accelerate their experimental ASAT system. And some people recalled the statements of the Soviet delegates in the United Nations during the rejection of international control of atomic energy thirty years before: the Soviet Union would go about taking care of its own security.

But what did this mean to the United States? "Window of vulnerability" advocates understood that the United States would be subject to Soviet blackmail. The people who made this case took it very seriously indeed, because they believed in Soviet ruthlessness, and privately said that we should back off if pressed by such power. Herman Kahn was not so sure. Colin Gray used to give "window of vulnerability" talks at Hudson seminars. Afterward Herman would revert to the theme of the secure bombers in Times Square and say, "Yes, there will be a window of vulnerability—*and the Soviets won't come in.*" In fact, Herman took a certain degree of paternal pride in reports of the activities of the nasty Soviets; he remarked to this effect: "Let's see, a secure second-strike force, plus a not-incredible first-strike capability, plus decent damage-limiting programs, with considerable conventional force for Type III deterrence. Why—it's the program of *On Thermonuclear War!*" All Herman's works had been translated into Russian, and the Soviet "journalists" and "counselors" who hung around Hudson hung on his every word. The Soviets adored Herman; on a visit to Moscow in the mid-'60s, he was accorded the VIP treatment of a Lenin Prize winner.

Perhaps the Americans would not listen, but it was too much to expect that both the superpowers would be stupid. So he was not much impressed by high-flying rhetoric about how "the Soviets are planning to fight and win a nuclear war." Of course they were planning to fight and win a nuclear war. They should be planning to fight and win a nuclear war. Should they be planning to *lose* a nuclear war? Should they be planning to surrender rather than fight? It was the responsibility of the military to plan to fight and win wars. The ability to fight and win a nuclear war gave leverage to the political authorities, which is what the military was supposed to be doing. The Soviets were constructing the preferred force level with which to deter us, and to pressure us and our allies if necessary. To be sure, Herman may have seen mirror-imaging. In any case, his analysis, however plausible and correct it may have been, was too subtle for the coarse public debate of the 1970s, and Herman slipped into debased ghostwritten "strategic" rhetoric toward the end.

## The Disarmers in the 1970s

At first the disarmament crowd had pooh-poohed the supposed Soviet buildup, and they continued to denigrate its significance, to deny that the Soviets were capable of achieving a first strike, to insist that strategic superiority was worthless and dangerous, and to support parity and mutual vulnerability as a desirable strategic regime. Yet as the numbers came in and were briefed on a classified level to those people with clearances and to members of the Congress, and as it became universally accepted that the Soviets were indeed making this military buildup, the arms controllers gradually became more disconcerted and demoralized.

Whatever the Soviets were up to, they were not playing the game that had been laid down by the high-minded Americans in the 1960s. The Soviets were not being educated in the true doctrine of mutual vulnerability. They seemed to be building weapons that coincided with the stated Soviet military doctrines which had long since been dismissed by the arms controllers. A new phrase was added to the arms-controller vocabulary: the Soviets held to "traditional military strategy"—which was foolishness, because the advent of atomic munitions had made everything all new. It was troubling to notice that what the Soviets said, and what the Soviets bought, indicated that they thought the purpose of weapons was to threaten people, and if the threats did not succeed, to beat them down. The arms controllers knew that this was a ridiculous idea in the nuclear age. It was very ominous that the Soviets seemed not to realize it—but we shouldn't reinforce their silly ideas by provoking them.

It did not occur to those people that the Soviets were right all along. Other Americans, who had forgotten what the "traditional" American strategy was in the '50s and early '60s, came around to the same view through a different route and with different goals. The chronicler recalls an Air Force general responding to an issue of nuclear operations with the query "What are the experts doing? What are *the Soviets* doing?" Actually, the idea of a distinction between American and Soviet schools of strategy was concocted in the 1970s. The major difference between the published Soviet strategy and the RAND strategy worked out in the 1950s was the spurious distinction between, quoting from Herman's briefing notes at the time, "war-avoiding" and "war-fighting." Short of surrender, war-avoiding strategies threaten war, which means a war-fighting strategy. The chronicler recalls challenging Herman on this point:

"You say the minimum deterrence position is 'deterrence only,' not 'war-fighting.' If smashing all the other side's cities and killing tens of millions of people isn't a war-fighting strategy, what the hell is?"

His response was "With minimum deterrence, you're not interested in the details of how the war is fought; you just push all the buttons and go home—if you have a home."

"That seems like a great reason *not* to worry about the details, Herman."

"Exactly. That's its appeal."

Since the Soviets had not responded to MAD theory, the arms controllers had to fall back a few steps. They denied that they had ever advocated mutual assured destruction as a strategy—they were merely describing it as a condition, as had Donald Quarles twenty-five years earlier. True, mutual vulnerability was a condition—a horrible condition—but the MADvocates belied their own apology by trying to block any attempts to alleviate it. They took the attitude of the concentration-camp guard who characterizes the inmates as docile and dirty. The most articulate of the disarmers, George Rathjens, showed real signs of weakening. To be sure, he could not abandon the Cambridge party line, but he hinted broadly that concentrating on the ABM opportunity raised by local opposition in 1969 was in retrospect a mistake. Blocking MIRV would have been better. Yes, it would—but MIRV could not have been blocked bilaterally, because a MIRV ban could not be verified. Only an American MIRV could have been stopped by Rathjens and company. In his ruminations we see the slide toward unilateral disarmament. "Arms control" had degenerated to blind opposition to any new weapons system, regardless of its characteristics: to any new *American* weaponry.

The harping on MAD by Brennan and his imitators was getting to the disarmers. An apposite riposte was by Panofsky and Spurgeon Keeny, who concocted a countersmear: Nuclear Use Theorists—NUTs. Herman, who was uncomfortable with the demagogy of MAD, was delighted by its appropriateness. Still, NUTs failed to take.

## The Empire Strikes Back

If anyone deserved to lose a reelection bid, it was Gerald Ford. His successor solicited support of all manner of disarming types. Jimmy Carter's appointments were peculiar, to say the least. For Secretary of State he selected poor Cy Vance, as if to balance the brilliantly competent Harold Brown as Secretary of Defense. Stanley Resor became the Undersecretary for Policy—the old ISA job. The National Security Adviser, Zbigniew Brzezinski, was as passionately anti-Russian as only a Pole can be. His deputy was David Aaron, one of the squishiest of the disarmers. To pay off his political debts, Carter had to put all sorts of odd creatures into minor back offices. The most glaring discordance was in the Department of the Air Force, where the Secretary became Hans Mark, one of Teller's boys, a stratospheric technocratic hawk, while an assistant was Antonia Chayes, whose only assets seem to have been her "gender" and her husband, Abram, of Chaysner. As if to illustrate the broader applicability of Yarmolinsky's Rule, the counsel for the Arms Control and Disarmament Agency was Adam Yarmolinsky.

Carter made a fatal error in neglecting to give jobs to members of the Scoop Jackson wing of the Democratic Party. Carter's most grievous nonappointment was Paul Nitze, who once again demonstrated that he was a dangerous man not to put into your administration. As the ACDA chief, Carter nominated Paul Warnke, one of the most vocal of the pooh-poohers of the Soviet menace. Nitze picked this appointment as an issue to show his claws, and incited "the battle of the Pauls." The political naiveté of the Carter administration is marvelously exposed by his aide Hamilton Jordan wandering over to Capitol Hill to ask Warnke's opponents what the hassle was all about. The Senate, as it always will unless there are extraordinarily negative reasons, recognized the prerogative of the President to select his own agent. The likes of Warnke were in, and the Nitzes were out.

With like-minded folk, Nitze organized a masterful lobby of Americans who were concerned about the strategic balance. Of course, the model was the Committee for a Prudent Defense Policy of the Safeguard fight. At its heart were the old "Cold War liberals," but it was rapidly expanded to include many Republicans. Among the names already seen in this chronicle were William Van Cleave, Frank and Ami Hoeber, Fred Ikle, Richard Perle, David Packard, Richard Whalen, Richard Allen, Johnny Foster, John Lehman, Edward Teller, Donald Brennan, Colin Gray, and dozens of others, including Ronald Reagan. (But not Dick Foster or Herman Kahn— Nitze had no trust in their judgment.)

It is incorrect to view The Committee on the Present Danger as an organization with any special interest in strategic defense. Its main function was to call attention to the Soviet military buildup and to agitate against attempts to restrain American efforts to at least match it. The committee was thin on concrete proposals, but insofar as it made any, it emphasized the offense. The most comprehensive statement of CPD advocated more bombers, strategic submarines, ICBMs, and intermediate-range ballistic missiles. The only reference to the defense was the advocacy of "expanded civil defense planning and preparations." In a thick analysis of the strategic balance drafted by Frank Hoeber, there was some discussion of the imbalance in civil defense and in air defense (although by disregarding the National Guard and Canadian squadrons he understated America's continental air defense). The CPD was in the business of advocacy of the offense—although, oddly, its analysis of U.S. vulnerability to a Soviet first strike implied a need for the defense of U.S. strategic forces.

### The Problem in Europe Revived

In the 1970s it was not only the Soviets' strategic forces that were troubling, but their intermediate-range "theater" forces against Europe as well. SALT had not restrained shorter-range missilery, and the Soviets considered that a buildup was consistent with "détente." A three-stage Soviet ICBM could work with only two stages. The Soviets began to deploy the stunted missiles to replace antediluvian IRBMs still in service from the 1950s; the West labeled the newcomers SS-20. The Europeans were decidedly becoming nervous, and it was felt necessary to cosset them. The first attempt was the "enhanced radiation," or neutron, bomb. Sam Cohen, out of Rand, surfaced as a leading proponent, and for a brief time became a minor public figure. The idea was that the neutron bomb would reassure the Europeans because it could kill attacking Russian troops while leaving European assets and sheltered civilians intact. This eminently sensible idea was bitterly attacked as "a capitalist bomb"— presumably, big-blast bombs are "socialist bombs." Objections were strong in both Europe and America for the usual spurious reasons, principally because people were against any new weapon as "accelerating the arms race." As with any more practical use of nuclear weaponry, it was objected to on the strategic ground that anything that made nuclear weapons more usable made nuclear war more likely. True enough—the neutron bomb made nuclear war more likely than abject surrender. On a more concrete level, neutron bombs were not optimal to the American strategic objective of denying western European assets to the Soviet Union. Carter embraced the neutron bomb, then, when the heat grew, abandoned it.

Helmut Schmidt had an even better idea. This canny man was one of the few national leaders who thoroughly understood nuclear-strategic issues. He had been involved in the global-strategic shmooz in the late '50s and early '60s (and had written the introduction to the German edition of Herman Kahn's *On Escalation*). The German Chancellor's quick-fix of The Problem was for the United States to station in west Europe intermediate-range nuclear missiles which could strike at the U.S.S.R. If the Soviets struck at western Europe with nuclear weapons, the Americans would hit back at the Soviet Union. (And by the way, exploiting an asymmetry in SALT favorable to the West: the treaty forbade missile defenses "of the national territory." The United States could put anti–tactical missiles in west Europe, and the Soviets could do the same in east Europe, but the Soviets could not legally put ATM in the Ukraine, and Schmidt's IRBMs could reach at least that far.)

With the older short-range missiles, a Soviet attack could have been met with a nuclear response in western Europe, especially in Germany, and the war could have been fought out without touching the U.S. or U.S.S.R. This was precisely what Helmut Schmidt did not want to happen. With the longer-range missiles, a Soviet attack would be met by an American attack on Soviet territory, which would certainly bring a Soviet response down on the American homeland, and the war could be fought leaving west Europe intact. It is a wonderful tribute to the incompetence of the Carter administration that it stepped into Schmidt's trap. Ordered deployed were Air Force ground-launched cruise missiles (GLCMs—"glick-ems") and Army intermediate-range ballistic missiles. IRBMs, in the missile wars of late 1950s, had been awarded to the U.S. Air Force; but the new Euromissiles were assigned to the Army because they were spuriously identified as a "modernization" of the older Pershing 1. So the Army, much against its will, found itself back in the long-range-rocket business, and Huntsville and White Sands were soon at work on new mobile Pershing 2s; like the SS-20s, they would fit in a truck.

In defense and arms control, the Carter people attempted the same line as the Kennedy people—to dress and undress at the same time, to initiate a defense buildup and to press negotiations with the Soviets. The principal thrust of the Carter administration was to expand upon the agreements of SALT I and to achieve a real limitation on strategic offensive arms. After terrible writhing, a deal was achieved that did not look bad on paper, although some minor advantages were granted to the Soviet Union in the shadowy Backfire medium bomber (which might reach the United States in a one-way mission—à la the late Tu-4—but almost certainly after the missile exchange had long since decided the issue of a nuclear war) and regarding the superior throwweight of the larger Soviet missiles. Upon these legitimate but hardly central points, the Committee on the Present Danger and company decided to fight the treaty tooth and nail. What was troubling to many objectors was that SALT II promised at best to restrain further expansion of offensive forces— which were already at debilitating levels. And there were fears— expressed openly by Dick Foster—that the Soviets wanted to put a cap on U.S. offensive forces so that they could achieve decisive advantage by deploying their strategic defenses. To be sure, SALT II was innocuous compared with SALT I—Salt I actually did something by forbidding serious antimissile defense, while SALT II was a plain and simple fraud. Nonetheless, the most glaring fault of SALT II was that it appeared to be an arms-control treaty, and therefore would perpetuate the myth of détente. As Herman had pointed out in a lecture in 1960, a grave drawback to arms control was that the United States would take it seriously as evidence of harmony and would slack off, while the other side would construe it narrowly, at best.

Still, SALT II probably would have been ratified had it not been for the growing suspicion of the Soviets' capabilities and intentions that they themselves had helped promote, and by the natural process of recovery from the Vietnam syndrome—because it was unnatural for the Americans to watch somebody else get ahead of them, especially in such a grave arena as the most puissant weaponry. That the Soviet Union intervened in neighboring Afghanistan was central: because the country had been neutralized ("Finlandized") for sixty years, it was zero threat to the Soviet Union, so the intervention and counterinsurgency against the ferocious mountain barbarians communicated that Soviet ambition had no limits. This was, by the way, the first time that Soviet troops had been used overtly outside the Soviet empire since the beginning of the Cold War. In addition was some funny business in Nicaragua created entirely by Carter's bungling, handing an American protectorate over to a gang of avowed Communists and then trying to bribe them into a sort of gushy Third World neutrality. And there was the Iranian debacle. Nitze *et al.* poured hot pepper on SALT II, Carter had to withdraw the treaty from consideration, and that was really the end for him.

Less publicized, and less noticed because it did not fit the ideological preconceptions of the major debaters, was that over in the Pentagon, with considerable support from some elements in the National Security Council, Harold Brown was turning around the defense structure to put America back on the road to military ascendancy. Among other programs, he ordered the long-delayed SAM-D, now named "Patriot," into production.

And other odd things were happening too.

## Jimmy Carter's Strategic Defense Initiative

At the same time, however, Harold Brown administered the last kick in the groin to continental air defense. The remaining Hercs and Hawks were withdrawn from Florida. The aging interceptor fleet was trimmed even further, and the last of the SAGE centers were ordered taken out of service. The Air Force's Air Defense Command followed the Army's into oblivion. The planes were transferred to Tactical Air Command, and the radars to SAC. The former Safeguard PAR radar in North Dakota, relabeled Perimeter Acquisition Radar Characterization System (PARCS—"parks"), was handed over to the Strategic Air Command. Nothing was left of NORAD except Cheyenne Mountain and its vulnerable command post. It was little more than a conduit, perhaps a superfluous one, for transmitting warning of incoming attack to SAC.

Among the many oddities of the Carter administration was the naming of Bardyl Rifat Tirana as the civil defense chief. We may doubt that his appointment was a conscious pitch for the Albanian vote. The original pick was Tina Hobsen, an "activist" with the high qualifications that she was black and female, but she turned down the job. Tirana was a local lawyer in Washington who handled transport in the Carter campaign and expected a DoD job—but a minute of conversation is sufficient to discover that Tirana is an archetypal candidate for the application of Yarmolinsky's Rule. Harold Brown dumped him into civil defense. The floundering CD bureaucrats received the appointment with enthusiasm, knowing that he was a graduate of Phillips Andover, Princeton, and Columbia Law School, perhaps another Steuart Pittman. Tirana was ambitious, aggressive, and naive. He took literally the academic "policy sciences" fiction that government has "policy" which it carries out with "programs." He noted numerous statutory mandates for civil defense—"policy"—but found no programs. But he found an adviser at hand.

Civil defense had found a new messiah, from a curious source. T. K. (Thomas Kensington) Jones was an old-hand Boeing engineer, who had worked on Bomarc. Boeing was the quintessence of the offense—Boeing built bombers and the ICBMs. But Jones became concerned with effects of that offensive weaponry on Soviet targets. How might the Soviet Union be nullifying the damage that Boeing's superb weapons might cause? From data provided by air intelligence, he concluded that the Soviets were not merely conducting paper evacuation exercises: they were digging in some important assets. There were substantial bunkers for military commanders, and for the political leadership. The Party cadres, given sufficient warning, which they certainly would have in a crisis provoked or stimulated by the Soviet Union, were secure from reprisal.

Of especial interest to Boeing were reports of efforts by the Soviets to harden their industries. No factory would survive a direct hit, but a 150-kiloton weapon tossed somewhat inaccurately on a city by an American submarine would impose grave damage only on a limited area. On paper, the city should be blown away by a few psi of overpressure; but what if the plants and machinery were protected by modestly sophisticated predesign and padding? And such technology might, by the way, help protect Boeing's own plants. Once again, the offense and the defense work together. So Boeing under T.K.'s leadership made some experiments using high explosive to simulate the atomics (and rather well simulated, because blast is blast no matter how produced) and found that these Soviet designs seemed to work. Our assured destruction of the adversary was not as assured as we believed.

T.K. took up the crusade of civil defense with a fanaticism only a convert could display. He was the right man at the place at the right time. All the previous major advocates of civil defense either had been spreading themselves thinly over many subjects, like Teller, or had become bored with a program going nowhere, like Herman, or had become wearied or disillusioned, like most of the full-time CD. It is not too much to say that T. K. Jones's innocence and enthusiasm singlehandedly revived civil defense as a major strategic defense issue. T.K. became involved in the technical support for the SALT negotiations, and came to the favorable attention of Paul Nitze, which was sufficient to make his reputation in the Business.

Hundreds of men knew more about CD, but T.K.'s name had been in the newspapers, so Tirana turned to him. Jones recommended the able Cliff E. McClain as deputy. The new CD team got into contact with the systems-analysis office of DoD, and among them was ginned up a revised civil defense program. It was not a new rationale—it was the old RAND rationale of twenty years earlier—but incredible as it sounds, especially in the atmosphere of the early days of the Carter administration, the concept kept being passed upward and it was not killed. A modest amount of civil defense was still as analytically persuasive as it had been under McNamara, and Harold Brown signed off on it.

In the White House, it had strong supporters in Zbigniew Brzezinski and Samuel Huntington, a token patriot on the Harvard political science faculty who was taking a year off to work at the National Security Council. Upward it went, dodging the antidefense group around David Aaron and up to the President's desk, whence it was promulgated as Presidential Directive 41. On paper, PD 41 was even more enthusiastic than Kennedy's adoption of civil defense. Kennedy merely endorsed the notion of civil defense as "insurance" against a nuclear war; PD 41 added the strategic argument, that a nation that could limit its damage could more credibly threaten with nuclear weapons. The new program was not to be anything so publicly disconcerting as shelter programs; it was strategic evacuation, relabeled "crisis relocation." In a severe crisis, the population would be evacuated from the cities to "host" areas. The civil defense apparatus was mandated to work up plans for moving people from here to there, and the staff began with eagerness. This was its first important function since completing the fallout-shelter survey in the late 1960s. To be sure, PD 41 was immediately leaked to the press, which provoked an uproar among the antidefense elements of Congress. President Carter didn't quite disavow it, but indicated that nothing was going to be done with it, and no more money was to be appropriated, except for planning.

Simultaneously, there was a separate development. Recall that in 1961 Kennedy had divided the civil defense functions—the life-protecting-in-war to the Defense Department, the residue of planning for postattack recovery to the Office of Emergency Planning in the Executive Office—and that Nixon had scattered OEP to several agencies. In his campaign, Carter had made a big to-do of his achievement reducing government agencies in Georgia—by the simple expedient of combining them. The ploy had been so politically successful that his staff thought to do the same in Washington. They found banging heads together in the national government harder to accomplish. They could consolidate only agencies that hardly anybody cared about, and civil defense fragments surely filled the bill— and many of the thoughtful people in civil defense had thought the separation to be irrational from the beginning. So with a wave of Carter's wand, the bits and pieces went into a hat and emerged as the Federal Emergency Management Agency (FEMA—"fee-mah"). The omission of the term "civil defense" from the title was no accident.

### The Shell Game

Still, as for the previous twenty years, the emphasis was on defending the deterrent. It must have been about 1975 that a plausible young Briton named Colin Gray came to brief the Hudson Institute with a bright new idea of how to defend the forthcoming MX supermissile. The concept was that the missiles would be mobile—not a radical idea, because rail mobility had been planned for Minuteman and been scrubbed by McNamara in favor of hardening—and would be shuttled between numerous modestly hardened places in a large military reservation. The attacker could not be sure where the MX missiles would be, so he would have to target all the places, requiring the expenditure of an enormous force to kill a few missiles. In effect, the multiple-protective-shelter (MPS) scheme reversed MIRV; to kill one missile carrying many warheads, the attacker would be obliged to expend many warheads. The scheme as laid out by Gray— and it was not original with him—was wonderfully complex and would have given credit to the conceits of the great cartoonist Rube Goldberg.

As he heard Gray's briefing, the chronicler was at first amused, then annoyed, and then appalled to learn that his colleagues were taking all this seriously. By this time he had little confidence in Brennan's judgment, but now even Herman was getting into it. The chronicler finally lost his patience and blurted out, "It's a shell game."

Brennan replied, "You don't understand the logic."

"And you don't understand the conclusion—you're not going to sell the American people on a wacko shell game."

Deceptive basing was not a new idea, nor was the "shell game" analogy original—both had appeared in the 1950s—and the screwiness of the scheme was widely perceived. The Air Force and the Department of Defense contrived dozens of other ways to try to defend MX. Indeed, despite SALT, BMD systems were always under consideration. That was the exact purpose of the Army's LoADS concept, which would mix the MXs with capsules containing interceptors and their own radars which, like the protected missiles, would pop up from their shelters and be fired at the appropriate time. One of many schemes was to fly MXs around in aircraft. This was an incredibly expensive option, not to mention the question of what happened when a plane crashed. And in the mid-'70s, discussion of these matters was no longer restricted to the professionals in the Business, but spread out to the wider public and was the subject of interminable investigations by dozens of congressional committees and subcommittees.

A major contributor to this brouhaha was Richard L. Garwin, of IBM's Watson Labs, just up the road from Herman Kahn's Hudson Institute. He was bubbling with bright ideas for alternative defenses of MX. Garwin was another *Wunderkind,* who had made important contributions to the mechanics of the final Super design, and was also a veteran of the air defense wars of the '50s. He went on to be a leading researcher at Columbia and at IBM, where he made valuable contributions to the emerging technology of that noble firm. His relationship with IBM allowed him to advise-and-consult on military matters, as long as he did not identify his views with IBM. That he surfaced in public in the anti–ABM campaign may merely reflect the long contact of IBM with the liberal Democrats, and a desire to attach IBM to the Kennedy camp. Burke Marshall, IBM's counsel, had been one of Attorney General Kennedy's principal assistants, and lent his name to an anti–ABM petition.

Or Garwin's surfacing may have been a result of his personality. He was convinced he had wonderfully unique and practical ideas. Unfortunately, in the closed scientific circles of the Business, Garwin's evaluation of the quality of his ideas was not widely shared. All too many of Garwin's peers believed his concepts were not as original as Garwin thought, or else were downright screwy. Perhaps Garwin felt the need to appeal to a wider audience. The orthodox defenders will certainly be appalled at seeing Garwin listed among them, but his difference from them was in emphasis and detail. Some people claim that he is a pure wrecker, always recommending alternative systems that he knows couldn't possibly work. Garwin denies this, and the chronicler believes him. Garwin is responsible and sincere in his efforts to improve national security—he merely inhabits a different realm of understanding than the rest of us.

A heavily pushed alternative to MX, not by Garwin alone, was itsy-bitsy submarines each carrying a few of these missiles, sailing in shallow waters waiting for the orders to launch. Seems effective, except for the vulnerability of submarines in shallow water to barrage attack by rocket or submarine-launched depth charges, which would create a tidal wave to crush these minisubs, bash them against the bottom, or pop them to the surface to be killed. Other drawbacks were the same that afflicted the deepsea subs—communicating in a crisis, and the loss of accuracy. But the most telling was what any Seaman Fourth Class with submarine service would have noticed— that it is impossible to keep crews in very cramped quarters for very long. Their efficiency would have fallen off rapidly, not to mention their reenlistment. But Richard Garwin and the other advocates of the minisubs, of course from MIT, are too upscale to take into account such mundane matters.

Another way of defending MX was also seaborne. A barge or something would drop off the missiles and let them float around until, in a crisis, they were tipped upright and fired at the enemy. You need not be even a Seaman Fourth Class to notice some disadvantages to having nuclear-tipped intercontinental ballistic missiles bobbing about in the ocean like old beer bottles waiting to be scooped up.

Garwin also pushed Swarmjet, a variant on the Project Charles Porcupine concept of 1951, whereby a battery of small, cheap non-nuclear rockets would fire like a monster shotgun at the incoming missile. A salvage-fused incoming would scatter Swarmjet like straw, and squash the radar. A neater idea was to defend missile silos by surrounding them with nuclear mines planted in the ground, which would be exploded upon the arrival of the attacking warhead, ejecting large amounts of debris into its path. Again, not impossible in theory, although not conducive to experimentation under a nuclear test ban. That the public, not to mention the silent silo-sitters in the adjoining command posts, might object to planting nuclear weapons in our soil and upchucking huge quantities of radioactive materials in the continental United States was again the sort of vulgar practicality that escaped the mind of Garwin.

So he came up with an even better scheme, elaborating what had previously been merely a distinction in nomenclature between the Army and Air Force. The Army spoke of "site defense" of a small area, while the Air Force used the term "point defense" to mean the same thing. Garwin considered that the two were separate and that instead of defending an entire missile field—"a site"—one should consider each silo "point" separately. This negated the ability of interceptors to defend all sites, but led to other possibilities. He proposed surrounding each silo with a hedge of huge spikes to skewer the incoming missile far enough above ground so that it could not blast the hardened silo. Paul Nitze called this "Garwin's dragon's teeth." Apparently Garwin forgot that the lead incoming would have salvage fusing to flatten the spikes, giving the remainder a free ride.

Garwin was also great for launch-on-warning—that we should announce and in every way attempt to convince the other side that we were prepared to fire when our early warning indicated incomings—so a computer glitch could destroy the Soviet Union, and the United States. But Garwin's favorite solution to nuclear-strategic problems was "mined cities." We would plant nuclear mines in their cities and they would plant them in our cities, so both sides would have perfectly assured destruction. This regime would make us all secure. The notion seems to have been first suggested by Leo Szilard, in a context wherein his seriousness is not certain. Garwin seems to have been dead serious; later he seemed to believe that our cities had already been mined. What is fantastic is that Donald Brennan employed the same concept rhetorically, as a parody of mutual-assured-destruction theory. Imagine the reaction to the announcement that the U.S. government is assisting the Soviet rocket forces in placing a 5-megaton bomb in a room on the eighty-sixth floor of the Empire State Building.

Garwin wrote regularly for Gerald Piel's *Scientific American,* lectured a lot, and wrote papers richly footnoted with references to his own books, which no one troubled to read. Among hackademics, he was considered quite an authority on advanced defense technology. Herman, who was loath to speak ill of any man, was finally provoked into awarding this accolade: "Garwin is a pain in the ass."

Many other schemes for defending MX were floated, but all were rejected for one reason or another. The least objectionable came down to the multiple protected shelters (MPS—"em-pee-ess"). Lavishly rococo strategic analyses and engineering calculations were made to get the best layout, whether long tubes underground, as originally conceived, or a great circle, or a web. One oddity of all schemes was windows in the roofs of the shelters so that from time to time they could be opened to examination by the Soviet satellites overhead, to reveal that the United States did not have missiles in all the shelters, but only those few permitted by the offensive-arms-limitation agreement. The Pentagon believed that the political fate of MX basing would require that this perversion be made part of the design. The arms-control deal had specified that both sides should determine verification through "national technical means," which meant radio eavesdropping and satellite observation, but no on-site inspections. Neither side was to interfere with the other's national technical means, but SALT did not say that either side had to make it easier for the other side to find out what was really going on. In the 1970s, American arms were being designed, not to attack or to threaten, but to be controlled.

## The Battle of the Great Basin

Eventually Carter determined to go ahead with the MPS system, selecting a scheme with 23 shelters per missile, requiring the Soviets to lay on 46 warheads to achieve near-certainty of kill of each MX; against 200 MX, 9,200 warheads would have to arrive nearly simultaneously—rather a tall order, even for the most ambitiously fractionated Soviet supermissiles. The shell game required an enormous area, and the only places suited for it were in the great American desert—the Great Basin between the Rockies and the Sierra Nevada, comprising the bulk of the state of Nevada and a good chunk of Utah.

So the Air Force sortied to emplace MX, a task even more ambitious than building the Army's Safeguard sites. Originally there was little local reaction, until an issue was made of it by a minor figure in arms-control circles who had returned home to be a professor at the University of Utah. He had perfectly absorbed all the precepts of the academic strategy, and did not like MX. In addition to being a law professor, he was an adherent of the Church of Jesus Christ of Latter-day Saints.

To people in the East, the Mormons, or LDS ("ell-dee-ess"), as they are known in Utah, appear terribly ultraconservative and odd. And in a very important military way, they are deviant. Most Americans believe the myth that the United States won all wars until Vietnam, that God is on their side, and that the justice of their cause has brought them victory. Two major groups are exceptions to this military optimism: the American South, which was crushed and pillaged a century ago, perhaps as a partial consequence is promilitary and the principal recruiting ground of the regular Army; the other losers are the Mormons, who fought a sixty-year war against the United States and were worn down and forced to capitulate.

Most lists of superfluous military bases include Utah's Fort Douglas, usually described by pinchpenny congressmen as a holdover from the Indian wars. Not true. The fort stands on a hill two miles to the east of the Temple, the Tabernacle, and the General Headquarters of the Church—optimum artillery range from the Mormons' Vatican. For three generations the guns stood there armed and ready, to remind the Saints of the secular power. Immediately adjoining Fort Douglas is the University of Utah, now a typical sprawling campus, but during the First World War this was America's greatest concentration camp, where pacifists, socialists, anarchosyndicalists, and others less than enthusiastic about the War for Democracy were incarcerated for the duration. That the camp was located right by Salt Lake City was no accident—it was originally intended for a different clientele, one immediately at hand. The psychological defenses were formidable in those days.

To the south of the university grounds is Little Cottonwood Canyon, where dug into the side of the mountains are great underground bunkers, officially to hold the sacred records of the Church. No one will say that these are command bunkers for the hierarchy of the Church, and perhaps for a few hundred healthy young couples (or perhaps merely healthy young women) to maintain Deseret after America is destroyed. Furthermore, the Saints have a structure of family and neighborhood defense. Every Mormon family is required to have a year's supply of basic goods stored in the basement. Every parish (ward) has an organization for mobilization and, if necessary, evacuation under attack. Military police are planned—although the official document states clearly (but certainly aesopically) that they shall be unarmed and subject to the civil authorities. The official rationale for this apparatus is generalized unnamed disasters, and the efficiency of the organization was demonstrated in the Utah floods of 1982, when General Headquarters dispatched tens of thousands of workers to fill sandbags and man the dikes, under better discipline than any of the secular authorities of Utah.

Sometime during the 1960s, when James Fletcher was president of the University of Utah, a radical speaker came to campus, and, imitating the style developed on other campuses, but with modifications for local conditions, exhorted the students to "kill your parents and desecrate the Temple." The word was flashed to General Headquarters, and in twenty minutes the neighborhood defense teams fell out: ten thousand armed men. Fletcher had to call down to Temple Square and inform the powerhouse that the speaker was just a hustler who posed no threat to the Kingdom of the Saints.

Well, in addition to having hardworking and serious men, handsome and prolific women, and an elaborate almost Bolshevik-style hierarchy, the Mormons also have scientists, who can make worldly calculations. The MX shell game in the Great Basin would have been an enormous undertaking with a disruptive ecological effect, involving huge amounts of water—precious to maintain the Mormons' farmland, the bedrock of their Zion. The construction would have attracted tens of thousands of outside workers—vagabond undisciplined Gentiles, corruptive of the moral order of the Kingdom of the Saints.

The physicists could calculate the effects of a Soviet attack on the MX complex. The obvious Soviet countermeasure was a great barrage attack, laying in tens of thousands of warheads to crush all the shelters at once and disrupt any scattered launches. This would raise hundreds of tons of radioactive dirt which would put clouds of fallout over Utah. The elaborate Mormon civil defense apparatus would be overwhelmed. Evacuation of the populace would be in vain. The bunkers might be overwhelmed. There might not be time to evacuate the Mormon high command into the mountains. The very soil of Utah would be polluted. Lew Allen, the Air Force Chief of Staff, made a rare gaffe in describing the Deseret deployment as a "warhead sponge."

Washington planned that MX would be inviolable to attack, and therefore would deter nuclear war. But the Mormons were not so sure; the Mormons, who knew that horrors can happen to their people, understood that deterrence might fail. Their prophet Joseph Smith had been lynched. The original LDS centers had been destroyed. The Saints had had to flee the territory of the United States, to go far beyond the mountains to carve out a new commonwealth in the desert, only to be tracked down and brought to heel by American democracy, Protestant Christianity, and the United States Army. MX threatened the Kingdom of the Saints. MX was intolerable.

The lawyer from the university got in touch with colleagues from elsewhere and brought in the arms-control propagandist Herb Scoville to agitate. The Church hierarchy complained that MX was A Bad Thing, and contrived an ingenious variant of Romish just-war theory to explain why MX was immoral. Utah's senators, those austere and high-minded conservatives Orrin Hatch and Jake Garn, followed the line.

Elsewhere in the Great Basin is Nevada, which is quite a different polity. Nevada is a reservation for the ferocious last-gasp frontier individualism, reflected in legalized gambling and prostitution, official flouting of national traffic laws, and perhaps the most thoroughly armed private population since the Zulus were forced to break their spears. Nevada, while less doctrinaire, was less than enthusiastic about MX also. Nevada's chief politician, insofar as Nevada can have a chief, was Senator Paul Laxalt, the closest congressional friend of one Ronald Reagan.

## The Weapons Labs Stir

In the 1970s, the weapons labs had to turn their attention to energy research and to other advanced technologies. At Livermore in particular there was enormous interest in controlled fusion, the harnessing of thermonuclear reactions to generate usable energy. Igniting hydrogen with a fission explosive did not lend itself to producing useful heat and electricity, so researchers turned to the possibilities of the high-energy laser to light a slow fire—but, although with some promise, without success. Other various and intermediate stages came to hand.

While most of the veterans in nuclear-weapons design were active, recruitment from university physics departments was drying up. The new blood in the field was young men who came directly to the weapons labs from graduate school. Edward Teller was supervising a network for recruiting promising talent. While no more eccentric and no more alienated than their predecessors, the new men tended to be from the lower middle class and alienated against the liberal establishment. Many of them had studied at the best schools—such as MIT—and despised their professors.

Both Los Alamos and Livermore had regularly sent personnel to Hudson Institute seminars to broaden their perspective as part of the labs' continuing-education programs. There they heard of the benefits of strategic defense and the evils of mutual assured destruction. In the mid-'70s, the young weapons designers were embittered at being pariahs to their scientific peers and the rest of polite society. Their morale noticeably improved toward the 1980s. They were just bursting to say things that they were not permitted to say. The phrase "third-generation weapons" was dropped. Fission was the first, fusion was the second, then what? Coy smiles and well-bitten tongues.

## The Space Cult

A separate story but one which becomes entwined with that of strategic defense is that of the cult of space. The idea of space as a "new frontier" had seized the imagination of some of the world's best minds early in the century, and always had something of a following among the high-tech forward-thinking types. It had early become vulgarized and circulated in mass form by science-fiction writers. Indeed, one space agitator was Jerry Pournelle, who combined popular science writing with science fiction and a little engineering on the side. In 1970 he coauthored a book advocating space defenses with Stephan Possony, an unalloyed old-line hard-line anti-Communist involved in the air-intelligence follies of the '50s, and a consultant to the 1952 Lincoln Summer Study. The book, by the way, "borrowed" Herman's defense-won't-work, will-work-too-well, and-both. Another popularizer was the writer Ben Bova.

The brutal cutback of the space program post-Apollo was a catastrophe to the space venture, which had assumed a straight-line projection to Mars, the outer planets, and the stars. The man-in-the-street had always been skeptical ("What did we get? A bunch of rocks"). When substantial elements of elite America gave up on high-tech, that dished an ambitious space program. (One of the most depressing experiences of the chronicler was briefing the NASA high command in 1971, forecasting that their budget would be low and stagnant, and that their agency would survive as a mobilization base and as a welfare program for aerospace engineers. Wernher von Braun listened dourly, and resigned three weeks later.)

But many enthusiasts did not abandon the vision. Herman didn't, nor did his friend the science-fiction writer Robert Heinlein. They shared with many others a very 18th-century positive vision of the future, combining technological progress, individual enterprise, and popularly-based nationalism. Heinlein's story "The Man Who Sold the Moon" epitomized the syndrome: a private syndicate organizing the first Moon expedition. In fact, only government could raise the resources, and only the high-volume computer could calculate the trajectories.

And governments cared for national prestige, and national security. The first space vehicle was the V-2 rocket, aimed not at the stars, but at London and Antwerp. Military and space hardware was dual-purpose: Any long-range rocket could also loft a satellite. Any satellite could have military reconnaissance or communication functions. Any exoatmospheric antimissile system could also kill a satellite. But space was a poor locale for weapons emplacement—

satellites were too visible and vulnerable. Weapons in space were hard to defend. The concept of space as "a new high ground" was discredited by the rejection of orbital bombardment systems and the dedication of the new low ground for the hardened ICBMs and the new low water for the SLBMs.

Still, the space cult is significant because it had a mass base which took for granted that humanity, and the United States in particular, should go out into space, that wonders could be accomplished there. Space was the future, not endless seminars on arms control, international cooperation, the Third World, limits-to-growth, animal rights, and other irrelevant, futile, and parasitic fashions.

One well-placed space enthusiast was Maxwell Hunter II, sometime chief rocket engineer for Douglas, who had designed all the Nikes, from Ajax to Zeus. In the '60s he did concepts work for a NASA affiliate in Washington before joining the space program of Lockheed. While it is disputed and perhaps indeterminable, Max Hunter may be the inventor of the space shuttle. The concept was adopted by the NASA chief Jim Fletcher in the early '70s, partly for technical reasons, but also to keep the manned space program alive by stretching it out and offering a plausible theory of lower launch costs.

Lockheed's work turned Hunter to space-telescope research: telescopes are optics, optics deal with light, a form of light is Light Amplified by Stimulated Emission of Radiation. Max Hunter's ingenious mind combined the emerging laser technology with his space work and his early and abiding interest in strategic defense. He was conversant, of course, with all the 1950s ABM research and with the concepts of Project Defender. In 1977 he published a personal paper, permitted but not promoted by Lockheed management, advocating a new look at strategic defense, and using BAMBI-Laser as the hook to grab the reader's interest. The paper was circulated throughout the Business by Xerox.

At a conference at the Institute for Foreign Policy Analysis, Hunter was seized upon by Angelo Codevilla, who arranged for his patron Malcolm Wallop to organize briefings for interested members of Congress. Three other experts briefed—Joseph Miller of TRW, Gerald Oulette of Draper Labs, and Norbert Schnog of Perkin-Elmer, the laser specialists; thus "the gang of four." Don Brennan helped prepare the briefings, and took the trouble to query Paul

Nitze about the concept's consistency with SALT. Nitze replied that it was illegal; the treaty unambiguously says, "Each party undertakes not to develop, test or deploy ABM systems or components which are sea-based, air-based, space-based, or mobile land-based." Fritz Hollings listened to the briefing with especial enthusiasm. Scoop Jackson reminded all of his support for ballistic missile defense— and may really have meant to remind them of how badly ABM had ended. Max Hunter gave the concept a veneer of plausibility by casting it in terms of what could be done with a Manhattan Project priority; the congressmen knew well that the conditions for the secrecy and urgency of the atomic-bomb program did not exist and were unlikely to appear. Hunter ruefully knew that too; he was deliberately using the concept as a draft to rekindle the flame of space dominance and strategic defense. Everybody knew that BAMBI-Laser was too iffy and too expensive to fly—except Angelo Codevilla.

## The Return of the Jedi

Ronald Reagan's military experience and interests were decidedly restricted. Before World War II he had been second in command of a Hollywood cavalry troop, committed to polo and venery. Lieutenant Reagan was known for wielding a formidable missile, but not one that the starlets found offensive. As Governor of California in 1969 he had participated in a futile attempt to get the Republican governors to endorse the ABM system. From time to time he made some passing remark in favor of strategic defense, but usually limited himself to generalities about making America strong again.

In his presidential campaigns he made no issue of strategic defense, although appearing in the Republican platform of 1980 was a phrase advocating "a strategic and civil defense which would protect the American people against nuclear war, at least as well as the Soviet population is protected." (Note the error—that strategic defense is something different from civil defense, a confusion arising from the passing of drafts among Madison-group staffers and ignorant pols.)

In a last-ditch stand to save NORAD and to preserve its commander from the shame of being reduced from four stars to three, the CINCNORAD, James Hill, practically opened up Cheyenne Mountain to any and all, and encouraged visitors to tour. They would be shown its impressive visual displays and be told of its wonderful communications capabilities and its far-flung system of sensors of Soviet attack. Someone in the group would inevitably ask what the United States would do when all this expensive and sophisticated equipment warned that the attack was coming in, and the answer, carefully prepared and perfectly precise, was "Nothing." And the good burghers would depart suitably shaken, as intended.

Among the sixty-five thousand visitors per year was a patriotic Hollywood producer named Douglas Morrow, who suggested to his old crony Ronald Reagan that he might find a tour enlightening. Reagan appeared with his aide Martin Anderson. Though entirely innocent of technical and strategic knowledge, Anderson had a good nose for a political strategy, and he urged Reagan to make an issue of strategic defense in the 1980 campaign. Calmer minds prevailed, and Anderson was relegated to the political second echelon of social policy. Another adviser who wanted to make a major issue of defense was General Daniel Graham, USA (retired), an intelligence officer, a canny operator, who became one of the intellectual leaders of the American Security Council, that aviary of decrepit hawks; but he too was denied and left the campaign. The primary goal in the dominant line of the Reaganites was that America had to restore its strength through augmenting its offensive forces.

Named to the top defense job was Caspar Weinberger, a Reagan loyalist and a man of immense personal charm. He knew nothing of defense, and saw no need to distract himself from foreign affairs to learn. He did realize that the campaign rhetoric demanded that something had to be done—and he asked the head of the transition team, William Van Cleve, what to do? This was unfair: Van Cleve was a "strategist" who had done yeoman work in exposing The Soviet Threat and the canards of Mutual Assured Destruction. Why should he be expected to know how to do anything? Weinberger sacked the entire transition team. Not one of them got a Defense Department job. Most of the medium slots in DoD were filled with sound men from the big contractors—the research chief came from TRW, and Boeing folk were scattered about the Building, including T. K. Jones. Pete Aldridge of SPC went in as chief of Air Force research and the National Reconnaissance Office, which ran the overhead program. Fred Ikle was made Undersecretary of Defense for Policy.

Ronald Reagan had originally been a solid New Deal Democrat, and he made a conscious decision to bring Democratic hawks into office. He had a list of candidates at hand. "Democrats for Reagan" had been formed under the nominal command of Admiral Elmo Zumwalt, whose office shared SPC's consultants' floor with Paul Nitze; but the official Democrats blocked the name in court, so the front became the "Committee for an Effective Presidency." Many of the members of the Committee on the Present Danger obtained appointments, and most of the rest honorary positions on advisory commissions and such. Richard Perle was Ikle's assistant, on paper. Ami Hoeber became a Deputy Assistant Secretary of the Army for research and development, where she had some shadowy authority over the doings at Huntsville, White Sands, and Kwajalein. Although Nitze was given the lowest job the administration dared— negotiating to rid us of the incubus of the Schmidt-Carter Euromissiles—he was not too aged to perform political gymnastics, and vaulted himself into control of arms control at State. Because he was still too hot for the flaming Right, the ACDA chair was occupied by a former SRI hand. Washington wags referred to the Committee on the Present Jobs.

As his National Security Adviser, Reagan picked Dick Allen, but he didn't last long. Harry Rowen went into the Agency. Hans Mark, a rare holdover from Carter, was deputy director of NASA. The secondary positions were filled, for the most part, by anonymities. In consequence, for the first time since World War II, the Department of Defense was dominated by the military, which was uneasy with its new role, having become accustomed to stronger political leadership. Fortunately, Shy Meyer of the Army, Lew Allen of the Air Force (who had worked on Zeus warheads at Los Alamos), and John Vessey, as Chairman of the Joint Chiefs, were all top men. But as the administration progressed and the original men were replaced, the quality of the military chiefs declined. Allen's successor as Air Force Chief of Staff declared publicly that an *advantage* of MX was that in war it would require the Soviet Union to attack CONUS.

The new regime was less than boom times for the think tanks. It was the Nixon years all over again—only worse. Anyone who used more than one polysyllabic word in a sentence must be a liberal. The Reagan people distrusted disinterested research and analysis. At a public meeting at the Brookings Institution, the Secretary of the Navy ranted against systems analysis. Everything ideological had to be divisive propaganda. Rand was considered an enemy—and kept on probation. The secessionist RDA was doing more defense business than its parent (and was flush enough to put Sam Cohen on the payroll). Wohlstetter's PanHeuristics kept its modest profile. Dick Foster's SRI shop picked up a little, but not much.

Hudson went from bad to worse. Anglophilia long has afflicted Americans, and Donald Brennan had a severe case. He was smitten by a plausible young Briton with a donnish pipe-smoking demeanor. A more sensitive social observer would have noticed that Colin Gray bore the stigmata of the lower middle class—he was the son of an RAF Bomber Command navigator. Gray's doctoral dissertation supported the massive-retaliation policies of the Eisenhower administration. Then he sojourned in Canada, where, adapting to the prevailing genteel anti-Americanism of the early Trudeau period, he sneered at NORAD and praised SALT I, citing Jay Stone approvingly. He then had a stint at the International Institute for Strategic Studies, where he was in concert with the mutual vulnerability theories prevalent there. Then he failed to get a job with Bernard Brodie at UCLA, and was recruited to Hudson by Brennan.

He made his mark with attacks on the "civilian strategists," and those of RAND in particular. The Air Force loved it. His product was not even on the same continent as early Hudson and RAND analysis, but no one before had dared to write sky-blue propaganda in a pseudoscholarly style. And the man had the incredible ability to repeat the same simple themes in myriad variations. Although lacking citizenship and access to classified material, Gray was able to generate a great deal of work from the Air Force.

Colin Gray was the right man at the right time. In the 1970s, there was no longer any real need for nuclear-strategic analysis, because all the valid ideas had been worked out in the '50s and elaborated to decadence in the '60s. What was needed was raw propaganda. Perversely, his notoriety was the work of the arms controllers, who promoted his reputation in order to discredit the hawks. They published his essays, which should have been considered a parody of the "war-fighting" school, claiming that America needed a credible theory of victory in a nuclear war. Warnke had the reply ready: sure, we "win," and the "winner" looks like Bangladesh in the aftermath. Although hundreds of men were more qualified, Gray was chosen as "token hawk" on a Carter administration arms-control panel that included Warnke, John Culver, Panofsky, and the president of Rand; Gray characterized the deliberations as "treason in high places," although he was not yet a U.S. citizen.

The 1970s had not been prosperous years for Donald Brennan in any professional or personal sense. He had peaked with the ABM fight. His ambitions far outranged his capabilities. Bill Schneider had put him in touch with the Buckleys, and he imagined he might be the Conservative Party candidate for U.S. senator. When J. Edgar Hoover died, Brennan fancied that he should be the director of *the* Bureau. He had no new ideas; his occasional attempts to float a minor strategic or arms-control concept were shot down by his colleagues in internal review.

His wife, Katie, was stricken with cancer and took an interminable time dying, lovingly nurtured by her husband. His last mistress was her West Indian nurse, whom he put through law school. And he became embroiled in a peculiar intrigue with the Chinese Communists. His connections with his former arms-control colleagues were nearly severed, and the last straw which infuriated him was when Paul Warnke became chief of ACDA and terminated his consultancy. There were also financial problems, because Brennan, while not living high, enjoyed the pleasures of the flesh and the table. The chronic financial crises of Hudson cut into his income. And Colin Gray was intriguing behind Brennan's back to seize control of Hudson's national-security research. Gray's ambition was not improper; Herman had long since nearly abandoned the field, and Brennan was rather less than productive, so Gray and a few henchmen had reason to believe that they were carrying the rest of the Institute on their backs.

It was Don Brennan's custom to work late in the evening and

leave instructions to his secretary on the tape recorder. In April 1980 his secretary listened to this tape:

> Hi Mary,
>    I'm sorry about the nature of this message, which I don't imagine that you'll appreciate getting and in many ways I don't appreciate leaving everybody this way, but I've become pretty well convinced that it's the most sensible thing for me to do. My financial circumstances have gotten simply terrible, even on full salary—that is to say, I'm on the ragged edge of bankruptcy as it stands—and of course the Institute situation is such that I would probably imminently have to go on three days a week, and there is no way I can meet current bills on that basis. So I was going to have to do something. The problem is exacerbated by the fact that my productivity on official reports has sort of gone to hell, and I don't have reports in hand for either DCPA [civil defense] or the DNA [Defense Nuclear Agency] escalation study, to say nothing of the old Air Force [contract] problem, and this has interacted with my energy in getting new contracts and that of course in turn interacts with the financial situation. Anyway, the only way I can see for anyone to pay up my bills is to use the insurance money, of which there is quite a bit, and my equity in the pension fund account, of which there is also quite a bit, and beyond that, there is a certain sense in which I have just simply grown tired of doing things like the DCPA study and the Air Force study and so on.
>    So why not choose a relatively pleasant and painless way out under the circumstances when at least I can arrange to take care of the major obligations that I shall be leaving behind.

He left directions for notifying kin and friends, his obituary for *The New York Times,* and some notes on winding up the boring contracts. The police found him with a shotgun—not against the calculating head but against the mere heart. A tremor went through the strategic community. In Bonn, Helmut Schmidt asked, had Brennan become demoralized by the tendency of the world? His ideas were on the upswing, and he had just been named to candidate Reagan's honorary defense advisory board. The tragedy seems to have had no more significant cause than a sense of personal failure. When he bought his Cadillac in the late '60s he had calculated that the probability of being killed did not warrant the annoyance of safety belts; indeed, the cost–benefit analysis proved it a worthwhile investment to pay to have them removed. In 1980, Don Brennan's calculation was that his own life was no longer cost-beneficial. But perhaps the very success of "MAD" did Don in—when the term became part of the common vocabulary, what need had the world of Brennan?

Gray succeeded him as director of national-security studies. After acquiring his U.S. citizenship, he fell in with an intriguing man believed to be an ex-spook and absconded with Hudson's defense contracts, to set up shop as a naked Air Force pitchman. Partly in desperation and partly because nuclear-warfare issues were again in the forefront of public attention, Herman went back to the topic that had made him famous. He was able to trot out his old ideas, and find them as new as ever—although less marketable than in the early '60s, because the intellectual standards of the high public audience had sunk so low. Still, old friends in the Building were willing to bail him out with subsidy contracts—for a time.

## The Dismemberment of Ma Bell

In 1974, the long-dreaded antitrust attack was thrown at Ma Bell. Despite the unified opposition of everybody with any sense, a coalition of left-wing and right-wing ideologues moved to dismember the American Telephone and Telegraph Company. The Defense Department was appalled—because AT&T was the vital element of the U.S. communications system. Ma Bell's rep manned a battle station in Cheyenne Mountain, outranking all mere colonels. The military well knew that hundreds of millions in communications costs were off-budget, being paid on the rate base. More ominous was the prospect of having to deal with dozens of telephone companies to maintain and to adapt the national communications network. (Without central control, the continental all-digit long-distance dialing system would not have been possible.)

To help make its case, AT&T engaged Dick Foster's shop to defend the national-security benefits of the existing single web. SRI compared the consequences of breakup to "paraplegia due to a severed spinal cord." Others pointed out that a dismembered telephone system would lack the resources to support the Bell Telephone Laboratories. The courts were not persuaded. In 1982, AT&T capitulated, and Ma Bell consented to be torn asunder.

## The Reagan Strategy

Fortunately for the country, the Reagan people arrived to find that the job of planning the defense buildup had already been accomplished by Harold Brown and his crew. Brown had programmed a well-thought-out and highly competent scheme for expanding U.S. forces over the next five years. On the offensive side, the Brown program included shell-game deployment of 200 MXs in the Great Basin, the Trident submarines, and air-launched cruise missiles for the bombers. But the Reagan people had to do something different.

The campaign rhetoric would suggest a quick-fix program, à la Kennedy-McNamara in 1961. Many lists had been prepared, by Herman among others. The B-1 bomber cut by Carter was restored. One man in the new administration who knew exactly what he wanted was John Lehman, one of the several aggressive young men whom the President found amusing; Lehman demanded the Navy secretaryship, and having got it, he wanted surface ships, so the strategic balance was to be rectified by additional aircraft carriers and demothballed battleships. This was to be the Reagan administration's major response to the Soviet threat. Military matters for several years would be befuddled by talk of a "maritime strategy." The fleet would fight through waves of Soviet bombers, gunboats, and submarines, and launch its handful of light bombers against the massed Soviet Troops of Air Defense. The sailors were less sanguine than Lehman, although no one could deny that fleet air defenses were puissant—the U.S.S. *America* was better defended than the United States of America.

The menace of the heavy-throwweight Soviet weapons was answered by continuing the Brown program to junk our heavy-throwweight Titan missiles, and in 1983 the administration committed itself to the tiny-throwweight Midgetman missile. The intolerable SALT II treaty was handled by an announcement that the new administration would adhere to its terms. SALT was relabeled START, and the administration demanded deep slashes in Soviet offensive forces, rather like the cuts that Carter had sought, and provoking Soviet belly laughs for his trouble. The arms controllers were inflamed—how dare the Reaganites ask for something the Soviets would surely refuse! To be sure, that was why they asked for deep cuts. Few troubled to mention that even very deep cuts would have not affected the vital issue—that the Soviets could still put America out of business in half an hour. The survival of the nation depended on the choice of the Soviet party bosses and generals.

On the defense, well . . . Bill Schneider was blackballed from DoD with the rest of the transition team. But a valuable consolation prize was the chief defense job in the budget bureau, where he had the agreeable task of taking the money that his colleagues stripped from domestic programs and jamming it into the defense budget. He was careful not to ignore ballistic missile defense research, and screwed it up as fast as he could.

**Ballistic Missile Defense (millions current $)**

|                     | 1980 | 1981 | 1982 | 1983 | 1984  |
|---------------------|------|------|------|------|-------|
| Last Carter Budget  | 241  | 268  | 346  | 410  | ——    |
| First Reagan Budget | 241  | 267  | 462  | 930  | 1,055 |

Some of the increase can be attributed to inflation—but most to Bill Schneider.

Brown had put plenty into command and control, and the Reaganites upped his ante. (The civilian Pentagon $C^3$ chief was Donald Latham, author of an intelligent pro–civil defense book in the '60s.) MITRE prospered with $C^3$, as did most of the technical consultants. Air Force plans for the upgrade of the archaic BMEWS radars were already in the program. Prospects for more ambitious strategic defense were the topic of the 1981 summer study of the Defense Science Board. The study was nominally headed by a political operator named Tom Reed—ex-Livermore and sometime Secretary of the Air Force under Ford (and who once had spoken publicly in favor of launch-on-warning). The project was actually run by Verne Lynn, ex–Lincoln Labs, the strategic defense chief in DoDR&E. Some familiar names appear: Fletcher, Nitze, Pittman, Schneider, Ron Easley of SPC, Bob Everett of MITRE, and Roberta Wohlstetter.

There were others from Lincoln Labs and MITRE, and people from McDonnell Douglas, TRW, Boeing, Livermore, and FEMA. Some old BMD hands included General C. J. LeVan (now retired and with RDA), Julian Davidson (ex-ABMDA), Vic Kupelian, Dan Fink of GE, and General Grayson Tate, the BMDO commander. The conclusions of the summer study were—yes, but no big deal; and nothing in hand could reliably defend MX.*

## JUSCADS

NORAD may have hit a new low, but did not disappear; indeed, it could not disappear. The paper wars were still being fought, and while the United States had a long lead, the Soviets would surely catch up with cruise missiles. So it became necessary to think about a defense against them. These gadgets were probably overrated, because there were all manner of ingenious countermeasures, up to and including merely putting up a high fence to block their terrain-hugging.

With the renewal of the NORAD agreement in 1978, the two parties arranged to conduct a joint study of future requirements— the Joint United States–Canada Air Defense Study (JUSCADS— "jus-cads"). SPC was a major contributor to the study, and Pete Aldridge was a leading analyst. The recommendations were to liquidate the remnants of the 1950s deployment and replace them. SAGE was a museum piece. The same could be said of the fighters—the American F-106s and the Canadian CF-101s were older than the pilots who flew them. Twenty years of radar development had made the pathetic remainder of the North American defense net obsolete.

The new administration continued the evolution of the plan, under the lead of the Undersecretary of the Air Force, Aldridge. A new system was to be put into place—not an impressive one, but at least modern, and sufficient to deny the other side a free ride. The DEW line was to be entirely replaced with a North Warning System and the continent ringed by perimeter coverage of radars. On the coasts the long-delayed Over-the-Horizon Backscatter radar was to go into

*A product of the study was a quick-and-dirty SPC history of strategic defense coauthored by Cliff McLain. It attempted to estimate expenditures for strategic defense back to the beginning of the Cold War. Unfortunately, the authors disregarded the largest defense item— the passive defense of the strategic forces. Very roughly two-thirds of the offensive-forces budget went for their defenses.

service. The key element was to be AWACS planes, to look down on the low-flying attackers. Of course modern computers were available. And a rich civilian air-traffic-control net had been made necessary by the burgeoning air travel of the '70s and '80s, and some interface could be arranged.

New fighters were programmed for air defense. The classic McDonnell F-4s were given dual roles for possible deployment overseas and for continental air defense. A few of the first-line F-15 fighters were assigned to continental air defense. Canada made a complicated deal for reequipment of its Air Defense Group with McDonnell's naval fighter, labeled the CF-18 north of the border. The last of the SAGE sites, the North Bay command bunker of Canadian air defense, was closed down in 1983 and part of its equipment shipped down to Boston to take an honored place in the computer museum along the Charles.

The planned revamping of NORAD wasn't much. Compared with what the Soviets had, it was nothing. The Soviets were finally working up a new long-range bomber, labeled "Blackjack." And the rule what-we-can-do, he-can-do still applied—the new NORAD would have to face Soviet cruise missiles.

### Ronald Reagan's Strategic Defense Debacle

In civil defense the Carter administration had left behind a reasonable program, considering the political climate. Reagan's people polished up PD 41 as NSDD 26. But the FEMA appointments were cronies of Edwin Meese, and Yarmolinsky's Rule was pushed to the extreme. Attempts to continue exercising the crisis relocation plans ran into stiff opposition in some local communities. A new accusation against civil defense appeared—that it was a Reaganite plot to persuade people that nuclear war is survivable. Ronald Dellums, the congressman from Berkeley, had wormed his way onto the House Armed Services Committee and gained seniority, so he had to be neutralized by being given responsibility for something that didn't matter—civil defense. Dellums had said that "America is all niggers," and seemed to favor a national lynching by the U.S.S.R. Civil defense funding could not get by that obstacle.

The White House gave up the fight. Over at the Pentagon, T. K. Jones protested, and was told to keep his damn-fool mouth shut.

Yes, the administration declared it favored civil defense, but did not push it on the Congress—it was the Johnson regime all over again, only worse. The civil defense agency wasn't doing anything at all. By the mid-'80s, the civil defense budget was cut to pre-1950 levels. No official at FEMA had the word "civil defense" in his job title. The miserable remnant looked back to the Carter years as a golden age. Jerome Weisner gloated.

Brown's people had also worked up a response to the Soviet antisatellite weapon—an Air Force system of an F-15 fighter plus the HIT nonnuclear missile originally designed by ARPA for ballistic missile defense. The opposition decided that it was A Bad Thing— it was Escalating the Arms Race: again demonstrating their belief that the way to prevent a race was to let the other side win in a walk. An aide to Senator Kennedy labeled the U.S. ASAT effort "Star Wars."

## Fratricide

On the strategic side, the early Reagan administration concentrated on finding a credible basing scheme for MX. Reagan had promised his friend Laxalt and the Utah senators that he would kill the shell game—but what to put in its place? All the ideas tried and rejected in the '70s were trotted out again, and gone over again, and again found wanting. An ingenious Air Force officer did score the unbelievable achievement of coming up with a new idea. As before and always the offense and the defense work together. The planning of attacks on ICBM silos had to take into account the effects of the blast of warheads upon following warheads. So elaborate calculations and underground experiments were made to assess the "fratricide" effect. Fratricide was turned on its head for defense. "Dense pack" was an ingenious idea; instead of the ordinary dispersion of missile silos so that each one had to be separately targeted, dense pack jammed them close together, so that the fratricide effects of attacking missiles prevented the silos from being attacked simultaneously. Pity that further analysis indicated that the enemy had too many plausible ways to overcome it, not the least of which was earth-penetrating warheads that would create shock waves to crush all the missile eggs in their nests—and generate tons of radioactive fallout to pollute the entire nation.

Another devilish countermeasure to the dense-pack defense was a "pin-down" attack, whereby the enemy would keep exploding warheads over the missile patch, filling the air with blast, debris, and radiation to prevent a launch between attacks. This would require quantities of megatonnage and precision of attack timing that were astonishingly high, but not incredible. Something else had to be tried. One advantage of dense pack, however, was that with the missiles jammed together, they could be more easily defended by a simple BMD system. The coverage need not be large, and the "threat tube," or avenue of approach, for ICBMs was fairly narrow and could be monitored fairly easily. In the end, the administration disavowed the "window of vulnerability" and put a few dozen MXs in the old Minuteman silos—not an appreciable augmentation of the offensive, and just as vulnerable as before.

The administration came to power full of the rhetoric of the war-fighting school of nuclear strategy, expressed in terms of "protracted" nuclear war. This was a short-term fix of The Problem—and the reason that Brown's people and Reagan's people took such interest in command and control. Maybe we couldn't win in a few hours, and maybe we couldn't win at all, but at least we could threaten to fight on and in defeat bring down the Soviet Union with us. Not an attractive prospect, but a credible threat to the other side. In the first eighteen months or so of its reign, the public statements of the Reagan administration were perfectly sensible and consistent with that line, and in the chronicler's judgment, admirably accurate in formulation, with a few minor rhetorical excesses. The opposition propounded the lie that the United States had never before been interested in nuclear war-fighting, only in "deterrence." Only that evil Reagan conceived of the abomination. So the administration line was not well received by the press, by substantial elements of academia, by officials of Allied governments, by the Soviet Union, and by large numbers of middle-class voting Americans. The notions that a nuclear war was unthinkable, unspeakable, and unwinnable had sunk in so deep that it was politically very dangerous to try to dig them out.

One unfortunate excess was laid on poor T. K. Jones, who was nailed by a lefty reporter late at night and blurted out, "With enough shovels, we'll all get through" a nuclear war. He was merely making the ancient civil defense case that most people would survive a nuclear war if they got away from the targets and got under cover; but the quote was stripped from the context of the broader interview and used to sandbag the administration. Nothing more was heard publicly from T. K. Jones after that.

## The Threat from America

Recall that in the 1950s and early 1960s the world was terrified by Soviet weaponry and threats; in the late 1970s and the early 1980s the Soviet Union had the weapons, but rarely made overt threats against anyone. Soviet propaganda was all sweet peace and harmony, merely advocating a recognition of the new realities of Soviet power in the world. In order to generate political support for the weaponry to counter the Soviet buildup, the rearmament advocates had to scream to high heaven to make the case of the Soviet threat. So the American hawks were broadcasting the Soviet threats against America and Europe. In the meantime, the Soviets had moved a long way from being the primitive goons of Stalin to roughly approximating the polished thugs of Wall Street and Madison Avenue.

When you pull on a cloth, the weakest threads give way first. To be sure, the rearmament agitation had the desired effect of bolstering the forces, but it had a debilitating effect on weaker constitutions. Millions of people, particularly in the more socially demoralized elements of the society—elite universities and media, atheist clergy, and pseudoeducated housewives—became threatened by the threat itself. It was civil defense all over again: It was not the Russians who were making all these terrible noises about nuclear war. In any event, we couldn't do anything about the Russians. So, fed by a residue of the late 1960s' antiestablishmentarianism at home and anti-Americanism abroad, pressure against the buildup built.

Although the Soviet-threat rhetoric was the trigger, it can be argued that the underlying basis was much more fundamental, as had been described by Herman nearly twenty years earlier:

> Even though the balance of terror suggests that the weapons
> have negated each other, this is not true. . . . there will remain
> a residual fear of war that would not exist if the weapons had

really canceled each other out completely. Under these conditions, the two antagonists will be living under a sword of Damocles; there will be pressures to evolve other arrangements for keeping peace. These pressures will result in both responsible and irresponsible arms control, in "ban-the-bomb" and "peace" movements. Either power might try to exploit these movements and the residual fear of war in order to disarm its opponent or at least to manipulate internal political movements of the other side to its own advantage. Each power will be able to develop persuasive arguments as to why the other side should make political concessions or accommodations to reduce the tensions as a prelude to bilateral disarmament negotiations. It can even create pressures on the other side for unilateral disarmament, or at least manufacture special situations . . . that create tremendous pressures for unilateral initiatives—"to break out of this self-fulfilling prophecy" or "arms race trap." Either power then, for example, might say, "One of us has to be responsible and it isn't going to be me, so it has to be you," or at least make it clear that initiatives will not come from itself: If they are to come, they will have to come from the other side.

In 1959, John F. Kennedy told an audience that the consequence of Eisenhower's deterrence-by-massive-retaliation doctrine was "The only choice is all or nothing at all, world devastation or submission." In 1969, Richard Nixon said the same thing rather better: that a President needed choices other than "suicide or surrender." Think on that—is suicide or surrender a choice? Would any decent or responsible person destroy his own country or devastate the world? Of course not. The only option is surrender. None would say it openly, but even the responsible (as distinguished from the hustler) hawks would surrender. While the advocates of mutual vulnerability proclaimed that deterrence would surely work, quietly they said they would surrender in the crunch. In an 1981 interview reminiscing about Project Charles, Jerrold Zacharias avowed that the lesson MIT had to teach America was summed up in this scenario: if the Soviets laid on a demonstration strike against one or two cities, our response should be to do nothing. Carl Kaysen nodded his agreement. While the economist Paul Samuelson remarked tartly that doing nothing might be extremely difficult in those circumstances, none of the assembled Cambridgites contradicted Zacharias. From a Hudson staffer who attended a Cambridge seance in the early '80s: "You know what they are teaching? They're teaching how to surrender!" Back in the '50s, Bertrand Russell was old and foolish enough to state the Cambridge position openly—negotiate, and if negotiations fail, surrender. "Better Red than Dead." Rather less than a robust negotiating position with Reds.

So the administration stopped talking about war-fighting and stuck to good old Deterrence, and pretty well got itself off the hook. In late 1983, the President told the Japanese Diet, "No one would win a nuclear war." No reporter had the wit to query the response of the parliamentarians from Hiroshima and Nagasaki. Later Richard Perle told the Senate Armed Services Committee that U.S. strategy was Deterrence, so it didn't matter if a nuclear war would destroy the world, and it was just as well if people thought it would.

## The Freeze

The domestic opposition, faced with a widespread public belief that the Soviet Union was dangerous and that a defense buildup was desirable to head it off, had to resort to other tactics. Nuclear policy is not terribly complicated, but not simple enough for a thirty-second television pitch, so the Freeze was born. There should be a "mutual and verifiable freeze on the testing, production, and further deployment of nuclear warheads, missiles, and other delivery systems; [with] special attention to de-stabilizing weapons." The principal document promoting the Freeze, written by Edward Kennedy's staff, was a compendium of the academic strategy—and illustrates the debasement of the strategic debate. The Chaysner anti–ABM book was Clausewitz by comparison. Especially objectionable were the conventional lies about civil defense, buttressed by a cynical denial of John Kennedy's civil defense initiative.

Among the "defense, foreign-policy, and scientific experts" who signed off on the Freeze fraud were many familiar names—Richard Barnet, Hans Bethe, Clark Clifford, John Culver, William Fulbright, William Foster, Mort Halperin, Seymour Melman, Herb Scoville, Jay Stone, Paul Warnke, Adam Yarmolinsky, and Herb York. From Cambridge were Abram Chayes, Paul Doty, Bernard Feld, Roger Fisher, George Kistiakowsky, Philip Morrison, George Rathjens, and—need it be said?—Jerome Wiesner. And some younger men who were running for SecDef in the next Democratic administration endorsed it. For the record, give credit to the names that are missing—among them, Harold Brown, McGeorge Bundy, Richard Garwin, and Robert McNamara.

At bottom, the Freeze was founded on a few buzzwords from the academic strategy—"arms race," "overkill," "action–reaction syndrome." It was a great marketing success, and it spread like fallout. And once again, people in the Business were called upon for token representation of the forces of evil "to give the other side" in phony debates. Again the Hudson Institute people took the road, and among them, the chronicler found himself at a dog-and-pony show for the American Association of University Women, coordinated by a mannish sociologist who spat "Reagan" like an epithet. Each worthy speaker gave a pitch for one thing or another—Congresswoman Ferraro laid it on for strengthening national security with aid to education. But something was missing. The beleaguered husband of a university woman approached the chronicler at the end of the meeting to say, "Nobody even mentioned the Freeze."

"Of course not. Everybody knows it's a hustle. We can't verify the nonproduction and nondeployment of nuclear weapons without turning the whole world into a police state tougher than Stalin imagined. Every log beside your fireplace could be a nuclear weapon."

A more amusing nonevent was a soiree at a minor university. Roughly from Right to Left were the chronicler, a State Department lady, the Freeze Lady, the Reverend William Sloane Coffin. The State Department lady gives the Reagan administration party line, which is repulsively tacky, and she is not yet sufficiently experienced at lying, so her voice cracks. More interesting is Randall Forsberg, the Freeze Lady. She learned strategy as a secretary at the Swedish International Peace Research Institute, which is widely believed to be a KGB front, but which I believe is actually a clever psychological defense operation of the Swedish secret police. Whoever picked her as front person pulled off a minor political coup. She is unthreatening and uncompetitive to a female audience. Her offices are in Wellesley, just up the road from Cambridge. On her letterhead is the name George Rathjens. Dully, she recites the academic strategy, and the specious history of the bomber gap and the missile gap, *ad infinitum.*

Then the true face of the enemy is exposed: the Reverend William

Sloane Coffin, sometime chaplain of Yale and now pastor of what was the Rockefellers' Riverside Church. He has not taken the trouble to learn even the most elementary aspects of the subject—his repertory is demagogic one-liners for extracting laughs from the sort of students who have nothing better to do than attend this sort of thing. The degenerative mind cannot stick to the subject for more than two minutes. Coffin wanders all over the anti-American landscape—touching Nicaragua, dwelling rather too long on supposed contra atrocities.

Rarely is something learned at these shows. But the chronicler recalls gossip about perverse goings-on at Riverside Church and takes note of the good Reverend's blasted eyes and remembers the same eyes on Senator John Culver, and thinks of all the "peace" polemicists who linger so longingly and lovingly on the gruesome horrors of nuclear war and who oppose attempts at mitigation, nay, reacting with revulsion to lifesaving, nation-saving, civilization-saving measures. Of course—these people *like* the vision of nuclear destruction. It turns them on. This is not policy. This is not ideology. This is nihilism. (At the closing, Coffin slaps the chronicler on the back—rather too hard.) The chronicler is refreshed. Our side may be thick with ordinary hustlers and cranks, but they have commonplace weaknesses; our people are not evil.

When the chronicler's turn comes, he offers what is essentially a ten-minute version of this book. He describes The Problem of restraining Soviet expansion in Eurasia (afterward, the fascinated State Department lady asks if this is written down somewhere; what do they teach their people at State?), and the theory and practice of deterrence, of the second-strike and of the not-incredible first-strike capability. "Borrowing" one of Herman's lines, he describes deterrence-by-reprisal as a lousy system, but the best we can do now, because the options are worse. Surrender won't work because the country is better armed than Afghanistan (with innuendo that the likes of Coffin will be executed before the occupiers arrive). Counterforce won't work because we cannot count on getting all the other side's forces. Civil defense is too expensive and/or cannot accomplish enough to secure the nation. But there is a long-shot way out: not today, but sometime in the future, it might be possible to design effective active defenses against nuclear attack; it might even be possible to conduct a nuclear war in which nobody gets hurt.

This was early in 1983; had anyone remembered, the speaker would have seemed impressively influential or prescient. He was merely keeping the flame alive. The bulk of the audience has to be written off as social offal, but afterward the speaker is approached by two young men—one seriously concerned that America can be destroyed, the other already knowledgeable about space reconnaissance technology from public sources—both lower-middle-class, both promising material for the Business. So the talk is a success.

## The Bishops Crack

The defense cannot be separated from the offense, or anything else either. As a consequence of the internal history of the American branch of the Roman Catholic Church in the mid–20th century, its staff was infiltrated by men who had gone down the path to perdition long since trodden by Protestants and Jews—toward making religion "relevant" in secular terms, which meant adapting the principles and programs of ecclesiastical institutions to whatever slogans were fashionable in the better universities last year. As academia became reagitated about nuclear war, so did the church staffs, who infected their superiors, the bishops. Manipulated by a superstitious fanatically antinuclear Jesuit, with the counsel of a screwball Yale professor, they evolved a crackpot combination of the academic strategy with traditional "just-war doctrine" (which had never guided the Roman Church in any of its thousands of wars).

Herman Kahn and Frank Armbruster tried to influence the bishops' deliberations in favor of defense advocacy, to no avail. The position that evolved was that nuclear weapons were A Bad Thing good only for "deterrence," and not for burning cities, because civilians should not be targeted—which if accepted would have meant that the Soviet Union would base its weaponry in its cities and pound the United States to rubble while the bishops prayed. This was not exactly what Saint Augustine had intended when he ginned up just-war theory to encourage the decadent Roman Empire to fight. Of course, the Soviets wouldn't take this sort of thing seriously, nor would any responsible American. Nonetheless, the Reagan administration, having made a befuddled public defense of its strategy, panicked. Unlike their Protestant and Jewish counterparts, the Roman clergy retained some vestige of moral influence. Many members of the administration, and the Right in general, were old-style flaming Papists. Over half the officer corps was of the Roman persuasion.

## Building the Political Defense

Danny Graham's "High Frontier" was a wizard packaging job. In a single ball of publicity wax, he tied up numerous strands: the need for U.S. strategic superiority, the Soviet space threat, high technology, nostalgia for the frontier, and capitalist investment—the economic benefits of going into space would more than pay the tab. But always up front was defense—ballistic missile defense, to be achieved in some manner. The High Frontier program was a potpourri of ideas that had been generated long ago and rejected as impractical and/or too expensive. To enthusiasts like Graham this was not an objection, nor was the little detail that the short-term BMD to be achieved through interceptors from "off-the-shelf components" was referring to a fictional shelf. The laser battle station down the path did not exist at all except as a promising concept. High Frontier's costs were estimated as no more than a tenth of what any responsible person would forecast. An effective cost-cutting calculation was the reduction of the number of space satellites over Soviet territory by the expedient of assuming that interceptor missiles would be fired fifty-three seconds *before* ICBM launch. And never mind Graham's assertion that an anti–ballistic missile defense could be built without violating the treaty prohibiting anti–ballistic missile defense.

Originally, the project was located at the Heritage Foundation, bankrolled by Karl Bendetson. Soon Graham determined to go into business for himself, with funding from Reagan's "kitchen cabinet" friend Justin Dart, and proselytized vigorously. Initially, he gathered to his banner many of the enthusiasts for strategic defense, including John Bosma, Frank Hoeber, Cresson Kearny, Arnold Kramish (ex-RAND), Orlando Johnson (Boeing), and Robert Pfaltzgraff. Some of those he enlisted were later embarrassed by the association of their names with his operation.

He wrote book after book that said the same thing, made quite a noise, and persuaded a lot of people to believe that he was the guru of strategic defense, but his influence in Washington was extremely limited because of his affectation of the persona of a genially transparent rogue. His private remarks exhibited the prudence and precision appropriate to a responsible general officer, but Danny Graham was better remembered as one of the intelligence officers who had helped provide the politic Vietnam numbers useful to Johnson and McNamara.

Angelo Codevilla, embittered at not obtaining an administration job, waged a guerrilla against the Pentagon's advanced laser program, which was deferring development of existing lasers in favor of research on more promising concepts. A Defense Science Board study group headed by Johnny Foster was dubious about the potential of existing laser efforts. Codevilla was convinced that his study of Aristotle gave him better understanding of intelligence than the entire intelligence establishment, and gave him more technical competence than the entirety of the defense science establishment. His thrust for rapid deployment of more immediate technology was useful to his patron, Senator Wallop of Wyoming, site of the Warren Minuteman fields. Wallop was a high-flying hawk, but also deeply concerned about the exposure of his state to a Soviet ICBM attack, and conscious of survivalistic sentiment among his mountaineer constituents. Wallop leaned on the President.

Another influence was Edward Teller, who was selling the "third-generation" ideas of his protégés with a vengeance. In 1981, one of the most fantastic concepts was leaked—Excalibur. Instead of using a laser to ignite fusion, bright young men at Livermore turned the process on its head, using fusion to drive a laser, to explode a thermonuclear weapon and aim its energy at a long distance, instead of letting it dissipate spherically, as in the first two generations of nuclear weapons. It was Al Latter's X-ray warhead with the energy channeled through a laser. Hard to think of some way to use Excalibur on Earth, but what about in space? And what might it be aimed at? Edward Teller was a great enthusiast for the concept. He had the ear of George Keyworthy, the President's Science Adviser, a Los Alamos man. And Edward Teller had direct access to the President.

The military also weighed in a peculiar way. An effective vacuum at the top of the Department of Defense had given them far more clout than they had had since the days of Harry Truman. They sought to restore the good old days of strategic superiority, yet they could also read the national mood. Bruised by dozens of fights with Congress, the soldiers recognized the increasing difficulty of bolstering the offensive forces, which left the defense as the only way out of the trap created by The Problem. General Vessey, the canny Chairman of the Joint Chiefs, had long been a strategic-defense sympathizer.

Teller had gotten to Admiral Watkins, the Chief of Naval Operations—not an aircraft-carrier admiral, but a nuclear-submariner, one of Hyman Rickover's boys, who had trust that competent and dedicated men could solve complicated problems. James Watkins was a devout Roman Catholic, a sincere man. He cared about his country more than he cared about aircraft carriers. In early 1983, the Admiral exercised his prerogative to give direct counsel to his Commander-in-Chief.

# THE DEFENSE

# DISCOMBOBULATED

*That is not to say that effective active defenses against the missile are technically impossible, or that their development should not be pursued; it is only to point out that one must have extraordinary faith in technology, or a despair of alternatives, to depend mainly on active defenses. The relevant problems are political and social as well as technological.*
BERNARD BRODIE

**R**onald Reagan's speech of 23 March 1983 toppled a row of rhetorical dominoes. Most of the content of the address dealt with decreasing reliance on nuclear weapons—the old RAND–liberal establishment–McNamara thrust of a generation earlier. Nine paragraphs gained all the attention, and they were carefully crafted. The President did not speak of making nuclear weapons "impotent and obsolete" but only long-range ballistic missiles; nor did he specify how this was to be achieved; nor did he offer a timetable; nor did he make any promise of deployment; nor did he use the phrase "strategic defense initiative," or even "strategic defense." All that came later. The initial document, National Security Decision Directive #85, was clearly titled "Eliminating the Threat from Ballistic Missiles." Reportedly, Reagan's single insistence was that the initiative be promoted as population defense. Defense of the deterrent is a professional issue that glazes the eyes of the populace; defending the people is something the people can understand.

Everyone in the Business was taken by surprise. The normal pro-

431

cedure is to research an innovation thoroughly, passing it through myriad committees to gain consensus and spread the word, and preparing the ground for its acceptance by disseminating favorable information. In this case, however, the usual procedure would have been counterproductive—so many players would have tried to abort the proposal in the womb. A directive by the Commander-in-Chief was necessary to whip the troops into line.

But what did he mean? Immediately at hand was a recent paper on space laser battle stations by Max Hunter in the classified *Journal of Defense Research*. Yes, it was BAMBI-Laser redux. The press picked up on the Kennedy staffer's sneer at ASAT and called the concept "Star Wars." Poor Weinberger and the White House and Pentagon flacks displayed their ignorance by talking of a perfect shield, and the opposition immediately shouted that any such thing was fantastic. And the public hype concentrated on space-based directed-energy systems—which were the most far-out and farthest from policy revelance.

And in response to sharp reminders that a perfect defense would provide cover for an American first strike, and thus be the very antithesis of making nuclear ballistic missiles "impotent and obsolete," the President glibly suggested that the United States might share its BMD with the Soviet Union—such information surely would assist the other side in degrading the perfection of the defense.

The administration named the whatever "The Strategic Defense Initiative," which immediately became SDI (ess-dee-eye), and SDI shortly came to mean ballistic missile defense. Civil defense and air defense presently followed passive defense of the strategic offensive forces down the memory tube.

A committee to take a quick-and-dirty look at the relevant technologies was appointed. The Defensive Technologies Study Team was headed by Jim Fletcher and included Harold Agnew, David Packard, Michael May of Livermore, Dan Fink of General Electric, and people from ARPA, Bell Labs, Lincoln Labs, Livermore, Los Alamos, MITRE, Raytheon, and RDA. Their mandate was to examine far-out stuff that might conceivably give perfect cover, not anything capable of short-term deployment. The contract was put through IDA.

Over in the Pentagon, Ikle and Perle, taken by surprise like everyone else, jumped into the fray and commissioned another committee to look into the strategic implications of SDI, and put the very best of the old hands on the job. Nominally headed by Fred Hoffman, the Future Security Strategy Study included Charlie Herzfeld, Frank Hoeber, C. J. LeVan, Andy Marshall, Larry O'Neill, Harry Rowen, Leon Schloss, and, of course, Albert Wohlstetter.

In the fall, Fletcher reported that there might be something to it—and had the draft kicked back by presidential Science Adviser Keyworthy; then reported that there might be a little more to it than that; had the report rejected again; then concluded that there definitely might be something to it—and the White House was satisfied. The results then were leaked to *Aviation Week*. Fletcher emphasized the potential of the layered defense—enough imperfect layers can become almost perfect.

The Hoffman team's output is one of the most brilliantly crafted reports that the chronicler has ever read. It didn't say that a reliable Star Wars defense of population was impracticable, but maybe something for the next century. It didn't advocate exploiting the loophole in the SALT treaty of anti–tactical ballistic missile defense, merely implying such a ploy in a masterpiece of *laissez-entendre*. The Hoffman report wasn't at all sexy and was publicly disregarded. Hardly noticed was that the 1983 Summer Study topic of the Defense Science Board was ATBM—Roberta Wohlstetter participated. Now the token conservative in the Department of State, Bill Schneider was deeply involved in the consultations with European allies.

The Air Force was delighted, and crafted a chart giving it total control, completely ignoring the Army's BMD research and the Army's mission in continental missile defense. Initially, the Army did not respond; it had been burned too badly in the past. Two years later, the Ballistic Missile Defense Organization was relabeled the Strategic Defense Command and its chief given a third star. Its first commander had no background whatever in the field. The Navy did nothing at all—except sweat privately in fear that strategic defense might divert resources from defense of the carrier battle groups.

The administrative problem was solved when the advanced BMD concepts work was put into a new Project Defender called "Strategic Defensive Initiative Organization" (SDIO—"ess-dee-eye-oh"), which parceled out money among the Air Force, Army, and ARPA. Hans Mark made the last round for its chief, but lost out to a highly regarded fighter jock/program manager Air Force general, and quit in disgust. The original SDIO program lumped all the relevant on-going programs into one. That way the budget looked considerable on paper.

Initially, the defenders were overjoyed. Old Bob Sprague was delighted. William A. M. Burden had his last hours brightened. Eugene Wigner and the Oak Ridge crowd were enraptured. But Bell Labs' Cliff Warren was bewildered by the declaratory goal of a perfect defense. Charlie Adams, semiretired from Raytheon, was also troubled by the rhetorical excesses. Freeman Dyson wrote a devilishly ingenious defense of strategic defense for the readers of *The New Yorker,* and turned to other matters. Charlie Herzfeld left ITT to become a high-tech investment banker, and to promote SDI on the Defense Science Board. Jerry Strope and Jack Devaney researched the implications of SDI for FEMA. Jake Shaefer retired as chief of Bell Labs' truncated military research—and soon there-after, the newly deregulated and dismembered AT&T concluded the heat was off, reconsidered its low-profile policy, and began to prepare Star Wars systems-architecture (ex–systems-engineering) proposals. Kissinger recanted completely and supported SDI; so did Brzezinski and Frederick Seitz.

Star Wars was a bonanza to the disarmament lobby. Its fickle market had become bored with the Freeze. Now there was a new abomination of the military-industrial complex to contest, and to stimulate fund-raising. Lobbies to defend SALT sprang into action. The Arms Control Association, formed in 1971 to promote SALT, flourished. The Union of Concerned Scientists enthusiastically gen-erated anti–Star Wars material. Those who remembered the ABM debate were charmed by a quick-and-dirty UCS study that grossly overestimated how many satellites were necessary to keep ICBM-killing devices over Soviet territory at all times. Among the authors were Richard Garwin and Hans Bethe—apparently theoretical physics does not require grounding in elementary solid geometry. There was the same old anti–ABM rhetoric about how easy and cheap coun-termeasures would be. To beat boost-phase burn by lasers, all the Soviets needed was to spin their rockets and/or accelerate them faster: in other words, all they had to do was buy a completely new missile force. Under the leadership of Jay Stone, the Federation of American Scientists went to work, although he ran a more knowl-edgeable operation, and recalled old bomber-disarmament days by commissioning a staffer to report on continental air defense and how it didn't work.

The ABM-killers got in on it—Herb Scoville, Sidney Drell, Herb York, Philip Morrison, Wolfgang Panofsky, George Rathjens, Jack Ruina, Victor Weisskopf, Jerry Wiesner, reinforced by some younger men, including Morrison's protégé Carl Sagan. Thousands of scientists and engineers signed petitions refusing to work on projects attempting to defend the nation from annihilation. And there were various save-the-SALT organizations formed of politicians left over from Nixon, Carter, and Ford years—including Nixon himself and Carter himself. Arms-control activists and ex-officials were incensed: while the President's announcement and subsequent program was within the limitations of SALT, its ultimate goal required abrogation of the anti–ABM treaty—the jewel in the crown of arms control—leaving America naked to attack forever. Stanley Resor said Star Wars was "destabilizing" and therefore "immoral." The Dean Acheson Professor of Political Science at Yale who had advised the Roman bishops preached that anything short of a perfect defense—which is to say, any defense—was contrary to Romish just-war doctrine and therefore satanic. The Utah anti-MX forces turned to opposing ballistic missile defense. The second "gang of four," including McGeorge Bundy and Robert McNamara, said it was A Bad Thing. Kennedy, Warnke, and the like jumped on board. Of course, Adam Yarmolinsky dutifully parroted the party line. "Experts" claimed that no existing computer program could handle the difficult data-processing requirements; Cliff McLain, who had gone into high-tech investment advising, was promoting a solution. Like a litany, the action–reaction syndrome was recited—but existing Soviet forces could utterly destroy the United States, so offensive reaction to defensive action could not possibly worsen the situation. Curtis LeMay in retirement, having given up cigars on doctor's orders, sneered at a "miracle shield" and "a Maginot Line." "Concerned" clergy picketed Raytheon's annual meeting, demanding that the company repent of its accessory role to defense. The arguments against Star Wars are readily summarized:

1. It won't work;
2. It will work too well;
3. Both.

General Glenn Kent, long since retired and working for a time in Rosslyn, had become a resident consultant for Rand and sniped at Star Wars. Rand lay low. Jim Digby, the last nugget of its golden age, retired and signed on with PanHeuristics. Johnny Foster of TRW, still the principal systems engineers of the offensive missiles, called SALT I one of the great achievements of our time which must be protected and maintained. Harold Brown elevated his skepticism to new heights. In the few months of life remaining to him, Scoop Jackson said not a word for publication about Star Wars. Bob Everett retired from MITRE and was succeeded by Charlie Zracket; MITRE worked up $C^3$ schemes for space-based defense—rather a SpaceSAGE, so elaborate that one could not but interpret them as reflecting Air Force skepticism. Bob Panero was brought in as a consultant to look again at very deep shelters for missiles. Paul Weidinger returned to hardening now, working no longer at psi but at $k$si strengths, to take blasts of thousands of pounds per square inch, so tough that an attack had to hit the edge of the silo cap to kill it. For MX, the Air Force reverted to the Minuteman railroad-mobile scheme.

Every "strategist" had something bright to say about Star Wars, rarely with reference to the corpus of twenty-five years of serious work. Colin Gray conveniently became converted to Air Force maybe-eventually but-certainly space-based ballistic missile defense. William Van Cleve produced a book claiming SDI was a response to Soviet defenses. What sounded identical to "arms control through defense" was advocated by a Harvard "strategist" without mention of Donald Brennan. *Daedalus* noted the twenty-fifth anniversary of its arms-control volume, and did not see fit to name its editor. Brennan's memory was shredded.

Dick Foster retired, and his Strategic Studies Center was liquidated by SRI. Frank Hoeber switched his consultancy base over to SPC, and advised SDIO on Red countermeasures. Ami Hoeber quit the Army for TRW, and quit Frank too. The morning after the Star Wars speech, Herman Kahn called his staff together to make a big push. The chronicler whipped up an op-ed for *The New York Times,* but was bumped by Teller. Herman died the day before a scheduled briefing of the Defensive Technologies Study Team. The substitute briefing by Frank Armbruster, the chronicler, and others (in SPC's Rosslyn suite, immediately above Nitze's old office) was the terminal institute effort. The Hudson fallout shelter was shut down, and the remnant of the Institute was sold to the Navy, so nothing more of strategic defense came from the Second Rome. Bill Davis retired from Huntsville and took a job with Teledyne Brown, but didn't last long. Sam Cohen retired to write "a scatological novel." Poor Angelo Codevilla fled Washington, carrying with him the fantasy that he was the father of Star Wars, and added the professional military to his private bestiary of demons. Ben Adams tried to get a job with SDIO, but couldn't. John Bosma bitterly split with Graham and moved to New Mexico. Max Hunter worked on space transportation projects before he retired from Lockheed and became a consultant to MITRE. The swelling funding drew the heavy hitters in the Business back to strategic defense, and there was no place for the marginal men of the '70s.

The issue became polarized, and those people in the Business who actually knew something about strategic defense were buffeted by both sides. Al Latter at RDA had the misfortune to have one of his papers leaked to the journalist who had previously smeared T. K. Jones, and found himself in a little trouble with the administration. His colleague C. J. LeVan was invited to be on a Cambridge television show about SDI; he consented, provided the producers agree that it be live or that he could approve the tape. They wouldn't, so he didn't; you don't make general without knowing how to defend yourself. Sid Graybeal of SDC produced a study which concluded that SALT I said what it said—no development, testing, or deployment of space-based defense systems—and was slapped down. The word had come down from the top of the Pentagon for people to hew to the party line of "replacing deterrence with defense" and defending "people, not hardware." Within about eighteen months it became quite uncomfortable for knowledgeable folk to comment honestly on SDI. One exception was Teller, who knew how vulnerable were space-based systems and promoted ground-based pop-up systems. Another man too powerful to muzzle was Paul Nitze, who offered a public exegesis of elementary BMD cost-effectiveness criteria in conventional mid-'60s Randish terms—and was hailed as an oracle by the arms controllers, and was damned as soft on the Soviets by Perle and company. T. K. Jones went back to Boeing. And the opposition charged that all involved were crooks.

The Republican Right rallied in support of Star Wars. Within three years, favoring SDI had become as much a part of the conservative syndrome as antidefense had become part of the liberal syndrome fifteen years earlier. All the New Right hustlers were all for it, and the conservative rank-and-file got right into step. Danny Graham formed a space alliance with Phyllis Schlafly, Robert Heinlein, and the Reverend Sun Myung Moon. Polls revealed that a large majority of the public at large supported ballistic missile defense—and that a large majority of the public at large believed the United States had ballistic missile defense. Few congressmen dared to oppose it altogether. Strom Thurmond and Fritz Hollings gave it full support. Ronald Reagan was reelected. SDI money poured into the Route 128 complex, and the governor of Massachusetts ran for President on a platform of the Commonwealth's economic success and his opposition to Star Wars. While viewing a contractor's show-and-tell, Edward Kennedy muttered, "I wish somebody would come up with a Star Wars for me."

Actually, the SDIO research was going very well. General James Abrahamson turned out to be an excellent choice as program manager. Many skeptics became more favorably disposed toward ballistic missile defense. Very interesting things were happening in the labs of the contractors and in tests under the Nevada desert. But nothing showed, except some Army shots of experimental ground-based Lockheed and Douglas antimissile missiles at White Sands and Kwajalein authorized by Harold Brown. It had been obvious from the beginning that the exotic systems—directed energy and "third generation"—would not be available until the next century. SDIO was forced to refocus on space-based kinetic kill systems—BAMBI. But they had the same drawbacks—to be sure, not as severe as in Project Defender days, but still impossibly expensive when considered in the context of the overall military budget and any reasonable sense of national priorities. BAMBI still lost the war of the numbers. One study estimated a space-based system for $174 billion—correcting for inflation, almost exactly the Project Defender estimate of a generation earlier. The Chairman of the Defense Science board, Robert Everett, ran review panels on SDI research, involving Fred Hoffman and the chief of Lincoln Labs. The leaked results were that research was progressing, but nothing was worthy of deployment in the immediate future. Understandably, nothing was done to procure the massive space lift needed to heft a satellite shield. After the space-shuttle debacle, the Air Force bought another batch of Max Hunter's Delta rockets.

It was still true that the optimal way to intercept ICBMs was not over their territory, where satellites were expensive and vulnerable, and not in mid-course, where the attacker could best decoy, but coming down on your territory: terminal defense—ABM—the scheme of Bell Labs of thirty years earlier, perhaps eventually using directed-energy-beam weapons. All the old ideas were worked over again, even the Gatling guns. Still, as it had been thirty years earlier, the way to kill incoming nuclear missiles was with nuclear ABMs. And the Corps of Engineers was selling off the old Nike sites that would be needed for terminal defense missiles.

Agitation appeared on the Right for immediate deployment of *something*—no matter what it did, no matter how well it worked, no matter what it cost, no matter how it would be paid for. Anyone who asked about those "details" was accused of MADness. Marty Anderson recommended that an experimental Lockheed ground-based system be deployed for insurance against accidental launch; the system might have worked reliably if there were twenty-four hours' notice of an accident. Bill Schneider (writing under his *nom de plume* "Jack Kemp") advocated reactivating the SALT-legal Grand Forks Safeguard complex, a shield for the Minuteman field and for the wheatfields of the Dakotas. A sometime SDIO research chief remarked on the puerile need for "instant gratification." To head this off, the administration discovered a reinterpretation of the anti–ABM treaty. The provision "not to develop, test, or deploy ABM systems or components which are . . . space-based" really meant *some* development and testing. As intended, the Congress went into orbit—so it could be blamed by the administration for blocking Star Wars. In truth, anything worth doing could have been bootlegged as something other than antimissilery, and the SALT treaty had a six-month escape clause if any necessary violation was in the national interest.

To be sure, the other side in the '80s continued to build and upgrade its strategic offensive forces, as well as its formidable conventional forces. Its air defense apparatus improved: small phased-array radars were placed on towers to help nail low-flying aircraft and cruise missiles. An apparent successor to the long-mysterious SA-5 Tallinn appeared in the SA-X-12, which stirred up the old concerns that it might have—or might be upgraded to—ballistic missile defense capability. The Moscow ABM defense was reduced from 64 to 32 missiles, and then the numbers built up again with what seemed to be a high-acceleration terminal defense missile. And new radars went in. Damned if it didn't look just like Nike-X.

And in the summer of 1983 the overhead picked up a new monster radar near someplace named Krasnoyarsk, located nicely to complete an ABM defensive net and thus violating the SALT I treaty. This stirred up old fears of a Soviet breakout. Spurgeon Keeny, the head of the Arms Control Association, avowed that it must have been some bureaucratic error. Soviet scientists agreed with their Cambridge compatriots that Star Wars was an abomination. American intelligence identified these fellows as the leaders of Soviet advanced-defensive-technologies research—the Soviet Jerry Wiesners. Soviet agitation against SDI became a principal selling point.

And since "strategic defense" had been made synonymous with ballistic missile defense, no one noticed when the Pentagon stripped another squadron from NORAD and when the administration let FEMA's budget be chopped to pre–Korean war levels. Finally a competent man, a former Army general, was put in command of FEMA. The next thrust was to manage "spontaneous" evacuation of the people fleeing the cities in crisis. The governor of Oregon said that this encouraged people to think they could survive a nuclear war, and a successor to Nelson Rockefeller announced that he would tolerate no evacuation of New Yorkers; whether he would order the state police to machine-gun the refugees or would request that SAC execute a preemptive strike against New York cities was left unspecified.

And finally, Raytheon's Patriot (né SAM-D) went into service; the stalling had cost the taxpayers half a billion dollars. And a tidy sum was awarded to the Brits to work up anti–tactical ballistic missiles, but this was attributed to the SecDef's urgent need for an excuse to conduct his affairs in England. In light of impressive Soviet IRBM accuracy, Pierre Gallois, the guru of universal vulnerability, reconsidered and declared for ATBM. America's allies heeded sharp admonitions that they dare not oppose America's self-defense. A partial exception was Norway, whose defense minister, Johan J. Holst, maintained that Star Wars should be a bargaining chip in negotiations with the Soviets.

Canada ostentatiously refused to participate in SDI research. Canada lacked the technical competence to contribute to SDI research. Planning for continental air defense upgrade—labelled Air Defense Initiative—went forward in a desultory manner. The Tories returned to power and restored blue uniforms to Canada's airmen.

The various radar upgrades went forward. Raytheon got the contract for the new BMEWS. The arms controllers claimed it violated the ABM treaty. George Rathjens flew to Denmark to try to persuade the Danish government to block the Greenland radar. Abram Chayes appeared in Managua as the legal defender of the Sandinista communists.

Arms control was given rhetorical support, but there were fears that the rhetoric was believed in the wrong quarters. In order to call the Commander-in-Chief's attention to the true doctrine, the Albertites connived to give Wohlstetter the Medal of Freedom immediately before the Geneva Summit; in order to get the attention of the First Lady, the medal was also awarded to Roberta. Again, the saga of strategic defense cannot be separated from other political events. Distrusted by the Congress and unable to employ the proper agencies, the White House staff fudged an amateur intelligence bureau. One of its missions was supplying spare parts for the Hawk air defense missiles of the Islamic Republic of Iran. At an inopportune time, the invaluable Albertite Donald Fortier of the N.S.C. staff died. Bill Schneider, the Undersecretary of State for Security Assistance, was the first to leave, and set up as a consultant in Rosslyn. To redeem itself politically, the administration moved toward the arms agreement it had resisted. In short order, Perle bailed out, and Lehman, and Ikle, and the ACDA director, and many lesser lights, and even Weinberger.

A treaty was signed to get rid of Schmidt's worthless Euromissiles, but the other side exploited the antinuke sentiment to euchre us into eliminating useful short-range missiles as well. A sweet bonus for the other side was the elimination of the major justification for ATBM development. And transparently pseudoverification of the mobile missiles was ballyhooed. There was more talk of building up conventional forces in Europe, and no money.

Like ABM before it, SDI became a bargaining chip. The other side cleverly demanded defense limits as the price for offensive-force reductions. The administration held firm, and thus strategic defense was cast as the impediment to arms control and "peace"— an engaging problem for Paul Nitze to solve.

So the Reagan administration was no more able to resolve The Problem than its predecessors. Not all the weak threads were on the fringes of the political fabric. As its strategic policy bogged down, the administration turned to traditional right-wing explanations for national failure—domestic treachery and the transfer of American capitalist technology to those dumb *muzhik* Commies.

Now, none of this would have been possible—or at least, one hopes not—had not the politicians and promoters felt themselves to be perfectly secure, or perfectly illusioned. You do not stage hustles when you perceive yourself to be gravely threatened. So in some sense we were safe. No one had seemed to notice that most concern about the nuclear offense and defense derived from fears of the continuation of the international crises of the 1950s; yet the last crisis was the Cuban missile crisis in 1962. America was safe, it seemed.

But what if the political fabric was tearing under the strain? What if America lacked a strong stomach and a strong pocketbook?

### The Next War in 1985

It looked no different from the next war in 1975. Whoever struck first won. But the other side had greatly improved its knowledge of America. Could the Soviets really credit the threat that we would strike first? In the mid-1980s, the Americans consoled themselves with conventional wisdom/wishful thinking/mirror-imaging of supposed Soviet economic difficulties and ethnic conflicts. (The Soviets had a balanced budget and balanced trade and superb internal security.) Their pocketbook was strong enough, and their stomach stronger yet. Their psychological defense was intact. In the early '80s they were becalmed by the triple loss of their number one. With a younger man at the helm, the Soviet state could take the wind of history. The other side had its Problem solved by the Americans.

And what if deterrence fails? Why should Soviet deterrence fail?
Still, the hard-core defenders will retain faith in another outcome.
In the words of a political hustler observing the successful strategic
defense of Baltimore:

> And the rocket's red glare, the bombs bursting in air,
> Gave proof through the night that our flag was still there.

# METHOD AND SOURCES

While the ABM wars were being fought in the Pentagon, the chronicler, in the conventional manner of restless young men of the privileged classes of North America, was idling in graduate school. There he was subjected to a course in historiography—the study of the study of history—which plotted inexorable progress from the origins of records to the present glories of the "discipline." The student did wonder who had improved on Admiral Thucydides, and he was especially impressed by the writings of a 14th-century monk called in English Sir John Froissart,* who hung about the courts and camps of west Europe and recorded and reported the doings, for good and evil, of the kings, captains, burghers, and noble ladies of England, France, and the Low Countries—terrific stories. But this wasn't *real* history, taught the teacher; history must be based upon documentation, preferably "primary" sources.

But one of the problems of doing history of the Business is that so much of what matters remains classified, and so much of what has been released is not true, and so much of what has been declassified is questionable. Most documents are for the record, reflecting official views and stating institutional interests. Because it is known that they will be closely held, they are not always crafted with care. They go "into the safe," and lie forgotten until some academic drudge troubles to have them declassified. Real information is transmitted orally—most formally in "briefings," verbal presentations buttressed by slides or handout notes. Records of briefings rarely survive.

---

*In addition to being the celebrator of chivalry, Froissart took note of an innovation in warfare—rocketry—and suggested improvement of accuracy by putting a spin on the primitive missiles.

So this book is not a history but a chronicle, based almost entirely upon hanging around the courts and camps of the Business and recording and reporting the doings, for better or worse, of politicians, soldiers, engineers, and analysts. An excellent place to hang out was Herman Kahn's Hudson Institute, where, until its collapse upon his death, all manner of exotic and informed people would congregate. The staff of the Institute were believed to be brilliant and knowledgeable people, so its visitors would attempt to show how brilliant and knowledgeable they were by offering informative briefings and shmoozing at conferences.

Almost everything in this book is derived from hanging out in that way, as well as decades of reading myriad "reports" and "studies." It was firm policy at the Hudson Institute to perform almost all research and discuss almost all matters "open source," and the material in this book was obtained that way. (In a very few cases, legitimately received information has been deliberately modified, the better to confound enemies of the Republic, and information in the public domain that may not necessarily be correct has not been repeated.)

In addition, the writer has been able to draw upon materials being gathered for a formal biography of the strategic analyst Herman Kahn, to be published sometime in the medium-run future. And some interviews were conducted specially for this book. Of course, there is always the question of the credibility of interviews, but they are often better than written materials. Interviewing delivers information not communicable by the mere words: for example, the retired Air Force general who would respond to a provocative question with a ———-eating grin and the comment "*Some* people might say that." Or the veteran defense analyst who would reply with widened eyes, "I wouldn't have said it that way myself." Or the wife of a distinguished strategist intently analysing her lap as her husband proclaimed his love for his bitter rival. The best example was a former high national-security official interviewed over a Japanese luncheon. Before relating his version of events contrary to reliable sources, he would carefully munch a sushi; prior to denying that his administration had overthrown a friendly government, he devoured a pair of the delicacies—thus adding a new term to the chronicler's family vocabulary: "the two-sushi lie." Indeed, the single credible published survey of these matters, the Anglo-American journalist Norman Moss's *Men Who Play God* (London, 1968), was founded almost entirely on interviews.

And some library research was undertaken. The citing of written materials should in no way be interpreted as endorsement of their overall accuracy. Many of these formal sources are listed below, but it should be repeated that these are not the principal sources of the chronicle, and therefore it should be understood that the listed sources were not necessarily the origin of accounts written.

On early days: Getting and Warren interviews; Hudson Maxim scrapbooks; Churchill, *Speeches*; T. R. Crouch, *The Eagle Aloft* (Washington, 1983); R. W. Clark, *Tizard* (Cambridge, Mass., 1965); Douhet, *The Command of the Air* trans. Ferrari (New York, 1942); L. Kennett, *A History of Strategic Bombing* (New York, 1982); F. A. Pile, *Ack Ack* (London, 1949); M. M. Postan *et al., The Design and Development of Weapons* (London, 1964); G. H. Quester, *Deterrence Before Hiroshima* (New York, 1966); Quester, "Historical Analogies to the Problems of Active and Passive Defense" in D. B. Bobrow (ed.), *Weapons System Decisions* (New York, 1969); A. Rawlinson, *The Defense of London* (London, 1923); A. J. Smithers, *Toby* (London, 1978); R. A. Watson-Watt, *The Pulse of Radar* (New York, 1959); *Five Years at the Radiation Laboratory* (Cambridge, Mass., 1946).

On Wasserfall: Lange interview; T. Benecke and A. W. Quick (eds.), *History of German Guided Missile Development* (Brunswick, FRG, 1957); W. Dornberger, *V-2* trans. J. Cleugh and G. Halliday (New York, 1954); F. I. Orway and M. R. Sharpe, *The Rocket Team* (Cambridge, Mass., 1982).

On early postwar period: Nitze interview; "U.S. Strategic Bombing Survey" (Washington, 1946); The Editors of Pocket Books (eds.), *The Atomic Age Opens* (New York, 1945); D. Masters and K. Way (eds.), *One World or None* (New York, 1946); W. W. Kaufmann, "The Evolution of Deterrence" (address before Air War College, 1958); D. Lang, *From Hiroshima to the Moon* (New York, 1959); D. MacIsaac, *Strategic Bombing in World War II* (New York, 1976); P. McC. Smith, *The Air Force Plans for Peace* (Baltimore, 1970).

On continental air defense in general: Barlow, Digby, Foster, Getting, James Hartinger (ADC, NORAD), James Hill, LeMay, Sprague interviews; Kahn, Killian, and J. A. Stratton (MIT) papers; "Problems of Air Defense" (Report of Project Charles) (MIT, 1951); "Project Charles Video History" (Sloan Foundation, 1981), courtesy Sloan Foundation; Lincoln Laboratory, "Final Report of Summer Study Group, 1952" (MIT,

1953); 1956 Senate (Symington) hearings, *Strategic Air Power*; C. M. Atkins and E. R. Jayne, "A Successful Laboratory and Science Policy: The Lincoln Case" (MIT, 1967); Getting, "Facts about Defense," *Nation* (22 December 1945), "Recollections of USAF in 1950–51" (typescript, 1973), "Vignettes of Air Defense" (typescript, 1982), and "All in a Lifetime" (typescript, 1985), all courtesy Getting; official Air Defense Command and NORAD histories; S. Huntington, *The Common Defense* (New York, 1966); C. H. Murphy, "The Decision to Curtail Strategic Air Defense Programs in FY 1975" (Congressional Research Service, 1974).

On SAGE: Everett and Zracket interviews; J. F. Jacobs, "A Personal History of the SAGE System" (MITRE typescript, 1985); "Special Issue, SAGE" (ed. Everett), *Annals of the History of Computing* (October 1983); Valley, "How the SAGE Development Began" and E. A. Weiss, "Review of the Computer Museum in Boston," *Annals* (July 1985); K. C. Redmond and T. M. Smith, *Project Whirlwind* (Bedford, Mass., 1975); R. C. Meisel and J. F. Jacobs, *MITRE: The First Twenty Years* (Bedford, Mass., 1979). MITRE deserves high marks for its support of technological historical research.

On Canada: D. Bell (Ministry of Defense), J. Collins (RCAF), and M. Sherman (Hudson Institute) interviews; William Bundy (ISA) communication; Annual Reports of the Minister for Defense; Committee on National Defense, "Canada's Territorial Air Defense" (Canadian Senate, 1985); C. Gray, "Canada and NORAD," *Behind the Headlines* (June 1972); P. C. Newman, *Renegade in Power* (Indianapolis, 1963); Newman, *True North* (Toronto, 1983); J. G. Eayrs, *In Defense of Canada*, III (Toronto, 1972).

On Sparrow, Hawk, and Raytheon: Adams and Getting interviews; M. W. Fossier, "The Development of Radar Homing Missiles," *Journal of Guidance* (Nov–Dec 1984); O. J. Scott, *The Ordeal of Change: The Story of Raytheon* (New York, 1974); S. J. Schoenberg, *Geneen* (New York, 1983).

On Bell Labs: Foster, Read, Shaefer, and Warren interviews; "Kwajalein Field Station" (Bell Laboratories, 1975); "ABM Project History" (Bell Laboratories, 1975); Foster *et al.*, "Basic Telecommunications Issues Affecting U.S. National Security and Survival" (SRI Tech Note SSC-TN-1232-2, 1980); Warren, "Ballistic Missile Defense Testing in the Pacific: 1960–1976," *Bell Laboratories Record* (September 1976); M. D. Fagen (ed.), *A History of Science and Engineering in the Bell System: National Service in War and Peace (1925–1975)* (New York, 1978); E. J. Kahn, *Micronesia* (New York, 1966).

On Ajax, Hercules, and ARADCOM: Foster, Hunter, Thomas Kee (Massachusetts National Guard), Shaefer, and William Staudenmeir (Air Defense Artillery) interviews; M. J. Cagle, "Nike Ajax" (Missile Command, 1959); Cagle, "Nike Hercules" (Missile Command, 1973); T. Osato, "Militia Missilemen: The National Guard in Air Defense" (National Guard Bureau, 1968); A. Parkman, *Army Engineers in New England* (Waltham, Mass., 1978); *Stations List of the U.S. Army* (Army Staff, 1950–1974); "Air Defense" file, U.S. Army Center for Military History; *Argus* magazine.

On early civil defense: Panero interview; "Fort Ritchie Briefing" (Fort Ritchie, 1985); *Bulletin of the Atomic Scientists* (1946–1957); Wohlstetter, "Views of Scientists" in J. H. Morse (ed.), "Problems Posed by Conflicting Views Concerning Nuclear Weapons" (SRI Summary Technical Report TR-5104-1 Annex, 1965).

On civil defense in general: William Brown, William Chipman (Wisconsin CD, FEMA), Devaney, and Strope interviews; Herman Kahn papers; sundry Hudson Institute, RAND, and SRI studies; House (Holifield) civil defense hearings 1956, 1958, and 1961; R. A. Gessert *et al.*, "Federal Civil Defense Organization" (Institute for Defense Analyses, 1965); B. W. Blanchard, "American Civil Defense: 1945–75" (U. of Va. Ph.D. dissertation reprinted by FEMA, 1980); Eugene Wigner (ed.), *Who Speaks for Civil Defense?* (New York, 1968).

On RAND civil defense studies: Brown, Hershleifer, Hitch, Ikle, Irwin Mann (RAND), Mitchell, Hubert Moshin (RAND), and Panero interviews; Kahn and Moshin papers; Kahn *et al.*, "Report of a Study of Non-Nuclear Defense" (RAND R-322-RC, 1958); Kahn, "Some Specific Suggestions for Achieving Early Non-Military Defense Capabilities and Initiating Long-Range Programs" (RAND RM-2206-RC, 1958); sundry Air Force–supported research and development documents "not to be quoted or cited." Collbohm refused interview.

On Eisenhower strategy: Sprague interview; Kahn and Killian papers; Council on Foreign Relations archives; Declassified Documents Reference Service; Killian, *Sputniks, Scientists, and Eisenhower* (Cambridge, Mass., 1977); Kistiakowsky, *A Scientist at the White House* (Cambridge, Mass., 1976).

On Sprague and Gaither Committee: Sprague, Nitze, and Wohlstetter interviews; Kahn, Saltonstall, and Sprague papers; "Deterrence and Survival in the Nuclear Age" (Security Resources Panel [Gaither Committee] of the Science Advisory Committee, 1957); M. H. Halperin, "The Gaither Committee and the Policy Process," *World Politics* (April 1961); Sprague, "Sprague Electric of North Adams" (Newcomen Society, 1958).

On Hardening: Brown, Panero, Rowen, Weidlinger, and Wohlstetter interviews; Kahn papers; NORAD sources: Wohlstetter and F. Hoffman, "Defending a Strategic Force After 1960" (RAND D-2270, 1954).

On Cheyenne Mountain: Panero interview; Kahn papers; NORAD materials; model of the COC at NORAD museum, Petersen AFB.

On Kennedy and McNamara strategy: Enthoven, Deirdre Henderson (JFK staff), Foster, Kaufmann, Kent, Rowen, and Wohlstetter interviews; A. W. Betts and D. Burchinal (Joint Staff) oral history interviews, USA Military History Institute; Posture Statements FY 1963–1969; Enthoven and K. W. Smith, *How Much Is Enough?* (New York, 1971); W. W. Kaufmann, *The McNamara Strategy* (New York, 1964); D. Lang, *An Inquiry into Enoughness* (New York, 1965). Ellsberg interview aborted when subject went berserk.

On civil defense under Kennedy: Armbruster, Bundy, Doty, Hirschleifer, Kaysen, Pittman, Ruebhausen, and Yarmolinsky interviews; Kahn papers; sundry congressional hearings.

On arms control: Brennan papers; Kent, "On the Interaction of Opposing Forces Under Possible Arms Agreements" (Harvard Center for International Affairs, 1962); Brennan (ed.), *Arms Control, Disarmament, and National Security* (New York, 1961); Schelling and Halperin, *Strategy and Arms Control* (New York, 1961); Halperin, "Arms Control: A 25-Year Perspective," *FAS Public Interest Report* (June 1983).

On BMD in general: Herzfeld interview; R. D. Holbrook and J. F. Gross, "On the Problem of Ballistic Missile Defense" (RAND P-2046-ARPA, 1960); T. Read, "Strategy for Active Defense" (Bell Laboratories typescript, 1960); sundry Hudson Institute reports; W. Davis, "BMD into the '80s" *National Defense* (November–December 1979) and "Ballistic Missile Defense Will Work," *loc. cit.* (December 1981); Holst and Schneider (eds.), *Why ABM?* (New York, 1969); A. B. Carter and D. N. Schwartz (eds.), *Ballistic Missile Defense* (Brookings Institution, 1984).

On ABM: Foster, David Harris (Missile Command flack), F. Hoeber, Robert Marshall (Safeguard Systems Command), Lange, Rosenthal, Ruina, and Schneider interviews; sundry SRI and Hudson Institute studies; Kahn, Brennan, and BBB papers; E. R. Jayne, "The ABM Debate" (MIT Ph.D. dissertation, 1969); Herzfeld, "BMD and National Security," *Survival* (January 1966); LeVan, "Remembering Nike Zeus" *National Defense* (July–August 1985); B. D. Adams, *Ballistic Missile Defense* (New York, 1971); A. W. Betts and H. K. Johnson oral-history interviews, USA Military History Institute; House and Senate hearings 1967–72; J. H. Kitchens, "A History of the Huntsville Division, U.S. Army Corps of Engineers, 1967–1976" (Huntsville Division, 1978).

On ABM warheads: Cohen, A. Latter, Lokke, Teller, and Robert Thorne (Los Alamos) interviews; private interviews; *Time* (26 May 1967); B.

and F. M. Brodie, *From Crossbow to H-Bomb* (Bloomington, Ind., 1973); *New York Times* (7 November 1971).

On Project Defender: Herzfeld, Holbrook, Kupelian, Nils Meunch (MICOM, IDA), and Cormac Walsh (Riverside Research) interviews; congressional hearings; Bosma, "Strategic Defenses in Space: A Road Once Travelled?" (High Frontier, circa 1984).

On Soviet active defense: Private interviews; V. Kriksunov, "The Interception Problems of Intercontinental Missiles," trans. W. I. Rumer (RAND, 1958); T. Greenwood, *Making the MIRV* (Cambridge, Mass., 1975); W. T. Lee, "The Possibility of a Soviet Breakout from the ABM Treaty" (Center for Strategic and International Studies, 1984).

On ABM politics: Enthoven, Foster, A. Hoeber, LeVan, Marshall, O'Neil, Resor, W. W. Rostow, Seitz, and Wohlstetter interviews; Betts and Brennan papers; calendar of Wiesner papers; Wohlstetter to McNamara 21 February 67, courtesy Wohlstetter; "The Missile Defense Question: Is LBJ Right?" (Republican [sic] National Committee, 1967); House and Senate Hearings; A. H. Cahn, "Eggheads and Warheads" (MIT Ph.D. dissertation, 1971); J. Bowman, "The 1969 ABM Debate" (U. of Nebraska–Lincoln Ph.D. dissertation, 1973); Rathjens, "The Future of the Strategic Arms Race" (Carnegie Endowment, 1969); "Xenophon," "Soviet Missiles: A Credible Threat Now," *Triumph* (February 1967); A. Chaynes and J. Wiesner (eds.), *ABM* (New York, 1969); W. Kintner (ed.), *Safeguard: Why ABM Makes Sense* (New York, 1969); D. Nelkin, *The University and Military Research* (Ithaca, 1972); E. J. Yanarella, *The Missile Defense Controversy* (Lexington, Ky., 1977); W. W. Rostow, *The Diffusion of Power* (New York, 1972); *Encounter* (February 1986).

On McNamara line: private interviews; [L. Gelb *et al.* (eds.)], *The Pentagon Papers*, Gravel edition (Boston, 1971).

On the Third Battle of the Numbers: A. Hoeber and Wohlstetter interviews; P. Morse (MIT) papers; *Operations Research* (September 1971); *FAS Newsletter* (December 1971): R. Sanders, *The Politics of Defense Analysis* (New York, 1973); Rathjens, "The ABM Debate," in Brodie *et al.* (eds.), *National Security and International Stability* (Cambridge, Mass., 1983).

On SALT I: Halperin and Lynn interviews; Brennan papers; congressional testimony; Y. U. Listvinov, *First Strike* trans. spook (Springfield, Va., 1972); J. Newhouse, *Cold Dawn* (New York, 1973); G. Smith, *Doubletalk* (Garden City, 1981); R. L. Garthoff, "BMD and East–West Relations," in Carter and Schwartz, *op. cit.*

On the defeated: William Carpenter (SRI), Garrett Scalera (Hudson, SRI), Barry Smernoff (Hudson) interviews; BBB papers; Wohlstetter, "Legends of the Strategic Arms Race" (U.S. Strategic Institute, 1975); "Proof of Evidence of Albert Wohlstetter on Behalf of Friends of the Earth Ltd." (California Seminar on Arms Control and Foreign Policy, 1977).

On SAM-D: Congressional hearings; Betts oral-history interview.

On Oak Ridge: Conrad Chester, Haaland, Kearny, and Wigner interviews; Oak Ridge reports; Chester and Wigner, "Population Vulnerability," *Orbis* (Fall 1974); Haaland and Wigner, "Defense of Cities by Antiballistic Missiles," *SIAM Review* (April 1977); Kearny, *Nuclear War Survival Skills* (pirated edition, 1982).

On Safeguard shutdown: George Mayo (Safeguard Systems Command), Robert M. Mullens (Grand Forks commander) interviews; *Congressional Record* (1975); "Report of the BMD Program Manager" (Washington, 1976?).

On Soviet civil defense: Kahn papers; 1961 Holifield hearings; Leon Gore, *Civil Defense in the Soviet Union* (Berkeley, 1962); Gore, "The Soviet Civil Defense Shelter Program" (Miami Center for Advanced International Studies, 1977); J. M. Collins and J. S. Chwat, "United States and Soviet City Defense" (Congressional Research Service, 1976); Director of Central Intelligence, "Soviet Civil Defense" (CIA, 1978).

On civil defense in the 1970s: Chipman, McLain, Strope, and Tirana interviews; FEMA materials; Carter, "Presidential Directive 41"; Comptroller General, "Civil Defense: Are Federal, State, and Local Governments Prepared for Nuclear Attack?" (GAO LCD-76-464, 1977); R. J. Sullivan *et al.*, "Survival in the First Year After a Nuclear Attack" (SPC, 1979). T. K. Jones would not be interviewed.

On the BMD underground: B. Adams, Bosma, Codevilla, W. Davis, Hunter, J. Jones (ABMDA), McLain, Schneider, G. Tate (BMDO) interviews; private interviews; Brennan and BBB papers; Hunter, "Strategic Dynamics and Space-Laser Weaponry" (Lockheed, 1977); G. Barash *et al.*, "Ballistic Missile Defense" (Los Alamos Labs, 1980); "M. Wallop" [Codevilla], "Opportunities and Imperatives of Ballistic Missile Defense," *Strategic Review* (Fall 1979); "J. F. Kemp" [Schneider], "U.S. Strategic Force Modernization: A New Role for Missile Defense," *Strategic Review* (Summer 1980); congressional hearings; W. J. Broad, *Star Warriors* (New York, 1985).

On Brennan: E. Brennan (brother), M. Mitchell (secretary), J. Perkins (wife's nurse), Schneider interviews; Brennan and BBB papers.

On Cohen: Cohen interview; Cohen, *The Truth About the Neutron Bomb* (New York, 1983).

On Dyson: Dyson interview; Betts, Brennan, BBB, and Dyson papers.

On Garwin: Garwin interview; Garwin, "Safeguard: Its Utility & Necessity as a Defense for Minuteman" (typescript, 1969), Betts papers; congressional testimony; *BAS* (January 1984); F. Griffiths and J. C. Polanyi (eds.), *The Dangers of Nuclear War* (Toronto, 1979).

On Gray: Brennan, Brodie, BBB, and Kahn papers: Gray, "The Defense Policy of the Eisenhower Administration" (Oxford Ph.D. dissertation, 1970); [BBB (ed.)], "Bibliographica Hudsoniensis" (Hudson Institute, 1976).

On Teller: Foster and Teller interviews; Teller, "The Nature of Nuclear Warfare," *BAS* (May 1957); Teller and A. Brown, *The Legacy of Hiroshima* (Garden City, 1962); SALT I ratification hearings.

On the Battle of the Great Basin: W. Evans (LDS flack), Fletcher, H. Fuller (Salt Lake City *Tribune*), G. H. Kaffer (Utah CD) interviews; "First Presidency Statement on Basing of the MX Missile" (LDS, 1981); "Spearhead Unit Operations Manual" (LDS, 1982); J. Edwards, *Superweapon* (New York, 1982); H. Scoville, *MX* (Cambridge, Mass., 1981).

On the road to Star Wars: Anderson, Howard "Dutch" Darrin (Hollywood cavalry), Graham, Hill, Morrow, Robert C. Richardson III (USAF, High Frontier) interviews; private interviews; BBB and Reagan papers; Anderson, "Reagan for President Policy Memorandum #3" (typescript, 1979), courtesy Anderson; J. W. Canan, *War in Space* (New York, 1982).

Epilogue: Fletcher, Hoffman, and Wohlstetter interviews; Hoffman Panel Report; private sources; press accounts.

The chronicler proffers his appreciation of the invaluable assistance of professional librarians and archivists, and his extreme gratitude to the interviewees who so generously gave of their time and hospitality. In particular, he thanks those gracious hostesses Roberta of Laurel Canyon, Penny of the Blue Ridge, the handsome unidentified woman who served a fine cup of tea at the Scarsdale lair of a mad scientist, and especially Jane of Chappaqua.

The chronicler apologizes for failing to record many distinguished contributors to the defense. He can only plead priorities and circumstances. And it is always to be regretted when characters are presented in print less handsomely than they appear in the mirrors of their own minds. Surely it is insufficient to remark that the importance of the subject makes individual sensitivities seem inconsequential by comparison. No egos will survive, if deterrence fails.

# Index